Hard Road to Freedom

Hard Road

to Freedom

The Story of African America

James Oliver Horton
and
Lois E. Horton

Rutgers University Press
New Brunswick, New Jersey, and London

Library of Congress Cataloging-in-Publication Data

Horton, James Oliver.
  Hard road to freedom : the story of African America / James Oliver Horton and
  Lois E. Horton.
      p.   cm.
  Includes bibliographical references (p.) and index.
  ISBN 0-8135-2850-X (alk. paper) — ISBN 0-8135-2851-8 (pbk. : alk. paper)
  1. Afro-Americans—History.   I. Horton, Lois E.   II. Title.
  E185 .H643 2000
  973.0496073—dc21   00-025568
                                                                            CIP

British Cataloging-in-Publication data for this book
is available from the British Library.

Copyright © 2001 by James Oliver Horton and Lois E. Horton

All rights reserved

Manufactured in the United States of America

Contents

Illustrations and Maps

Maps

Acknowledgments

This book could never have been completed without the support, assistance, and cooperation of a host of friends and colleagues. Norbert Finzsch provided much of the inspiration and encouragement for this sometimes overwhelming undertaking. John Vlach, Laurence Glasco, and Alan Isaacman read and provided valuable suggestions for our discussion of African history. William Chafe took time from his busy schedule to read chapters dealing with the modern civil rights era and Michele Gates Moresi and Paul Gardullo also provided important commentary on several chapters. Rod Paolini shared his knowledge and personal experience about Chicago politics.

Denise Meringolo and Stephanie Batiste read and commented on various sections of the entire manuscript and were enormously helpful in the seemingly unending paperwork and inquiry associated with picture research. Michael Siegel from Rutgers University produced the beautiful maps included in this volume, and archivists and librarians, at too many institutions around the country to mention individually, were enormously helpful in our research and tolerant of our many requests. We are indebted to students in classes at George Mason University for reactions to early chapters and to the faculty and students at George Washington University's American Studies Department for listening to our ideas and frustrations and for providing valuable insights into history and American culture. We benefited enormously from their comments, experience, and support. We also express our gratitude to the George Washington University and the National Museum of American History at the Smithsonian Institution for partial funding of this project.

We give special thanks to Leslie Mitchner, Editor in Chief of Rutgers University Press, to Managing Editor Marilyn Campbell, and to the entire staff at the press for their professionalism and hard work. We truly appreciate their encouragement and their competence. Finally, we thank Dana Jeffrey Horton-Geer for his good nature, his amazing curiosity, and his naturalist lectures.

Hard Road to Freedom

Introduction

People are often surprised, fascinated, even shocked when they first learn about the history of African Americans. Sometimes outraged, they demand to know why they haven't heard this story before. Why did their textbooks ignore the dramatic tales of the black experience? Why has no one told this story? It is true that until recently, general American history textbooks and courses have paid little attention to this aspect of the country's development, save for a few references to slavery, usually discussed in connection with the period just before the Civil War. But it is not true that the story of black America has not been told.

Black people told their own stories again and again during their time in America. Over the past three hundred years, they told it in oral testimony, in written petitions to the government, in autobiographical narratives, in poetry and song, in dance and religious ceremonies. In an autobiography published in 1760, Briton Hammon told of his enslavement in New England, his ship-wreck in Florida, his imprisonment by the Spaniards, and his service aboard a British warship. In the many autobiographies that followed, Africans and African Americans recounted their lives in West Africa, and they remembered African history and culture. They described the horrors of capture and enslavement, and the restrictions on those who gained a limited freedom. Published at the end of the eighteenth century, the influential autobiography by the African Olaudah Equiano related how he had been captured and brought to America when he was only eleven years old.[1]

A flood of slave narratives telling the stories of those who had experienced the inhumanity of slavery was published in the early and mid–nineteenth century, becoming a powerful weapon in the fight against slavery during the decades before the Civil War. Some former slaves—Frederick Douglass, Nat Turner, Harriet Jacobs, William Wells Brown, and Jarena Lee among them—wrote or dictated widely read autobiographies that countered proslavery propaganda. James W. C. Pennington, a slave blacksmith and carpenter who taught himself to read and write, wrote two books after he escaped from slavery in 1827. The first, a general African American history called *A Textbook of the Origin and History of Colored People,* was used in the Free African School in Hartford, Connecticut. Since he was still a fugitive from slavery, he had to flee to Britain after his 1849 autobiography, *The Fugitive Blacksmith,* revealed his identity and location. In the 1850s William Cooper Nell, a free black man and community activist in Boston, published two histories detailing the role of African Americans in the Revolution: *The Services of Colored Americans in the Wars of 1776 and 1812* (1851) and *Colored Patriots of the American Revolution* (1855). Nell hoped to counter charges that black people had no history worth recording and to establish black entitlement to American freedom and citizenship.[2]

Other African American histories followed. Former slave and autobiographer William Wells Brown published *The Black Man: His Antecedents, His Genius, and His Achievements* in 1863. He followed this with several works of fiction and a play dealing with race during the Civil War. George Washington Williams's landmark *History of the Negro Race in America,* published in 1882, influenced most of the important chroniclers of the African American experience who came afterward. Williams carefully documented his work with extensive footnotes, hoping to prevent his account of the role and accomplishments of African Americans from being dismissed as propaganda or wishful thinking. More than a half century later, when John Hope Franklin was preparing his classic study, *From Slavery to Freedom,* he was greatly impressed with Williams's scholarship.[3]

Scholarly African American histories, biographies, and autobiographies continued to flourish in the early decades of the twentieth century. W.E.B. Du Bois published his Harvard University doctoral dissertation, *The Suppression of the African Slave-Trade,* in 1896 and went on to produce a host of important historical and sociological studies. Du Bois's work ranged from a landmark analysis of the Reconstruction period after the Civil War to a study of the black community in Philadelphia that anticipated the mid-twentieth-century social history movement. Carter G. Woodson was born in West Virginia to a former slave and received a Ph.D. from Harvard University in 1912. Determined to raise popular awareness of the contributions of blacks to America, he organized the Association for the Study of Negro Life and History in 1915 and established the *Journal of Negro History.* Historians Charles H. Wesley, Luther Porter Jackson, Lorenzo J. Greene, and L. D. Reddick were among the first black scholars to publish in this journal. In addition to scholarly articles, the journal made many important historical documents available for study.

Meanwhile such black institutions of higher learning as Howard University, Fisk University, and Morehouse College began offering courses in Negro history. In 1926 Woodson and his organization established Negro History Week. Celebrated at first almost exclusively in black schools and churches, this one-week observance introduced black history into school curricula, encouraged the publication of work dealing with African Americans, and stimulated the black press and a few white newspapers to run related stories. By the 1930s the government aided this work, as the Federal Writers' Project of the Works Progress Administration gathered the recollections of elderly people who had been slaves before 1865. Until World War II there were few black Ph.D.s in history, by 1940 only eighteen, more than half of whom had earned their degrees at Harvard University and the University of Chicago.[4] Among the recipients were Rufus Clement, Benjamin Quarles, and John Hope Franklin. Along with those still active from the earlier years, these scholars set the stage for a major breakthrough in the study of African American history. Their advances in the field were capped by the publication of Franklin's *From Slavery to Freedom* in 1948.

Black scholars played a critical role in the Supreme Court's *Brown* decision, which struck down the concept of "separate but equal" in 1954, fueling the postwar drive for civil rights. Their work, which laid the foundation for arguments for racial equality by challenging the segregationist assumptions that dismissed the importance of black people to the nation, presented historical evidence placing black people squarely in the center of the American experience. White scholars, too, contributed to this work during the 1950s. Studies focused on the history of slavery were especially relevant to policy discussions during the civil rights era. Kenneth Stampp and Stanley Elkins corrected earlier contentions that slavery was a benign institution, and by the late 1960s, federal social policy advisers debated whether the destructive effects of slavery served as an explanation for twentieth-century African American poverty. Some scholars argued that slavery had robbed blacks of their African heritage, disturbed black family and community values, and left them without culture. The debates inspired a new generation of historians to undertake social history studies to examine the validity of such claims. These young scholars called for a "history from the bottom up" that broadened the vision of American history to include those at the lower socioeconomic levels of society.

During the 1970s studies of slavery established the existence of a slave community, a social and cultural space that allowed slaves to resist much of slavery's destructive intent. Studies by such historians as John Blassingame, Herbert Gutman, Eugene Genovese provided convincing evidence of the resilience of African American families and culture. Lawrence Levine's study of black folklore and culture proved conclusively that black people had shaped a remarkably rich social and cultural life and had preserved a considerable African heritage. By the 1980s African American history had moved beyond demonstrating the significance of black contributions and celebrating first blacks. Newer works took up Du Bois's task—the study and analysis of black communities and culture—with modern research techniques and technologies. Important studies of Boston, Cleveland, Detroit, Philadelphia, Providence,

New York, and many other black communities began to illuminate the too-often-obscured interior world of black urban America, and a few scholars investigated black rural life. Meanwhile historians produced critical works of political history that drew on the social data to describe and analyze race in America in new and valuable ways. The last generation of African American scholarship has brought us a great distance toward a fuller, more useful understanding of the historical experience of black people. In our 1997 book, *In Hope of Liberty,* we attempted to add to this scholarship not only by investigating the lives and relationships of northern blacks during the eighteenth and early nineteenth centuries but also by showing that the African American culture created during that period helped to create the general American culture developing at the time. Our aim in that book was to link the historical experience of blacks to that of other Americans, making the point that no American history happened in isolation from other American experiences. We have tried to continue that theme in this book.

One major undertaking of the most recent work in African American history has been the creation of a narrative that brings together stories formerly told separately. In *Hard Road to Freedom* we tell the story of black people in America as an expression of one of the nation's fundamental principles: the pursuit of freedom. The story begins with African cultures and the slave trade in which many Africans lost their freedom. Those speaking out against the trade that dominated New World development and created so much wealth were voices crying in the wilderness of greed and economic windfall. The evolution of American slavery is the recapitulation of the development and codification of racial slavery and the story of cultural resistance to that hardening system.

The age of the Revolution brought the promise of African American freedom, raised along with the colonists' cries of liberty. Whether black men fought for the British or for the independence of the new American nation, they fought for their own freedom. For them the Revolution was an antislavery struggle, which freed more African Americans than did any other act before the Civil War. In its aftermath the nation was regionally divided by the issue of slavery or freedom. In newly formed northern black communities, African Americans called on the country to live up to its founding principles, while in the South, slavery expanded its territory, tightened its grip, and increasingly stifled dissent. Slaves resisted a hardening bondage, forming communities of support that sustained the hope of freedom in desolate times. They found encouragement in the increasing strength of antislavery voices. Slavery's opponents saw the Civil War as a second American Revolution, a blow for freedom that would complete the first. Though the sacrifice and anguish of war did end slavery, they brought an ambiguous freedom. The promise of Reconstruction faded into southern sharecropping and segregation, policed by organized terrorism.

At the turn of the twentieth century, reformers focused on economic freedom. Progressive movements struggled to create interracial alliances among farmers and industrial workers, and blacks pursued strategies for the internal development of economic and political institutions. As expanding industries drew more African Americans north, a cultural renaissance in northern cities gave voice to sophisticated and varied forms of self-expression that broadened arguments for black freedom. The Great Depression of the 1930s was especially devastating for black communities, but it also created the opportunity for new alliances among the growing numbers of poor displaced laborers. World War II made the dangers of racism abroad clear, and U.S. domestic racial policy became an international embarrassment in the context of the ensuing Cold War competition with Communism for the loyalty of the world's people of color. In Korea and elsewhere, African American soldiers had fought for a double victory, to bring freedom to the world and equality at home. Their demands and expectations helped spawn a massive modern civil rights movement that gathered force during the post–World War II period, seeking freedom first through the courts and then through nonviolent protest. Martin Luther King, Jr., became the best-known spokesman for the movement, marshaling the moral power of the nation's principles, but masses of blacks and whites raised their voices together, speaking truth to power.

Southern resistance to civil rights demands, the federal government's equivocal support and its distraction by American involvement in the Vietnam War, and the assassinations of progressive leaders, including Martin Luther King Jr., deepened the anger and widened divisions in the movement by the late 1960s. Voices of rage demanded "freedom now." With the war abroad and riots and upheaval at home, a political backlash brought into power racial and economic conservatives who advocated the strategy of a "color-blind" emphasis on individual rights in their acrimonious debates with those pleading for a continued focus on racial equality. At the beginning of the twenty-first century, the American people are aware of the nation's racial and cultural diversity—diversity emphasized by the historians who continue to recover the story of the nation's multiracial past. African American history is a critical part of American history, and African Americans have figured prominently in the creation of American culture. An awareness of their quest for racial equality will help advance all Americans, and the nation itself, along the hard road to freedom.

Chapter 1

Africa and the Atlantic Slave Trade

O laudah, whose name meant "the fortunate one," was born in 1745 to an elder among the Ibo (also called Igbo) people living in Benin, the eastern area of present-day Nigeria, in West Africa. Olaudah Equiano was his full name, although later in his life he would also be called Gustavus Vassa. His first few years were fortunate indeed. Indulged as his mother's favorite, he was the youngest son in a large family of comfortable means in a warm, productive land, "almost a nation of dancers, musicians, and poets."[1] Trade with neighboring settlements linked Equiano's people to a far-flung commercial network, but most daily contacts were local, and most disputes were decided by the village elders. Living more than a hundred miles from the coast, the young boy had no contact with European traders and knew nothing of their society. Through local oral histories, however, Equiano probably had heard stories of his own people, the Kingdom of Benin, and the ancient empires and great civilizations to which it was tied. Beginning in ancient times, African storytellers memorized proverbs and tales from their people's history and could recite them to educate and entertain the villagers. As the archivists of their people, these talented and specially trained men were often trusted government advisers respected for their skill.

Equiano lived in a small corner of a vast continent. Second only to Asia in size, Africa has a land area of 11,700,000 square miles, stretching from the Mediterranean to the Cape of Good Hope, almost six times the size of Europe. Its geographical characteristics vary from the dry Sahara Desert in the north, an area the size of the United States, or the Kalahari Desert in the south to the grasslands of the Sudan to some of the most beautiful tropical rain forests in the world, situated in the central regions of the continent. It is a land infinitely diverse in climate, terrain, wildlife, and human culture. Between 6000 and 2500 B.C.E., a desert gradually emerged in Africa where once a green belt had existed. Equiano knew that his homeland was but a small corner of this vast expanse; that his nation and its people were rooted in an ancient civilization, indirectly descended from those who migrated south from the fertile Sahara as that region became too dry to sustain agriculture.

Long before, in the fourteenth century B.C.E., the Egyptians had retaken much of northern Africa from the darker skinned peoples of Kush, who retreated southward. Archaeological records reveal that the people of Kush established a strong kingdom based on agriculture, commerce, and iron manufacturing. They built urban centers and massive stone structures and dominated the trade routes to the Red Sea and the ivory markets of northern Africa for many centuries. In the third century C.E. their power was challenged by another emerging nation, occupying the region of present-day Ethiopia centered in the commercial city of Axum. Finally, around 350 C.E., the commercial conflict between these two nations became open warfare that ultimately destroyed Kush, scattering its people among other national groups to the east and to the west, toward the Atlantic coast.[2]

The contentions creating critical changes in northeastern Africa during this period included religious conflicts. Christianity was taking root in Egypt and spreading to the south and west, challenging traditional religions in those regions. After Rome became Catholic, most African Christians broke away from the Roman Church and formed the Coptic Church. ("Coptic" comes from a Greek word meaning "Egyptian church.") Over many centuries, as it spread, Christianity faced stiff competition from the many traditional local religions and from Islam, which was particularly influential in the region of the Sudan. In regions where Islam was accepted, oral historians added the Koran to their other recitations; in Christian areas they incorporated the Bible.

In the fourth and fifth centuries, a powerful trading nation arose to the southwest of Egypt. It took the name "Ghana" from the title given to its ruler, and by the eighth century it dominated West Africa. It controlled the trade routes across the Sahara that connected Africa with Mediterranean Europe, its people acting as middlemen between the people of West Africa and the Arabs of the north, and imposing tariffs on salt, gold, rubber, ivory, brass, and the small numbers of slaves that flowed north from the grasslands of central Africa. The tariff collected on this trade increased Ghana's wealth, and the wealth made it militarily strong. By the eleventh century Ghana's rulers commanded an army estimated at two hundred thousand warriors. From the north Ghana received the influence of Muslim merchants, Arabic as a written language, and the Islamic faith. The Muslim influence was apparent in its capital city of Kumbi-Saleh, which had not only a national palace and other opulent state buildings but also a Muslim quarter with twelve mosques and guest accommodations for Muslim visitors; Kumbi-Saleh was a center for education as well.

Ghana's wealth was enhanced still further by the gold brought from the mines of the Senegal River region and by the craftsmanship of its ironworkers, who were skilled at making weapons for warfare. This empire too was constantly challenged by its neighbors, who sought to acquire its wealth. Muslim warlords chipped away at the territory and trade that were the source of Ghana's power, and in 1076 they captured the capital, executing all who refused to convert to Islam. As the result of military losses and successive droughts, Ghana finally ceased dominating its region in the late twelfth century.

The successor state to Ghana was the Kingdom of Mali, which became extraordinarily wealthy and powerful during the thirteenth century. Travelers from the Middle East and southern Europe came in caravans to trade in Gao, Kangaba, Jenne, and other commercial cities of the empire. In the fourteenth and fifteenth centuries scholars came to Timbuktu to study Koranic theology, diplomacy, and law at the University of Sankore. The city and its university became a major center of Islamic learning, offering special education in geography and mathematics. European visitors were impressed with the grandeur of Mali and the grace and adroitness of its rulers. Under Mansa Kango Musa, a devout Muslim who made regular pilgrimages to the holy city of Mecca, Mali reached the zenith of its power between 1312 and 1332. With these pilgrimages Mansa Musa made a mighty impression on rival states. In 1324 five hundred slaves wielding heavy golden staffs heralded his arrival at the gates of Mecca. His camel caravan, escorted by many thousands of his servants, carried thirty thousand pounds of gold.[3] In terms of wealth, governmental organization, and military power, fourteenth-century Mali dominated its region and rivaled any nation in Europe. Centuries later British historian E. W. Bovill wrote that Mansa Musa ruled over a nation as "remarkable for its size as for its wealth, and which provided a striking example of the capacity of the Negro for political organization." J. C. DeGraft-Johnson believed that Mansa Musa "came nearest to building a united West Africa." "Whether you lived in the Gambia, Sierra Leone, the Ivory Coast, the Gold Coast, Togoland, Dahomey, or Nigeria," DeGraft-Johnson asserted, "you could not help but feel the power and strength of the Mali Empire, the empire which sought to fuse all of West Africa into one whole." Thus Mali and its glory were directly connected to Benin's history. Through his ancestors Equiano was linked to all West Africans who were dominated by, and shared in, the ancient kingdom's power.[4]

In the late fifteenth century Mali's power waned, and Songhay (Songhai), a nation in the western Sudan that had been converted to Islam in the beginning of the eleventh century, rose to power. Songhay, with its capital city of Gao on the banks of the Niger River, became a mighty trading nation. Under its control Timbuktu and Jenne flourished, their markets and schools drawing an ever-increasing economic and intellectual traffic from North Africa, the Middle East, Asia, and southern Europe, especially Spain and Portugal. At the height of Songhay's power Timbuktu alone had 180 schools, and white and black scholars at the University of Sankore studied grammar, literature, geography, science, law, surgery, and diplomacy. African scholars from Songhay carried their learning to the educational centers of southern Europe. Its

government was a complex structure, comprising elected and appointed officials. Its military was a professional corps distributed throughout the provinces
of the nation under the command of provincial governors. Its economy
revolved around trade, agriculture, and herding, and its economic success
attracted the attention of rival states in North Africa.[5] In 1591 the sultan of
Morocco dispatched troops, many of whom were Spanish mercenaries, to attack
Songhay. The resulting war was a costly one for both sides. Despite their superior weaponry, which included firearms previously unknown in the region,
twenty thousand Moroccan troops fell. However, the warfare weakened Songhay's ability to withstand internal conflicts and pressures from neighboring
states, and the empire disintegrated by the early seventeenth century.[6]

Equiano's nation of Benin had gained importance in the fifteenth century, growing from a walled city to a nation state as a result of its conquest
of states west of the Niger River. The religion and science of his people
reflected the long history of diverse influences in the region. They were not
Muslim, although there were strong Islamic influences. Equiano reported that
his people had no public places of worship but were attended by "priests and
magicians, or wise men." There were strict religious rules governing funerals,
food preparation, and cleanliness. The people believed in only one "Creator
of all things" but also believed that spirits could affect the world. There was
a close link between religion and science. Religious "magicians" also practiced
the art of bleeding, much like Europeans at the time (and Americans well into
the nineteenth century).

Although religious practices varied widely in West Africa, the importance
of ceremonial music and dance was universal. Special dances, songs, or
poems marked any significant event, victory in battle, marriage, birth, death,
or an agricultural festival. Public dances were highly stylized, with special
positions occupied by married men, married women, young single men, and
"maidens," representing battle, domestic life, sports, and courtship. Later in
his life, after he left Africa, Equiano saw Greeks dancing in ways that reminded
him of the dances done by his people.

Benin was an agricultural nation and a land of traders. By the end of the
fifteenth century its cloth products were popular with European traders, and
its bronze and ivory art was found in Europe. The farmers of Benin were famous
for their pepper, and the Portuguese established a trading post to deal largely
in this one coveted spice. Africans received copper, coral beads, umbrellas, and
guns in exchange for pepper and some slaves taken from the interior as prisoners of war. Increasingly after 1500 the Portuguese became more interested
in the slave trade to supply labor for their sugar plantations on the island of
São Tome in the Gulf of Guinea, in southern Portugal, on Madeira, and later
on Cape Verde and in Brazil. Their plantation system drew on the earlier expe-

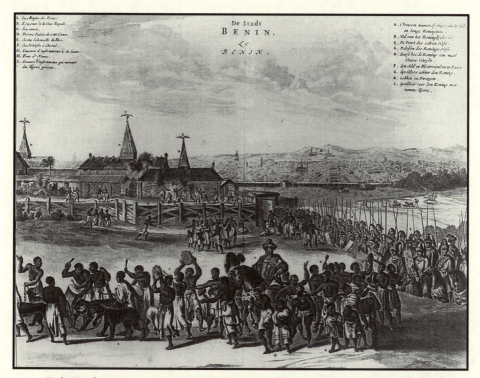

Eighteenth-century engraving depicting a celebration near the city of Benin
on the Guinea Coast of West Africa.

Museum of African Art, Smithsonian Institution, Washington, D.C.

rience of Mediterranean sugar plantations in Cyprus, Crete, and Sicily, which
used Muslim war prisoners and Slavic forced labor from the port towns of the
Black Sea. In fact, so closely were eastern Europeans identified with this
forced labor that the word "slave" originated in the ethnic designation of Slav,
only gradually coming to denote bound laborers of African origin. Over the
next three centuries Europeans competed for control of the massive Atlantic
slave trade, which provided much of the labor for their colonization of the
Americas.[7]

Slavery was already well established in Benin and other areas in North
and West Africa before European involvement. Those held in bondage were
generally taken in war, the losers of some battle who might have been killed
but for their capture. Traditionally a slave's value increased with the distance
from the slave's home. Before the fifth century Romans were willing to pay
higher prices for North African slaves because their remoteness from their homeland made them a more secure investment. In the Muslim world slaves at a
distance from their homes were valued as "strangers" who might be provided

with trusted positions because they were thought to have no local loyalties other than to their master. These slaves were often used as special military guards in their master's household or harem. As a logical consequence of this reasoning, as a slave became more familiar with the social customs and the politics of a region, that slave also became less suitable for slavery in that region. This might have critical implications for a slave's children, whose familiarity with the local society might brand them as unfit for slavery.[8]

In Benin slaves became servants, tenders of the livestock, domestic workers, and agricultural field laborers. They were denied the freedoms accorded to others in the society and were subject to harsh punishment for infractions of the rules that governed master-slave relationships. Slaves endured harsh, restricted lives, but they had hope for a better future.[9] Among Equiano's people a slave might rise from that lowly position to become a full citizen, equal in rights and status to any others in the society. Equiano had witnessed many slave sales as a child. Well-armed traders with large sacks traversed his region offering to buy or sell slaves. Before travelers were allowed to transport slaves through Benin lands, however, they were required to certify the lawfulness of their acquisition. Kidnappers were themselves enslaved as punishment for their violations of the rules. Equiano claimed that only war prisoners and criminals were held by his people or sold to passing traders. This was the expectation with which Benin's traders initially participated in the slave traffic with the Portuguese. Their understanding eventually changed, however, but by that time their principles had been compromised by the allure of the guns that came in return for slaves and greatly magnified the military might of Benin.

Equiano explained the process. "When a trader wants slaves, he applies to a chief for them, and tempts him with his wares." "It is not extraordinary," he observed, "if on this occasion [the chief] yields to the temptation with as little firmness, and accepts the price of his fellow creature's liberty, with as little reluctance as the enlightened [European] merchant's."[10] Benin was among the first nations in its region to be supplied with substantial numbers of firearms and horses, which facilitated the expansion of its empire beyond the Niger Delta to Lagos and from the Atlantic coast into Yorubaland.[11]

As with other powerful nations, Benin was constantly challenged by rivals, and as the pressure to maintain a strong military presence was unrelenting, trading slaves for weapons of war increased. Eventually, during the eighteenth century, Benin's power waned so that by the time Equiano was born its military might was overshadowed by competitor nations who controlled more of the area's trade. The Yoruba empire of Oyo largely supplanted Benin in the Portuguese trade during much of the eighteenth century. Oyo and Ashante became two of the most powerful nations of the region, controlling much of the slave trade and defending their commerce against the military incursions of Muslim traders. Their power allowed them to require tributes and taxes from Europeans in return for the privilege of trading in the region. Access to the coast was important for participation in the European trade. Along the coast from the Senegal River in the northwest to Angola in central Africa, European nations established trading posts that grew with the slave trade into a chain of more than fifty forts dotting three hundred miles of coastline. The greatest concentration of forts was along the Gold Coast, reflecting the original impetus for European involvement in African trade. The largest of these forts were called castles, elaborate walled settlements providing accommodations and offices for European traders, storage facilities for supplies, and holding pens for more than a thousand slaves. In 1481 the Portuguese built Elmina, one of the first of the large castles, on the Gold Coast in present-day Ghana. From coastal garrisons like these, European nations contended for control of the slave trade, as African nations contended for internal control of the trade. Elmina fell to the Dutch in 1637; the Cape Coast castle built by the Swedes in 1653 had been held successively by West Africans, the Dutch, and the English by 1665.[12]

Dahomey, a non-Muslim inland nation, broke through to the coast and replaced the coastal traders who had served as go-betweens selling Dahomean goods and slaves to the European coastal traders.[13] Among the people of Dahomey, slaves often filled out the ranks of military forces used to capture more slaves, who were then sold to strengthen Dahomean military power further. Perhaps it was a group from Dahomey who came to Equiano's village while the adults were away in the fields. But it was no military unit that found the eleven-year-old Equiano and his sister alone in their compound. This was a small slave-raiding party of two men and a woman, who seized the pair and took them off into the woods, where they were bound and placed in large sacks. They were taken first to a neighboring state where their own language was spoken, and were sold to a chieftain. Equiano's owner was a blacksmith, and the boy was employed working the bellows at the forge. The children remained in this "very pleasant country" for only a short time before they were sold again and separated. Equiano was eventually taken to the Atlantic coast, where he was shocked by his first encounter with Europeans. "Their complexions . . . differing so much from ours, their long hair, and the language they spoke (which was very different from any I had ever heard)" reinforced his fear that he would be killed by these "white men with horrible looks, red faces and long hair" whom he considered "bad spirits." He was also surprised by the ethnic and linguistic diversity of the other Africans he met, and astonished by his first sight of the ocean and the great ships lying at anchor.

Although Equiano had never seen Europeans before, contact between southern Europeans and African people was already centuries old. The North

African conquest and occupation of the Iberian Peninsula, beginning in 711, lasted for hundreds of years. For more than seven centuries Africans and Europeans shared this region, with the Africans wielding power. There was regular interaction between the races until the Spaniards pushed these Moors, as they were called, back across the Mediterranean in the eleventh century and finally retook control of the entire peninsula in 1492 with the conquest of the Kingdom of Granada. By that time the region had become what the historian Ronald Sanders called "the most racially varied society in western Europe."[14]

Yet, Iberians were ambivalent on the question of color. The numbers of blacks in the society encouraged both racial tolerance and racial restriction. Although the black population was eventually absorbed into the society, legal prohibitions, such as those that separated burials by race, relegating Africans to a common grave (*"Pocos dos Negros"*), narrowed interracial associations, limited black movement, and lowered African social and political status in the society. Still, it is likely that the region's historical experience made the Spaniards and the Portuguese more aware than the English of the nuances of ethnicity, culture, and skin color among the Africans they encountered in West Africa.[15] Mid-sixteenth-century Spanish traders' and travelers' impressions of Africa evidenced an awareness and an appreciation of the human variety they came in contact with. As the English observed, many Spaniards considered differences in skin color to be "[o]ne of the marveylous thynges that god [sic] useth in the composition of man." They were conscious of white and black as the extremes of human skin shades, "utterlye contrary," but they also recognized yellow, tan, brown, and other colors as well.[16] Other Europeans tended to simplify or even ignore cultural differences between Africans and to call them all "black." The English especially, who came to West Africa in the fifteenth and sixteenth centuries, were much more likely to see an indistinguishable African blackness. As the English became increasingly important in the growing Atlantic slave trade, "blackness" gradually imputed to African people the negative characteristics associated with the term in the English language. According to the fifteenth-century *Oxford English Dictionary* "blackness" was evil, sinful, ugly, and unclean, and the English identification of Africans as black marked the African character with these connotations in the English mind.

Contrary to British stereotypes, Africans were ethnically, linguistically, religiously, and culturally varied peoples. In fact, the wide variety of African cultures and histories makes it difficult to tell their story except in the broadest terms. The family was central to African social, economic, and political life. Family lineage was traced through the father in West Africa and through the mother in west central and central Africa. In most regions the lands

Olaudah Equiano;

or

GUSTAVUS VASSA,

the African?

Published March 1 1789 by G Vassa

Olaudah Equiano,
as shown in the
frontispiece to
*The Interesting
Narrative of the Life
of Olaudah Equiano;
or Gustavus Vassa,
the African.*

Prints and Photographs
Division,
Library of Congress,
Washington, D.C.

were controlled by large extended families. Three families generally collab-
orated in selecting national leaders. The royal family supplied eligible male
candidates, another family selected the leader from among the candidates,
and still another family invested him with the power of office. As in other
traditional societies, individuals were connected to their history through
their family. Africans removed from family, from their ancestors and their land,
were separated from an important part of their identity and were truly lost
and alone. In the months and years after his enslavement, Equiano preserved the memory of his family and traditions as best he could; writing and

publishing his autobiography decades later, in 1789, helped him preserve a part of his identity.

During the days that Equiano was held on the coast, he and his fellow African prisoners learned much about their white captors, and after he found an African with whom he could communicate, he began to understand his situation. He was to be taken far away to the white man's country in one of the great ships. He was relieved once he was convinced that these strange men were not going to eat him, a common fear among those who had never before seen Europeans, and he began to believe that life might be no worse for him than for slaves in his land. Still, what he saw worried him—"the white people looked and acted . . . in so savage a manner, for I had never seen among any people such instances of brutal cruelty." He was terrified not only by the way white men treated the Africans but also—especially—by the way whites treated one another. "One white man in particular I saw . . . flogged so unmercifully with a large rope . . . that he died." The man's body was tossed overboard in a manner unthinkable to an African socialized in a society that held funeral ceremonies sacred.[17]

After several days the ship came that was to carry the Africans from their homeland. They marveled at the ship's arrival under full sail and wondered at the magic that brought this machine and these men to this place. In the next days and weeks, life for these Africans became almost unbearable as they endured the transatlantic voyage that has come to be called the Middle Passage. A cargo of "black people of every description was chained together" belowdecks in the hold of the ship for six to eight weeks. As Equiano remembered,

> The stench of the hold while we were on the coast was so intolerably loathsome that it was dangerous to remain there for any time, and some of us had been permitted to stay on the deck for the fresh air; but now that the whole ship's cargo were confined together, and the heat of the climate, added to the number in the ship, which was so crowded that each had scarcely room to turn himself, almost suffocated us.[18]

The passage from the west coast of Africa to America was one of the most agonizing and dangerous parts of the enslavement process for the Africans. As if to testify to Equiano's description, hearings on the slave trade were held by the English Parliament in the 1780s. In these hearings a diagram of a slave ship, the *Brookes,* sailing out of Liverpool, depicted the unbelievably crowded conditions aboard one vessel. Resulting legislation prescribed the space to be provided to each slave aboard. Even if these rules of space allocation had been enforced—and they seldom were—slaves would have had half the room allowed to European immigrants brought to America during the seventeenth

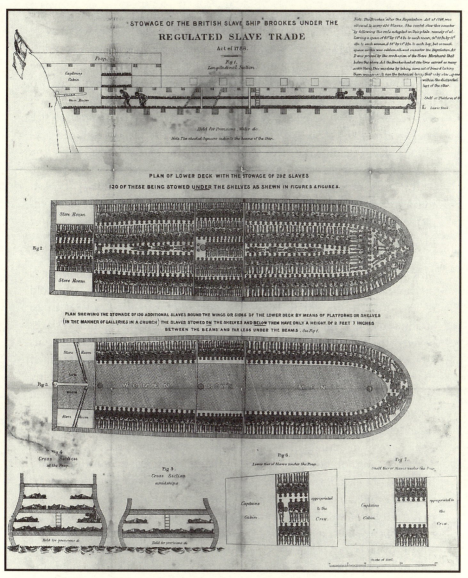

Schematic drawing of the slave ship *Brookes,* used to illustrate British
regulations for the number of humans to be loaded aboard during the
Middle Passage from Africa to the Americas. British law required no more
than 451 slaves to be carried by a ship of that size. Abolitionist member
of Parliament William Wilberforce produced records to show, however,
that this ship had transported as many as 609 slaves on some of its voyages
to North America.

Prints and Photographs Division, Library of Congress, Washington, D.C.

century as indentured servants, or even to prisoners transported to colonies such as British colonial Georgia or Australia. On the slave ships shelves were added to increase the capacity of the hold, dividing the area into two sections. A space six feet by one foot four inches was allotted for each adult man, five feet ten inches by one foot for each adult woman, five feet by one foot two inches for each boy, and four feet six inches by one foot for each girl. Using these calculations, British lawmakers estimated that a ship of the *Brookes's* size could reasonably transport up to 451 slaves, albeit in the most cramped conditions. The full horror of the Middle Passage is barely suggested by the impersonality of reducing human beings to deck-space dimensions. The whole story was even more grotesque, and many in Parliament were shocked to learn from a former crew member's testimony that the *Brookes* had completed the trip several years before carrying over 600 slaves, and they had lost many during the voyage.[19]

Alexander Falconbridge, a British surgeon, made the voyage from West Africa to the West Indies thirty years after Equiano's journey. Dr. Falconbridge's description of the hardships of the trip and the crowded conditions in the hold reveals little improvement. When the doctor ventured belowdecks in an attempt to attend the sick, he was forced to step on chained bodies, as slaves covered the entire floor. He reported that each slave was locked in irons attached to a long chain fixed to the lower deck, binding fifty or sixty men to the ship and to one another. Twice a day, at about eight in the morning and at four in the afternoon, weather permitting, these slaves were allowed abovedecks for food and exercise. As Falconbridge described it, their food consisted "chiefly of horsebeans, boiled to the consistence of a pulp; of boiled yams and rice, and sometimes of a small quantity of beef and pork."[20]

Conditions on board ship made death from disease, malnutrition, mistreatment, or lack of fresh air, frequent. Slaves who resisted their bondage by refusing nourishment were force-fed by the application of special jaw screws to force their mouths open. The whip was liberally employed to discourage protest of any kind. Equiano told of a group of Africans on his ship who elected suicide over slavery, making their way through the deck netting and flinging themselves into the ocean to drown. The crew "rescued" several of them and pulled them back aboard. Those who survived were severely and brutally punished as an object lesson to others who contemplated such action.

While some Africans sought freedom through suicide, others watched for opportunities to escape or to rebel. Slavery's defenders often argued that the dangers of ocean crossings in general accounted for the high death rate among slaves. In reality slave ships were floating prisons that held men and women for weeks under the most inhumane circumstances. The crew members were essentially prison guards, and there was great incentive for these guards to take their work seriously, since all knew the danger of slave rebellions at sea. Capt. Philip Drake, an experienced slave trader, explained to those seeking to enter the business that "the Negroes [fight] like wild beasts" and warned that "slavery is a dangerous business at sea as well as ashore."[21]

Slave ships generally carried more crew members than did other vessels, partly because of their special security needs. Many captains felt it essential to have at least one crewman for every ten slaves, and although this was not always the case, a ratio of one to twelve or fifteen was not uncommon. Some captains increased the security aboard their vessels by keeping male slaves chained belowdecks for the entire trip. This may have helped protect the crew, but it devastated the health of the slaves, killing many more than died during the average voyage.

Life on a slave ship was dangerous and uncomfortable even for the captain and crew. The crew's diet was almost as meager as the slaves', except that they received regular and larger portions of meat and a ration of rum. Disease was far more dangerous belowdecks, but the crew was not immune to the deadly plagues that were common on slave ships. Under these conditions the mortality rate was very high, 15 to 25 percent, reaching 33 percent for the slaves and almost that for the crew. Slave ships attracted a steady escort of sharks because the dead were tossed over the side each morning. Most captains endured the hardships in return for a share in the profit from the sale of the slaves. While profits fluctuated, returns from 100 percent to 150 percent on investments per voyage were usual. Some crew members were paid; others were impressed into service or were convicts offered duty aboard a slave ship as the only alternative to prison. Yet, even under the worst of circumstances, the voyage abovedecks could not be compared to that in the hold. Slaves, of course, had no choice and profited not at all.

African women received somewhat different treatment aboard ship than did the men. They were sometimes confined to a separate section of the hold and were often allowed to remain abovedecks for longer periods of time because they were believed to be less dangerous. Thus they were somewhat less likely to suffer the health hazards and extreme physical hardships of the crowded quarters in the hold. However, because they were abovedecks, the women were at the constant mercy of the crew. Although all women were at risk, young slave women were especially likely to be raped and otherwise abused by the captain and crew while they were at sea. Often the captain depended on the crew's access to the women to quiet dissatisfaction during long difficult voyages.

Although captains generally allowed women and children to remain untethered above deck, many knew better than to underestimate their female captives. As one captain was cautioned, "putt not too much confidence in the

Women nor Children least they happen to be Instrumental to your being surprised which may be fatal."[22] Women too were responsible for deadly shipboard rebellions. An unnamed woman played a key role in an abortive escape attempt by three slaves being transported aboard the English ship *Robert* in 1721. Because she was allowed to move about the ship more freely, she was able to carry information from one captive to another and coordinate the attack. The strike killed two of the crew, but it ultimately failed, and the slaves involved were executed. Adding a gruesome touch to the deadly business, the captain forced the three insurgents to eat the heart and liver of one of the dead white crewmen before he killed them. As if to make a special example of the woman, the captain had her hanged by her thumbs, whipped, slashed with knives, and allowed to bleed to death.[23]

Horrifying as these events were, they were not unique. The slave trade was one of the bloodiest, most brutal aspects of African, European, and American history. After Europeans established settlements in America their labor needs increased greatly. The Spaniards in Latin America used native American Indians at first, but they died in such large numbers and at such a rapid rate that they provided an inadequate supply. King Charles II of Spain had prohibited the use of African labor in New Spain, but was persuaded to lift the ban by those who, like Bishop Bartolomeo de Las Casas, advocated the importation of African labor as a "humanitarian effort" to keep the Indian populations from total destruction. Later, after witnessing the brutality of African enslavement, Las Casas reconsidered and opposed the importation of Africans, but by the mid–sixteenth century Africans had become the favored substitute for Indian labor.

The African slave trade, which had progressed at a trickle during the fourteenth and fifteenth centuries, became a torrent during the next four hundred years, as it was redirected from southern Europe to South America, the Caribbean, and to a lesser extent North America. The first slave ships, mainly Spanish, to come directly from Africa to the Western Hemisphere traded in the West Indies as early as 1532, while the Portuguese brought Africans to supply their sugar plantations in Brazil after the mid–sixteenth century. The wealth extracted from the Americas by the Spaniards and the Portuguese was directly connected to the increased demand for sugar, which outpaced the supply from southern Europe. As the number of Europeans who could afford to indulge a taste for sweets grew, the value of sugar increased, and the demand for slaves to cultivate this extremely labor-intensive crop climbed sharply. By the end of the century sugar production in the Caribbean and Brazil was absorbing two thousand African slaves a year. The Africans imported to the Spanish colonies of South America were not all used in sugar production immediately. They replaced Indian laborers in the gold mines of New Spain and suffered comparably high death rates. By the end of the eighteenth century, however, sugarcane had become the Americas' major slave crop.

Other Africans came not as slaves but as sailors or as part of the Spanish military forces. Ancient cultural artifacts found in Latin America suggest to some scholars that Africans may have traveled to the Americas hundreds of years before the arrival of Christopher Columbus, although this hypothesis is not universally accepted.[24] Certainly many came during the age of European exploration. At least one of Columbus's crew is believed to have been of African ancestry, and thirty blacks traveled with the Spanish explorer Vasco Núñez de Balboa when he became the first European to discover the Pacific Ocean in 1513. In 1519 when Hernándo Cortez defeated the Aztecs in what is now Mexico, more than three hundred Africans were there to position his cannon. Other Africans entered the American West with the early Spanish expeditions. They produced the first wheat crop harvested in America, and in 1565 helped to build St. Augustine in Florida, the first city established by Europeans in North America.

Estevanico, a black Spaniard who acted as a guide for Cortez, excited the Spanish imagination by relating the Indian tales of the "Seven Cities of Gold." In 1539, with Estevanico guiding the way and acting as Indian interpreter, Father Marcos de Niza led Spanish troops through the American Southwest (in the areas that are the present-day states of New Mexico and Arizona) in search of the mythic treasure site. Posing as a medicine man, Estevanico enlisted the aid of several Indian villages in the search. The Spaniards hoped to discover these cities, with their limitless supply of gold, but their dream was never realized. Estevanico was killed by Indian forces, and the expedition retreated to the main Spanish settlement in Mexico. Yet the journey had fueled the Spaniards' fantasies of great wealth, and the story of Estevanico encouraged many other expeditions to continue the search. Centuries after Estevanico's death the Zuni Indians of the Southwest still tell of the black man who died searching for the golden city. Although Africans played various roles among the Spaniards in America, they were most likely, by far, to be slaves in South and Central America. It is fair to say that Spain's ascension to economic and military dominance during the fifteenth and sixteenth centuries rested on African and American Indian slave labor.[25]

The Portuguese produced great quantities of sugar in Brazil, using slave labor supplied from its trading posts in the Congo and Angola. Although they gained an early lead through their involvement in the slave trade, the government did not officially sponsor the activity until the late seventeenth century, and Portugal was overshadowed by other European traders who rose to power with the full support of their government. After Holland emerged from Spain's control at the end of the sixteenth century, it established a government-assisted slave trading effort that resulted in the formation of the Dutch West India Company in 1621. This company, which held a monopoly on all slave trading between Africa and the Dutch New World, produced spectacular profits for the nation and company stockholders. Holland translated its economic power into a strong naval force and managed to push Portugal out of its Gold Coast trading posts. Rivalries with neighboring France and, later, England eventually weakened the Dutch hold on the slave trade and allowed other Europeans to participate in the profits, but Holland continued to trade slaves for at least another one hundred years.

As Europeans realized the economic potential of the African trade, more nations established slave-trading centers in West Africa. During the seventeenth century Sweden, Denmark, and the German principality of Brandenburg took part in the lucrative trade.[26] Thus by the eighteenth century the African continent was supplying great wealth and power to Europe and to Europe's emerging American settlements. Meanwhile Africa was being drained of one of its greatest assets—many of its young, strong, healthy people.

England entered the slave trade later than most of its competitors, but it quickly eclipsed the field. The English had traded gold and ivory in Africa for more than a century before Sir John Hawkins became one of the first English traders to bring African slaves, in a ship called *Jesus,* to be sold in New Spain. Initially there was resistance at home to British participation. Queen Elizabeth I was afraid that God would punish her nation for selling human beings, but her fears of a catastrophic event were calmed when Hawkins demonstrated the vast profit to be made. Subsequently she encouraged him to undertake another slave trading voyage and invested her own money in the enterprise. Thus, long before England established its own colonies in America, it profited from the New World through its participation in the slave trade.

Three times during the 1560s Hawkins sailed between Africa and America, and each time the returns were considerable, so much so that several English merchants followed his example. British colonists in America entered the slave trade in 1644 when Boston merchants sponsored their first commercial voyage to Africa. Their ship, the *Rainbow,* brought slaves and other merchandise to British colonies in the Caribbean. In 1655 Britain established plantations in Jamaica and imported slaves to grow sugarcane. The increasing profit from sugar encouraged increased slave importation so that by 1673 there were ten thousand Africans and only eight thousand English settlers in Jamaica. Within fifty years Africans accounted for almost 70 percent of the island's population.

In 1672 the Royal African Company was formed to coordinate the slave trade, by then partly underwritten by the Crown. The company entered the trade just at the point of its most rapid expansion. Clashing with Holland over its move into Dutch-controlled West African areas, England expanded its participation. The trade became so lucrative that even though the Royal Africa Company secured a grant of monopoly from the Crown in 1673, it could not prevent other English dealers from infringing on its trade. Finally, in response to mounting pressure, Parliament rescinded the company's monopoly in 1711 and opened slave trading to all Englishmen. By that time Britain had established colonies in North America and was supplying them with African slaves.

The economic rivalries developing in Europe bore striking similarities to those in existence hundreds of years earlier in West and North Africa. Both centered around the African and European intercontinental trade. On both continents powerful nations had risen to preeminence based on their ability to control and profit from that trade, only to be supplanted by competing nations. Whether Ghana or Portugal, Songhay or Spain, each owed its economic and consequent military power to the profit from that trade. Old World dominance was constructed on traditional commodities, which included gold and slaves. From the eighth to the sixteenth century, most of the western world's gold came from the Sudan, controlled there by African merchant powers. Much of the struggle in the fifteenth and sixteenth centuries focused on Europe's attempt to circumvent that control. Europe's incursion into the Americas was a part of this effort. There, too, gold, and the slaves to extract it, became central to increasing wealth and power. By the mid–sixteenth century, sugar grown in America became ever more significant, overshadowing production in southern Europe. The wealth generated by trade in these commodities underlay the political and military power of Europe, as it had for Africa.

Figures are disputed, but the best recent scholarship estimates the total number of Africans brought to the Americas at something under fifteen million. The vast majority of those taken as slaves were males, a fact only marginally affected by economics. Generally male slaves brought higher prices as labor for the early American sugar plantations and gold mines, but after the late seventeenth century, women were in demand and brought prices comparable to those for men. African merchants, however, were less willing to sell African women. Women were valued at home as the bearers of children and, in most African societies, as the chief agricultural producers. There were also fewer female slaves available to African coastal traders because slaves were likely to be taken in battle, making men most likely to be captured. Very few children were taken because they brought prices too low to make their trade profitable. Only about 10 percent of the slaves who made the Middle Passage were under the age of ten.[27]

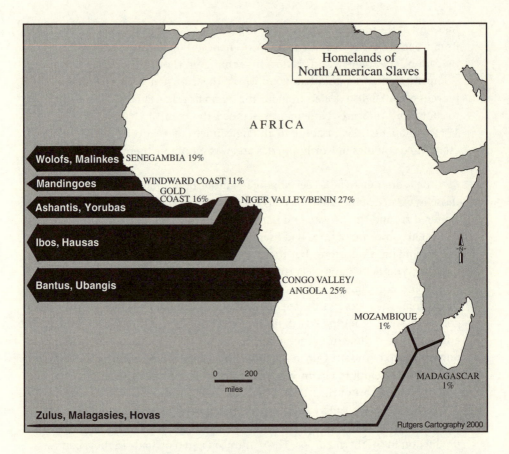

Homelands of
North American Slaves

AFRICA

Wolofs, Malinkes SENEGAMBIA 19%

Mandingoes WINDWARD COAST 11%
GOLD
COAST 16% NIGER VALLEY/BENIN 27%

Ashantis, Yorubas

Ibos, Hausas

CONGO VALLEY/
Bantus, Ubangis ANGOLA 25%

MOZAMBIQUE
1%

0   200

miles

MADAGASCAR
1%

Zulus, Malagasies, Hovas

Rutgers Cartography 2000

Economics did substantially determine the slaves' destination, however, and since the return on slave labor used in sugarcane fields was great, African slaves brought the highest prices in the sugar-producing regions south of the present-day United States. Ninety percent of all the slaves brought to the Americas were sold to those regions. During the first 350 years of the slave trade to the West (1502–1860), more than 50 percent of the Africans were enslaved in the West Indies by Spanish, French, Dutch, Danish, Swedish, and English sugar planters. Slightly less than 40 percent were bound to the Portuguese in Brazil; only 6 percent of enslaved Africans brought to the Western Hemisphere were held in the British colonies of North America. Initially most of the slaves brought to North America were transported through the large slave markets and plantations in the West Indies. After 1700, however, North American officials, slave importers, and their customers became convinced that West Indian traders sold the strongest and healthiest Africans to the more lucrative Caribbean market and shipped the less able, or sometimes the more rebellious, workers northward. Joseph Dudley, colonial governor of Massachusetts,

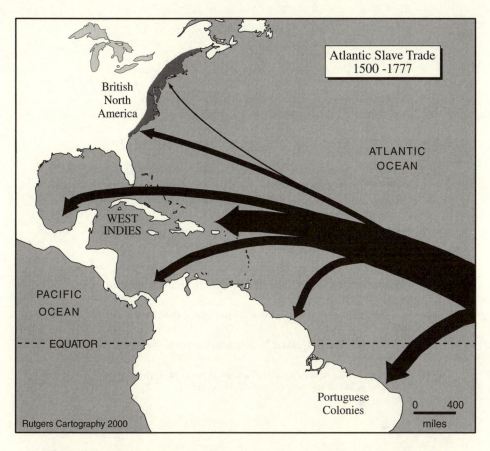

Atlantic Slave Trade
1500 -1777

British
North
America

ATLANTIC
OCEAN

WEST
INDIES

PACIFIC
OCEAN

- - - - EQUATOR - - - - - - -

Portuguese
Colonies

0   400

miles

Rutgers Cartography 2000

complained that slaves imported from the West Indies were "usually the worst Servants they have." Many suspected that they were "Criminalls or otherwise of Little worth." By the mid–eighteenth century, traders were bringing an increasing majority of those enslaved in North America directly from Africa.[28]

Fifty years before Equiano was enslaved, the average annual importation of slaves to the Americas had reached more than twenty thousand, and it increased so rapidly that by the 1780s it stood at more than eighty thousand.[29] Perhaps it was this staggering increase in the Atlantic slave trade that fueled the stories Equiano heard about the white men's cannibalism—stories that provided one possible explanation for the Europeans' voracious appetite for African slaves. Equiano was landed in the West Indies in the 1750s and eventually was taken to the colony of Virginia. He spent more than a decade struggling to regain the freedom he had lost. Once free, he raised his voice on behalf of the millions kidnapped from their homelands in Africa and cast into the wilderness of American slavery.

Chapter 2

1607 Founding of Jamestown, Virginia, first permanent English settlement in North America

1619 First Africans brought to British North American colonies landed in Jamestown, Virginia

Virginia General Assembly, the House of Burgesses, first representative government in colonial British North America

1620 Pilgrims arrive on the *Mayflower* at New Plymouth, Massachusetts

1635 African Anthony Johnson freed

1651 Anthony Johnson receives 250-acre land grant in Northhampton, Virginia

1670 Repeal of Virginia law that had allowed free blacks and indentured servants to vote

1676 Bacon's Rebellion in Virginia; participants include slaves and white indentured servants

1688 Germantown Protest; Quakers in Germantown, Pennsylvania, denounce slavery and the slave trade

1712 Slaves and Native American allies burn sections of New York City. Nine whites killed and twenty-one slaves executed

The Evolution of Slavery in British North America

*I*n Virginia, Olaudah Equiano became one of the tens of thousands of Africans and African descendants who tended the tobacco fields, maintained the households of planter families, and provided the skilled labor to build their homes and establish their settlements. By the time of Equiano's arrival, colonial law in British North America had transformed a loose system of African long-term labor into codified, perpetual, and inherited racial slavery. Virginia was a corporate venture financed by the sale of stock in the Virginia Company of London. The company employees who settled Jamestown in 1607 had not intended to build a society based on African slave labor. Drawing their lessons from Spain's extraction of gold from America, they hoped for riches from a similar enterprise employing American Indian labor. Despite a desperate first decade during which many Indians and many colonists died, the English settlers soon recognized that Virginia held a different sort of promise. With some instruction from the Indian population, farmers hoped to take advantage of the mild climate and fertile soil to supply both food and cash crops to sustain the colony. Tobacco, not gold, was to become the source of Virginia's wealth, and the unexpected arrival of twenty Africans aboard a Dutch trading ship in 1619 presented Virginians with another potential source of the labor to harvest this wealth.

Britain saw great potential for the colony of Virginia. It might provide produce that could not be grown at home and offered a place to transplant the growing numbers of unemployed people who crowded English cities and threatened the peace and stability of British society. Taxes on goods traded from Virginia brought needed revenue to the national treasury, and merchants and Virginia Company stockholders looked forward to reaping great profits. This lucrative potential could not be realized, however, without a stable, reliable labor force. Attempts to force Indians to labor were unsuccessful, as most escaped back to their own people, rebelled against British demands, or died of European diseases. When American Indian labor proved infeasible, the Virginia Company turned to Britain's poor, launching a campaign enticing them with promises of a new start in a place with virtually limitless land and great potential wealth. The land was strewn with gold, they were told, and a man could get rich quickly with little work. Those unable to pay their own passage were allowed to sign indentures, pledging five to seven years of work in return for the cost of the trip. Many believed the company's promises, and these indentured servants provided much of Virginia's work force during the early seventeenth century. But as the British birthrate fell, and wages and the prospects for employment in Britain rose after the 1630s, they became a less reliable labor source. As fewer of the English poor were willing to become indentured servants in Virginia, the company turned to African laborers, and the number of black servants in the colony began to increase steadily.

At the same time British holdings in the West Indies were turning to the cultivation of sugarcane for a reliably profitable crop and importing growing numbers of African slaves to supply the labor. Many slave traders believed that Africans' resistance to enslavement could be broken by the harsh system of gang labor in these sugar plantations. Accordingly, until well into the eighteenth century, many slaves bound for the mainland were taken first to the West Indies for a process called "seasoning." In his short stay in the West Indies, the young Equiano was horrified by the brutality of the life sugar plantation slaves were forced to endure. It was under these conditions that the British developed the customs and laws governing the operation of their slave system, providing the precedents in English law that were applied to mainland colonies. Gradually, over the next hundred years, the British colonies established a uniquely American form of racially based slavery.

North American slavery emerged slowly and unevenly, simultaneously manifesting different stages of development in different locations. The early black laborers in Virginia, not yet slaves but less free than white indentured servants, were sometimes allowed their freedom after a set period of time, almost always serving a longer indenture than white servants. There is evidence that some black servants were already serving for life by the middle of the seventeenth century. This implication can be drawn from the fact that when masters recovered seven escaped servants in Virginia in 1640, all were whipped, branded, and put in chains for a year, but only the whites' terms of service were extended as punishment. No such adjustment was necessary for the African, Emanuel, whose original service was apparently not limited by time. In the same year three other Virginia servants ran away from their master. When they were caught, two of them, a Dutchman and a Scot, received four additional years in servitude but the third, a black servant named John Punch, was ordered to serve for the rest of his life. In some instances blacks and whites of similar circumstance seemed to be treated similarly. When a white man and a black woman were found guilty of fornication in 1650, the church required them both to stand in shame before the congregation, clad only in white sheets, following a customary form of church-administered justice.[1]

Anthony Johnson

In the early 1620s slave traders captured a man in Angola, gave him the name Antonio, and brought him to the Americas, where he was sold to a colonist in Virginia. During these early days in British North America, before the system of slavery was strictly codified, some bound Africans were treated much like indentured servants. Although, unlike European servants, they had no contracts, some Africans were freed after a period of servitude. Perhaps this was how Antonio and his wife, Mary, also African, gained their freedom. Antonio may also have been granted a tract of land as the customary freedom dues for an indentured servant. By 1641 Antonio, a free man known as Anthony Johnson, was the owner of a small farm with livestock on Virginia's eastern shore. By midcentury, the Johnsons' farm had grown to about 250 acres, and the family held servants of their own.

During the formation of slavery, although race was a factor, color did not yet define life chances as comprehensively as it would by the nineteenth century. The Johnsons suffered a setback in 1653 when fire burned many of the buildings on their farm. The colonial court, noting that Johnson and his family were respected members of the community, granted them tax relief. A few years later, however, the Johnsons' white neighbor, Edmund Scarburgh, forged a letter in which Anthony Johnson appeared to acknowledge a debt. Though Johnson clearly was illiterate, the court granted Scarburgh a substantial portion of his land on the strength of that letter. The family purchased more land in Maryland and continued to live on their Virginia land. But when Anthony died in 1670, an ominous court ruling foreshadowed a more precarious future for free blacks. A white planter was allowed to seize the Virginia land because, the court said, as a black man, Anthony Johnson was not a citizen of the colony. His children maintained their hold on enough land to remain independent farmers, but they faced greater racial restrictions. By the turn of the eighteenth century, slavery was defined by laws that restricted the lives of all black people, both free and slave.

By midcentury it was becoming clear, however, that Africans would not be treated like other colonials. In 1652 Virginian John Pott's purchase of ten-year-old Jowan included "her Issue and produce duringe her (or either of them) for their Life tyme. And their Successors forever."[2] African slavery was thereby hereditary and perpetual, a condition recognized in law in 1660 in Virginia and 1663 in Maryland.[3] In 1662 the Virginia assembly reversed the English common law tradition whereby a child took its father's status by declaring that bondage passed to a child if the child's mother was bound. In this way Virginia assured that the offspring of Englishmen and African women remained in service and provided a larger supply of perpetual servants. During the same decade another potential avenue to black freedom was closed when the question of whether an African convert to Christianity could be held as a slave was resolved by a General Assembly ruling that baptism did not protect an African from perpetual bondage.[4] As more Africans served for life, the punitive value of lengthening the time of service was lost, and masters demanded that they be allowed to use corporal punishment against slaves who resisted their control. Virginia authorities agreed, and in 1669 they ruled that masters would not be held liable for such punishment even if the slave were killed, since it was presumed that no person would intentionally destroy his own property.[5]

In Maryland, the Chesapeake colony established by Cecilius Calvert in 1634 as a haven for Catholics, indentured servitude played a greater role in the labor system for a longer period, and British convict labor was imported when voluntary servants became more difficult to find. Many Africans served terms much like white indentured servants, and their similar situations increased the likelihood of interracial cooperation in such ventures as running away. In 1664, in an attempt to help protect slaveholders from the loss of their slaves, Maryland passed legislation aimed at discouraging the most intimate form of interracial association. The law declared that any white woman marrying an African slave could be forced to serve her husband's master for as long as her husband lived. By 1700 heavy penalties were imposed for interracial marriage, Africans commonly served for a lifetime, and slaves' children became slaves. Eighteenth-century advertisements for runaway slaves demonstrate that legislation could not entirely prevent such liaisons. Isaac Cromwell, a forty-year-old mulatto slave, escaped from northern Maryland with Ann Greene, an Englishwoman who was an indentured servant in the same area. They fled on two of Isaac's master's horses, and his master believed they were living together in Philadelphia as husband and wife. When Peggy, a black slave who spoke with a Welsh accent, escaped from slavery, she left with her Portuguese lover, who was an indentured servant.[6]

The status of some blacks in both Chesapeake colonies remained ambiguous until the end of the seventeenth century. There were exceptional experiences like that of Anthony Johnson, who was brought to Virginia in 1622, gained his freedom, and eventually prospered as a middling planter. Freed after a term of service, he married and acquired substantial acreage and a herd of cattle. Johnson held slaves of his own, turned a reasonable profit from his land, and even used the colonial court system to protect his right to the labor of his slave against a claim by a white neighbor. He was one of a few free blacks who moved to the ranks of small planters before 1700. By the eighteenth century Africans constituted 80 percent of the unfree workers in the region, largely

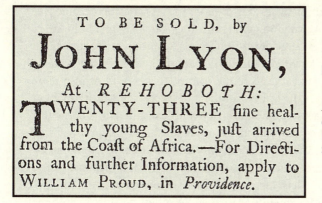

TO BE SOLD, by

JOHN LYON,

At *R E H O B O T H:*
TWENTY-THREE fine heal-
thy young Slaves, juft arrived
from the Coaft of Africa.—For Directions and further Information, apply to
WILLIAM PROUD, in *Providence.*

"To Be Sold
by John Lyon,"
Providence Gazette,
June 11, 1763.
Graphics Division,
Rhode Island Historical
Society, Providence.

replacing the Chesapeake's white indentured servants, and slavery had evolved from an ambiguous form of indenture to a permanent, inherited status. Increasingly whites came to assume that any black person was a slave unless there was explicit evidence to the contrary.[7]

To the south of the Chesapeake the British established the colony of Carolina in 1663. The initial settlers in the southern part of the colony that later became South Carolina produced timber and livestock for the British colonies in the West Indies, but within a generation rice became the chief money crop. Carolina settlers came mainly from the British West Indian colony of Barbados, where African slaves worked in the sugarcane fields. Unlike the Chesapeake, Carolina relied on slavery from the beginning, with slaves first herding livestock and felling the timber to be shipped to Barbados, then cultivating rice. Since Africans had grown rice for hundreds of years in the region south of the Gambia River in West Africa, many were brought to South Carolina as slaves to teach rice culture to their English masters and to grow rice in the lowlands along the Atlantic coast, where tidewater flooded the fields and West African techniques were most successful. Blacks were the vast majority of the population in this region, especially during the summer months, when the danger from malaria drove whites farther inland. They were 90 percent of the population by the mid–eighteenth century in the wealthiest, most established plantation areas near the capital city of Charleston, and more than 60 percent in the entire region. The largest plantations in the British North American colonies were located in tidewater Carolina, where the subtropical heat and humidity in the summer were much like those in the areas from which these Africans had been taken. Those who had spent their childhood in these regions had generally developed some resistance to such diseases as malaria, giving them an advantage over the British, who had a high mortality rate from tropical diseases.[8]

Carolina's demand for slaves was so great that Charleston became the major port of entry for Africans brought to the American mainland from Africa and the Caribbean. By the time of the American Revolution almost one hundred thousand slaves had entered through Charleston harbor, most of them bound for the rice-growing regions of the colony. Its majority African population made it more like the Caribbean than other parts of North America. The great number of blacks in Carolina enabled Africans there to retain more of their languages and cultural practices for longer than perhaps anywhere else in North America. The plantations of Carolina became the home of large African slave communities, with internal social and political structures based on West African models. Especially in the low country of southern Carolina, an amalgam of African cultures shaped an American African culture. In Africa traditional rivalries might have made many of these people deadly enemies, but in Carolina their suffering and shared disadvantage brought them together.

The large number and high proportion of Africans in Carolina created other similarities with slavery in the West Indies—heightened white fears of slave rebellion and harsh measures to control the slave population. Rumors of slave unrest in Charleston in 1711 and 1720 led to death by burning for suspected rebels. White slaveholders' insecurity undoubtedly helps to explain the extremely harsh slave codes enacted in South Carolina in 1696, even harsher than the Barbadian codes on which they were modeled. These codes were so restrictive that some masters complained that they infringed on slaveholders' property rights. Slaves without written permission were restricted to their master's property, and any white person who discovered a slave violating this rule could whip the slave, although the punishment could not exceed twenty lashes. Fines were imposed on any white overseer who discovered an unknown slave on his plantation and did not report and whip the slave. No master could allow his slave to hunt except with a special license, renewed monthly. Masters were required to inspect all slave quarters regularly to ensure that no weapons were available to their slaves. Volumes of regulations detailed punishments ranging from whipping for many offenses, branding for petty theft, cutting off the right ear for the first offense of striking a white person, castration for a fourth escape attempt, and death for rape, attempted murder or murder of a white person. Those who administered punishment were not held liable if death resulted inadvertently. These sanctions were among the most draconian anywhere in the Americas.[9]

Yet even in South Carolina there was occasional evidence of surprising tolerance during the colonial era. One striking example of this was the establishment of a school in Charleston for area slaves. The plan, sponsored by the Society for the Propagation of the Gospel in Foreign Parts, an auxiliary of the

Anglican Church, was to train slaves in the Christian religion and to have them instructed by a slave specially educated to be the schoolmaster. In 1743 the school opened under the direction of Harry, considered a "genius" by some local whites, and the student body quickly rose to sixty. Although some whites were concerned about the experiment, the school continued for more than twenty years until Harry died in 1764. The coexistence of this school with South Carolina's harsh slave codes illustrates the contradictory nature of American slavery.[10]

On the southern border of South Carolina lay the colony of Georgia. Granted by the Crown to James Edward Oglethorpe in 1732, this colony was intended to serve an important military function as a strategic outpost separating British North America from Spanish Florida to its south, standing against the expansionist ambitions of one of England's most powerful rivals. Among its earliest British settlers were the abject poor of English society, many drawn from the nation's debtor's prisons. British liberal reformers saw this new land as an asylum in which these unfortunates of society might be rehabilitated. Their dream was to establish Georgia as a utopian community of independent small farmers. No one person could own more than five hundred acres, and the inheritance of land was restricted. To encourage hard work and civility among the settlers, alcoholic drink was outlawed, and in the interest of public tranquillity slavery was forbidden. Further, since white Georgians feared that Africans might join with the Indians and the Spanish in military action against them, both slaves and free blacks were prohibited from entering the colony.

This commitment to a slave-free colony was not universally accepted among the colonials, and many bent on rapid economic development argued for the necessity of slave labor. These "malcontents," as other Georgians called them, claimed that white laborers could not grow rice as profitably as slaves did in South Carolina. Opponents of slavery, motivated as much by antiblack prejudice as humanitarian sentiment, countered by citing the example of German planters from Salzburg who were successfully growing rice in the small community of Ebenezer, near Savannah. After a decade of debate it became clear that the original vision of Georgia as a utopian community would not be sustained. In 1742 the ban on alcohol was lifted, and eight years later restrictions on slavery and large landholdings were repealed. Thereafter Georgia moved rapidly in the direction of other southern colonies, establishing large plantations where great numbers of slaves supplied the labor on which the wealth of a powerful planter class was based.[11]

North of the Chesapeake there were a few large plantations, but most slaveholdings were much smaller, and blacks accounted for a tiny proportion of the population, especially in New England. Whereas in 1750 slaves constituted

61 percent of the colonial population in South Carolina, 31 percent in Maryland, and 46 percent in Virginia, they were only 2 percent in Pennsylvania, 7 percent in New Jersey, and 14 percent in New York. In New England, except for Rhode Island's 10 percent, no colony's slave population exceeded 3 percent of the total. Although slavery was not the major enterprise in the northern colonies that it was in the South, it was still economically and socially important. Slavery became an issue for debate early in the life of Pennsylvania, a colony established by English Quakers on Maryland's northern border in 1661. In 1682 its founder and governor, William Penn, who had envisioned a refuge for Quakers persecuted in England, proposed to limit slavery in the colony. Two years later 150 Africans were imported to help clear the land. Penn preferred to have Pennsylvanians rely on indentured labor, with African indentures for fourteen years of service, and many blacks received land as their customary freedom dues. But demand for labor in the colony was too great to be satisfied by the supply of indentured servants. Within three years of his original proposal, Penn decided that perpetual slavery was more economical than temporary service, abandoned his plan, and became a slaveholder himself. As the number of white servants declined, Pennsylvania came more and more to rely on African slave labor, and its capital city of Philadelphia became a major slave-trading center.[12]

By the 1760s almost 8 percent of the inhabitants of Philadelphia were of African descent. Estimates of the black population in Pennsylvania vary widely, ranging from 2,500 to 5,000 in 1721 and 2,900 to 11,000 by mid-century. After that time a large and relatively sudden influx of German and Irish indentured servants reduced the demand for slaves and curbed the growth of the colony's black population. Whenever the supply of white servants was disrupted, however, Pennsylvania slaveholders imported more African slaves. Some Pennsylvanians expressed concern about the colony's growing number of slaves. In fact, as early as 1707 and 1722 white laborers complained of competition from slaves. Others expressed fears that the increasing number of Africans would bring a greater danger of slave rebellion. Acting partly on these fears and partly on a desire to generate revenue for the colony, the Pennsylvania Assembly imposed a tax on the importation of slaves. Still, the continuing demand for slave labor made it difficult to control the number of importations effectively. Pennsylvania's taxes were easily circumvented by landing slave cargos in neighboring New Jersey and smuggling them overland into the colony, and smuggling became so common that New Jersey seaside towns such as Perth Amboy and Cape May became major slave ports.[13]

Yet Pennsylvania's Quakers had always been uneasy about slavery, and their discomfort grew with the increasing slave population, while their disquiet moderated the institution. In fact many visitors reported that slavery in Penn's colony was milder by far than in colonies farther south. Many Quakers favored providing opportunities for the colony's blacks, and in the 1750s, Israel Acrelius, a visiting minister, was impressed by the better treatment of Pennsylvania slaves. In 1758 a Philadelphia Quaker educator, Anthony Benezet, established a school for blacks and used the educational achievement of his students as the basis for his arguments against the notion of African intellectual inferiority, calling it "a vulgar prejudice founded on . . . pride and ignorance."[14]

Sometimes the tolerance extended to slaves provided them with opportunities that approached independence. Many slaves were allowed to "hire out" their time, providing most of their earnings to their master but keeping a portion for themselves. Although slave marriages were not legal, there were apparently some efforts to prevent the separation of families when slaves were sold. So long as slaves did not seem dangerous, few restrictions were imposed on their movements, and they associated freely during their nonwork hours with family and friends among other slaves, free blacks, and even white servants. The lax enforcement of slave codes angered some colonists, but by the mid–eighteenth century sentiment against slavery had gained strength in Pennsylvania, and the annual Quaker meetings debated ways to discourage the importation of more African slaves and encourage the manumission of slaves already there. Despite an increase in antislavery sentiment, slave codes still restricted slaves in Pennsylvania. Slaves were clearly distinguished from free people in colonial law and were not guaranteed legal protection. Curfews; restrictions on slave gatherings; pass systems; and harsh penalties including whipping, castration (for attempted rape), and death (for burglary, murder, or rape) were used to control Pennsylvania's slave population, as they were in the southern plantation colonies.

Discussions among the Quakers continued, and by 1693 the Yearly Philadelphia Meeting asserted that no Quaker should buy slaves except as a means of freeing them. More radical Quakers called on all slaveholding members to free their slaves. During the 1730s Benjamin Lay, a Quaker from Barbados who had witnessed large-scale slavery, testified at one annual meeting after another about the horrors of the institution and once even abducted a slaveholder's child to dramatize the pain slavery caused to families. He was expelled from the meeting for this action and for the publication of *All Slave-Keepers That Keep the Innocent in Bondage,* in which he roundly condemned all Quakers who participated in or condoned slavery. Other influential Quakers opposed to slavery included John Woolman from New Jersey, whose writings on antislavery were widely read among Quakers, and Anthony Benezet. By 1758 the work of the Quaker antislavery activists bore fruit—Penn's Yearly

Meeting declared that Quakers who imported, bought, or sold slaves after that year should be expelled from the congregation. Further, it strongly suggested that slaveholding members free their slaves and provide them with Christian training. These were tentative steps, but they marked the start of a conviction among Quakers that spread from Pennsylvania throughout the middle colonies into New England and even into the South, where Quaker settlements became centers of antislavery philosophy.[15]

The middle colonies continued to import white servants throughout the pre-Revolutionary period. Interracial relationships developed as black slaves often worked with white laborers and indentured servants in ways not common on the larger southern plantations. These workers associated with one another in iron manufacturing in New Jersey and Pennsylvania, as dock laborers in New York City, and even in the skilled trades of the urban centers. Consequently Africans in the middle colonies were more likely to learn about English culture and to learn the English language faster and better than Africans in the large, insular African communities on southern plantations. Whereas most slaves in the South were required to know only enough English to be able to carry out the work-related orders of masters and overseers, in the middle colonies slaves often lived in the master's household and spent much of the day with European Americans.

Differences in background and experience help to explain the differences in linguistic abilities reflected in newspaper advertisements for runaway slaves. Blacks imported from the West Indies often spoke French and Spanish. One slave named John, who was born in Dominica and ran away soon after coming to Philadelphia in 1745, was described as speaking French well but only a little English. Another fugitive, it was said, spoke Spanish but no English, while a third was fluent in English, French, and Spanish. One runaway from Pennsylvania spoke both English and "Swede," and a New Jersey runaway, Claus, spoke "Dutch and good English." Blacks in the region that had been controlled by the Dutch frequently spoke both English and Dutch. When Toney left his master in Philadelphia, he was well-dressed in a "Striped Linsey Woolsy Jacket," a "Tow shirt," matching pants, and a felt hat. His distinguishing characteristics included his being "a likely lusty" twenty-four-year-old who spoke English and "High Dutch" (actually, proper German).[16]

Because the British colony of New York began as the Dutch corporate colony of New Netherland, slavery there had a slightly different foundation. Although the first eleven slaves were landed in New Netherland in 1626, slave labor was never an important part of the colony's economy. African slaves worked the Dutch West India Company's great Hudson River Valley estates as they did the plantations of the South, but most slaves were employed on smaller farms or were part of the Dutch military forces that defended the colony against the Indians during the early 1640s. The Dutch intended their reliance on slave labor to be temporary, but white workers moved quickly from agricultural work to trades, leaving the colony with too few farmhands and an unstable labor supply. By the 1640s the Dutch regularly imported African slaves to fill their labor needs.

The Dutch West India Company employed a flexible style of bondage called "half freedom." Africans were allowed to live independently in exchange for their agreement to pay a yearly tax and provide labor to the company when needed. Under these circumstances slaves' daily lives were much like those of free persons. Married slaves lived in family units and supported their own families. Despite the fact that the children of slaves bound under the system owed their labor to the company for life, it was still one of the mildest forms of slavery practiced in North America. If they were freed, blacks were accorded the same rights as whites in the colony. They could own property, pursue trades, and even intermarry with whites. Race was a factor in that being black carried with it the probability of being enslaved, but blacks were treated as free people so long as their white neighbors knew that they were free.[17]

In the 1660s England went to war against Holland, attempting to eliminate Dutch trade competition and to gain control of the Hudson River fur-trading region. When the British took over the colony in 1664, they gradually made slavery there conform to the system in their other American colonies, and slaves lost the advantages of the half-freedom arrangement. As the number of slaves increased, rising colonial anxieties encouraged harsh restrictions. In 1682 flogging was prescribed for any four or more slaves caught meeting together without white supervision. A sunset curfew was imposed on all adult slaves in New York City, but when that arrangement proved inconvenient for masters, the provision was changed, and slaves were required to carry lighted lanterns when they moved about the city after dark. A slave-regulating act was passed in 1702, in 1708 whipping became mandatory for minor infractions, and after 1710 colonial courts rejected several cases brought against masters by slaves claiming wages for unpaid labor. By the early eighteenth century virtually all that remained of New York's Dutch past were a few large estates in the Hudson Valley, Dutch cultural festivals and traditions, and the Dutch language spoken by many blacks and whites.[18]

Under the British during the first half of the eighteenth century, New York became the major slaveholding colony north of Maryland, with more than ten thousand slaves, constituting about 15 percent of the population by 1750. With continued growth, there were more than nineteen thousand slaves in New York on the eve of the Revolution. Slaves were provided with

Venture Smith, an African, Tells of His Capture and Enslavement

I was born at Dukandarra, in Guinea, about the year 1729. My father's name was Saungm Furro, Prince of the tribe of Dukandarra. My father had three wives. Polygamy was not uncommon in that country, especially among the rich, as every man was allowed to keep as many wives as he could maintain. . . . I descended from a very large, tall and stout race of beings, much larger than the generality of people in other parts of the globe, being commonly considerable above six feet in height, and every way well proportioned. . . .

[At word of a planned attack by an army supplied and incited by whites] my father and his family set off about the break of day. The king and his two younger wives went in one company, and my mother and her children in another. We left our dwellings in succession, and my father's company went on first. We directed our course for a large shrub plain, some distance off, where we intended to conceal ourselves from the approaching enemy, until we could refresh ourselves a little. But we presently found that our retreat was not secure. For having struck up a little fire for the purpose of cooking victuals, the enemy, who happened to be encamped a little distance off, had sent out a scouting party who discovered us by the smoke of the fire, just as we were extinguishing it and about to eat. As soon as we had finished eating, my father discovered the party and immediately began to discharge arrows at them. This was what I first saw, and it alarmed both me and the women, who, being unable to make any resistance immediately betook ourselves to the tall, thick reeds not far off, and left the old king to fight alone. For some time I beheld him from the reeds defending himself with great courage and firmness, till at last he was obliged to surrender himself into their hands.

They then came to us in the reeds, and the very first salute I had from them was a violent blow on the head with the fore part of a gun, and at the same time a grasp around the neck. I then had a rope put about my neck, as all the women in the thicket with me, and were immediately led to my father, who was likewise pinioned and haltered for leading . . . my father was closely interrogated respecting his money. . . . But as he gave them no account of it, he was instantly cut and pounded on his body with great inhumanity. . . . All this availed not in the least to make him give up his money . . . until the continued exercise and increase of torment obliged him to sink and expire. . . . I saw him while he was thus tortured to death. The shocking scene is to this day fresh in my memory. . . .

The army of the enemy was large, I should suppose consisting of about six thousand men. . . . After destroying the old prince, they decamped and

(continued)

immediately marched towards the sea, lying to the west, taking with them myself and the women prisoners. . . . The enemy had remarkable success in destroying the country wherever they went. For as far as they had pene- trated they laid the habitations waste and captured the people. The distance they had now brought me was about four hundred miles. All the march I had very hard tasks imposed on me, which I must perform on pain of pun- ishment, I was obliged to carry on my head a large flat stone used for grinding our corn, weighing, as I should suppose, as much as twenty-five pounds; besides victuals, mat and cooking utensils. Though I was pretty large and stout of my age, yet these burdens were very grievous to me, being only six years and a half old. . . .

[At the end of the long march and more slave-raiding battles, in a coastal settlement called Anamaboo] the enemy's provisions were then almost spent, as well as their strength. The inhabitants, knowing what con- duct they had pursued, and what were their present intentions, improved the favorable opportunity, attacked them, and took enemy, prisoners, flocks and all their effects. I was then taken a second time. All of us were then put into the castle and kept for market. On a certain time, I and other prisoners were put on board a canoe, under our master, and rowed away to a vessel belonging to Rhode Island, commanded by Captain Collingwood, and the mate, Thomas Mumford. While we were going to the vessel, our master told us to appear to the best possible advantage for sale. I was bought on board by one Robertson Mumford, a steward of said vessel, for four gallons of rum and a piece of calico, and called VENTURE on account of his hav- ing purchased me with his own private venture. Thus I came by my name. All the slaves that were bought for that vessel's cargo were two hundred and sixty.

After all the business was ended on the coast of Africa, the ship sailed from thence to Barbadoes. After an ordinary passage, except great mortality by the small pox, which broke out on board, we arrived at the island of Bar- badoes; but when we reached it, there were found, out of the two hundred and sixty that sailed from Africa, not more than two hundred alive. These were all sold, except myself and three more, to the planters there.

The vessel then sailed for Rhode Island, and arrived there after a com- fortable passage. Here my master sent me to live with one of his sisters until he could carry me to Fisher's Island, the place of his residence. I had then completed my eighth year. After staying with his sister some time, I was taken to my master's place to live.

———
Venture Smith, *A Narrative of the Life and Adventures of Venture, A Native of Africa, But Resident Above Sixty Years in the United States of America. Related by Himself* (1798; reprint, Middletown, Conn.: J. S. Stewart, Printer and Bookbinder, 1897), 4–10.

virtually no legal protection, and no slave could testify against a free person in court. As in other northern colonies, slavery was not the basis of New York's economy, but slaves did provide an important part of the labor supply, and there were many slaveholders in the colony. In the rural areas outside New York City, slaves accounted for between one-fifth and one-third of the population. The estates on Long Island and in the Hudson River Valley, as well as those in the tobacco-growing areas of the Narragansett region of Rhode Island, continued to use large numbers of slaves throughout the eighteenth century, functioning more like the plantations of South Carolina than did most other regions in the North. New York City was the major urban slaveholding center. Only Charleston surpassed it in slave ownership, and although the proportion of slaveholders in New York City's population declined as the century progressed, the actual number of slaves in the city increased, so that by the mid–eighteenth century slaves were a common sight. In the early 1770s one foreign visitor to New York was surprised by slavery's visibility, remarking, "It rather hurts the European eye to see so many negro slaves upon the streets."[19]

There were fewer blacks in New England than in the Middle Colonies, but even there slavery was a familiar aspect of colonial life. From 1624, when Samuel Maverick became the region's first slaveholder, New Englanders imported small numbers of Africans, mainly from the British West Indies. The slave population increased slowly—only a few arrived each year before 1700, and only a few dozen each year during the first part of the eighteenth century. By 1700 there were barely one thousand Africans in all of New England; about half of those were in Massachusetts.

The Puritans of New England seem to have struggled more with the morality of slavery than did the planters of the Chesapeake or Carolina, though somewhat more legalistically than the Quakers in Pennsylvania. In the Massachusetts Body of Liberties of 1641, colonial authorities justified slavery only for those who sold themselves or who were taken captive in "just wars." Previously, in 1637, the colony's need for labor had encouraged a tortured interpretation of this principle, allowing several hundred Indian men captured during the Pequot wars to be taken to the West Indies and traded there for Africans who were then brought to New England as slaves. Pequot women and children captured during the wars remained in Massachusetts and were treated as servants. This interpretation hardly satisfied the spirit of the colony's principles, but it provided justification enough given the rising expense of white labor.[20] The Massachusetts General Court clarified this issue with a ruling in 1645 that the importation of slaves was legal so long as the purchase was made from "legitimate" slave traders. By 1670 the question of the status of children born to slave women and white men was resolved by following the precedent, set in Virginia, that such offspring took the status of their mother. Massachusetts set the example for other New England colonies, and by the early 1700s slavery was legal and well-established in the region. Economic pressures had overcome theological and philosophical reservations to allow slaveholding in the region, but the number of slaves remained very small. Massachusetts was the largest slaveholding colony in New England, but even in Boston, where slaves were concentrated, there were only 150 Africans by 1690 and fewer than 500 in 1710. The average slaveholder held only two slaves, and only about 12 percent of Boston's white population owned even a single slave.

With such small slaveholdings, slaves were as integrated into the colonial household and society in New England as they were in the Middle Colonies. This situation not only facilitated their learning English but often provided them with other advantages. The experiences of the slaves in the household of a physician in Plymouth, Massachusetts, provide examples of the potential benefits from this form of slavery. The slaves Pompey; Phyllis, his wife; Quasho; and Prince, the household cook, lived in two rooms above the kitchen in the home of Dr. LeBaron, a widower with many children. LeBaron exercised authority over his slaves, but he also allowed them privileges not generally granted to southern slaves. Phyllis controlled her own money and successfully invested in the business ventures available in the busy commercial port. With part of the profit she made for her share in the cargoes of a schooner, she bought a set of "Guinea-gold beads" that she wore along with her "portentous turban" to express her own African sense of beauty and style.[21]

When disagreements arose between a northern master and the slaves who lived in his household, compromises were likely to be reached, or the slaves might even be able to impose their own wills. When Dr. LeBaron decided to extend the classical allusions in his household by adding "Julius Caesar" to the Pompey already there, he suggested that Quasho accept that name. The slave refused, saying that his mother in Africa had called him by the name of Quasho Quando, and he did not intend to take another. LeBaron attempted unsuccessfully to change Quasho's mind with punishments ranging from the deprivation of food to whipping. He then tried bribery but finally dropped the matter.[22]

Although colonies in New England had fewer slaves, and they were less likely to be strictly controlled than in the South, African slaves were an integral part of New England's labor system. They worked mainly on small farms or as domestic servants, unskilled workers, or even skilled artisans in the cities.

> **Newport, *July* 6, 1764.**
> Juſt imported in the Sloop *Elizabeth*, from *Africa*, and to be ſold, by
> # John Miller,
> At his Houſe, or Store ;
> ## A Number of healthy
> Negro Boys and Girls.
> Likewiſe to be ſold,—*Tillock's* and *Kippen's* Snuff, by the Caſk or Dozen.

"Just imported in the Sloop *Elizabeth,* from Africa," *Providence Gazette,* July 6, 1764. Graphics Division, Rhode Island Historical Society, Providence.

Most whites in Massachusetts agreed with colonial Governor John Winthrop that the colony could not survive without "a stock of slaves sufficient to dow [*sic*] all our business."[23] Except perhaps in the areas with large estates, the economic importance of slavery in New England and New York was more a matter of slave trading than of slaveholding. New England sea captains often commanded the slave-trading vessels, merchants from New England and New York often financed the ventures, goods produced in these regions served as items traded for slaves, and vessels built in New England moved the trade across the ocean. Slaveholding was important to the trade, since African workers in New England provided labor for the distilling industry that turned West Indian sugar into rum. The New England ships that brought sugar to North America, finished goods and rum to Africa, and Africans to American slavery were built with slave labor.[24]

Although much of the colonial economy rested on slave labor, and many whites believed that slavery was the only suitable institution for controlling Africans, not all Africans were slaves. As slavery evolved and the number of slaves increased, especially in the plantation South, and legal measures for the protection of slaveholders' property rights were established, free blacks were increasingly seen as a threat to those rights. It became more difficult for slaves to gain their freedom, as a few had before the mid–seventeenth century. Thus, the development of slavery was closely tied to a deterioration of the rights of free blacks, and prosperous former slaves like the Anthony Johnson family of seventeenth-century Virginia became increasingly rare. In 1691 Virginia's General Court declared that no slave might be set free unless that freedom was accompanied by enough money to transport the freed slave out of the colony within six months of emancipation. In 1723 the judgment was strengthened by a declaration that a slave could only be manumitted for some "meritorious service" certified by colonial officials. Those blacks who did acquire their freedom were not truly free; their rights were severely restricted by special regulations devised to control them. In Virginia free blacks had no right to vote or to a jury trial, and they could be sold into slavery for minor infractions.

Since the free black population in Maryland was smaller than that in Virginia, it was less threatening, and there were fewer restrictions on the manumission of slaves. An attempt to prohibit emancipation failed to pass the colonial legislature in 1715, but by midcentury the requirement of special written freedom forms issued by the colonial authorities made freeing a slave more difficult. Concerns that freed slaves might become public charges prompted other regulations, requiring that a manumitted slave be healthy, capable of self-support, and not over fifty years of age. As in Virginia many of the restrictions placed on the movement of slaves also applied to free blacks, and these restrictions made it extremely difficult for them to find employment outside of indentured servitude.

A series of slave rebellions in Barbados from 1639 to the 1690s made South Carolina planters, many of whom came from that island, uneasy about their growing black population. They were especially concerned about the potentially disruptive influence of free blacks on their slaves and took measures to discourage the growth of the free black population. In 1715 the colony passed a regulation preventing the emancipation of any runaway or rebellious slave, although a master could free a slave for loyal and faithful service. Once freed, however, just as in Virginia, a black person was required to leave the colony within six months. In what might seem an unnecessary addition, a 1721 colonial statute limited the right to vote to "free white men."[25] Planters' apprehension intensified after a major slave uprising at the Stono River in South Carolina in 1739, and with the expanding number of African arrivals in the colony.[26] Between 1735 and 1740, slave traders brought twelve thousand Africans to work the South Carolina rice fields. In 1741 this prompted futile efforts on the part of colonial officials to control the size of the colony's black population by levying a tariff on further importations. Although the number of free blacks remained relatively small, the slave population soared. Within a decade Africans and their descendants accounted for almost two-thirds of South Carolina's population. Controls on slaves and free blacks were tightened, and a new law prohibited freeing any slave except for some exceptionally honorable service, and with official approval. Even such loyal slaves could only remain in the colony for six months after gaining their freedom.[27]

Despite the restrictions the number of free blacks increased all over the South, and a few even prospered. Some free blacks became landowners, a few grew wealthy, and a small number became slaveholders themselves. In North Carolina those few who could meet the property requirement became eligible to vote after 1737 when the king lifted the colony's prohibition against voting by blacks and Indians.[28] It is surprising that Carolina slaveholders tolerated even their small free black population in the eighteenth century, but some were tied by blood to the most powerful planters, who saw them as trusted allies, a protective buffer against slave rebellion. Though this trust was sometimes misplaced, as when free blacks were implicated in slave conspiracies, free blacks could often use it to their advantage.[29] Still, their lives and freedom were precarious, and restrictive and exclusionary laws could be enforced whenever the white minority felt threatened.

There were more free blacks south of Maryland and Virginia, but a larger percentage of the total black population was free in the Middle Colonies and in New England. Many factors encouraged the growth of a free black population in these areas—many blacks gained their freedom after serving their terms as indentured servants; Quaker opposition to, and Puritan reservations about, slavery led to fewer restrictions on manumissions. Philosophical and moral reservations also seemed more persuasive in regions where slavery was not the dominant labor system and where there were relatively few Africans.

Especially where there were small slaveholdings, the lives of free blacks and slaves were intertwined, and often they were members of the same family. Marriages involving slaves were not generally recognized in the colonies, and even under the best circumstances, they were maintained only at the master's convenience. The tenuous existence of slave families is illustrated by the advertisement in a New England newspaper offering for sale a "likely negro woman about 19 years and a child of about six months of age to be sold together or apart."[30] One way for free black people to protect slave members of their families was to secure their freedom, and free blacks often spent years working and saving to purchase the freedom of family members. Laws restricting free blacks often made it more difficult to gain the freedom of family members in the southern colonies. On occasion, because newly freed blacks could not legally remain in a colony, it was more efficient for a free black person to purchase a family member and hold that person as a slave. Such ownership would be a legal convenience allowing the newly purchased slave to remain with the family. Many of the slaves listed as the property of free blacks in South Carolina, Virginia, and elsewhere in the South were "owned" under these circumstances.

Dealing with the problem of enslaved family members was only one of many problems faced by free blacks. Even the most fortunate were not truly free to take advantage of opportunities open to whites. In New England, Lucy and Abijah Prince were well off by the standards of the day, though both had been slaves in Deerfield, Massachusetts. Lucy had been kidnapped into slavery at the age of five in her native Africa. She was known in Deerfield for her narrative poem describing the Indian attack she witnessed on the village in 1746. Abijah Prince gained his freedom through his master's will, which also gave him a sizable plot of land. This land provided the funds to buy Lucy's freedom and to give the couple a comfortable start when they married in 1756. The Princes acquired additional land in nearby Vermont, where they raised their six children and settled into a life as respectable members of the community. Despite their exemplary lives, when their oldest son, Caesar, reached college age, he was refused permission to enroll at Williams College in western Massachusetts. Not easily discouraged, Lucy set their case before the college trustees, presenting a three-hour argument drawing on the law and the Bible, but to no avail. The college held fast to its policy that no black person, no matter how qualified, could attend Williams.[31]

If the financially stable, determined Prince family faced obstacles to its advancement in New England, one of the most tolerant regions in the colonies, it is not surprising that less well-situated free blacks in less tolerant surroundings fared poorly. North or South, they were discriminated against, restricted, and generally despised. Free blacks were often limited to the least desirable sections of a town for their residences or to the least productive land in the countryside for their farms. In most public places they were segregated, and regardless of the weather they were relegated to the outside of carriages, the outside decks of ships, and the unsheltered decks of ferries. If they were allowed to attend white churches at all they were often limited to seats in the rear or in out-of-the-way areas, and they were barred from or segregated in places of public entertainment. More important economically, free blacks also faced occupational restrictions and were often unable to take up even the trades they had practiced in slavery. As early as 1717 the Connecticut colony required that blacks get special permission from colonial officials before they could open any business. Under such conditions it is not surprising that most free black people were poor, and they faced all the hardships of poor people as well as some problems peculiar to blacks. Many New England towns, for example, could simply order transient poor whites deemed undesirable, and any free blacks presumed to be undesirable, out of town.

The sea offered one of the few areas of employment open to free black men, and a great many worked as sailors throughout the eighteenth century. Unlike life ashore, life at sea was generally unsegregated, partly because of the limitations of the ships' quarters and partly because conditions for everyone were so harsh that any attempt at fine differentiation would have been futile. The sea offered some of the best opportunities for black men during the period, even though blacks were generally relegated to the lower ranks and the least desirable, most dangerous jobs and often got a smaller share of the profits from the voyage. For free black women, there were few desirable alternatives to domestic service, and black women provided the domestic labor for many rural and urban colonial households. In the South almost all of these women were slaves, but in the North both slaves and free women were in the domestic workforce. On occasion a skilled black woman might be employed as a seamstress or a weaver, among the most desirable jobs available to blacks in any region.

There was no clear place for free blacks in the society of the colonies. Yet they were not the only marginalized peoples in British North America—they shared this position with American Indians. Most of the Native Americans who had survived the wars with the English and exposure to European diseases lived on the fringes of colonial society, trading and occasionally working for the colonists, their presence on the frontier a constant source of conflict and concern. When officials were slow to act, frontier settlers—who continually demanded that colonial authorities protect them from local tribesmen—were sometimes willing to take matters into their own hands. Often the informal colonial forces that defended frontier settlements or attacked Native American neighbors included blacks as well as whites.

In 1676 Nathaniel Bacon, a white frontier planter, led an interracial army of poor whites, servants, and slaves against the Native Americans of western Virginia. Incensed when colonial authorities condemned his actions, Bacon turned his interracial force against the governing elites. The colonial governor declared Bacon and his men outlaws and moved against them with a substantial force. Bacon died and his army was defeated, but among those who held out longest were eighty blacks and twenty whites. This incident alerted Virginia's elites to the dangers of interracial alliances among the lower classes. In fact many laws were designed to control the perceived threat to the public order, and to slavery, represented by such relationships. In Virginia the first racially based laws prohibited interracial marriages. In 1705 Massachusetts also prohibited such relationships, providing that black men and women in interracial relationships be whipped and sold into slavery outside the colony. White men would be whipped, fined, and held responsible for any children resulting from the relationship, and white women would be whipped and bound into a period of indenture. A 1726 Pennsylvania law declared that any free black person who married a white person could be sold into slavery.[32]

Bacon's Rebellion also illustrates the complex, shifting interracial alliances that emerged during the eighteenth century. British colonials found both enemies and allies against rival Europeans among American Indians. Blacks often found common cause with Native Americans against white colonists, but even in the areas of greatest slaveholding, they sometimes helped defend the colonies against European or Native American enemies. In 1747, for example, South Carolina expressed formal appreciation to the black militiamen who "in times of war, behaved themselves with great faithfulness and courage, in repelling the attacks of his Majesty's enemies."[33] Both free blacks and Indians, however, were generally viewed with suspicion by white settlers. Indeed, the fact that they occupied similar statuses sometimes brought blacks and American Indians together in political and personal alliances. On occasion they were allied in military action, as in 1657, when a combined force attacked and burned part of Hartford, Connecticut; or in 1727, when blacks and Indians terrorized Virginia settlements. Fearful whites responded to such incidents with restrictive regulations. In 1690 several Connecticut settlements set a 9 P.M. curfew for both Indians and blacks. Boston officials prohibited blacks and Native Americans from carrying canes or sticks that might be used as weapons. In order to discourage slaves' attempts to escape to the Indians or to the French in Canada New Yorkers enacted harsh laws calling for the execution of any slave caught traveling forty miles north of Albany.[34]

Blacks and American Indians frequently developed close personal relationships as well. Large numbers of Native American men had been killed or exiled from New England in the wars in the seventeenth century, leaving a society with a gender imbalance heavily favoring women. The preference for importing male slave labor, on the other hand, resulted in a higher proportion of men in the area's black population during the late seventeenth and early eighteenth centuries. Colonial records document the significant number of American Indian–African marriages that resulted partly from these complementary imbalances. The customary practice of treating the offspring of these marriages as black was made official in 1719 in South Carolina by the colonial governor's proclamation that all those "not entirely Indian" would be counted as black. The records of colonial New Jersey indicate that that colony also listed those of Indian and African parentage as black. Under this provision Cyrus Bustill, Jr., the son of a black baker and a Delaware Indian woman, was listed on official documents as "negro." As an adult Bustill was a successful Quaker businessman, an advocate of antislavery, and a powerful spokesman for the black community.[35]

Some people of American Indian and African heritage functioned as members of both groups. Paul Cuffe of Massachusetts was born to a Native American mother and an African father. Although Paul spent most of his life outside Indian society, he claimed his Indian heritage and signed separate political petitions representing both Indian and African interests. Several of his siblings lived alternately in Indian and non-Indian settlements in Massachusetts.

His older brother, John, married an American Indian woman and remained with the Indians.[36] Intermarriage between blacks and American Indians was so common that treaties struck between colonial authorities and several Indian nations to prevent their sheltering fugitive slaves commonly threatened to separate families. Such treaties were generally ineffective, and cooperation between Africans and American Indians was always a potential source of instability for colonial slaveholding societies.[37]

By the middle of the eighteenth century, colonial British America had developed the beginnings of a distinctly American culture, a culture shaped by the influence of Africans and American Indians and by the limitations and possibilities of the New World. Black celebrations through the eighteenth and well into the nineteenth century illustrate one aspect of this cultural evolution. Negro elections or black coronation festivals were popular seasonal celebrations generally held in the spring or early summer. Especially in the northern colonies, but also in the Chesapeake region, slaves selected a ceremonial king or governor and celebrated with several days of merrymaking. In New Amsterdam (capital of New Netherland), Africans participated in a two-day observance of Paas (or Easter), vying for the honor of having baked the best Paas cake and competing in traditional Paas cake-throwing. The Dutch celebration of Pinkster, or Pentecost, in New Amsterdam and, later, New York and New Jersey, was eventually dominated by Africans and their traditions. Blacks celebrated all these festivals in similar ways, often electing "kings," sometimes from among families known to be from the ruling class in Africa. Celebrations combining African and European traditions and resembling those in the West Indies and Latin America featured parades with high stepping and baton twirling, athletic competitions, great feasts, and abundant music and dancing. Whites were often fascinated by the performances of African celebrants. One white observer in Albany, New York, reported that at one festival the slave king, a "Guinea man" dressed in an elaborate costume and wearing a yellow lace hat, led a long parade sitting astride one of the finest horses in the region provided for the occasion by his master. Later he led the "Guinea dance," an "original Congo dance as danced in [the slaves'] native Africa." Dancers were accompanied by music provided by musicians playing traditional African instruments including banjos, violins, and drums.[38]

What was less apparent to European observers of these celebrations was their connection to West African theology and religious practice and their function as a form of cultural resistance. Equiano observed the centrality of dance and music among his people not only for secular purposes but as sacred ritual. Singing, drumming, and dancing were part of the worship of African ancestors and gods. These were ancient expressions of spirituality. "So essential [were] music and dance to West African religious expression," the historian Albert J. Raboteau observed, "that it is no exaggeration to call them 'danced religions.'" These rituals helped form the connection between worlds. For the African enslaved in a foreign place, the music and dance of these African American celebrations provided outward expression of the African cultural traditions and familiar practices of worship passed down over generations of American slavery. Preserving these traditions provided links with African cultural homelands, helping African Americans resist slavery's attempt to define their identity. During the seventeenth and eighteenth centuries, African religions were more important than Christianity in the spiritual lives of the vast majority of American blacks. African religions were especially strong among the large African American populations of the lower South, where traditional African religious beliefs and forms of worship remained well into the nineteenth century.[39]

In the American colonies religion was just one aspect of many of these multilayered black celebrations. Some whites, especially indentured servants, attended and even participated in these celebrations, as a poem composed in 1760 made clear. According to the poet, the merrymakers were "of black and white, and every sort." Colonial officials were not comfortable with such associations of white and black servants. According to a white observer from Lynn, Massachusetts, "black celebrations" included so many of "the lower class of . . . our own complexion" that it alarmed the elite, who feared they might lead to dangerous political alliances among the "mean" classes against the "better" classes of the colonies. The eighteenth-century poet echoed these apprehensions, describing the revelers as "a motley crew of Whites and Blacks and Indians too."[40] Colonial elites also attended the festivals, perhaps to oversee such associations but also to enjoy the merriment—merriment undoubtedly made especially attractive by what these staid white European Americans perceived as African abandon. Children of the upper class were sometimes taken to the celebrations by black servants. Years later James Eights remembered a Pinkster celebration he attended as a boy with a household servant and his wonderment at the music, the baskets, and the other wares being sold by Native American families, and the exotic animals, including a lion and tiger, on display.[41]

Each group in the colonies contributed to the amalgam shaping American culture. Africans provided their knowledge of agriculture to make the rice culture of South Carolina profitable, and African techniques for inland river navigation greatly enhanced the ability of planters to move their goods to market.[42] Both African and American Indian medicine, though sometimes discounted by Europeans as superstition, were widely used and incorporated into eighteenth- and nineteenth-century American medical practice, especially in the southern colonies. Planters called on African doctors to treat their slaves

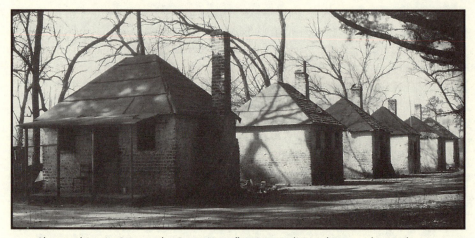

Slave cabins in Savannah, Georgia, reflecting traditional West African design.
Photographs and Prints Division, Library of Congress, Washington, D.C.

and their own families. In South Carolina a slave named Caesar was granted freedom and a cash reward for developing antidotes for several poisons based on African herbal cures. In Massachusetts, the Puritan minister Cotton Mather learned the principle of inoculation as a defense against smallpox from his black servant. Mather reported interviewing several Africans, who explained that the practice of inserting a small amount of material from an active smallpox pustule into a small cut on the arm of a healthy person was used with great success to prevent death from the disease in West Africa. Although the patients did become mildly ill they never developed smallpox. Africans used this rudimentary inoculation technique for protection against several diseases in other colonies in North America and in the West Indies. African medical knowledge, including the use of barks and herbs to treat everything from headaches to syphilis, eventually blended with European medical practices and a host of American Indian medicines to form early American medical practice.[43]

Though Americans of European origin probably owed the greatest part of their culture to their European roots, much of what they came to consider American had African roots. Before the end of the eighteenth century African music changed white Americans' musical sense. African foods like okra, collard greens, and yams became the foundation of American southern-style cooking and the American greeting "Howdy" was blended from the English "How do ye" and the African American "How de" or the Afro–West Indian "Hodi."[44] An emergent multiracial and multicultural America was apparent in the British colonies. This culture developed in the context of the important political and social changes facilitated by colonization. The lines of social status among whites that were so fundamental in England underwent a gradual erosion, a process already noticeable by the eve of the Revolution. The availability of cheap land dampened Europeans' willingness to accept extended indentures or to work for wages any longer than was necessary to become landholders. This propensity for personal independence encouraged a political commitment to individuality that by the late eighteenth century came to be known as the republican ideal. Ironically this passion for personal independence grew simultaneously with a reliance on a system of racially defined slave labor that became the very antithesis of freedom. The presence of an enslaved African people provided the contrast by which white Americans defined liberty. Black Americans, however, refused to accept a definition of liberty that excluded them, and they remained determined to claim freedom for themselves.

Chapter 3

Slavery and Freedom
in the Age of Revolution

*J*ust before 10 A.M. on a Sunday morning in September 1739, William Bull, the lieutenant governor of South Carolina, and his four companions confronted their worst nightmare on the road near Charles Town (later called Charleston). Suddenly the horrified party faced an army of armed slaves, hesitated for a moment, and then wheeled their horses around and rode for their lives.[1] The slaves' military action had begun in the early morning hours, when twenty black men, captives from the Kingdom of Kongo, met at the Stono River about twenty miles west of Charles Town.[2] Led by an African named Jemmy, these former warriors hoped to take advantage of the distraction provided by the war being waged between Spain and Britain to fight their way to freedom.

Colonial Spanish Florida, bordering Georgia, was barely 150 miles south of South Carolina. Hoping to disrupt the British plantation economy, in 1693 the Spanish Crown granted freedom to slaves who ran away from the British colonies. Thereafter many South Carolina fugitives escaped to Fort Mose, near St. Augustine; and in 1738 the Spanish governor of Florida granted these blacks homesteading lands where they founded Gracia Real de Santa Teresa de Mose. Fiercely loyal to the Spanish Crown, this first free black settlement in colonial North America became an asylum for fugitives, who formed a sizable military force to man its garrison. The Spanish Fort Mose discouraged the British raids that endangered settlements in the St. Augustine area throughout the early eighteenth century.[3]

Hoping ultimately to make their way to Florida and the protection of the Spaniards, the South Carolina rebels near the Stono first broke into a store to acquire guns and ammunition and killed two shopkeepers in the process. As they marched south they stopped at plantations, and other slaves joined them. By midmorning at least fifty boldly marched down the road "with Colours displayed, and two Drums beating."[4] Their banners were "like the unit flags that African armies flew in their campaigns."[5] By afternoon they numbered more than a hundred. Those of the original rebels who had been soldiers in their Kongo homeland provided the battle strategy. They were skilled with firearms and conversant with Kongolese military rituals, and they joined in the traditional battle dance that in Africa served as a military drill in preparation for meeting the colonial militia that had formed during the day. Most of the large slave army that engaged the militia, however, were agricultural workers without military training. The initial battle took place in an open area, leaving the Kongo men, who traditionally fought in a skirmish style, without cover against a force of superior arms. Forty blacks fell in the initial engagement. As they were driven from the field, military men withdrew to regroup, but many untrained fighters fell away, hoping to return to their masters with their rebellion undiscovered. The military men marched thirty miles toward Florida before they were overtaken by the militia. Most of the rebels were killed, but some escaped to the swamp and the woods. A year later, colonial authorities were still pursuing members of the fugitive band, and one rebel eluded capture for more than three years.[6]

The rebellion at the Stono River reinforced fears among planters of both the possibility of slave rebellion and the threat of Spanish invasion. Within a year James Oglethorpe led the South Carolina and Georgia militia in a land and sea attack on Fort Mose and drove the black forces out of the settlement to the safety of nearby St. Augustine. Spanish blacks rebuilt the fort, but British raids continued intermittently throughout the next two decades. In 1742 South Carolina was again shaken by word that a Spanish force, with at least one black battalion, threatened an invasion. These uncertain times prompted colonial authorities to place greater restrictions on slaves and free blacks. Instability may also have prompted some efforts to forestall rebellion, perhaps explaining the 1740 regulation that provided fines for slaveholders who failed to give slaves sufficient food or clothing or to allow them the customary Sundays off from work.[7]

The threat of slave uprising and the growing size of the colony's black majority made most South Carolina slave masters intolerant of any perceived challenge to their control over slaves. When, during this period, evangelical missionaries moved into the colony seeking to convert not only whites but blacks as well, planter reaction was decidedly cool. Hugh and Jonathan Bryan were at first persuaded by Methodist preacher George Whitefield that their slaves ought to be brought to Christianity. When planters in the vicinity suspected that the slaves were drawn mainly by what they took to be an evangelical antislavery message, however, the experiment was brought to an abrupt conclusion. Still, elsewhere in the colonies evangelical missionaries were successful in converting thousands of whites and many blacks.[8]

A religious fervor called the First Great Awakening emerged in England during the 1720s and brought a new spirit of equality and democracy to the American colonies in the 1740s and 1750s. Revivals swept in with plainspoken, emotion-laden preaching, a contempt for formal church hierarchy, and a greater emphasis on believers' ability to communicate directly with God. The new sects formed under this movement, the Methodists and the extremely decentralized Baptists, converted thousands in the British North American colonies. Their appeal was especially strong for ordinary white people, and they even made converts among less isolated African Americans in northern colonies and in the Chesapeake region. The strength of African cultures in the large slave communities of the Lower South, however, hampered conversions there.[9] Evangelical revival services of prayer, song, and testimonials, often held in tent encampments, created a far different atmosphere from the more staid services of established churches. Some of the difference was attributable to the democratic nature of participation; congregations included blacks and Native Americans as well as whites; slaves as well as free people; and men, women, and children. Some of the difference was due to the influence of African music and styles of worship. Much as whites were drawn to African performances in the celebrations of Pinkster and governors' elections, evangelicals found that the style of worship practiced by Africans and African Americans was a great attraction to white yeoman farmers, servants, and the nonelites. Some preachers relied on the participation of blacks to help "bring down the spirit," allowing whites in the congregation to throw off their inhibitions, commit themselves fully to the religious spirit, and accept the call to God's salvation.[10]

Informal evangelical worship practices allowed interracial gatherings to incorporate many aspects of African spirituality and worship styles, such as call-and-response singing, and this form and context gave the message of Christianity greater appeal to the slaves. Particularly in the Upper South, evangelical religion became a mixture of African and European practices, providing another arena for interracial interaction. Massive numbers of white people were attracted to the simple, more democratic theology and the more emotional worship style, which might include both music and dancing. Fearing such associations and disapproving of such practices, many of the churchgoing colonial elite vehemently objected to this brand of worship.

An especially dangerous aspect of evangelical religions in the eyes of the elites was that virtually anyone seemed to be able to assume a position of leadership. One Boston reporter was upset by the fact that "there are among the exhorters . . . young persons, sometimes lads, or rather boys; nay women and girls; yea, Negroes, have taken upon them to do the business of preachers." From the perspective of the established clergy and other colonial authorities, this was the unmistakable sign of their diminishing control over potentially dangerous elements of society, as "private persons of no education and but low attainments in knowledge" were allowed to preach the gospel.[11] The stand that many evangelical preachers took against slavery, even in the South, provided sure proof of the dangers. For those already uncomfortable with the work of educating slave children and adults, being conducted by the Anglican Church's Society for the Propagation of the Gospel in Foreign Parts, the antislavery language of the evangelicals was especially disconcerting.

The interaction of blacks and whites, especially poor servants and slaves, in religious gatherings, festivals, and cooperative political actions, was so prevalent in the North during the colonial period that authorities passed legislation to block such alliances, much as they had done to curb black and Native American interaction. An ordinance adopted in Rhode Island in 1708 forbade any free person, white or black, from entertaining a slave except in the presence of the slave's master, but such regulations did not keep evangelical reformers from their ministry among servants and slaves. Sarah Osborn of Newport, Rhode Island, was one who opened her home to the poor of all stations and conditions. She conducted a school during the week and held educational religious services on Sunday evenings. An average of seventy African Americans attended her Sunday evening gatherings by the 1760s. From these meetings sprang a small religious community of free blacks and slaves, many of whom became prominent in the religious life and the antislavery struggle of the revolutionary period. Newport Gardner, a slave who later gained his freedom and opened a music school for black and white students, regularly attended Osborn's religious meetings. Also a part of this group was a young African-born woman named Obour Tanner, who occasionally held her own services. Tanner's preaching deeply affected Phillis Wheatley, a Boston slave who was also a well-known poet, and the evangelical message often appeared in her poetry. This evangelicalism brought blacks and whites together in religious worship in a manner that allowed them near equality in their participation. The potential social disruption of evangelical practice was exacerbated by the nature of the evangelical message itself: a theological equality that became part of the foundation of early antislavery thought.

There is little doubt that colonial authorities feared the potential disruptiveness of interracial associations, although moralistic arguments often obscured their political concerns. In New York officials claimed that such socializing was "destructive to the morals of servants and slaves." The influential editors of the *New York Weekly Journal* described these associations as "the principal bane and pest of the city."[12] Elite concerns were well founded, since there were many occasions when interracial actions challenged colonial authority. In New York City two white saloon keepers, John Romme and John Hughson, operated theft rings that included a number of slaves and free blacks. Romme and Hughson made arrangements to sell the stolen goods supplied to them by their associates. By the 1740s each man's tavern served as a criminal headquarters catering to an interracial clientele that included street gangs. Hughson's pub was especially popular with New York slaves, and on their Sundays off many spent the afternoon after church services enjoying the special dinner served there. Blacks and whites partook of goose and mutton served with freshly baked bread, rum, cider, and punch. There were music, dancing, and conversations about unjust masters and inconsiderate bosses, all reinforcing the commonalities of their social and economic status.[13]

These commonalities were said to have shaped the discussions at Hughson's tavern into a major "slave plot" to burn New York City and kill many of its white inhabitants in 1741. Mary Burton, who lived at the tavern, informed the authorities of the plot, which she insisted she had overheard being discussed by three black Spanish sailors. A major investigation concluded that this plot was indeed being planned, and 150 blacks and 25 whites were prosecuted for their alleged roles in the conspiracy. Although the evidence presented at the trial was circumstantial at best, 32 blacks and 4 whites (including Hughson and his wife) were executed. Historians disagree about whether there was actually a plot or whether it was an exaggeration of a scheme to cover criminal activity and made believable by the general fear of such plots. There may well have been some New Yorkers old enough to remember the attack on the city in 1712, when slaves and Indians set fires, killing 9 whites and wounding several others. The proven existence of the 1712 slave plot lent credibility to testimony about the 1741 plot. Real or not, anxiety about interracial joint action was strong enough to create near panic among the white citizens of New York: strong enough to lead to the execution of thirty-six people.[14]

Attacks by the resentful poor became an increasing threat to authorities during the mid–eighteenth century as wealth and power became more concentrated in the hands of those at the top of colonial society, a trend reflected in the tax rolls, and an increasing display of wealth. The economic disparity was most apparent in the South, but after midcentury it was clear everywhere that the poor were less likely to rise above poverty than they had been before. In the cities growing relief roles testified to the relative permanence of poverty—three times as many people received relief in Philadelphia in 1765 as had in 1750.[15] The consolidation of wealth was accompanied by a concentration of power, and economic and political advantages were reflected in the application of the law, as colonial courts were likely to favor those of higher rank over those of lesser status.[16] In 1767, for example, the court refused to render a judgment against a military officer and governor designate on behalf of a "yeoman." The court justified its refusal on the grounds that a "[g]entleman by office" might "abate [such a] writ." Gentlemen also seem to have been immune from certain punishments routinely prescribed for crimes. Although whipping was a common sentence for those found guilty of even petty offenses in New York, and gentlemen were occasionally found guilty of such offenses, no gentleman was ever whipped in colonial New York City.[17]

The increasing distance between rich and poor did not go unnoticed by those at the bottom of colonial society, and officials were concerned about a "general murmuring against the government and the rich people." The problem was evident as early as the 1730s, when unemployment and inflation worked a special hardship on the poor in some cities, while yeomen farmers in the surrounding countryside received decreasing prices for their produce from urban merchants. Poor people from Boston tried to solve this problem by bypassing local merchants, traveling into the farm areas, and buying directly from producers, but by the end of the decade evidence of the merchants' continued price manipulation provoked them to mob action. Like those who gathered in Romme's tavern in New York, according to contemporary accounts, these poor urbanites who eventually forced price reforms were "young People, Servants and Negroes."[18]

Another important issue that prompted interracial action was British impressment, the practice of drafting young men into British naval service in a summary fashion that amounted to virtual kidnapping. British "press gangs" roamed rural areas and towns, taking young men whenever naval personnel needs required it. Men were taken immediately and without warning, fathers forced to leave their work in the fields, sons forced from their dinner tables. Taverns and other places where the common people gathered were the favored sources of manpower, and poor people of all races were vulnerable. Public reaction to impressment was strong and often violent. In the 1740s Bostonians battled press gangs in the streets in what one inquiry called a "riotous, tumultuous assembly of foreign seamen, servants, Negroes and other persons of mean and vile condition." At one point in the melee several thousand people attacked the governor's house. Local authorities expressed sympathy for those unfairly impressed, but they vigorously condemned this interracial, lower-class mob violence.[19] In the 1760s impressment attempts provoked riots in Maine, New York, Maryland, and Virginia. Five hundred "seamen, boys and Negroes" resisted the press gangs in Newport, Rhode Island, in the summer of 1765. Clearly this was an issue that galvanized popular opinion into concerted action. While the revolutionary cry of "No taxation without representation!" might have rallied those in the middle and upper ranks of colonial society in the 1770s, in the eyes of the poor impressment was the most serious sign of English disregard for American freedom. For the poor impressment was at least as devastating as the taxes imposed by Britain.

Developments in the colonies by the 1770s had created some divergence of interests between groups of colonists, according to their place in the
economy. Poor people reacted most strongly to colonial policies that inflated
prices, threatened jobs, and deprived them of their liberty. All colonials were
concerned with these issues, but the elites were not generally sympathetic to
the freedom demanded by slaves and servants. They were determined to
wrest additional political power from England and to establish control over
trade policies. In the years after the mid–eighteenth century the growing numbers of middling Americans, not at the bottom but below the elite, were less
likely to protest impressment than they were to react when the crown tightened controls on the American economy and threatened what they saw as the
"rights of Englishmen." Nevertheless they often joined the poor in mass
action, especially on economic issues.

In 1765, when Parliament passed the Stamp Act in an attempt to force the
colonies to reimburse the Crown for expenses incurred during the French and
Indian War (1754–1763), colonials claimed that Britain had no right to levy
a tax designed to raise revenue rather than to regulate trade. The regulation
required that fees be collected in the colonies, as they were in Britain, for stamps
to be affixed to newspapers, wills, contracts, marriage licenses, and other legal
documents. This had the effect of raising the cost of doing business and was
especially burdensome for merchants and lawyers. Although poor people were
seldom involved in such transactions, colonial leaders fostered their opposition by drawing a parallel between the Stamp Act and impressment, arguing that in both cases Britain ignored the rights of Americans. The resulting
mob actions that erupted all over the colonies included a far more diverse group
of protesters than had many earlier actions, bringing together black and
white, poor and nonpoor. In New York City mob leaders, who were beginning
to be thought of as revolutionaries, gathered at the Queen's Head Tavern to
lay plans and discuss strategy. Owned and operated by "Black Sam" Fraunces,
a West Indian mulatto, the tavern became notorious as the revolutionaries'
headquarters during the 1760s and 1770s. From the Queen's Head, New
Yorkers launched their equivalent of the Boston Tea Party in 1774.[20]

As the political debate between the colonies and the mother country over
economic control continued, colonial leaders called on the mobs with increasing frequency. Mob actions supported the cause of well-to-do colonials, but
mob participants often had their own interests, and mobs always presented
the troubling prospect of uncontrolled popular excess. Samuel Adams and other
members of the "better" classes who had ties to the lower ranks attempted
to direct the mob but occasionally lost control, as in 1770 when sailors,
dock workers, and the unemployed attacked British soldiers in Boston. This
particular revolutionary mob was reacting to the specific grievances of its

members, and its leader was not controlled or trusted by the colonial elites. He was Crispus Attucks, a former slave in his late forties who had escaped from his master outside Boston in 1750 and had remained free for twenty years. In an ad placed by his master in the *Boston Gazette and Weekly Journal* the year he escaped, he was described as a "well set" mulatto, twenty-seven years old, six feet two inches tall, with short curly hair and "knees nearer together than common." Attucks was part African and part Nantucket Indian, and during the years of his freedom he worked as a seaman on whalers sailing out of Boston and in a rope factory in the city's North End.[21]

As a seaman Crispus Attucks faced the danger of impressment, the economic pain of inflation at the end of the French and Indian War in 1763, and the uncertainty of irregular employment. When Britain redoubled its efforts to regulate colonial trade under the Navigation Acts and other tax legislation, it dispatched soldiers to American ports. In Boston, as elsewhere, British troops were a constant reminder of the authority of the Crown and the power of the Parliament over daily life in the colonies. For ordinary working people the soldiers were also competitors in the job market. With full-time employment to satisfy most of their needs, soldiers could afford to accept part-time work below the customary wages. This competition for jobs lowered the wages that employers were willing to pay and imposed great hardships on the colonial work force. This was an important aspect of workers' resentment of British soldiers and contributed greatly to the tensions between the two groups. In Boston during the winter of 1770, seamen and laborers instigated sporadic attacks on the British troops.

These were the issues that dominated the conversation of the seamen and laborers who gathered to drink in a Boston pub on the afternoon of March 5, 1770. Tempers flared when an unsuspecting newly arrived British soldier entered the pub, ordered a drink, and inquired about part-time employment in the city. The crowd became hostile; one seaman suggested that the soldier clean his outhouse, another made similarly insulting propositions. Confronted by such anger, the young soldier left the pub. For the rest of the afternoon and into the early evening, the men continued drinking, and their talk became bolder. Finally the club-wielding crowd of twenty or thirty "saucy boys, negroes and mulattoes, Irish teagues and outlandish jack-tarrs," led by the former slave Crispus Attucks, spilled into the street and snaked its way to the Customs House on King Street. There they confronted the British soldiers standing guard. Attucks took the lead in harassing the sentries, poking one of them with a stick and calling him a "lobster," an allusion to the British soldiers' red coats. Some threw snowballs, then chunks of ice, and finally stones. The situation escalated rapidly— "the multitude shouting and huzzaing, threatening life, the bell ringing, the mob whistling and screaming like an Indian yell,

Eighteenth-century romanticized sketch of the Boston Massacre of 1770.
Prints and Photographs Division, Library of Congress, Washington, D.C.

the people from all quarters throwing every species of rubbish they could pick up in the street." "The way to get rid of these soldiers is to attack the main-guard," Attucks shouted. "[S]trike at the root: this is the nest."[22]

Deadly violence swiftly followed. As word of the Customs House confrontation spread, crowds gathered in other parts of the city to challenge British soldiers, and in one skirmish a soldier stabbed a young boy with his bayonet. At the Customs House Attucks and his compatriots grew still bolder until finally a British officer, fearing the mounting danger to his troops, gave the order to fire into the crowd. When the order was ignored it was given again, but once more the soldiers failed to react. The people in the crowd assumed the troops would retreat, not fire, but they were wrong. A third order rang out: "Damn you, fire, be the consequence what it will." This time soldiers responded with a volley; three in the crowd were killed, and two others were wounded. Attucks was hit twice and died instantly, the first casualty in what became the revolutionary cause of American independence.[23]

The events of March 5, 1770, became known as the Boston Massacre, mythologized not as the reckless actions of a few intoxicated seamen and laborers, but as the symbol of American colonists' willingness to stand up to armed troops to oppose British tyranny. Attucks's role was central to the event and is crucial for the understanding of the social and political relations in the late eighteenth century. When Massachusetts held a trial, the British soldiers were defended by Boston attorney John Adams, a future revolutionary leader. Adams was troubled by the Crown's disregard for the rights of the colonials as English citizens, but he was even more disturbed by the increasingly frequent "mob violence." He denounced the mob's taunts and rock throwing, and condemned Attucks for having "undertaken to be the hero of the night," but he expressed no surprise that the mob was interracial or that its leader was an African American.[24] Nor were racial distinctions made during the funeral services held for those who died at the Boston Massacre. Despite Adams's condemnation the fallen were treated as patriots. Their funeral procession was a "vast multitude of people, walking, six deep, and a long train of carriages belonging to the principal gentry of the town." Their bodies were given a place of honor in one of the city's most prestigious cemeteries. The ceremony, it was said, attracted "the greatest concourse which had then ever assembled upon one occasion in America." Crispus Attucks was buried along with the three other fallen patriots.[25]

John Adams later acknowledged that the Boston Massacre opened the rift with England that became American independence. The presence of the British army continued to be an irritant; as Sam Adams put it, a standing army was "always dangerous to the liberties of the people." During the 1770s even those who feared the excesses of the mob came to accept them as useful to building the revolution. In his diary John Adams recorded a letter to the royal governor of Massachusetts, Thomas Hutchinson, signed with the name "Crispus Attucks." Holding Hutchinson responsible for the troops under his authority, and arguing that his crimes against "the people in general" were "chargeable before God and man, with our blood," the letter was dated 1773, three years after Attucks was killed. Thus it is likely that Adams wrote the letter and signed Attucks's name recognizing the former slave as a revolutionary symbol and acknowledging the important role blacks played in the cause of American freedom.[26]

As the rhetoric of revolution escalated, whites concerned about the loss of their freedom used the word "slavery" to describe the relationship with Britain they wished to avoid. African Americans pointed out the hypocrisy inherent in the use by slaveholders of the rhetoric of slavery and freedom.[27] In 1773 and 1774 Massachusetts slaves confronted colonial authorities with the question of their freedom. "We expect great things from men who have made such a noble stand against the designs of their fellow men to enslave them," they declared. Their demands were not revolutionary, simply that slaves be allowed one day a week to labor for their own benefit so they might accumulate funds to purchase their own freedom. This petition was refused, but

Petition for Freedom by Massachusetts Slaves

Boston, April 20th, 1773

Sir, The efforts made by the legislative of this province in their last sessions to free themselves from slavery, gave us, who are in that deplorable state, a high degree of satisfaction. We expect great things from men who have made such a noble stand against the designs of their *fellow-men* to enslave them. We cannot but wish and hope, Sir, that you will have the same grand object, we mean civil and religious liberty, in view in your next session. The divine spirit of *freedom,* seems to fire every humane breast on this continent, except such as are bribed to assist in executing the execrable plan.

We are very sensible that it would be highly detrimental to our present masters, if we were allowed to demand all that of *right* belongs to us for past services; this we disclaim. Even the *Spaniards,* who have not those sublime ideas of freedom that English men have, are conscious that they have no right to all the services of their fellow-men, we mean the *Africans,* whom they have purchased with their money; therefore they allow them one day in a week to work for themselves, to enable them to earn money to purchase the residue of their time, which they have a right to demand in such portions as they are able to pay for (a due appraizement of their services being first made, which always stands at the purchase money). We do not pretend to dictate to you Sir, or to the Honorable Assembly, of which you are a member. We acknowledge our obligations to you for what you have already done, but as the people of this province seem to be actuated by the principles of equity and justice, we cannot but expect your house will again take our deplorable case into serious consideration, and give us that ample relief which, *as men,* we have a natural right to.

But since the wise and righteous governor of the universe, has permitted our fellow men to make us slaves, we bow in submission to him, and determine to behave in such a manner as that we may have reason to expect the divine approbation of, and assistance in, our peaceable and lawful attempts to gain our freedom.

We are willing to submit to such regulations and laws, as may be made relative to us, until we leave the province, which we determine to do as soon as we can, from our joynt labours procure money to transport ourselves to some part of the Coast of *Africa,* where we propose a settlement. We are very desirous that you should have instructions relative to us, from your town, therefore we pray you to communicate this letter to them, and ask this favor for us.

(continued)

(continued)

In behalf of our fellow slaves in this province, and by order of their Committee.

Peter Bestes,
Sambo Freeman,
Felix Holbrook,
Chester Joie.

For the Representative of the town of Thompson

———

Herbert Aptheker, ed., *A Documentary History of the Negro People in the United States* (New York: Citadel Press, 1951), vol. 1, 7–8.

others followed, each carefully worded to highlight the parallels between their cause and the colonists' desire for a "free and Christian country."[28]

Colonials organized Committees of Correspondence to protest Britain's denial of their rights as Englishmen, while Africans in Massachusetts called on the Enlightenment ideal of the natural rights of man to petition for an end to their enslavement. Some colonial leaders had made the connection between their desire for freedom from English tyranny and the slaves' longing for liberty. When James Otis asserted in 1765 that all those born in the colonies were "British subjects" entitled to civil rights, he concluded that all blacks as well as whites were "by the law of nature free born" and argued therefore that slavery must be ended. Abigail Adams pointed forcefully to the incongruity in a letter to her husband in 1774: "It always seemed a most iniquitous scheme to me to fight ourselves for what we are daily robbing and plundering from those who have as good a right to freedom as we have."[29]

African Americans found themselves in a complex situation at the start of the Revolution. They had grievances against both the British and the Americans. When Parliament closed down the Port of Boston as a punishment for the Boston Tea Party, black seamen and dock laborers suffered the consequences just as their white counterparts did. Both blacks and whites were endangered by impressment and angered by the passage of the punitive "Intolerable Acts" forced on the colonies in 1774. Despite their shared circumstances, however, most American patriots seemed willing to pursue freedom from England without acting against slavery at home. Black protests created fears among some southern patriots. After "some Negroes had mimicked their betters in crying Liberty," as Henry Laurens of South Carolina put it, their focus shifted from the threat of British tyranny to the more pressing prospect of slave insurrection at home.[30]

Phillis Wheatley

In the summer of 1761, a young African girl no more than seven or eight years old arrived in Boston on the ship *Phillis*. Slave traders had captured her in the Gambia River region of West Africa in the Fulani nation. In Boston, John and Susanna Wheatley bought her and called her by the name of the ship that brought her to the colonies. Phillis was extraordinarily bright, and the Wheatleys allowed her to learn to read and write. Within sixteen months she was proficient in English, and within three years was literate in Latin. In 1767 Phillis published a poem in Rhode Island's *Newport Mercury,* and by the mid-1770s published several others, many about freedom. She joined Boston's Old South Church, where the Wheatleys were members. The church served as a forum for patriotic meetings during the 1770s, although John and Susanna Wheatley remained loyal to Britain. In 1772 Phillis accompanied her owners to England, where she met the British abolitionist Granville Sharp and Benjamin Franklin, who was in London at the time. Franklin was impressed by her talent, and the Londoners helped her publish a book, *Poems on Various Subjects, Religious and Moral,* in 1773. Phillis returned to Boston as America's first black published author, and that fall, the Wheatleys granted her freedom.

Then in her early twenties, Phillis Wheatley strongly supported the American Revolution. Her poem dedicated to George Washington drew an enthusiastic reception from the commander of the Continental forces and an invitation to visit him at his headquarters. Her views on freedom may have influenced Washington's personal struggle over slavery. In 1778 Phillis Wheatley married John Peters, a free black man. The couple struggled financially while Phillis worked on an ambitious three-hundred-page manuscript, a project she did not live to publish. She died in childbirth in Boston in 1784. One of her last poems, written in honor of the Treaty of Paris, ending the Revolution, was entitled "Liberty and Peace." As manumission societies were formed at the end of the eighteenth century, Phillis Wheatley came to symbolize the Africans' longing for freedom and became a reminder of talents to which the slave system generally denied expression.

Frontispiece from a book of poems written by Phillis Wheatley in 1773. Prints and Photographs Division, Library of Congress, Washington, D.C.

The ambivalence many blacks felt toward the American cause continued as political protest became a war for independence. Africans and African descendants took up arms along with their fellow Americans when the British marched through Lexington, Massachusetts, on their way to capture American arms in the nearby town of Concord. Some were Minutemen who served with the special militia, while others volunteered as the British army approached. Massachusetts black men, like Peter Salem of Framingham, Samuel Craft of Newton, and Cato Wood and Cuff Whittemore of Arlington, stood their ground in Lexington and Concord with their white compatriots when the "shot heard around the world" was fired, signaling the beginning of the Revolutionary War. "Prince the Negro" was wounded in the battle that followed. Titus Coburn, Salem Poor, Grant Cooper, and Peter Salem, who eventually served seven years in the Continental army, were among those who held out against the British at the Battle of Bunker Hill, near Boston. Several blacks who participated in the battle were commended for bravery, and Peter Salem's hometown later erected a monument to his courage as a Revolutionary soldier.[31]

Despite blacks' participation in initial Revolutionary military actions, their presence in the Continental forces was questioned. On July 9, 1775, just five days after he was appointed commander of the American troops, George Washington, a slaveholder from Virginia, ordered that although those already on active duty might remain, no new black recruits should be enlisted. Black participation was heatedly debated by the Continental Congress. Representatives from southern areas struggling to control their large slave population were keenly aware of the danger of arming blacks. At the same time they contended that blacks were too servile and timid by nature to make good soldiers and asserted that white southern military men could not be induced to serve beside black soldiers. Edward Rutledge, the delegate from South Carolina, led southerners in demanding that all slaves and free blacks be removed from the army. Northerners, less fearful of slave revolt, were more likely to see the benefits of black enlistment and argued that blacks had proved their worth in early battles. The attempt to remove blacks failed, and Washington's compromise stood as a recognition of the courage of the African Americans who had already served. The strength of southern fears is apparent in light of the fact that blacks had already served in all the colonial wars, including King William's War (1690–1697), Queen Anne's War (1702–1713), King George's War (1744–1748), and the French and Indian War (1755–1763). In 1747 South Carolina had officially thanked black troops for helping defend the colony. Further, Africans had formed the major body of the Spanish army in the American Southwest as early as the sixteenth century, had served the Dutch in New Netherland before British occupation, and were used by the British in Barbados. Given this evidence it seems likely that it was the fear of arming slaves, not skepticism over their fitness for military service, that was at issue.

White southerners had good reason to be concerned about arming slaves and to fear the specter of interracial uprisings. There were many rumors about servant and slave conspiracies planning to provide military service to the British and to strike against southern plantations. According to one southerner many believed that the "malicious and imprudent speeches of some among the lower classes of whites . . . induced [the slaves] to believe that their freedom depended on the success of the King's troops."[32] In South Carolina, newspapers reported that large bands of "the most infamous banditti and horse thieves [which included] a corps of Indians, with negro and white savages disguised like them," were raiding settlements and "stealing slaves" throughout the region. These banditti were groups of fugitive slaves, indentured servants, Cherokee, poor farmers, and backcountry Tories who worked independently and with British forces and were commanded by men like "Captain" Jones, "Colored Power Man," or the mulatto William Hunt. These guerrilla bands burned and looted plantations, stole horses, and attacked Continental forces in many regions. In New Jersey, a band under the leadership of Tye, "a Negro who [bore] the title of colonel," attacked American fortifications and a number of large slaveholding estates, freeing slaves and indentured servants. Guerrilla fighters continued to operate even after the end of the war. For more than half a century bands of blacks calling themselves the King of England Soldiers harassed southern plantations and freed slaves when possible. Ironically the persistence of these bands bore testimony to the power of the revolutionary message of liberty.[33]

Many patriots argued that the only way to discourage black participation in loyalist groups like the banditti was to enroll them in the American cause. It was the colonial governor of Virginia, Lord Dunmore, however, whose actions quickly forced the Americans to reconsider their policy on black enlistment. In November he struck at the heart of the colonials' contradiction with a strategy designed to infuriate and humiliate them, especially the slaveholders. Dunmore promised freedom to all slaves and indentured servants who escaped from their rebellious masters and fought on the side of the British.

In light of the ruling in the *Somerset* case a few years before, slaves were inclined to believe the British offer of freedom. James Somerset was a slave who had run away from his master in England in the early 1770s. When he was recaptured and his master threatened to ship him to Jamaica to be sold, abolitionist Granville Sharp persuaded the court to take up his case. In a carefully worded decision the British court ruled that no slave could be forcibly taken from England. Some American slaves acted on the promise of the Somerset ruling directly, as their masters attested when they advertised for their return. One Virginia slave, a master speculated, would probably "board a vessel for Great Britain . . . from the knowledge he has of the late Determination of the Somerset Case." Another master believed his runaway slave couple was on the way to Britain, "where they imagine they will be free," adding, "a Notion now too prevalent among the Negroes." Drawing the implication from the court ruling that slavery was incompatible with the rights granted by English common law gave the hope of freedom to slaves in England and in the colonies and gave credence to Dunmore's promise of freedom in return for military service.[34]

The promise of "liberty to slaves," as the insignia on the uniforms of Dunmore's Ethiopian Regiment proclaimed, was wildly successful. In a few months three hundred blacks served in the regiment, and by the end of the war eight hundred blacks had served, constituting more than half of Dunmore's troops. Other effects of the proclamation were to provide the British with support troops and to deprive many slaveholders of their labor supply. Wherever the British went, nearby slaves sought sanctuary with them, though only the approximately one thousand slaves who fought in the army were promised freedom. Estimates are that the Americans lost as many as one hundred thousand of their approximately five hundred thousand slaves to the British during the war. The disruption of wartime itself, of course, also provided opportunities for slaves who did not need the motivation of British promises to escape from bondage. By 1778 Thomas Jefferson reported that thirty thousand Virginia slaves had run away to the British; others have estimated that South Carolina lost at least twenty-five thousand and that Georgia lost more than twelve thousand of its fifteen thousand slaves before the war's end.[35]

Lord Dunmore's strategy forced the patriots to compete for the loyalties of African Americans and reconsider their policy against enlisting blacks. The threat of conspiracies and guerrilla actions by allied white loyalists and slaves became reality in many communities and was rumored in many others. In a letter to one of his officers, Washington worried that Dunmore's black troops would draw more and more slaves to the British lines. Indeed Washington predicted that the use of black troops would make Dunmore "the most dangerous man in America," and that ultimately "success [would] depend on who [could] arm the Negroes the faster." Under these circumstances he saw little recourse but to reverse his policy on black recruitment. Recruiting blacks into the Continental forces would also help address the problem of a growing troop shortage. White soldiers were reluctant to serve for longer than short three-month enlistments or to serve great distances from their homes, and the availability of black troops might ease this situation. On January 6, 1776, Congress acted on Washington's recommendation and set into motion a series of orders that eventually opened the Continental ranks to African Americans. Eventually all the states except South Carolina and Georgia enlisted black soldiers. The

dwindling white enlistments as the war continued created economic hardships and reinforced the argument for recruiting blacks. In the end most states
matched Dunmore's promise of freedom for slaves who served in the army.[36]

Some states allowed the enlistment of slaves as replacements for whites
unwilling or unable to serve the American cause. This proved a boon to
many slave masters, who sent their slaves to service in their stead. Nathan Dib-
ble and his son Eli, both of Connecticut, avoided military service by sending
their slave, Jack Anthony, to serve in their places. After a term of service that
lasted until the end of the war Anthony was granted his freedom. London Haz-
ard, a Rhode Island slave, served for several members of his master's family
in order to secure his freedom, and Cezar Negro, who had been born at sea
during his mother's crossing from Africa, won his freedom after serving in place
of his master's son. James Armistead served as a spy for General Lafayette and
was granted his freedom by the Virginia legislature in 1786. Blacks served with
Francis Marion, "the Swamp Fox," and his guerrilla band in South Carolina.
Thousands of slaves gained their freedom by helping to win freedom for the
United States, many serving in place of their masters or members of their masters' families. In doing so these blacks generally served for long periods,
often two to three years longer than white soldiers. Prince Hazeltine served
in the Second Massachusetts Regiment for six years and was not discharged
until the end of the war. He received two badges of merit for his heroism at
Worcester, where he rescued several of his fellows from an explosion and fire
that cost many lives. He was so badly injured in the process that for the rest
of his life he was unable to work regularly.[37]

Not all who fought were slaves fighting for their own freedom; free
blacks also served in the Continental army. Since few free blacks could afford
to pay for a substitute, and because most believed that their lives might be
better in an independent United States, a great many served. Abijah Prince
served with the Green Mountain Boys of Vermont, under the command of
Ethan Allen. As a part of the French allied contingent, five hundred freemen
from Haiti also took their places among the American forces. Henri Christophe,
who later became the King of Haiti, was one of them. The official count of
black revolutionary soldiers and seamen was five thousand, but many more
served as spies, guides, laborers, and musicians. Unknown numbers of black
women served the Continental forces as nurses and cooks, and a few may have
disguised themselves as men and served as regular soldiers. Many blacks
served as merchant seamen and military sailors in both the American and the
British navies. Even whites who objected to arming slaves on land were generally willing to allow slaves and free blacks to serve on warships. Blacks served
either in integrated units or in a few all-black regiments.[38]

After the British took the capital city of Newport, destroyed many farms,
and occupied two-thirds of the state, Rhode Island raised its own black unit.

Portrait of Lemuel Haynes, former Revolutionary War soldier and African American minister to a white congregation in eighteenth-century Vermont.

Photographs and Prints Division, Schomburg Center for Research in Black Culture, The New York Public Library, Astor, Lenox, and Tilden Foundations.

Most of its troops came from the Narragansett region, an area with some of the few large slaveholding estates in the North. As in the South the large planters in Rhode Island objected to arming slaves and were successful in ending slave enlistments, but were too late to stop the black unit from going into action. The First Rhode Island Battalion, as it was called, was commanded by Col. Christopher Greene, a white Quaker who violated the pacifist tenets of his religion to join the war effort. The battalion served in its home state and in Virginia and New York. Greene had led a unit of four hundred black troops in Delaware before taking charge of the Rhode Island unit, and other black units were formed in Connecticut and Massachusetts. New York, New Jersey, and New Hampshire enlisted blacks in the ranks of its general military units. In Maryland the state legislature rejected the idea of raising an all-black regiment and integrated slaves and free blacks into its regular state militia. Virginia allowed free blacks to join its militia but refused to arm slaves, although some slaveholders enrolled slaves in their stead by claiming that the slaves were free. No amount of persuasion could break the resolve of Georgians and South Carolinians not to allow black troops to be raised within their borders, however. Several plans were proposed, one supported by Alexander Hamilton of New York, that would have provided three thousand blacks to assist Georgia and South Carolina in filling their quota of troops, but they were soundly rejected. As one South Carolinian wrote, "We are much disgusted here at the Congress recommending us to arm our Slaves, it was received with great resentment, as a very dangerous and impolitic step."[39] A counterargument was advanced that by enlisting slaves in common cause with slave masters, slave uprisings might actually be averted, but it was to no avail, even when it appeared that South Carolina and Georgia would fall to British forces. White Georgians tolerated having black troops from the French West Indies defend the port city of Savannah, but fear of the consequences of arming slaves prevented them from making any further concessions. Georgia fell to the British in early 1779, and Charleston, South Carolina, was taken in the summer of 1780, but still no black troops were enlisted.[40]

Yet black soldiers fought in every theater of the war, even in the South. They saw action in the Green Mountains of Vermont and in the Blue Ridge Mountains of North Carolina. They endured the snow and freezing temperatures alongside the white troops at places like Valley Forge, Pennsylvania. Cato Cuff was frostbitten so badly there that he could never work outdoors in cold weather again. At the Battle of Lake Champlain in New York, Samuel Coombs, though wounded himself, tended the wounds of other injured men. Prince Whipple and Oliver Cromwell were among those who manned the oars of the boat carrying George Washington across the Delaware River to the battle at Trenton, and blacks like African-born Prince Bent of the Rhode Island regiment were serving with Washington when Cornwallis surrendered.[41]

The Revolution brought independence to the new American nation and freedom to thousands of African American slaves, but not all blacks who were promised freedom were freed even after they had completed military service. Many substitution agreements between masters and slaves consisted only of a verbal promise, which masters easily denied at war's end. Some slaves successfully brought suit against these masters, but the national government did little to ensure that masters abided by state legislation freeing slaves who had served. Although many were properly freed and some freed themselves by simply walking away from slavery during the postwar disruption, many others remained in slavery.[42]

The last British contingent, which surrendered New York in November 1783, took four thousand blacks with them. More than fourteen thousand blacks departed that fall, and most of those who had not served with the British forces but had simply escaped to British lines remained in slavery. Some went to Canada with Loyalists or to England with the troops. Others ended up on sugar plantations in Jamaica or some other British West Indian colony, where life was unspeakably harsh for slaves. The British granted some people a choice of destination; Phyllis Thomas, "a free black woman," was granted passage to the West Indies or "elsewhere at her option." Other free blacks traveled to Britain, Europe, Canada, or parts of Latin America. Some found opportunities abroad that they would probably not have had in the United States. Bill Richmond, a slave of the duke of Northumberland on New York's Staten Island, went to London with his master when the duke withdrew from the United States. There Richmond was educated, became a boxer, and by 1800 was billed as "the Black Terror," a bare-knuckle contender for the national championship. Although Richmond lost to champion Tom Cribb in a brutal one-and-one-half-hour contest for the title, his fame enabled him to retire from the ring and establish the Horse and Dolphin Inn and his own boxing academy at the Royal Tennis Court; he trained many well-known British personalities, including Lord Byron, who attended regularly.[43]

Hundreds of blacks who went to Canada settled in Nova Scotia, accounting for at least 10 percent of those who settled the Halifax area during the early 1780s. Many were families like Charles and Dolly and their five children, who had been slaves in New York and settled in Port Roseway, Nova Scotia. There Charles found work as a carpenter with the British army engineers, they survived the harsh winters, and the family built a life in freedom. Others who settled in Canada were not so fortunate, and with increasing urgency the new black Canadians reported that land and employment were difficult to secure, racial intolerance was increasing as the black population grew, and life was generally hard. Even though these blacks valued their new freedom, neither Canada nor England offered most blacks the opportunities they sought for progress and self-determination, and many migrated elsewhere. A few went to other countries in Europe, but by 1790 many American-born blacks were among the settlers of the British West African colony of Sierra Leone.[44]

In the new United States, antislavery forces continued their agitation during the war, arguing that slavery was inconsistent with both Christianity and the values of the Revolution. Many colonies—even including Virginia, North Carolina, and Georgia—had temporarily outlawed the slave trade during 1774 and 1775. In 1775 the first antislavery society in the world was established in Philadelphia, calling itself the Society for the Relief of Free Negroes Unlawfully Held in Bondage. Two years later Vermont became the first state in the nation to abolish slavery within its borders, adopting a state constitutional provision that declared, "All men are born equally free and independent." Local abolitionists attacked slavery everywhere but in the Deep South.[45] In 1779 a group of slaves petitioned the legislature in New Hampshire for their freedom. They argued that their being kidnapped from their native Africa and held in the United States against their will was plainly against all natural law, since the "God of nature gave them life and freedom, upon the terms of most perfect equality with other men." But New Hampshire officials were deaf to the slaves' plea, though the 1783 state constitution seemed

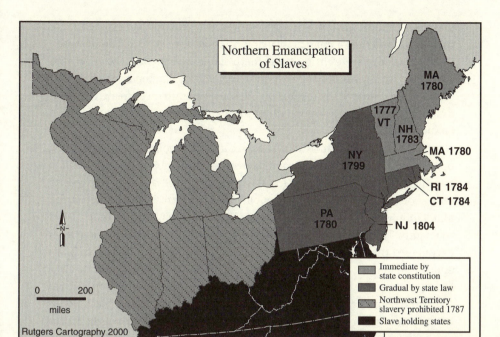

to deny slavery's ligitimacy. Although slavery waned in the state, and the number of slaves dwindled to practically zero before the nineteenth century (eight slaves were recorded in the state in 1800), the institution was not officially abolished there until 1857.[46]

The antislavery arguments of slaves and their abolitionist allies were more directly successful in other northern states. Most of these states abolished slavery through strategies of gradual emancipation that were less economically and socially disruptive than immediate emancipation, at least from the perspective of the white society. In Connecticut a combination of economic depression and antislavery pressure encouraged the legislature to institute a plan that freed the children of slaves when they reached the age of twenty-five. In Pennsylvania any slave born after 1780 was to be set free at twenty-eight, being treated as an indentured servant until that time. New York and New Jersey enacted gradual emancipation plans in 1799 and 1804. Massachusetts answered the revolutionary rhetoric in a slave petition with immediate emancipation, after the state supreme court ruled in 1783 that slavery was incompatible with the state constitution of 1780. By 1800 slavery was abolished or in the process of being gradually abolished throughout the North.[47]

The ideals and the rhetoric of the Revolution made arguments for emancipation difficult to ignore, but other factors also contributed to the demise of slavery in the North. Urban white workers, wanting to limit both employment competition and the number of blacks in the local population, pressured officials to abolish slavery. Northern employers found free labor sufficient for their needs and thus a financially viable alternative to slavery. The relatively small number of slaves in most northern states, and the fact that northern economies were generally not built on slavery, meant that there were few powerful voices in favor of the institution. All these circumstances created the conditions under which the arguments of those working for emancipation could be successful.

In the Lower South, where planters held the political and economic power, the impact of Revolutionary idealism was negligible. As South Carolina and Georgia had resisted enlisting slaves in their militia during the war, so they stood fast against the winds of abolition drifting across the northern states. Maryland, Virginia, and North Carolina retained slavery too but far less adamantly. There, for a generation or more, state regulations allowed and even encouraged the voluntary manumission of slaves. As a result the free black population in those Upper South states grew substantially during the late eighteenth century and the first two decades of the nineteenth. By 1810 more than 107,000 free blacks, almost 58 percent of the nation's total free black population of 186,000, lived in the southern states. The rate of growth of the southern free black population declined after the 1820s as fewer southern slaves were freed. The numbers of slaves grew substantially, to 1.5 million by 1820 and to more than double that number by midcentury. Thus slavery became more significant in the South as it was gradually abolished in the North, and the social and political distance between North and South increased steadily.[48]

The divergence between the North and the South regarding slavery created new dangers for northern slaves. When it seemed clear that slavery would be abolished in the North, many slaveholders rushed to sell their slaves farther south before freedom prevented them from doing so. Even after the passage of emancipation laws, children and young adults particularly faced this risk. Under gradual emancipation, young slaves might be held as servants only until they reached their mid-twenties. Although the practice was illegal, handsome prices for young slaves in the plantation South provided an incentive for northern masters to sell their slaves to the South before they reached the age of manumission. In Connecticut in 1792 one slaveholder was charged with attempting to circumvent state law by "exporting" two slave children.[49] The closer northern slaves lived to the South, the greater the danger of their being transferred into southern slavery, and many traveling slave traders roamed the southern regions of the North in search of good buys. Some masters tricked slaves, sending them into the South for temporary employment and selling them once they were there. Eighteen-year-old Harvey had only a few more years to serve when he was persuaded to travel from Middlesex County, New Jersey, to Louisiana to work "temporarily." He was enslaved there for the rest of his life.[50] In this way many young slaves never gained their promised freedom, and the tragedies of slavery continued for them long after official emancipation in the North. Isabella, a slave with a strong Dutch accent who lived in New York State, understood the dangers as well as anyone. She looked forward to freedom for herself and her children under New York's emancipation law, but before freedom came her youngest son was given as a wedding present to her master's daughter who was leaving New York for Alabama. When a distraught Isabella confronted her mistress, the white women refused to take her concerns seriously. "A fine fuss to make about a little nigger! Why, haven't you as many of 'em left as you can see to?" Many parents carried such painful memories into freedom as slavery came to an end in the North. Isabella was eventually able to recover her son, but the incident contributed to her determination to fight against slavery and for the rights of women. In that fight she took the name Sojourner Truth.[51]

With the prolonged process of gradual emancipation in most of the North, many African Americans throughout the country continued to suffer the hardships of slavery after the Revolution. Even those who were freed faced hard times in the postwar period, as all Americans were confronted by economic uncertainty and an unstable currency. The situation was especially difficult for the poor, including ex-slaves and indentured servants, and those who had gained their freedom by fighting in the war often carried additional burdens. Cato Howe, freed from bondage in return for his years of service for Massachusetts, returned to his wife and farmwork. The Howes settled in a section of Plymouth, Massachusetts, known as New Guinea or Parting Ways, with the families of three other black war veterans—Plato Turner, Quamony Quash, and Prince Goodwin. The depression of 1784 meant that the farmers received low prices for their produce. When Howe developed rheumatism from his war wounds he had trouble working around the farm and his life became even harder. Recognizing the hardships suffered by these veterans, in 1792 the town of Plymouth granted the men the rights to 106 acres of the land where they were living in return for the labor it would take to clear it. Despite this aid, the support and friendship of his comrades, and the pension to which his wartime service entitled him, Cato Howe was forced to rely on public assistance in his old age.[52]

For African Americans the Revolution brought an incomplete freedom and a precarious status in the United States. In Georgia and South Carolina nearly all the slaves who did not escape to the British lines remained in slavery. In the Chesapeake region, slavery remained as an institution, but the conditions under which masters could free their slaves were liberalized so that the number of free blacks increased. In the North slavery was ending, but freedom brought limited benefits to former slaves. The lingering revolutionary spirit held promise, but the future of black people in the United States was even more uncertain than the future of the new nation.

Chapter 4

1787	Adoption of the United States Constitution
	Northwest Ordinance outlaws slavery in the territory northwest of the Ohio River
	British found Sierra Leone as West African colony for freed slaves
1789	George Washington elected as the first president of the United States
	Olaudah Equiano publishes his *Narrative*
1790	First United States Census records nearly 4 million residents, more than 750,000 (19 percent) of whom are black
1791	Benjamin Banneker assists in surveying area to become District of Columbia
	Slaves revolt in French Haiti
1793	Eli Whitney invents the cotton gin
	Congress passes the first federal Fugitive Slave Law
1800	U.S. population 5,308,483; black population 1,002,037 (19 percent)
	Gabriel's massive slave revolt in Virginia is betrayed
	Thomas Jefferson elected president, the first president to reside in Washington, D.C.
1803	Louisiana Purchase more than doubles the land area of the United States
1804	Haiti achieves independence from France
1808	United States prohibits the African slave trade
1809	Thomas Paul organizes the Abyssinian Baptist Church in New York City
1812–1814	War between the United States and Great Britain
1815	Andrew Jackson commands U.S. troops, including a large force of African Americans, in the Battle of New Orleans
1816	American Colonization Society established
1820	West African colony of Liberia founded by colonization society for settlement of freed slaves
	Missouri Compromise maintains balance of slave and free states (twelve each); Missouri admitted as slave state and Maine as free

The Early Republic and the Rise of the Cotton Kingdom

*J*ames Forten returned from the Revolution to a Philadelphia that was the new nation's largest city and its financial, intellectual, and scientific center. This commercial hub had more than thirty-two thousand residents and a rapidly growing black population of more than eleven hundred, which would double in the next decade. The fourteen-year-old Forten, born free in Philadelphia, had served aboard the colonial ship *Royal Louis* and been captured by the British and held for seven months on a prison ship before finally returning to his family in his home city. Forten learned the trade of sailmaking and was so talented at the work that by the age of twenty he was foreman of a shop owned by white sailmaker Robert Bridges. He became a prominent member of the city's free black community, which by the mid-1780s accounted for almost 90 percent of the African Americans in Philadelphia. The small slave population continued to dwindle in the city and in the state, but the nation remained largely committed to the institution, no matter how it contradicted the national purpose.[1]

The United States was beginning to work out the meaning of citizenship for its people; and African Americans, having sacrificed to make independence possible, were determined to gain both liberty and full citizenship. Especially in urban areas the establishment or expansion of free black communities provided crucial economic and social support. The willingness of reformers to aid the newly free with services like education was a hopeful sign, as was the emergence of antislavery organizations. The debate over slavery was critical to the future of the United States as the new nation contemplated the construction of its government. The documents of the Revolution were filled with the language of equality, arguing for the right to liberty and self-determination. These sentiments had contributed to the decisions to abolish slavery in nearly all the northern states, and African Americans now called upon the nation to live up to its principles. Indeed historian Gary Nash has called the 1770s and 1780s the "opportune time for abolishing slavery" in the country. According to Nash the new nation could have outlawed slavery at that time because antislavery sentiment was strong; the Lower South, where slavery was dominant, was too weak to stand alone; a belief in innate black inferiority was not yet widespread; and western lands might have been used

to compensate slaveholders for freeing their slaves or for black colonization.[2] Post-Revolutionary leaders, however, having rebelled against a strong
colonial power, were acutely aware of the dangers of governmental central-
ization, and wartime disagreements had exposed the divergent interests of the
new states. Thus they limited the power of the federal government to impose
its will on the states by establishing a relatively weak, decentralized system
of government under the Articles of Confederation, leaving the issue of slavery to the separate states.

The turbulent decade of the 1780s exposed the vulnerability of a limited
federal government. In the years after the Revolution, economic pressure
increased as returning soldiers faced deteriorating conditions. The Continental
scrip with which they were paid was practically worthless, their debts had accu-
mulated, and the prospects for financial improvement seemed remote. Britain
had been the major market for colonial goods before the war, and the loss of
that market, combined with England's restrictions on American trade with the
British West Indies, fueled a depression, further demoralizing urban workers
and small farmers. In western Massachusetts debt-ridden farmers led by
Daniel Shays, a Revolutionary War hero and prominent landholder, revolted
against the increasing number of farm foreclosures. From August 1786 to March
1787, under Shays's leadership, thousands of armed farmers closed the local
courts and prevented authorities from foreclosing on their property. One of
Shays's inner circle was Moses Sash, a free black laborer from Massachusetts
who had also served in the war. Sash had received land as part of the payment
for his service—land he too was struggling to retain. For those in authority
concerned with political and economic stability, Shays's Rebellion was especially distressing. Congress had neither the funds nor the authority to raise
troops to put down the revolt. Black war veteran Prince Hall offered to take
a force of seven hundred Boston area African American volunteers to quell
the rebellion, but Massachusetts preferred to raise a force of white troops paid
by wealthy Boston merchants. By the spring of 1787 the privately financed
militia had routed Shays and his followers, many of whom then turned to state
politics to redress their grievances. Boston blacks were greatly offended by the
rejection of their offer of service to the new republic. Three months after Shays's
Rebellion ended, Prince Hall and more than seventy others petitioned the Massachusetts General Court for funds to transport all blacks who wanted to go
to Africa.[3]

At the same time representatives were meeting in Philadelphia in a constitutional convention to consider broad new powers for the federal government. As the founding fathers sat in hot, humid, summertime Philadelphia
arguing, compromising, and finally composing the Constitution, slavery was
a major point of contention, a point on which the Lower South especially

Portrait of Prince Hall, founder of the Colored Fraternity
of Free and Accepted Masons, Boston, Massachusetts.

Photographs and Prints Division, Schomburg Center for Research in Black Culture,
The New York Public Library, Astor, Lenox, and Tilden Foundations.

resisted compromise. Northern states were already moving toward the abolition of slavery, and delegates like Pennsylvania's Benjamin Franklin and New York's Alexander Hamilton had expressed the expectation that the new nation would follow their example. Virginia delegates George Washington, Thomas Jefferson, and Patrick Henry and others had assumed that an end to slavery would have to be negotiated at the Constitutional Convention. Yet northern delegates did not press the South, especially resistant South Carolina and Georgia. Perhaps feeling their weakness as part of a fledgling nation faced with continuing European designs on its territory and resources, the framers of the Constitution avoided a confrontation on the contentious issue. The harmony purchased at the cost of leaving the slavery question unresolved allowed the convention to construct a Constitution that provided a strong tripartite central government with access to financial resources and increased control over a military that might be called on to meet foreign threats or contain popular unrest. As it was finally written the Constitution never referred to slavery directly but did accommodate slavery in three respects. First it protected property rights in slaves by providing slaveholders with the assurance that runaway slaves would be returned even if they crossed state lines. Second it allowed the African slave trade to continue for a period of twenty years (and to reopen in places like South Carolina, where it had been closed), protecting it until 1808. Finally it provided additional representation, and thereby greater political power, in the federal House of Representatives to slave states by allowing three-fifths of the slaves to be counted in determining the basis for a state's representation. The Constitutional Convention did not define the requirements for citizenship, in effect reaffirming the traditional political system that gave citizenship rights to propertied white males. Although the Bill of Rights, the first ten amendments to the Constitution, seemed to offer the possibility of some legal protection for African Americans, the position of free black people remained unclear. The general term "person," occasionally with the qualifier "free," was used to refer to American citizens, while the term "other" delineated slaves, to whom no constitutional rights were guaranteed.

Although the silence of the Constitution on slavery left the existence and regulation of this institution to each state, the new Congress did concern itself with slavery in the territories directly under federal control. In 1787 Congress passed the Northwest Ordinance, governing territories north of the Ohio River that were not yet ready to gain admission to the Union as states. This ordinance outlawed slavery in these northwestern territories, but by not mentioning the southwestern territories gave tacit approval for the introduction of slavery there. As a concession to slave owners, slaves already in the northwestern territories, including those brought in by the French before British settlement, could remain in slavery. Strong proslavery feeling in the portion of the territory that later became the states of Indiana and Illinois led to continual attempts by officials to circumvent the ordinance.[4] As each new state was admitted to the union, the issue of black status was debated by state constitutional conventions. During the next two generations, western and southern territories applying for admission either protected slavery or outlawed slavery and restricted black migration. In Kentucky in 1792 antislavery elements raised religious and philosophical objections, but strong proslavery forces made Kentucky the first new slave state admitted to the Union. Four years later Tennessee, with more than ten thousand slaves, applied and was admitted as another slave state. In areas covered by the Northwest Ordinance, new states tried to limit the size of their black population. Indiana, Michigan, Wisconsin, and Iowa prohibited black immigration, and Illinois threatened bondage for blacks who attempted to settle there permanently. Ohio passed a series of "black laws" requiring that free blacks post a five-hundred-dollar bond of good conduct and denying blacks the right to vote in most areas, to hold public office, or to testify against a white person in court. Free blacks were prevented from serving on juries and testifying against white people in many states. Restrictive laws were irregularly enforced, however, and the free black population continued to grow, especially in areas bordering the South.[5]

Discouraged about their prospects for equality in America, members of African societies in Newport and Providence, Rhode Island; and in Boston and Philadelphia expressed cautious interest in the British colony of Sierra Leone in West Africa during the late 1700s. They were especially encouraged for a time in 1787 when the English committee for Sierra Leone hired the African Olaudah Equiano, then known as Gustavus Vassa, as the clerk in charge of outfitting and loading the ship bound for the colony. In his long route from his capture in Africa as a boy to this responsible position, Equiano had indeed been fortunate under adverse circumstances. He had spent only a few weeks in Barbados in 1756; as no one purchased him for plantation work there, the traders took him to Virginia, where they sold him to a tobacco planter who named him Jacob. He spent a month of terrible isolation. He could not speak English, and no one spoke his language. While working around the master's house and yard, he caught the eye of a visiting sea captain, who purchased him, took him to England, and named him Gustavus Vassa. When this new owner received an appointment as a naval officer in 1756 during the French and Indian War, Equiano embarked on a dangerous life. During his five years at sea, he had a fair amount of freedom for a slave, learning to read; accumulating some clothing, books, and cash; and sharing the perils and camaraderie of ships at war. At the end of the war, however, he was stripped of his possessions, sold to the West Indies, and resold in Montserrat to a Quaker man from Philadelphia. Equiano's fortunes changed again as his new master allowed him to work for wages and to purchase his freedom in the summer of 1766. For the next two decades the free African sailed the Caribbean and traveled in various parts of Europe, returning to London several times and working there for extended periods. In 1785 he visited the United States, spending time in Philadelphia. By this time Equiano had become a part of the antislavery movement, and within a year he was a major figure, appointed by Britain to supervise efforts to supply the Sierra Leone colony.[6]

In 1789 readers of English in Britain, the United States, and Europe were captivated by an extraordinary new autobiography. Published in London, this two-volume account was the work of an African of indisputable intelligence, imagination, talent, and humanity. *The Interesting Narrative of the Life of Olaudah Equiano; or Gustavus Vassa* was Equiano's powerful first-hand account of his life in Africa, his capture and enslavement, and his life under the British-American slave system. It was so popular that at least eight editions were sold in the first five years of its printing. Equiano's writing provided a glimpse of what Europeans and Americans saw as the exotic society in his African home, but it was also a morality tale that condemned Christians' complicity in slavery's destruction of African lives and families and unequivocally blamed the avarice of Christian slave masters and their accomplices

At Salem, " *Cæsar Pratt,* a black man, aged 65—remarkable for his inftinctive facility in numbers, by which he was able to make, in an inftant, calculations which would require in common perfons the aid of many figures; his memory was alfo the regifter of every perfon's age of which he had ever been informed, and which he was fure to remind them of as the anniverfary of their birth came round; and in other refpects he was a convenient chronologift."

"Eulogy for Caesar Pratt," *Providence Gazette,* May 19, 1804.
Graphics Division, Rhode Island Historical Society.

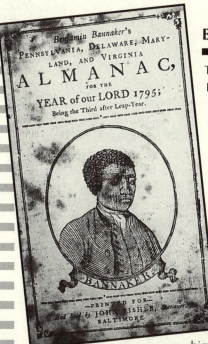

Benjamin Banneker

The scientist, mathematician, and astronomer Benjamin Banneker was born free near Baltimore, Maryland, in 1731. His father came to North America from Guinea, West Africa, as a slave and was later freed. His mother was also free, the child of an English indentured servant and an African who had gained his freedom before she was born. Benjamin's white grandmother taught him to read, and he became an avid reader with a natural aptitude for mathematics. He once constructed a mechanical clock on mathematical principles alone, having never seen one. Banneker farmed until rheumatism made it impossible, but retirement at middle age allowed him to take up mathematics and astronomy in earnest. In 1791 the presidentially appointed surveyor, Andrew Ellicott, asked Banneker to help him survey the area for the new national capital of Washington, D.C. For three months Banneker made the astronomic calculations each night that Ellicott used for his surveying the following day. Returning to Baltimore, Banneker organized his calculations, and in 1792, published them as the first of several almanacs.

Banneker was more than a man of science. He was also a man of keen political understanding, who used his learning and accomplishments to argue for racial equality. Ellicott and other scientists familiar with his work were impressed, but some were unwilling to acknowledge his obvious talent. Learning of Thomas Jefferson's doubts about the intelligence of African Americans, Banneker sent Jefferson copies of his calculations. Jefferson returned a polite reply but privately expressed doubt that a black man could have produced such intricate work. Curiously Jefferson, one of the most intellectually inquisitive men in America, never tested his doubts and never invited Banneker to demonstrate his skill.

Banneker's almanac sold widely in the United States and Great Britain, and at least twenty-eight editions were published before his death in 1806. Benjamin Banneker died in his sleep at his home in Baltimore, just one month short of seventy-five years of age. In 1980 the U.S. Postal Service issued a postage stamp in his honor.

Benjamin Banneker, astronomer and mathematician who assisted in the surveying of Washington, D.C. Prints and Photographs Division, Library of Congress, Washington, D.C.

for the horrors of the slave trade. Equiano's literary skill created a powerful argument for antislavery forces, which used it to refute notions of African inferiority.[7]

In the face of post-Revolutionary antislavery sentiments in much of the United States, and the growing international interest in abolition, slavery became more firmly entrenched in the American South during the last decade of the eighteenth century. Thomas Jefferson had published his suspicions of black inferiority in his *Notes on Virginia* in 1787. Although he was troubled by slavery, his reflections later formed the core of a powerful proslavery argument. In his writing Jefferson ignored the accomplishments of such prominent blacks as Equiano, the impressive poetry of Boston slave Phillis Wheatley, or Benjamin Banneker's sophisticated mathematical computations and observations in his scientific almanac. Jefferson was anxious that his reflections not be taken by his fellow slaveholders as an attack on slavery. Southern slave states were deeply affected by events on the French-held island of St. Domingue in the Caribbean. The spirit of the revolution spread from France in 1789 to St. Domingue as slaves there determined to secure freedom for themselves. In the late summer of 1791, slaves rebelled against their masters with such fury that the French government sent troops to the colony to subdue them. By the time the French forces arrived, blacks had organized themselves under the leadership of a former slave carriage driver named Toussaint L'Ouverture. In 1793 slaves and free blacks defeated the French army stationed in the capital and captured the city. Whites fled in ships bound for the United States, and on their arrival American newspapers were filled with their accounts of the horrors of the rebellion, stories that terrified southern slaveholders.[8]

Meanwhile, in St. Domingue, full-scale war frustrated Napoleon's plans for American expansion. Finally, in 1800, he resolved to end the resistance and sent a force of 25,000 men. The French offered to negotiate a peace with the rebels, but when L'Ouverture arrived for the talks, he was captured, shackled, and taken to Paris. Nevertheless, the revolt continued, and on the first day of January 1804 Jean-Jacques Dessalines, its new leader, proclaimed Haiti's independence, the first independent black nation in the Western Hemisphere. France's defeat ended Napoleon's dreams of a New World empire and encouraged him to dispose of his American lands while some profit could still be derived from them. In 1803, in exchange for fifteen million dollars, approximately four cents an acre, France sold the United States a huge tract of land. The Louisiana Purchase, as it was called, amounted to 828,000 square miles, stretching from the Gulf of Mexico northward to the Canadian border, and from the Mississippi River on the eastern boundary to the Rocky Mountains in the west. President Thomas Jefferson's acquisition of this new

Benjamin Banneker's letter to Thomas Jefferson

Maryland, Baltimore County.

Near Ellicott's Lower Mills August 19th. 1791

Thomas Jefferson Secretary of State.

Sir, I am fully sensible of the greatness of that freedom which I take with you on the present occasion; a liberty which Seemed to me Scarcely allowable, when I reflected on that distinguished, and dignifyed station in which you Stand; and the almost general prejudice and prepossession which is so previlent [*sic*] in the world against those of my complexion.

I suppose it is a truth too well attested to you, to need proof here, that we are a race of Beings who have long laboured under the abuse and censure of the world, that we have long been looked upon with an eye of contempt, and that we have long been considered rather as brutish than human, and Scarcely capable of mental endowments.

Sir, I hope I may Safely admit, in consequence of that report which hath reached me, that you are a man far less inflexible in Sentiments of this nature, than many others, that you are measurably friendly and well disposed towards us, and that you are willing and ready to Lend your aid and assistance to our relief from those many distresses and numberous calamities to which we are reduced.

Now, Sir, if this is founded in truth, I apprehend you will readily embrace every opportunity to eradicate that train of absurd and false ideas and oppinions [*sic*] which so generally prevail with respect to us, and that your Sentiments are concurrent with mine, which are that one universal Father hath given being to us all, and that he hath not only made us all of one flesh, but that he hath also without partiality afforded us all the Same Sensations, and endued [*sic*] us all with the same faculties, and that however variable we may be in Society or religion, however diversified in Situation or colour, we are all of the Same Family, and Stand in the Same relation to him. . . .

Sir, Suffer me to recall to your mind that time in which the Arms and tyranny of the British Crown were exerted with every powerful effort, in order to reduce you to a State of Servitude; look back I intreat you on the variety of dangers to which you were exposed. . . .

This, Sir, was a time in which you clearly saw into the injustice of a State of Slavery, and in which you had Just apprehensions of the horrors of its condition, it was now Sir, that your abhorrence thereof was so excited, that you publickly held forth this true and invaluable doctrine, which is worthy to be recorded and remembered in all Succeeding ages. "We hold

(continued)

(continued)

these truths to be Self evident, that all men are created equal, and that they are endowed by their creator with certain inalienable rights, that amongst these are life, liberty, and the persuit [*sic*] of happiness."

Here, Sir, was a time in which your tender feelings for your selves engaged you thus to declare, you were then impressed with proper ideals of the great valuation of liberty, and the free possession of those blessings to which you were entitled by nature; but Sir how pitiable is it to reflect, that altho you were so fully convinced of the benevolence of the Father of mankind, and of his equal and impartial distribution of those rights and privileges which he had conferred upon them, that you should at the Same time counteract his mercies, in detaining by fraud and violence so numerous a part of my brethren under groaning captivity and cruel oppression, that you should at the Same time be found guilty of that most criminal act, which you professedly detested in others, with respect to yourselves. . . .

This calculation [his almanac sent as a present], Sir, is the production of my arduous study . . . altho you may have the opportunity of perusing it after its publication, yet I chose to send it to you in manuscript previous thereto, that thereby you might not only have an earlier inspection, but that you might also view it in my own hand writing.

And now Sir, I Shall conclude and Subscribe my Self with the most profound respect,

Your most Obedient humble Servant

Benjamin Banneker

Sidney Kaplan, *The Black Presence in the Era of the American Revolution, 1770–1800* (Greenwich, Conn.: New York Graphic Society Ltd. / Smithsonian Institution Press, 1973), 118–121.

territory doubled the size of the United States, and slaveholders saw the promise of a vast new area open to slavery.

Although most of the estimated ten thousand French slaveholders who fled the Haitian revolution for the United States settled in the South, some brought their slaves to northern cities such as Philadelphia and New York. In 1792 they petitioned Pennsylvania for the right to keep their slaves, noting that congressmen who brought their own slaves to the national capital at Philadelphia when Congress was in session were exempt from the abolition laws. In answer to their petition, authorities reaffirmed Pennsylvania's constitutional commitment to freedom and recommended that the legislature immediately and totally abolish slavery in the state. Between 1787 and 1810, of the 508 French slaves freed in Pennsylvania, 45 were granted immediate freedom, 2 purchased their own freedom, and the rest were indentured in accordance with the gradual emancipation law.[9] The French slaves' association with the Haitian revolution, their extreme poverty, their tendency to settle together in the least desirable part of the city, and their practice of the island-developed voodoo religion all aroused white fears of disorder. These fears were confirmed in New York City in 1801, when twenty people tried to prevent a white Haitian immigrant from selling her slaves out of the state, threatening to "burn the house, murder all the white people in it, and take away a number of the black slaves." The incendiary potential became even clearer when hundreds of blacks congregated at the house that evening and clashed with fifty watchmen attempting to keep order. The authorities prevailed, the slaves were not freed, and twenty-three rioters were jailed.[10]

The Haitian revolution itself aroused the fears of southern Americans. White nightmares of the spread of slave revolts seemed to be coming true in 1800 when a slave plot was unearthed just outside of Richmond, Virginia. As was typical in the Upper South, Richmond area slaves enjoyed a good deal of geographic mobility. They were often able to hire out their time to planters who needed extra help. Most of their pay was claimed by their masters, but they were generally able to retain a portion of it. Some saved to purchase their freedom or that of family members. While working on William Young's plantation just a few miles northeast of Richmond, Ben Woolfolk, a slave hired during the summer of 1800, was approached by one of Young's slaves and asked to take part in a slave uprising. As the details of the plan became known over the next few months, it became clear that only slaves on the Young plantation and several slaves from Richmond were involved. Three brothers—Martin, Solomon and Gabriel—all skilled blacksmiths who were slaves on a plantation in Henrico County, near Richmond, belonging to Thomas Prosser, were involved at the beginning of the plot; and Gabriel eventually became the leader. The number of recruits grew as black boatmen and other "traveling" slaves carried the word from plantation to plantation and into the cities of the region. The plan was to attack Richmond, take Governor (and future President of the United States) James Monroe prisoner, and use the victory to encourage a general slave revolution in Virginia. These plans took shape in the context of a bitter dispute between the two major political parties in the United States, the Federalists and the Republicans, during the election year of 1800, and growing tensions between the United States and France. There were general fears that the election of 1800 would result in armed hostilities between Federalists and Republicans. Gabriel and his followers planned to take advantage of any disruption that might occur.

Gabriel attempted to enlist the cooperation of local whites, apparently believing his attack on slavery could become the foundation for a larger inter-racial class-based revolt against the privileged. He sought the cooperation of a Frenchman who might aid in devising military strategy, and hoped that white artisans in Richmond, angered by the merchants' use of skilled slaves to curb wages, might join as the revolt progressed or at least might not take up arms against it.[11]

The initial strike was planned for August 30, but it was postponed because of a fierce rainstorm. The delay proved fatal to the revolt's success, as the plan was revealed to whites by slave informants. Word soon reached the governor, state forces were assembled, and within a few days scores of slaves were arrested. A white seaman's efforts to help Gabriel escape failed when two slave seamen informed officials of his hiding place. At the trial, testimony revealed the extent of the conspiracy—apparently thousands of slaves were ready to join the revolt once it began. Gabriel was one of twenty-seven slaves convicted and hanged for their participation. For years after Gabriel's defeat other slaves in other parts of Virginia remained ready to revolt, and authorities un-covered a number of conspiracies, one reportedly involving hundreds of slaves in at least eight counties in southern Virginia and northeastern North Carolina. Other plots were uncovered in South Carolina, though it is unclear how many of these were slaveholders overreacting to the Haitian Revolution and Gabriel's plot. Real or not, fears of slave uprisings led to the execution of twenty-five more blacks in Virginia in 1802 and to the passage of laws in Virginia, North Carolina, and South Carolina regulating slaves and free blacks. Laws established slave patrols, restricted the movements of free blacks and slaves, limited the emancipation of slaves, and mandated the removal of free blacks from the state of their manumission. By the middle of the first decade of the nineteenth century, the South had tightened its grip on slav-ery, reversing the trend toward a more flexible system of bondage and a less restrictive policy of manumission that had been most prominent in the Upper South.[12]

Southerners urged Congress to bar blacks from Haiti or elsewhere in the French West Indies from entering the United States lest they infect Ameri-can slaves with a rebellious spirit. Congress responded in 1803 with regu-lations restricting West Indian immigration. It had also restricted mail carrying to whites in 1802, since black post riders had helped to spread the word of rebellion among slaves in Virginia. The government also feared that, as U.S. Postmaster General Gideon Granger said, carrying the mail allowed blacks to learn of their human rights and disseminate that knowledge. As a further safeguard some in the South called for the removal from the country of all free blacks and troublesome slaves. At James Monroe's suggestion, President Thomas Jefferson considered the American West as a place to establish a colony for this purpose, but Jefferson decided that eventual American expansion into the West should not be blocked by a black colony. He considered the West Indies, particularly Haiti, as a place where unwanted black Americans might be shipped. The South, however, feared any arrangement that might enlarge the population of the black West Indian revolutionary forces. There was a brief flirtation with a plan to ship unruly slaves to the British African colony of Sierra Leone, but many were concerned that this would reward rebels with freedom, thus the idea was at least temporarily abandoned. Finally the purchase of Louisiana from France and the opening of the southern regions of that area to slavery partially solved the problem of the disposal of unwanted slaves. In 1812 Louisiana was admitted to the United States as the first slave state carved from the new territory. Of the thirteen states formed in the territory, four—Louisiana, Alabama, Missouri, and Arkansas—allowed slavery.

Initially the heart of Louisiana's economy was sugar. Cane could not be grown as easily as in the West Indies, and yields were not as great, but cultivation of the crop required slaves, and rising prices encouraged masters in the Upper South to sell any extra hands into the new western South. Since the gang labor of sugar plantations called for a largely male workforce, Louisiana quickly acquired a slave population of relatively young males who outnumbered whites in many of the large plantation areas.

A shift to cotton production in the western South dramatically increased the demand for slaves in that region. Cotton had been grown in limited quantities in a few coastal areas of the eastern South since the seventeenth century, but South Carolina planters generally preferred to concentrate on rice cultivation. A few small planters grew cotton, and slaves made their clothing from cotton they grew in small gardens. During the Revolution a boycott of English cloth encouraged home production, but the most desirable long-staple cotton could be grown only near the coast. The short-staple cotton could be grown inland, but the tedium involved in removing the seeds from the fiber of this type of cotton made its production difficult and costly. The invention in 1793 of a simple device called the cotton gin by Eli Whitney, a Yale-educated teacher who traveled to South Carolina to tutor planters' children, made it economically feasible to expand the production of this crop. Using this new machine, essentially a box containing a rotating cylinder with protruding nails, a worker could remove seeds fifty times faster than by hand. The Louisiana Purchase provided fertile land, treaties and skirmishes subdued the Creek, Chickasaw, Choctaw, and Cherokee Indians who lived there, and Whitney's new technology made it possible to create a new "Cotton Kingdom" in the western area known as the Deep South. The new states of Mississippi, Alabama, and Arkansas joined western Georgia to become the prime cotton-growing region of the nation. Its rich black soil (hence the area's designation as the Black Belt) produced the crop that became the foundation of the nineteenth-century southern economy and plantation culture. The Black Belt's demand for slaves increased just after Congress ended the African slave trade in 1808, and this reduction in the supply increased the value of the slaves in the Upper South who might be sold to the Deep South. The average price of a prime field hand grew fitfully during the first half of the nineteenth century from about six hundred dollars in 1802 to as much as eighteen hundred dollars by 1860. Over the same period the number of slaves in the nation increased dramatically from about seven hundred thousand to nearly four million.[13] Although cotton prices fluctuated, they generally increased during the early decades of the century, and production rose dramatically in response. By 1815 cotton, the chief slave crop in the United States, was also fast becoming the country's single most valuable export, supplying the raw material for the textile mills of Britain and France. It continued its growth throughout the antebellum years, representing one-third of the value of all American exports by 1820, more than half by 1840, and almost 60 percent by the time of the Civil War. Mississippi alone produced ten million pounds of cotton in 1821, thirty million pounds in 1826, and eighty million pounds by 1834.[14]

In Louisiana sugar was also an important slave crop and like cotton its cultivation exacted a terrible toll. In 1830 a New Orleans newspaper estimated that there was a death rate of at least 25 percent among slaves transported from the Upper South to work in the cane fields, and one contemporary observer speculated that the life expectancy of a slave in the cane fields was no more than seven years. Historian Charles Duncan Rice described sugar-producing Louisiana's reputation as "the most terrifying of all the various hells of the Deep South to which blacks from the older slave economies of the tidewater states could be sold."[15] Sugar profits generally grew throughout the antebellum years and soared after midcentury, as the demands of this crop absorbed the labor and the lives of thousands of slaves. Yet cotton remained king even in Louisiana, and the steady increase in its economic value ensured its political power. Whatever the crop, especially after 1830, slavery was the dominant labor system in the South. Its centrality to the economy of that region, and thereby to the nation, made its abolition unlikely, especially where it was most concentrated.[16]

The development of the Deep South expanded the internal slave trade, and as the trade became more profitable, the major cities of the eastern and

Upper South became primary trading centers. During the late summer and early fall, traders in Washington, D.C., and Alexandria and Richmond, Virginia, bid on likely workers to be sold in New Orleans, Louisiana, and Mobile, Alabama, in December and January, when planters had marketed their summer crop and could afford cash payment. It was also in winter that planters returned to the Deep South from their retreats to more healthful climates where they routinely sought escape from summer's malaria and yellow fever. Then too, newly-arrived slaves had time to become acclimatized before the onset of summer heat and humidity. Traders generally auctioned slaves in urban slave markets, but they traveled around to local plantations selling individual slaves when market sales were slow. In the Black Belt, slaves generally found the work harder, the hours longer, the climate nearly unbearable, and the treatment more brutal. Since many planters were absentee owners during the heavy growing season, overseers with no personal financial investment in slaves to safeguard were left to handle the day-to-day operation of the large plantations.

A slave's life expectancy was diminished by severe conditions in the Deep South. The hot, humid climate so good for growing sugarcane in Louisiana was also ideal for breeding malaria-carrying mosquitoes. Cane cultivation in Louisiana was more intense and physically demanding than in the West Indies, where the growing season was slightly longer. Even after the worst summer heat was over, the work was hard. During the sixteen- to eighteen-hour days between mid-October and late December, when the crop was harvested, slaves worked at an exhausting pace, and masters increased the amount of cane each slave was expected to harvest as new agricultural techniques and new varieties of sugarcane increased the yield per acre. On the expansive cotton plantations of Mississippi and Alabama, established during the first three decades of the nineteenth century, slaves not only cultivated and harvested the crop but also did the backbreaking labor of clearing the land during the early years of settlement. Lewis Clarke, a slave from Kentucky, reported that slaves knew that being taken to the Deep South was a horrible fate because they were "driven very hard there, and worked to death in a few years." Even the threat of being "put in the master's pocket" (that is, traded South for money the master could put in his pocket) was enough to cause rebellion, flight, or even suicide. James Williams, an Alabama slave, knew of some slaves who, when they learned that they were to be sold South, died "of grief, and others [who committed] suicide on account of it." One made himself unfit to be sold South by cutting off the fingers of his left hand with an ax. Another drowned herself, and a third cut her own throat with a razor. All were terrified of labor in the Deep South, a fate some regarded as worse than death. Masters often used this fear to control their slaves.[17]

The burgeoning internal slave trade increased the splintering of slave families in the Upper South. Prior to 1820 a southern planter or a planter's son was likely to move west with many of the slaves from his eastern plantation, but the opening of the Deep South changed this pattern. By 1820, 70 percent of the slaves who were taken South were moved by slave traders who realized great profits from the relatively high prices brought by young male slaves in the markets of the Black Belt. Between 1820 and 1830 a quarter of a million slaves were traded south, with a devastating impact on slave families and communities. In New Orleans, Natchez, Montgomery, and elsewhere in the western South, male slaves between the ages of ten and thirty were considered "prime hands" bringing the best prices. About 10 percent of all Upper South slaves in their teens and 9 percent of slaves in their twenties were sold south during the 1820s. One recent study has estimated that after 1815, about one-third of all adults were sold south before they were forty years old. High transportation costs discouraged conveying small children or other family members so that generally only the most valuable were taken. A major route for transporting slaves was the Mississippi River, and so great was the likelihood that a family might lose a member, especially a son or a young father, to this internal slave trade that a new phrase, being "sold down the river," was added to the American lexicon and came to describe the disastrous consequences of these sales. Statistics on slave families tell the story of the trade's impact and the harsh conditions in the Deep South. Ann Patton Malone found that just over half (57 percent) of the slaves in the rural Louisiana parishes she studied were able to establish two-parent or couple households. Most of the young male slaves brought from Kentucky to work on Walter Bashear's plantation in Louisiana, for example, never married. Messages exchanged with their families in Kentucky made clear that old relationships were not ended by their forced migration. "If you see Daddy," "poor little Hannah" instructed her mistress, "give my love to him." The opening of the Deep South may have brought great economic opportunity for the planter class, but it increased the misery of their slaves.[18]

During this same period, as slavery ended in the North, black families there were reunited or established. Expanding trade with Europe and economic prosperity attracted many free African Americans to the eastern port cities in search of work and the relative security provided by a black community. Even during the colonial era, free blacks had been largely city dwellers, and most had congregated in the Atlantic seaport towns and cities where work was available and new black communities were beginning to take shape. This trend continued during the late eighteenth and early nineteenth centuries with the black population of the major northeastern coast cities growing in actual numbers

Free African American Population

City	1790	1800	Percentage of Increase 1790–1800	1830	Percentage of Increase 1790–1830
Boston	761	1,174	54	1,875	146
New York	1,078	3,499	225	13,960	1,195
Philadelphia	1,420	4,210	197	9,795	590

Sources: *Negro Population in the U.S., 1790–1915,* 55; Leonard P. Curry, *The Free Black in Urban America, 1800–1850* (Chicago: University of Chicago Press, 1981), 250.

and as a proportion of the city's population. Free blacks were, in fact, the most urban group in America.[19]

Paul Cuffe, living in coastal Massachusetts, was one of the free blacks who profited from the growing post–Revolutionary War trade. By the time the Revolution was over, Cuffe was a mature man of twenty-five with many years of experience as a sailor fishing the waters around Nantucket and in the North Atlantic and whaling off Mexico and the West Indies. He had grown up in relative security with close ties to his many siblings and his mother's people in the Indian community at Chilmark on Martha's Vineyard. When his father, the African freedman Cuffe Slocum, died before the war, he left Paul's mother, Ruth, and her ten children settled on their 116-acre farm in Dartmouth, Massachusetts. After the war Paul Cuffe married an Indian woman, Alice Pequit, and established a partnership with his brother-in-law Michael Wainer. By the early 1790s Cuffe and Wainer had two schooners fishing and whaling off the coast of Newfoundland, the beginning of a successful, life-long business partnership.[20]

As the urban free black population increased, black families formed the basis for more stable, expanded, and diverse community institutions. Among the first institutions were mutual-aid societies, cooperative organizations formed to provide funds for burials and aid to members' widows, the sick, and the unemployed. Racial prejudice and often, ironically, their desperate poverty frequently disqualified blacks from the sources of aid available to most whites. Early charitable institutions were loath to aid those they did not consider to be a local responsibility or those whose extreme poverty, poor character, or bad habits, they believed, did not make them good candidates for reform. Thus African Americans were likely to be forced to rely on the resources of their own communities. This necessity, a traditional African communal ethic, and the African religious significance of a proper burial all contributed to a proliferation of mutual-aid societies among free blacks. There was a general increase in associations in American society after the Revolution, but their

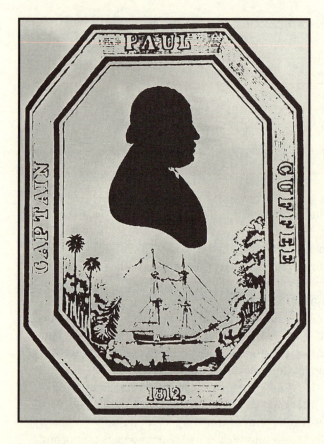

Paul Cuffe,
sea captain,
shipbuilder, and
merchant, with an
engraving of his ship,
Traveller, 1812.

Photographs and Prints
Division, Schomburg
Center for Research
in Black Culture,
The New York Public
Library, Astor, Lenox,
and Tilden Foundations.

growth among blacks also drew on the African traditions still vivid in the memories of thousands of African-born Americans. In many African societies an individual's identity was derived from the family, an individual's primary responsibility was to the family, and the community was simply an extension of the family. This communalism became the basis for social organization in the black communities established in the West Indies and North America. "What is mine goes," instructed one African proverb, but "what is ours abides." One of the earliest mutual-aid groups, the African Union Society, was organized in Newport, Rhode Island, in 1780. The Free African Society was formed in Philadelphia in 1787 by free blacks in cooperation with white anti-slavery Quakers, and blacks in Boston organized the African Society in 1796. Through these organizations, people contributed to the support of the spouses and orphans of deceased members and to disabled, unemployed or destitute members and their families. The Philadelphia organization, with two prominent community leaders, Richard Allen and Absalom Jones, among its founders, also provided aid to ex-slaves. Both Allen and Jones had been slaves, and each had bought his own freedom shortly before establishing the Free African Society.[21]

Another early African American community organization was the Masons. Even before the Revolution, a small black Masonic group was organized in Boston by Prince Hall, a native of Barbados and the son of a free mulatto mother and a British father. After he arrived in Massachusetts, Hall had become a soapmaker and eventually a Methodist lay preacher. Under his leadership the black men applied to the white Masonic order in Boston for an official license as a lodge, but the Boston Masons refused to recognize an organization of black Masons. Hall then turned to the British order, through an Irish military regiment stationed in Boston, and they accepted his application. In 1775, just before the British troops were expelled from the city by American forces, fifteen African Americans were initiated into the British lodge, and they continued to meet during the Revolution. After the war Hall, who had served six years with the American troops, again applied to the American Masonic order for recognition, and again was refused. Finally he turned to the Grand Lodge of England, which officially granted permission in 1784 for the formation of the African Lodge Number One of Boston. Formally established in 1787 and renumbered Lodge 459, it was the first black Masonic lodge in the United States. It became a center for community mutual aid, political action, and a catalyst for other black Masonic organizations in Providence and Philadelphia. By the turn of the nineteenth century, there were several black Masonic lodges, some initiated with the support of the Boston group. Philadelphia was rapidly becoming an important center of Masonic activity; one of its lodges was established by black sailors with the aid of the Grand Lodge of Germany in 1798. The proliferation of lodges throughout the North established regular lines of communication among many black communities, facilitating political organization in the nineteenth century. Like other African American associations, Masonic organizations were multipurpose mutual aid, religious, and political action groups.

By the turn of the nineteenth century, African Americans had formed hundreds of mutual aid societies, fraternal organizations, and community service groups boasting thousands of members throughout the North. Often these groups included both males and females, although some—like the African Masonic lodges in many cities or the Female Benevolent Society of St. Thomas in Philadelphia—were restricted. Membership dues provided the funds for the operation of these groups and the benefits they provided. Membership in the African Benevolent Society of Newport, Rhode Island, required a fifty-cent initiation fee, and the African Marine Fund in New York City required an initiation fee of one dollar. Additional monthly dues ranged from twelve and a half to fifty cents. Boston's African Society, for example, charged twenty-five cents to enter the society and another twenty-five cents for monthly dues. These were considerable fees for a generally poor people, but these organizations provided essential services in a manner congruent with African Americans' values, and a great many people joined. Various contemporaneous studies of the benevolent societies in Philadelphia provide some measure of the growth and importance of such organizations. In 1830 there were almost fifty societies, sixty by 1836 and one hundred by 1838, paying out approximately six, nine, and fourteen thousand dollars in annual benefits, respectively. Though there was undoubtedly an overlapping membership, the nearly 7,500 members in 1838 represented a remarkable level of organization in the city's black community of 10,507 people.[22]

Early black organizations concerned themselves not only with the financial and social needs of community members but also with their spiritual and political needs. Free African Societies often provided religious services, and some were the forerunners of African American churches. Philadelphia's Bethel Church, founded by Richard Allen, and the African Church (later called the African Episcopal Church of St. Thomas), founded by Absalom Jones, both grew from the membership of the Free African Society. In Boston the African Baptist church grew out of the African Society of that city and drew its original membership from that organization. As in traditional African life, the distinctions between secular and sacred institutions were never great in African American society. Black churches—the communities' most important public institutions—served as social centers where community drama groups, bands, youth organizations, men's and women's clubs, and debating societies met. They often hosted community educational facilities and served as political forums and convention halls. The first black school in Boston met originally in the basement of the African Meeting House, the home of the African Baptist Church. The building also provided space for William Bassett's music classes for black children, for community band concerts, and for the rehearsals of the Social Harmonic Society, a popular local choir. Similar activities found rooms in the churches of Philadelphia and New York City. In almost all African American communities across the North, whenever community meetings were held, most were held in the black churches.[23]

As the political center of most black communities, the church was also a training ground for black leaders. In white society a young man aspiring to political prominence might enter law, run for minor local office, or work for a politician. In black society the most common route to community leadership was through the church. Black ministers were both the guardians of the spiritual life of the community and its political leaders. Their activities might range from leading worship services, ministering to the sick, and feeding the hungry to hiding fugitive slaves escaping from bondage.[24]

It was much more difficult for free blacks to establish organizations in the South, since southern slaveholders were greatly suspicious of free blacks not under their direct control. Laws prohibiting black gatherings without white supervision limited the movements of all African Americans. Restrictions grew stronger and were enforced more rigorously during periods when rumored or actual slave revolt made slaveholders more apprehensive. Still, southern free blacks formed societies to meet the spiritual and practical needs of their communities. Although some societies managed to meet secretly, public gatherings required white sponsorship. Typically a white clergyman was responsible for the oversight of a black church and its many related organizations. Despite white obstructions African American communities in major southern cities with sizable black populations, such as Charleston, Richmond, Baltimore, and Washington, D.C., were nearly as well organized as those in the North. By 1836 Baltimore blacks, for example, had about forty fraternal, literary, religious, and temperance associations, many attached to churches.[25] One type of free black organization in the South, the oldest of which was the Brown Fellowship Society formed in 1790 in Charleston, South Carolina, seemed to pose little threat to the slave system. Some of the membership was drawn from mulattoes who fled the Haitian Revolution after siding with the French colonials against the black revolutionaries. The color consciousness of these light-skinned Haitians found expression in groups like the Brown Fellowship, groups of economically and socially privileged African Americans whom whites judged less threatening to white supremacy. These mixed-race people were often related to prominent local white families, and many slaveholders hoped they would provide information about the slave population, warning of unrest and conspiracies.

The position of southern free blacks was complex. Since they were unable to depend on southern law for protection, patronage from powerful southern whites was the only buffer between them and the systematic injustice they were liable to suffer in the slave South. Indeed, some slave conspiracies were betrayed by other African Americans, both slave and free. But even elite black groups were involved in the common political issues of central concern to all African Americans: the opposition to slavery and the protection of fugitive slaves. Northern groups were the most visible proponents of black freedom, since even the limited white southern tolerance for antislavery expression had disappeared by 1830. The abolition of slavery, the most serious and immediate problem, was but one of many political concerns for blacks in America. As the new nation defined the rights of citizens through the passage of state constitutions, the rights of free blacks were increasingly limited.[26]

Discrimination and an uncertain future in America continued to spark interest in emigration, especially among African-born blacks. Capt. Paul

Cuffe, with an African father and a Native American mother, was one of those interested in African colonization. In 1810 he set sail in his ship, *Traveller*, with his nephew Thomas Wainer as first mate and an all-black crew, to explore the prospects for settlement in and trade with Sierra Leone. Cuffe was impressed by the settlement he found and hopeful that he could eventually demonstrate that a profitable trade not including slaves could be established between Africa and the United States. Among the 3,500 settlers were former American slaves who had come to the British colony by way of England or Canada, where they had gone with withdrawing British forces after the Revolution. There were also local Africans, blacks from the British West Indies, and people rescued from slave trading ships off the African coast. A handful of Europeans, approximately 1 percent of the colony's population, controlled almost two-thirds of the property in Sierra Leone. Recognizing that initial support for any trading venture would have to come from the British merchants who financed the European property holders, Cuffe sailed for England.

By April 1812, when Cuffe and Wainer returned to the United States, continuing tensions with Britain had escalated, and the United States had instituted a trade embargo. Since the *Traveller* had been in England, U.S. customs authorities confiscated Cuffe's cargo when he entered port in Rhode Island, an inauspicious beginning to his African trading venture. Through his connections with wealthy Quaker merchants, Cuffe was able to meet with President James Madison and Secretary of the Treasury Albert Gallatin, who helped him gain the release of his ship and cargo. But his standing in the business community did not protect him from the indignities of discrimination in public lodging and on public transportation, discrimination that increased his commitment to African settlement. In New York, Philadelphia, and Baltimore, Cuffe met with black leaders, reporting on the promise of Sierra Leone and encouraging them to establish organizations to promote Sierra Leone and organize potential settlers.

The trading ventures of merchants and captains like Paul Cuffe were deferred by the growing hostility between Britain and the United States. Many common sailors suffered more directly, losing work and wages as trade diminished. Americans complained that Britain acted with intolerable arrogance, not respecting the new nation's shipping rights, violating its territory, and impressing its citizens. Contrary to the peace agreements ending the Revolutionary War, British troops remained in western forts, and Britain seized neutral American ships to prevent them from trading with its enemy, France. English impressment gangs roamed European ports and boarded American ships at sea, forcibly taking the most likely sailors to serve aboard British vessels. Many blacks were among the American sailors British naval authorities abducted.[27]

During the spring of 1812 relations between England and the United States deteriorated further, and in June, President James Madison issued a formal declaration of war. Despite the Revolutionary War service of African Americans, American authorities again heatedly debated the question of black participation in the military. For southerners the prospect of arming their enormous, generally enslaved black population again evoked the terrifying specter of the Haitian Revolution. Meanwhile the British once again promised freedom to American slaves who joined their forces. Thousands of slaves escaped to the British army lines, some volunteering for military service. One alarmed southerner reported that blacks were "flocking to the enemy from all quarters."[28] African Americans served aboard British vessels in battles in the Great Lakes and Chesapeake Bay, and when British troops attacked Baltimore and invaded and burned the capital city of Washington in 1814, newly freed slaves were among them. When the United States offered to free slaves in return for military service, many volunteered, even when the terms were unattractive and discriminatory. New York slaves had to serve for three years before they were freed, and the cash payment normally provided to soldiers was generally paid instead to their masters. As in the Revolution, slaves fought for both Britain and the United States, joining whichever forces promised liberty.

Many free African Americans, motivated by patriotism or local loyalties, served with American forces on sea and land. They formed separate units in New York, Philadelphia, and other cities along the Atlantic coast. One New York "Citizen of Color" argued that it was the "duty of every colored man resident in this city to volunteer" when British forces threatened the coast. He argued that white Americans would see this as a "test of patriotism."[29] The spirit and unity of the builders of New York's fortifications were reflected in a popular song called "The Patriotic Diggers." "To Protect our rights / Gainst your flints and triggers," the lyrics challenged, "See on Brooklyn Heights / Our patriotic diggers," claiming, "Men of every age, / Color, rank, profession."[30]

In New England strong antiwar sentiment discouraged residents from participating in the war, and African Americans there were also less likely to join the American army. Black sailors from New England, however, were prominent participants. Cmmdr. Isaac Chauncey, who engaged the British on the Great Lakes, counted the fifty blacks under his command as "among [his] best men." At first Capt. Oliver H. Perry was uncomfortable with his integrated crew, one quarter of whom were black, but after defeating the British fleet in 1813, he praised the action of his black sailors and singled out several for special commendation.[31] Likewise Capt. Nathan Shaler lauded his black sailors, telling of one who after "a twenty-four pound shot struck him in the hip, and took away all the lower part of his body," urged his shipmates on, saying, "Fire away boys!—No haul a color down." Captain Shaler asserted that "while America has such tars, she has little to fear from the tyrants of Europe."[32]

Many American sailors were captured and spent time as prisoners of war in British jails, and some black sailors who had been impressed into British service chose to go to prison rather than fight for England when the war broke out. As many as eleven hundred black and five thousand white Americans were confined in England's Dartmoor prison by 1814. At first the British housed the Americans together, but as the population grew, they eventually segregated the prison barracks by race. Still, visiting between barracks and continual inter-action among the prisoners gave Dartmoor an interracial cultural life. The black barracks became an important center of prison life, where interracial casts per-formed Shakespearean plays, interracial audiences enjoyed African music and dance, and regular church services were held by a black minister. Box-ing classes were conducted by Richard Seaver, a black sailor from Salem, Massachusetts. Classes in reading and writing were taught by inmates of the black barracks. Dartmoor was no interracial utopia—it was a prison filled with sailors where racial tensions occasionally erupted into conflict, but it also had a lively interracial political, economic, and social life. Although the prison was segregated, shipboard habits, identifications, and friendships carried over to prison life. One black prisoner from Newburyport, Massachusetts, for example, made a point of sharing his card-game winnings of "a two penny loaf and a pint of coffee" with his white mates from his hometown.[33]

In December 1814 Britain and the United States negotiated an end to their hostilities with the Treaty of Ghent. Napoleon had abdicated as emperor of France, ending the war in Europe and removing the issue of neutrality rights for American shipping. The issue of impressment was not resolved, but the war's end reduced England's need for sailors. Britain did drop its demands for territorial concessions and for American recognition of an independent Indian state and finally withdrew from the western boundaries of the United States. Ironically, the battle of New Orleans, the best-known battle of the war, was actually fought after the war was over, and it involved blacks as combatants on both sides. In New Orleans, Gen. Andrew Jackson, future president of the United States, faced a British invasion. Jackson commanded a force of fron-tier militiamen which included at least six hundred mulattoes and free blacks. He was uncertain of blacks' willingness to engage the English in battle and so made plans to move them to the rear rather than risk their joining the British troops. In a desperate effort to secure the loyalty of the city's people of color as British forces approached, Jackson promised black troops the same pay, equipment, food, and 160-acre land grants as white troops. Years later Jack-son confided to President James Monroe that he had been uncomfortable recruiting black troops but had employed them largely to prevent the British from using them against the city.[34]

Contrary to Jackson's fears black Americans and white Americans successfully defended New Orleans, inflicting heavy casualties on the invaders and providing the United States with an important victory. Jackson kept his promise to the free blacks and rewarded them for their service, but the slaves who fought with him were not so fortunate. James Roberts, born a slave on the eastern shore of Maryland, was twice unlucky. He had earned his freedom for service in the Continental forces during the Revolutionary War, but his master sold him to a slaveholder in New Orleans for fifteen hundred dollars instead. Decades later, when the call went out for slaves to defend the city against the British invasion, Roberts volunteered, hoping to gain his freedom. After the battle Jackson extolled the bravery and skill of the blacks who had stood with him but insisted he was powerless to interfere with masters' rights over their slave property. Roberts returned to slavery a bitter man, feeling he had once again been "duped by the white man."[35] Many of the slaves who escaped to the British fared little better and were sold to the West Indies by British officers who made considerable profit from this illegal trade. In response to persistent complaints by New Orleans slaveholders, England finally agreed to pay more than one million dollars in 1826 to compensate them for the loss of slaves who escaped during the battle.[36]

Winning the war reinforced the developing American identity and heightened nationalism especially for whites, but some blacks continued to contemplate emigration to Africa. Less than a year after the peace had been signed, Paul Cuffe set sail for Sierra Leone on the *Traveller,* carrying goods for trading and fifty-eight African American passengers. Cuffe settled his people on the land he purchased in the colony and by the spring of 1817 returned to the United States to promote colonization. He soon found powerful allies among a number of white men who had formed a group in 1816 to promote the colonization of blacks in West Africa. Hoping for congressional financing, and calling their organization the American Colonization Society, they included some of the era's most prominent men. Virginian Charles Fenton Mercer, New Jersey minister Robert Finley, and Francis Scott Key, composer of the present-day national anthem, the "Star-Spangled Banner," were among the society's founders. Members included powerful political figures such as Henry Clay, the U.S. representative from Tennessee, Daniel Webster, U.S. senator from Massachusetts, future president John Tyler, Supreme Court Justice Bushred Washington, and Gen. Andrew Jackson. The fact that this distinguished group was composed mainly of slaveholders aroused black suspicions, but Paul Cuffe's commitment to promoting African settlement and trade led him to an association with some of the society's members. Cuffe's knowledge of shipping, of West Africa, and of Sierra Leone were extremely useful to the colonizationists. He was able to persuade several black leaders in New York and Philadelphia to consider the organization's project, but most rank-and-file black community members in northern cities rejected any association with the American Colonization Society. The black masses of Philadelphia remained unconvinced even though many of the city's important leaders, James Forten and Richard Allen among them, originally supported colonization. Cuffe's African Institutions provided organizational support, prominent white leaders addressed large crowds promoting the society, and Cuffe himself spoke in black churches extolling the wonders of Africa and the opportunities opened by colonization.

In 1820, with financial help from the federal government, the society founded its own colony and called it Liberia. Daniel Coker, one of the country's most prominent black ministers, led eighty-six African American settlers who set sail on the *Mayflower of Liberia* for a new life in the West African colony. There was significant black support for the American Colonization Society in the states of Virginia and Maryland in the Upper South. There opportunities for free blacks were extremely limited, and some masters were willing to free slaves who agreed to emigrate. Several blacks from Richmond, Virginia, were members of another group, which set off in 1821. Lott Cary, a former slave who bought his own freedom, was one of them. His emigration was sponsored by Richmond's First Baptist Church, an interracial congregation who sent him as a missionary to the African people. Like many settlers Cary had many reasons for emigrating. "I am an African," he declared, explaining that he wanted to regain his heritage and hoped to develop his talents without the restrictions burdening black people in America. For black Americans born in Africa, colonization offered the opportunity to rejoin the friends and family they had been forced to leave behind many years before. African-born Boston Crummel, originally from the region of Sierra Leone and enslaved in New York for many years, was anxious to go home, but Crummel's wife, who had been born on Long Island in New York, was far more skeptical about emigration and about the colonization society. During the years before the Civil War the colony of Liberia survived, but it drew only small numbers of emigrants from the United States.

The establishment of the colonization society was directly connected to the growing importance of cotton, slavery, and the planter class. Even though slavery became increasingly isolated in the South as northern states abolished the institution during the early years of the nineteenth century, the national power of slaveholders grew. Slaveholders such as James Monroe, Andrew Jackson, Henry Clay, and John C. Calhoun held the highest political offices in the nation. New York bankers financed southern cotton production, and

Massachusetts textile mills depended on a steady supply of raw cotton. The American Colonization Society provided a convenient vehicle for whites uneasy about slavery but unwilling to confront the power of cotton and its slave system directly. The society allowed the discomfited to subscribe to somewhat contradictory aims. They could advocate removing free blacks to Africa, thereby placating slaveholders seeking a more secure slave system without the danger posed by free blacks, they could reassure the northern white workers who were becoming increasingly concerned about competition from black labor, and they could use the language of freedom and opportunity in campaigns to recruit blacks for colonization. The multiplicity of goals accommodated by the American Colonization Society's program help to explain both its popularity with whites and its failure to attract most northern blacks. Remembering blacks who had participated in the Revolutionary struggles and defended the new nation in the War of 1812, many African Americans were insulted and offended by colonization schemes sponsored by slaveholders.

As black people struggled to define their place in the United States after the war, there were confusing signals from white authorities. Northern states abolished slavery, but many restricted African Americans' civil rights. Colonization seemed to provide incentives for slaveholders to free their slaves and allow them to emigrate, but the increasing power of the Cotton Kingdom promised an entrenched slave system in the South. As regional tensions between slave and nonslave states grew, Congress became the arena for the struggle to maintain their balance of power. When the Missouri Territory applied for admittance to the Union early in 1819, northern congressmen tried to exact the gradual release of its ten thousand slaves and a restriction on the further introduction of slaves in return for Missouri's becoming a state. The southern congressmen argued that this was unconstitutional, but a crisis was avoided by a compromise providing for the simultaneous admission of Missouri as a slave state and Maine as a free state, and an agreement that Missouri's southern border would be the northern limit of slavery. The Missouri Compromise of 1820, as it was called, was one of a succession of confrontations between the slaveholding and nonslaveholding states, increasing in seriousness and marking the country's widening sectional rift. Years later black abolitionist Frederick Douglass identified the Missouri Compromise as the first of those "shocking development[s] of that moral weakness in high places which [attended] the conflict between the spirit of liberty and the spirit of slavery."[37]

Chapter 5

Slavery and the Slave Community

During the eighteenth century, when Equiano was captured and enslaved, slavery was a profitable but still relatively small institution in British North America. By the nineteenth century slavery had grown, filling a large part of the labor needs of the new nation and following the westward expansion of the plantation South. The number of slaves had increased from fewer than seven hundred thousand in 1790 to more than one million by 1810. Even after the constitutional ban on the African slave trade went into effect in 1808, the institution of slavery continued to grow. Illegal imports combined with natural increase to result in a population of nearly four million slaves by 1860. As the northern states completed their abolition of slavery during the first decades of the nineteenth century, nearly all of slavery's growth occurred in the southern states, especially in the western South. These developments increased sectional differences and exacerbated tensions growing from the diverging interests of North and South.[1] The great increase in the slave population was especially notable in light of the fact that the number of slaves imported directly from Africa had actually declined during the last half of the eighteenth century. The experience of many slaves in the nineteenth century was very different from Equiano's in the previous one. All Africans were separated from their families and homelands; with the opening of the western South, even slaves born in America faced the danger of being separated from their families as members were sold to the large plantations in places such as Mississippi and Louisiana. The voracious appetite of this labor system for new workers increased the danger for free blacks even in northern states. In the 1840s musician Solomon Northup, a freeborn man in his early thirties, lived in New York State with his wife and three children. One day while his wife was out of town, he was enticed by the promise of a job playing his fiddle and traveled first to New York City and then to Washington, D.C., where he was kidnapped into slavery. He was taken through Virginia to the auction block in New Orleans. On the way he encountered two other free men who had also been kidnapped, one from Cincinnati, Ohio, and the other from Norfolk, Virginia. Northup labored twelve years as a slave on the sugarcane and cotton plantations of Louisiana before he could get word to his family in New York and gain his freedom.[2]

Abd al-Rahman Ibrahima
(1762–1829)

Abd al-Rahman Ibrahima was the son of the ruler of the warlike Muslim Fulbe people from the West African interior, traders of ivory, livestock, gold, and slaves to coastal settlements. Ibrahima received a traditional Islamic education and pursued advanced studies in Macina and Timbuktu, more than a thousand miles from home. At seventeen he returned home and joined the army; by the time he was twenty-six, he was a husband, father, experienced horseman, and army commander. After a battle in 1788, he was ambushed, taken prisoner, and sold to slave traders, along with fifty warriors.

Eight months, six thousand miles, and a series of sales brought Abd al-Rahman, or Abduhl Rahahman, to Natchez in Spanish-controlled territory. Tobacco planter Thomas Foster, a man of little learning, bought him and another African on credit for $930. The striking, six-foot-tall Rahahman, with shoulder-length hair and a dignified, intelligent appearance explained to his owner, probably through a Mandinka translator, that his father would pay a king's ransom in gold for his return. Foster responded by naming him Prince.

Six years later Foster bought Isabella, an American-born Christian woman, and soon Ibrahima and Isabella were married. Rahahman endured the rigors of slavery while maintaining his religion and some Arabic literacy. His integrity gained his owner's trust, and on weekends he was able to take produce to the Natchez market where occasionally newly imported Africans gave him news from home. In 1807 he encountered John Cox, a man who had known him and his father in Africa. Cox tried to arrange Rahahman's freedom, but Foster refused to sell him. Cox publicized the story, Rahahman became a celebrity, and eventually Secretary of State Henry Clay and President John Quincy Adams became his advocates. Foster agreed to sell him, but only if he agreed to go to Africa. Aided by the African Colonization Society and a one-year fund-raising tour, Ibrahima and Isabella sailed for Africa in 1829. During forty years of slavery Rahahman had continued to hope for freedom and to return home, but he died in Africa before

Abduhl Rahahman (Abd al-Rahman Ibrahima), West African prince, son of the King of Timbo, enslaved in America for almost forty years. Prints and Photographs Division, Library of Congress, Washington, D.C.

he could get home. Two of his nine children and five of his grandchildren joined Isabella in freedom in Liberia the following year.

During the nineteenth century an increasing proportion of North American slaves had been born in the United States, and the changing character of the slave population had important consequences. African-born slaves suffered the torment of lost liberty and forced labor and the anguish of separation from their cultural homes and extended families. The many languages people from West and Central Africa spoke were often so distinct that communication between Africans was initially difficult. Over time, however, multiple tongues mingled on the plantations in British North America and combined to form a language not native to any but that made communication between Africans possible. The longer slaves lived in the United States, the more familiar they became with the English language and with the society of their captors. African linguistic styles continued to influence the English spoken by even those Africans who had lived in the country for an extended period or had been born there, and in areas with many blacks they influenced white speech as well. Following African speech patterns, African Americans sometimes dropped the unstressed syllables of English words or eliminated the verb in an English sentence, as in "Henry, he in field."[3] Although African- and American-born slaves suffered equally under the slave labor system, the African Americans' greater knowledge of European ways, their more sophisticated understanding of the slave structure, and wider support system better equipped them to cope with their situation. Their greater facility with English and the Creole languages developed by these American-born blacks made it possible for them to communicate with whites beyond simple work-related matters. This also allowed them greater access to information, an important tool in their struggle to deal with the power of slaveholders and the white society.

African-born slaves—reputedly more difficult to control, more likely to run away, and more likely to risk their lives in resistance or escape—were also more likely to fail in their attempts and to be recaptured or killed. They lacked experience dealing with masters and overseers and were unfamiliar with the countryside. The defiant stance or bold action of proud Africans that has provided material for heroic historical drama could mean death for slaves. In the early nineteenth century, when a night patrol with dogs barking at their heels galloped around the Virginia countryside to discover blacks lingering in revelry past their curfew, most slaves could have been expected to disappear safely into the darkness. Instead Robert, "an athletic, powerful slave, who had been but a short time from his 'father land' [and] whose spirit the cowardly overseer had labored in vain to quell" sent the women to a nearby cabin and rallied the men to stand their ground. He stationed two men just inside the door of a darkened cabin with orders to rush out and chase off the patrol's horses when they broke in. In the violent encounter that ensued, two whites

$200 Reward.

RANAWAY from the subscriber, on the night of Thursday, the 30th of Sepember,

FIVE NEGRO SLAVES,

To-wit : one Negro man, his wife, and three children.

The man is a black negro, full height, very erect, his face a little thin. He is about forty years of age, and calls himself *Washington Reed*, and is known by the name of Washington. He is probably well dressed, possibly takes with him an ivory headed cane, and is of good address. Several of his teeth are gone.

Mary, his wife, is about thirty years of age, a bright mulatto woman, and quite stout and strong.

The oldest of the children is a boy, of the name of FIELDING, twelve years of age, a dark mulatto, with heavy eyelids. He probably wore a new cloth cap.

MATILDA, the second child, is a girl, six years of age, rather a dark mulatto, but a bright and smart looking child.

MALCOLM, the youngest, is a boy, four years old, a lighter mulatto than the last, and about equally as bright. He probably also wore a cloth cap. If examined, he will be found to have a swelling at the navel.

Washington and Mary have lived at or near St. Louis, with the subscriber, for about 15 years.

It is supposed that they are making their way to Chicago, and that a white man accompanies them, that they will travel chiefly at night, and most probably in a covered wagon.

A reward of $150 will be paid for their apprehension, so that I can get them, if taken within one hundred miles of St. Louis, and $200 if taken beyond that, and secured so that I can get them, and other reasonable additional charges, if delivered to the subscriber, or to THOMAS ALLEN, Esq., at St. Louis, Mo. The above negroes, for the last few years, have been in possession of Thomas Allen, Esq., of St. Louis.

WM. RUSSELL.

ST. LOUIS, Oct. 1, 1847.

Reward notice for fugitive slaves, St. Louis, October 1, 1847.

Prints and Photographs Division, Library of Congress, Washington, D.C.

and six blacks were killed, and several on both sides were injured. Three of the slaves, including the African, left widows and children, and all the slaves in the area suffered the consequences of their resistance. "[White] people flocked from every quarter, armed to the teeth, swearing vengeance on the defenseless slaves." The most experienced understood that all would suffer for the defiant acts of a few.[4]

The slaves' violent retaliation against slavery, feared by slaveholders and their allies, was a realistic and ever-present danger. Spontaneous violence, an emotional outburst resulting from some long-simmering grievance or suddenly unbearable outrage, was most likely. Overseers were most vulnerable to such attacks because they worked more closely with slaves than other whites, because their job was to force compliance with the work routine and plantation discipline, and because they were the ones most likely to administer punishment. It was during the administration of punishment that overseers were particularly susceptible to angry slave reprisals, as when an overseer punished a young slave in Marksville, Louisiana, for failure to complete assigned work. The slave explained that he had been unable to complete his work because the overseer had sent him on an errand that had taken much longer than either of them had anticipated. The overseer was unmoved by this argument and forced the slave to kneel for a severe whipping. After the first few blows, the slave, smarting from both the whip and the particular injustice, leaped to his feet, grabbed an ax, and hacked the overseer to pieces.[5]

While an angry reaction to some specific injustice or brutal treatment may have triggered violence, rarely was the slave reacting to a single act. More often a long line of such abuses culminated in violent retaliation. Some slaves created detailed plans and organized their movements carefully, as when a group of slaves came together on one South Carolina plantation to plan a strategy for doing away with their abusive overseer. Understanding southern class antagonisms, they planned to take advantage of their master's prejudice against working-class overseers. The slaves surprised the well-armed overseer when he was alone, beat him to death, and carried his body to a nearby swamp and burned it. When the overseer did not arrive for work, his planter employer assumed that he was irresponsible and had simply walked off the job.[6]

The most radical kinds of resistance were those that struck not simply at injustice from an individual slaveholder or overseer but more consciously against the institution itself. There were fewer of these full-blown slave revolts, but they were extremely important for what they symbolized for both master and slave. The Stono rebellion in mid-eighteenth-century South Carolina, the Haitian Revolution at the end of the eighteenth century, and Gabriel's rebellion in early-nineteenth-century Virginia all created fear in white communities. In an effort to guard against revolt, governments sometimes placed severe restrictions on the movements and activities of slaves. Fear drove planters to constant vigilance. Some masters sat up all night, armed and on guard against expected violence, and both masters and slaves understood why. "How can men, who know they are abusing others all day," one slave asked rhetorically, "lie down and sleep quietly at night . . . when they know that men feel revengeful, and might burn their property, or even kill them?"[7]

Such was the fear in the early 1820s when the word was passed in Charleston, South Carolina, that carpenter Denmark Vesey, a former slave who had won his freedom in a lottery, was planning a revolt. In one of the most extensive slave plots in American history, potentially involving up to nine thousand slaves, Vesey and his aides worked for over a year, drawing up plans, fashioning weapons, and participating in West African war rituals under the supervision of slave conjurer Gullah Jack. Their plan to attack Charleston, capture guns and ammunition from the city armory, and march into the countryside liberating slaves as they went was discovered. South Carolina's governor, whose slave had been part of the plot, called out troops to crush the rebellion before it could get under way. The conspirators were captured, thirty-seven were banished from the region, and thirty-five, including Vesey, were executed. The Vesey conspiracy caused near panic in South Carolina as rumors circulated that it had been inspired by northern opponents of slavery and free blacks outside the state. There were theories that educated blacks were the main conspirators. Throughout the region new restrictions were imposed on slaves and free blacks, and old regulations that had languished were rigidly enforced. During such times black southerners were especially vulnerable, and most kept out of public view until white fears had subsided.[8] The most successful slave revolt during the antebellum period took place in Southhampton County, Virginia, in the summer of 1831. Under the leadership of slave preacher Nat Turner, a slave army of seventy or more attacked and killed fifty-seven whites, driving others into the swamps and creating hysteria in the entire region. It took a superior force of some three thousand, including militia from surrounding areas and neighboring states, to end the slave revolt. In a frenzy of retribution, whites killed hundreds of slaves, many of whom had played no role in the rebellion. By early winter, Turner was arrested, tried, and convicted of insurrection and murder, and on November 11, he was hanged in Jerusalem, Virginia. Turner's rebellion was the embodiment of white southern nightmares, swift and deadly, involving more and more slaves as the revolt progressed. Such open violence, however, was the exception in the antebellum South. Slaveholders were protected by a broad array of military forces from other communities, surrounding states, and ultimately the national government. This realization tempered revolutionary actions among most slaves, but some were willing to resort to violence despite the nearly inevitable deadly consequences.[9]

In order to control its slave population in the face of continuous resistance and periodic unrest, the South became a police state. Both slaveholding and nonslaveholding whites were charged with manning the slave patrols that watched transportation routes and gathering places to ensure that slaves were not off plantations without permission and did not meet in unauthorized groups. This martial atmosphere helped encourage a southern attitude of militarism, as John Hope Franklin argued in his classic study *The Militant South*. In order to enslave millions of African people and to maintain them in bondage, southern society was forced to tolerate and came to honor a military social climate that accepted violence as a necessity, brutalizing and dehumanizing all those involved.[10]

Slavery's brutality helped define a general climate of sanctioned violence in southern society and also spawned violence among whites. The historian Bertram Wyatt-Brown, studying pre–Civil War southern culture, argued

Nat Turner, leader
of a slave revolt in
Southhampton, Virginia,
1831.

Prints and Photographs Division,
Library of Congress,
Washington, D.C.

that the concept of honor was the centerpiece of southern relationships, especially among white males.[11] Presumably honorless blacks were the defining "others" against whom even poor white men could measure their own status. Violence against blacks was a display of white power and a defense of white honor. Insults to other whites could also lead to the violent defense of a man's honor. To be without honor was to be lower than a white person, to be more nearly black, and graphic accounts of heroic violence among southern white men became part of the regional folklore. "Honor in the Old South applied to all White classes, though with manifestations appropriate to each ranking." Among the southern elites, dueling was the classic means of defending honor, and savage fistfights were common among lower-class men, and both were tolerated by authorities. Murder and assault rates in the slaveholding South were ten times or more higher than in New England. The South was equal in its rates of violence to the West, which had less organized legal authority and a much higher proportion of the young single men who were most likely to be violent. "Violence in the South," as Wyatt-Brown has argued, "had its unique source in slavery and the structures of black subordination."[12]

In the face of the formidable power exercised by slaveholders, most slaves wisely limited their protests to covert actions. It was widely believed that the most effective and practical protest was action that could not be traced to its perpetrator. Most slaves asserted themselves in ways less likely to result in severe punishment. Many resisted the slaveowners' authority by actions slaveowners viewed as deceitful and dishonest, including such tactics as breaking tools, setting barns afire, or lying to and tricking the master. Stealing was another way slaves could exert control while also obtaining necessities or small luxuries. Slaves frequently justified it with the argument that taking something belonging to the master was simply redistributing the master's property, since they themselves were also the master's property. For slaves, stealing from the master was generally acceptable or even admirable; however, stealing from fellow slaves was not.

To the slaves slavery was more than the absence of freedom, it was the denial of their humanity. Theirs was a constant contention for human dignity and for some measure of autonomy within the plantation society. Masters held the great advantage, of course. Backed by local and national laws, they could punish with impunity or even kill slaves who threatened their authority. Resisting slavery was a complex matter involving many kinds of action and inaction. It was not always a confrontational refusal to submit to the authority of owners or overseers. Resistance was also a matter of surviving, of trying to protect loved ones, and remaining loyal to friends and fellow slaves.

Some earlier historians believed that the master's influence was absolute. It is true that slaves were required to adapt to the culture of the slaveholders, but more recent scholars have uncovered other influences. They have noted a wide variety of "significant others"—people other than the master, who played important roles in a slave's life—and have described the two separate interlocked communities that developed on the plantation. One community revolved around the "big house," where the master and his family had the greatest control and where the slaves were most likely to apparently acquiesce to white authority. This was where most white people gained their impressions of slavery and of southern black people, and this was the plantation community that formed the popular image of the genteel, courtly South in the American imagination. There was another very different plantation community in the slave quarters, however, where white people held far less direct power and the expressions of the slaves were less guarded. It was in this community that slaves could maintain some degree of dignity and control. In view of masters' attempts to be the only significant influence on the slaves, the maintenance of a slave community was a form of resistance to slavery.

By the nineteenth century most slaves lived on large plantations. Although three-quarters of southerners held no slaves, and most slaveholders owned fewer than five, three-quarters of the slaves lived in groups of ten or more, and half lived in slave communities of twenty or more. The growth of the institution, the development of the western South, and more equal numbers of men and women resulted in living arrangements for slaves that ranged from small households or extended "families" to complex slave communities. Solomon Northup's experience of being kidnapped into the Lower South in the 1840s illustrates many of these possibilities. His autobiography gives a remarkable firsthand account of the unpredictable life and degradation of the slave and provides an unusually detailed picture of the lives of slaves in the Lower South during this period.[13]

When first sold in New Orleans, Northup was taken several hundred miles north up the Mississippi River and the Red River to a lumbering camp maintained by his owner, William Ford. There Northup lived near the master's family, with ten other slaves. Working in or around the house were Rose, a slave from Washington who had been there five years; Sally, the mother of two toddlers; John, a sixteen-year-old who worked as the cook; and Eliza, who had been purchased by Ford along with Northup. Eliza had been the slave mistress of a wealthy man near Washington, living for years as his wife and bearing his child. She had the bad fortune, however, to be part of her owner's property, which fell to his lawful wife in their divorce settlement, and was sold. Rose and Eliza became immediate friends on the basis of their both having come from Washington, but the Fords were dissatisfied with Eliza's work, and she was soon sent to the fields. According to Northup's account she was disconsolate and never recovered from being separated from her two young children when they were all sold separately into slavery. In addition to two men who worked at the mill—Sam, also from Washington; and Anthony, a blacksmith from Kentucky who had been with Ford for ten years—there were three slave lumbermen—Northup; Walton, Rose's husband, who had been born a slave on Ford's plantation; and Harry, who was also purchased with Northup. These eleven slaves—some related by birth and some by common background, some many years with the same master, and others newcomers—were all united by their status and lived and worked together in a kind of extended family.[14]

Yet unpredictable change was the awful norm of a slave's life. Northup lived with these people a relatively short time, though he did remain in the same area for his entire time in slavery and so maintained contact with them. After a few years working there, and on Ford's large plantation farther south, he was hired out and eventually sold. He continued to be hired out periodically during slack times on his home plantation or busy times for others, and so worked and lived in different situations. He was employed as a carpenter, hired out to assist a white carpenter or to work on his own, as a fiddler for local plantation parties, and as part of the gang labor cutting cane on large sugar plantations. For most of his remaining ten years in the South, Northup worked on a small cotton plantation as the slave of Edwin Epps, an uneducated and harsh man who had worked as a slave driver and overseer before renting and then purchasing his own plantation. On the plantation where he spent the last eight years, Northup joined an established group of eight other slaves who had been together for many years.

The slaves' fortunes were directly linked to their master's financial stability, and the consequences of a master's insolvency were often dire for his slaves. All but the youngest of Epps's slaves had belonged to a county sheriff in South Carolina named James Buford. When Buford fell on hard times, these seven slaves were put in chains and marched the long distance across the Mississippi River to the plantation of Archy B. Williams, who used them to pay his overseer, Edwin Epps. Five of Epps's nine slaves belonged to the same family. Phebe, her husband Wiley, Phebe's two grown sons by a former husband, and Edward, born to Phebe and Wiley after their purchase by Epps. In addition to this family the small community in the slave quarters included Susan, the elderly Abram, and a young woman named Patsey. Abram was a storyteller and philosopher who had been born in Tennessee and lived there until the 1830s, when a slave trader sold him to Buford in South Carolina. He regaled his fellow slaves with tales of Tennessee's Gen. Andrew Jackson and the exploits of his black soldiers in the War of 1812. Such resourceful slaves could sometimes carve personal space from the largely inflexible world of the plantation.[15]

Special talents or abilities, like Abram's storytelling or Solomon's fiddling, gained some slaves respect and authority among their fellow slaves. Slave conjurers and preachers who ministered to the spiritual needs of the community were influential, although the preacher's role was especially complex. Some slave masters insisted that their slaves convert to Christianity, and large numbers of slaves had professed the Christian faith by the mid–nineteenth century. Yet even converts did not simply adopt European religious beliefs. Many Africans and African Americans never adopted Christian beliefs, and those who did generally adapted them to their own African cultural and spiritual traditions, using them for their own practical purposes. The planters encouraged the acceptance of a religion emphasizing obedience, sin, and gentleness, but slaves were drawn to the Old Testament stories from Exodus, featuring themes of escape from bondage and freedom from oppression. Slave preachers who supported the slaves' longing for freedom were sure to find favor within the slave community. Many relatively benevolent planters saw religion as a vehicle for reinforcing their power, arguing that God commanded slaves to obey their masters and to be loyal, leaving any relief from bondage for the next life. Slaves privately rejected arguments that slavery was the will of God visited on Africans as punishment for an ancient sin. "I was not very long in finding out," recalled Frederick Douglass, that "it was not color, but crime, not God, but man, that afforded the true explanation of the existence of slavery."[16]

African Americans not only adapted Christian beliefs to their previous belief systems and their present condition, they also incorporated African styles of worship into their Christian services. Far less staid and solemn than Europeans in their worship, Africans celebrated their religion with rhythmic song and dance. The ring shout, a ritual circle dance done by the Dahomey, the Kongo, and other societies of West Africa, symbolized a oneness with nature and with ancestors and the solidarity of community. It linked the sacred and the secular worlds and was an important display of religious emotion.[17] As Europeans and Africans met in America, some American religious customs took on African characteristics. This was especially true in the South for blacks and whites, but it was most obvious among African American slaves. As one Virginia slave recalled:

> The way in which we worshiped is almost indescribable. The singing was accompanied by a certain ecstasy of motion, clapping of hands, tossing of heads, which could continue without cessation about half an hour; one would lead off in a kind of recitative style, others joining in the chorus. The old house partook of the ecstasy; it rang with their jubilant shouts, and shook in all its joints.[18]

Whites had different reactions to African American forms of Christian worship. Some found it attractive for what they saw as its unpretentious simplicity. Some were repulsed by what they called its primitive heathenish display. Masters sometimes found it threatening and unnecessary, and a few refused to allow their slaves openly to practice any form of religion. One slaveholder discouraged his slaves' religious interests, saying, "You niggers have no souls, you are just like those cattle, when you die there is an end of you, there is [nothing] more for you to think about than living."[19]

Efforts to curb slave religious worship were generally unsuccessful. A particular brand of African American Christianity remained a central part of slave activity and identity throughout the pre–Civil War period, and the slave preacher remained an important actor in the slave community. The preacher's job was neither comfortable nor safe. Planters who tolerated slave preachers were especially watchful for any hint of their subversion of plantation authority. Thus, most slave preachers were forced to either provide the master's message of obedience, or to speak only indirectly about the worldly concerns of their congregations. Some preachers became expert in a kind of theological doublespeak, or what historian Charles Joyner refers to as the African tradition of "indirection," which allowed strong criticism of authority without direct confrontation. The preacher might appear to be in compliance with the master's wishes but instead provided theological reassurance and expressed the grievances of their fellow slaves.[20] Slaves generally dismissed preachers who appeared to believe the master's message. Frederick Douglass commented, "I could entertain no such nonsense as this [affirmation of the master's beliefs]; and I almost lost my patience when I found any colored man weak enough to believe such stuff." John White, like most slaves, assumed that when a preacher spoke in support of slavery's rules, "the old preacher was more worried about the bullwhip than the Bible." Those who provided support or access to power had standing in the slave community, but those perceived as working for the master were generally dismissed.[21]

While the role of slave preachers gave them distinction in the community, others commanded respect for their strength or skill or their influence with the master or other whites. Some planters took great pride in individual slave athletes who represented the plantation in competitive races and boxing matches. Skilled blacksmiths and carpenters were especially important to plantation maintenance and often had particular leverage with masters. For example, slave musicians who entertained at plantation functions could often use their prestige to influence the master and benefit the community. The same might be said for favored servants or the skilled cooks important to the success of the master's dinner parties. In the fields slave drivers, often slaves themselves, were also important. They worked under the direction of white overseers, and the whips they carried symbolized their power and their responsibility for enforcing plantation rules. They turned slaves out into the fields in the morning, ensured continuous work during the day, and enforced the curfew at night. A driver might have some privileges but was also required to do a share of the work. His was a difficult position because he often lived among those he was expected to discipline. Thus, he often worked out informal agreements with the other slaves, making him and his position useful to the community. Solomon Northup recalled that he developed such skill with the whip that he was able to simulate a whipping by snapping the whip close to but not quite touching the skin, "throwing the lash within a hair's breadth of the back, the ear, the nose, without, however, touching either of them." From a distance he could make a light touch seem like brutal punishment. The victims must play their roles convincingly lest the driver be found out, and all would be punished. "I would commence plying the lash vigorously, when according to arrangement, they would squirm and screech as if in agony." Unfortunately, slaves could not depend on this level of skill or a driver's willingness to risk punishment to spare his fellows, but compromises were often worked out between drivers and community members.[22]

The cluster of interlocking relationships and roles constituting the slave community enabled many to survive the hardships of slavery. Some people were connected by blood, but most were joined by a shared condition and a common place in the power structure. Though all did not agree on the best ways of coping with their situation, the slave community provided important support, helping sustain them in the face of continual assaults on their dignity and humanity. The institution of slavery was predicated on the assumptions that slaves were subhuman and powerless, valuable only for the work they produced. Though, like any human group, the slave community had conflicts, tensions, betrayals, and animosities, it was in the slave quarters that African Americans were likely to find recognition for their accomplishments, respect for their strength of character and virtue, compassion for their suffering, and love. The community was important because it contradicted slavery's message and provided a partial shield from the institution's most devastating effects.

The family was central to the formation of the community, and its maintenance became far more possible as more black women were added to the African American population by the late eighteenth and early nineteenth centuries. The historian Ann Malone found that in Louisiana, two-thirds of the slaves in the 1830s and nearly three-quarters in the 1840s lived in what she called simple family households. Such households were composed of a couple with or without children or a single parent, usually a mother, with children. Family and household composition were greatly influenced by the actions of the slaveholders, who responded to economic difficulties and opportunities by buying or selling slaves. Therefore household composition statistics are an incomplete indication of the history of family formation and dissolution. Still slaves' difficulties and adaptations to adversity are reflected in Malone's findings that fewer than one in five slaves lived alone and fewer than one in ten lived in households of more than two generations. This household data gives little information about the family relationships that may have linked separate households and different plantations, but it confirms earlier studies that found that the nuclear family structure of parents and children was the most common family form among slaves throughout the South before the Civil War.[23]

Slave marriages had no legal standing, and all such unions took place at the pleasure of slaveowners. Planters often encouraged marriages between slaves on their own plantations, since those who married off the plantation would inevitably want the privilege of visiting spouses elsewhere, removing them from the master's direct control. Some masters acquiesced in their slaves' choices of mates from other plantations and attempted to arrange a hire or purchase to unite the couples. When a Colonel Barsdale of Virginia, for example, received a letter asking that he consider hiring or selling a slave woman, the request came from a planter whose slave, Israel, the blacksmith, seemed "much attached to her." Large plantations offered the greatest opportunities for slaves to find mates in their local community, but even there, many

sought partners elsewhere. The selection of a partner living off one's plantation limited the time a couple could spend together and increased the likelihood of permanent family separation. Since any offspring became the
property of the mother's owner, it also made the father less able to influence
his children's upbringing. Yet, many slaves chose marriage partners from other
plantations, thereby exercising some control over their lives, and many slave
marriages were carried on at a distance.[24]

Family life for a slave was always problematic, since slaves had no legal
rights to protect a family or keep it intact. In marriages between free people,
husbands controlled their wives' property and were assumed to protect their
rights, standing as the legal representatives of the family. Slave marriages put
husbands and wives on an equal footing: Neither had any property rights or
legal standing. Slave masters had absolute authority to separate the family and
discipline or reward any family member, theoretically making parental
authority and marriage rights meaningless. Many families were devastated by
the internal slave trade which transported slaves from the eastern Upper South
to the plantations of the western Lower South. Even under these circumstances
many families managed to maintain contact for decades, many had the support of nuclear families, and some maintained extended kinship networks.[25]

When forced sales made separations unavoidable, some slaves maintained symbolic contact with lost family members through the names they
chose for their children. Many followed African traditions, naming children
for their grandparents or other relatives. Although many sons were named
after their fathers, slave women whose children were fathered by whites were
likely to name sons after black male relatives. Elizabeth Keckley was separated from her mother at age fourteen and taken from Virginia to North Carolina, where she eventually had a son by a white man to whom she was hired
out. The child was named George, not for his white father, but for his black
grandfather, whom Elizabeth had barely known.[26]

The gender assumptions of the white society combined with the laws regulating the slave system and the conditions of servitude to minimize enslaved
men's roles as husbands and fathers. Slave women, on the other hand, were often
allowed time during the workday to care for their children. Sometimes children
were brought to the fields with their mothers, who nursed them and tended
to their needs during work breaks. On a few of the larger plantations slaves ran
nurseries for the estate's children, often including the white children. On most
of the smaller farms, slave mothers provided care for their own children and
were sometimes given time off from work to do so. Often husbands worked
longer hours to make up for the time allowed their wives for child care.

Although slave parents could frequently make arrangements for caring
for their children, when the demands of work were especially great or when

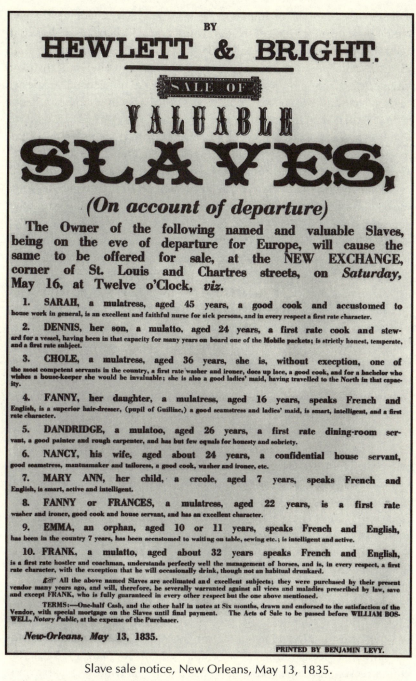

BY
HEWLETT & BRIGHT.

SALE OF

VALUABLE

SLAVES,

(On account of departure)

The Owner of the following named and valuable Slaves, being on the eve of departure for Europe, will cause the same to be offered for sale, at the NEW EXCHANGE, corner of St. Louis and Chartres streets, on *Saturday,* May 16, at Twelve o'Clock, *viz.*

1. **SARAH,** a mulatress, aged 45 years, a good cook and accustomed to house work in general, is an excellent and faithful nurse for sick persons, and in every respect a first rate character.

2. **DENNIS,** her son, a mulatto, aged 24 years, a first rate cook and steward for a vessel, having been in that capacity for many years on board one of the Mobile packets; is strictly honest, temperate, and a first rate subject.

3. **CHOLE,** a mulatress, aged 36 years, she is, without exception, one of the most competent servants in the country, a first rate washer and ironer, does up lace, a good cook, and for a bachelor who wishes a house-keeper she would be invaluable; she is also a good ladies' maid, having travelled to the North in that capacity.

4. **FANNY,** her daughter, a mulatress, aged 16 years, speaks French and English, is a superior hair-dresser, (pupil of Guillac,) a good seamstress and ladies' maid, is smart, intelligent, and a first rate character.

5. **DANDRIDGE,** a mulatoo, aged 26 years, a first rate dining-room servant, a good painter and rough carpenter, and has but few equals for honesty and sobriety.

6. **NANCY,** his wife, aged about 24 years, a confidential house servant, good seamstress, mantuamaker and tailoress, a good cook, washer and ironer, etc.

7. **MARY ANN,** her child, a creole, aged 7 years, speaks French and English, is smart, active and intelligent.

8. **FANNY or FRANCES,** a mulatress, aged 22 years, is a first rate washer and ironer, good cook and house servant, and has an excellent character.

9. **EMMA,** an orphan, aged 10 or 11 years, speaks French and English, has been in the country 7 years, has been accustomed to waiting on table, sewing etc.; is intelligent and active.

10. **FRANK,** a mulatto, aged about 32 years speaks French and English, is a first rate hostler and coachman, understands perfectly well the management of horses, and is, in every respect, a first rate character, with the exception that he will occasionally drink, though not an habitual drunkard.

☞ All the above named Slaves are acclimated and excellent subjects; they were purchased by their present vendor many years ago, and will, therefore, be severally warranted against all vices and maladies prescribed by law, save and except FRANK, who is fully guaranteed in every other respect but the one above mentioned.

TERMS:—One-half Cash, and the other half in notes at Six months, drawn and endorsed to the satisfaction of the Vendor, with special mortgage on the Slaves until final payment. The Acts of Sale to be passed before WILLIAM BOSWELL, *Notary Public,* at the expense of the Purchaser.

New-Orleans, May 13, 1835.

PRINTED BY BENJAMIN LEVY.

Slave sale notice, New Orleans, May 13, 1835.

a master insisted on maintaining a steady work pace, slave children were often left on their own for much of the day. Former slave Frederick Douglass characterized the early years of a slave child's life as relatively carefree, spent in play and generally in close association with the white children of the plantation. Before age eight or nine, slave children were not generally expected to do demanding work, and Douglass described his childhood as a happy time.[27] Others remembered their early years in slavery differently, recalling that the work of the plantation was so demanding that parents had little time for child care until evening or Sunday, the slaves' traditional rest day. As J.W.C. Pennington recalled, his childhood was marked by a "want of parental care" as his parents "were not able to give any attention to their children during the day." By necessity, parenting was a community responsibility, with other adults filling in for parents where possible and taking complete responsibility for children separated from their parents. Among slaves, the process of informal adoption helped to provide for children whose parents were absent or incapacitated.[28]

Slavery was harsh for all slaves, but not all slaves experienced that hardship in the same way. "Slavery is terrible for men," explained former slave Harriet Jacobs, "but it is far more terrible for women." Her belief was based on the fact that slave women were often forced to endure all the hardships and indignities imposed on men but were also regularly subject to sexual exploitation. The history of slavery is filled with the stories of masters sexually abusing their female slaves, and plantations were populated with the offspring of such relationships. From trading block to whipping post, slave women's modesty was not respected; they were stripped and exposed to public view. Sexual relationships with slave women marked young white boys' passage into puberty and satisfied the masters' lust. Occasionally slave women could exercise some control over these exploitations. Harriet Jacobs made a conscious decision to take a white lover to shield her from other white men and to give some protection to her child. The vast majority, however, had no choice but to submit to the sexual demands of white men.[29]

Slave women were also vulnerable to the anger of white women who could not punish their husbands, the slave masters, but could and did punish their slaves for these relationships. As a child, Patsey told Solomon Northup, she had been a great favorite around the Epps household in Louisiana. She was proud of the fact that her father was an African, carried, she said, to slavery in Cuba before being sold to South Carolina. She was a skilled teamster and rail-splitter, a speedy runner, an accomplished horsewoman, and the fastest cotton picker on the plantation. She was also the unwilling sexual favorite of frequently drunken Edwin Epps and paid dearly for this in severe whippings at the behest of Epps's extremely jealous wife.[30] Many whites believed that black women were highly sexual and promiscuous, and white men used these stereotypes to absolve themselves of responsibility in these sexual associations. Thus slave women were vulnerable to abuse by planters and punishment by planters' wives, and suffered from the stereotypes that protected white men from guilt.

Both women and men did heavy labor in the fields with little accommodation to gender differences. The specific nature of the work depended on the crop being grown and the time of year, but generally both male and female slaves spent long days in strenuous work. Indeed Solomon Northup reported that some cotton and sugar plantations were worked entirely with female labor. When extra hands were needed at Ford's lumber operation, four black women, Charlotte, Fanny, Cresia, and Nelly, were sent to help the men. They were "excellent choppers," according to Northup, "equal to any man" at piling logs. On the largest plantations slave life was generally more regimented than on small farms or in urban areas. Northup recalled that each workday on the large cotton plantations in Louisiana began with the blowing of a horn about an hour before dawn. After a hurried breakfast (typically warm cornmeal cake) slaves filled gourds with water, packed lunches of cornmeal cake and, occasionally, cold bacon, and went off to the fields to work.[31]

During March and April the ground was prepared for planting. Where Northup labored, a mule pulling a large plow made a straight furrow; a young woman followed sowing cotton seeds from a huge sack hung around her neck. Then came another mule pulling a harrow, which covered the seed. In one pass two mules, two mule drivers—most often men but sometimes women—and one planting woman could plant a row of cotton several hundred yards long. This was the beginning of the process that by fall produced the tens of thousands of pounds of cotton that were the foundation of the South's economy. After planting came the hoeing season, which lasted from April until July, during which time slaves worked their way down each row, cultivating and keeping weeds from choking the growing cotton plants. In August slaves began picking the cotton, the hardest part of the process, as each picker worked with a huge sack on a strap slung around the neck and shoulders. An experienced hand was expected to pick about two hundred pounds of cotton each day.[32]

Landscape architect, abolitionist, and sometime journalist Frederick Law Olmsted reported seeing plantations on which thirty plows and thirty to forty people with hoes, mostly women, moved together across the wide fields of Mississippi well into the night. Often he saw a black slave driver walking along, brandishing a whip and cracking it over the heads of the other slaves. After their work in the fields, slaves had additional tasks, such as gathering wood for supper fires, feeding the animals, and carrying heavy sacks of cotton to be stored or ginned. Slaves had little time to do things for themselves or their families, for at least some planters insisted that their workers be in bed by ten in the evening and forced them to the fields before daylight. One planter told Olmsted, "Well, I don't never start my niggers 'fore daylight except 'tis in pickin' time, then maybe I got 'em out a quarter of an hour before," in this way, confirming his self-image as a kind slave master. Other masters were not so considerate and sent their slaves to the fields as early as necessary to get the day's work done. No matter what time slaves began their day, the work was constant. "I keep 'em right smart to work through the day," Olmsted's informant declared.[33]

Masters and overseers set quotas for the amount of work to be done, generally taking into account the experience, skill, and strength of the individual; and slaves who did not make their quotas were often whipped. According to Northup the most accomplished slaves picked cotton with extraordinary quickness. Patsey, for example, used both hands and could easily pick five hundred pounds of cotton in a single day. When darkness forced slaves from the fields, the day's picking was weighed, a process that provoked extreme anxiety for the slaves. Those who had not picked their quota were whipped, and those who had picked substantially more than expected had their quotas raised. Often slaves cooperated and reduced their pace to protect weaker or slower workers. The fastest and cleverest could always be expected to make their quotas, but others were never able to pick the standard poundage and after repeated beatings were finally removed from the fields, sold, or given other jobs to do. The style of work generally employed on cotton plantations was called gang labor because slaves worked in large gangs, moving through the fields from morning to night, under the threat of the overseer's whip.[34]

In the rice fields of South Carolina and the low country of Georgia, slaves often worked under a task labor system, focused less on the amount of time they labored than on the tasks they completed. Ben Horry, a slave on the Brookgreen plantation in South Carolina, explained that as soon as the fall rice harvest was completed, the slaves started to ready the fields for the next season. Using mules and oxen, they plowed under the remains of the harvested rice plants before the winter arrived. They plowed the fields again in the spring, cut deep trenches into the soil, planted the new rice, and flooded the fields. Then, as the fields were alternately drained and flooded, slaves worked in water or thick mud for the rest of the season, finding respite during the summer only when they moved to higher ground to plant and tend the crops that supplied food for the plantation. In midsummer, when the fields were drained, slaves worked long days in intense heat, with thick mud making their every movement an effort. During the harvest season they gathered the grain with rice hooks and threshed the rice by hand, pounding and fanning it in baskets designed like those used in African rice culture to make it ready for market.[35]

The flies and mosquitoes, the disease and fungal infections, and the general discomfort of working long hours in wet soil in heat and humidity combined to make rice cultivation onerous work. John Brown, a slave who worked in the rice fields of Georgia, thought that rice cultivation was the most unhealthful of all slave agricultural work. He contended that working knee-deep in the foul-smelling water that reflected the heat brought on fevers and contributed to sunstroke. With the constant dampness causing cracks in their skin that allowed insects to lodge just under the flesh, slaves suffered infection, rheumatism, asthma, consumption, and other painful and chronic maladies. Brown also recalled the danger from the water moccasins, which were always plentiful in low-country rice fields. Generally, he said, rice work was "very much more trying than either cotton or tobacco cultivation."[36] Yet the task system employed on most rice plantations provided slaves with some degree of autonomy. A skilled rice worker might complete the assigned work hours before sundown and then have time to perform personal tasks, to grow, gather, or hunt food for his or her own family, to develop a skill that might provide some personal or family advantage, to handle other family matters, or to rest. Completing one's task early could be a backbreaking proposition, but slaves generally preferred the task system of rice over the gang labor of cotton.[37]

Slaves employed in cotton production, although forced to labor in gangs, also found ways to exercise some control over the nature and pace of their work. Many slaves sang their way through the ordeal of gang labor. White observers agreed that slaves seemed to sing all the time they worked. Although a few slaves reported, "Dey didn't allow us to sing on our plantation, cause if we did we just sing ourselves happy and get to shouting and dat would settle de work," slave songs were never successfully banned.[38] These songs ranged from field hollers, like "The Carolina Yell," described as "a loud musical shout, rising and falling, and breaking into falsetto," to more structured combinations of words and complex rhythms.[39] Songs sung during work helped encourage a sense of community among those sharing the hardship of agonizing labor. They helped pass the time during boring work and distracted attention from painful work, but they had an even greater practical value. Slaves working to music set the rhythm for that work. Since on cotton plantations, fast workers often amplified a master's frustration with slower workers and increased the likelihood of their punishment, it was useful for all slaves to maintain a moderate but steady work pace. Work songs helped to coordinate a common pace, allowing the slowest workers to keep up without alerting the master or overseer. This singing also often convinced whites that their slaves were contented and relieved some of their anxieties about the possibility of slave rebellions.[40]

Another way slaves could control their work was by running away for a few days. There were many reasons why slaves left their plantations without permission, including visiting friends and family, courting potential mates, or being angry at masters, but they also ran away to the woods or swamps to rest from their labor when they were exhausted or sick. When Patsey was sick and could not keep up her usual fast pace picking cotton, Northup reported, she ran away. On Epps's plantation slaves faced frequent whipping if they picked too slowly and were whipped again when their pickings weighed too little. Patsey stayed away nearly all summer to recover from an illness, living in the woods a short distance from the plantation and depending on the other slaves to share what little food they had. Her respite was bought at the price of a severe beating, five hundred lashes being the standard punishment at that time in Louisiana for running away. Across the South whipping was universally employed as the punishment for a slave's infraction of the rules, the severity determined by the type of infraction and the mood and temperament of the master or overseer. Northup reported that fifty lashes might be administered for a minor annoyance such as a leaf found in the cotton bag, and one hundred lashes for the offense of "standing idle in the field." Other punishments ranged from longer work hours or loss of the privilege of visiting one's family to more horrifying measures like the amputation of limbs or gruesome, terrifying mutilations that resulted in death. The last was obviously meant to serve as a lesson to other slaves. For controlling slaves, each plantation functioned as an independent fiefdom.[41]

Information was critical to the slaves' ability to exert a measure of control over their situations. Henry Clay Bruce, recalling his slave experience, explained that every plantation had its own spy network. House slaves were particularly well situated to acquire valuable information about the master, his family, his political concerns, and his financial matters. On their breaks from duties in the master's house, domestic slaves often brought news of local, regional, and national events to the slave quarters. News that someone was to be sold or punished, or information about friends or kin on neighboring plantations, might provide the warning that allowed a timely escape or the formulation of a plan of action.[42]

Booker T. Washington reported that what he called the "grapevine telegraph" was a regular and reliable conveyer of information for both slaves and free blacks.[43] Networks of informants included new slaves purchased or hired out from other areas, slave artisans and house slaves who came into regular contact with whites, and any African Americans who traveled to nearby areas or to towns and cities. Slave drivers or personal servants often accompanied planters on business trips or vacations, sometimes even to the free states. Body servants attended the southern planters who regularly visited northern border cities like Cincinnati, and often visited local blacks while their masters did business. The Dumas Hotel in Cincinnati was a favorite gathering place where southern slaves and Ohio free blacks mingled, despite the attempts of many slaveholders to discourage such associations.[44] Slaves returning from such trips faced lengthy interrogation by fellow slaves, seeking word of family members who had gone north, or simply wanting news from the outside world. Information helped break the isolation of the plantation, gave slaves a broader sense of the world, and equipped them with important strategic knowledge. If a cotton broker was about to make an appearance to bid on the plantation's produce, slaves knew that the master might be under special pressure to get the crop baled and shipped to market. As the contract date approached, a planter's dependence on the laborers' efficiency increased, and though his anxiety might lead to additional whippings, it also provided an opportunity that slaves could sometimes exploit to their advantage. At such critical times a work slowdown by slaves could be especially effective.

The internal slave trade threatened the stability of slave families, but it also provided a valuable source of information on distant family members. New slaves brought into an area often carried news of loved ones left behind. Although many plantation slaves lived in relatively isolated areas of the country, the business and social life of the plantation provided many opportunities for the exchange of information. The plantation business brought in new supplies of workers and necessitated contacts with buyers and shippers for agricultural products, and the plantation's social life often brought the personal servants of slaveowners together. Typically slaves from neighboring plantations might gather for holidays like Christmas and, ironically, Independence Day. Through informal networks of information, many slaves managed to maintain family ties. Willie Lee Mathis of Cincinnati, for example, kept in touch with her mother, a slave in Virginia, for thirty years. Others smuggled letters to children, parents, and other relatives in bondage in many areas of the South. Contacts between slaves and between slaves and free blacks, North and South, provided information that enabled some people to escape from slavery. These links created the hazardous informal route to freedom that became known as the underground railroad. Contacts with the world beyond the plantation, as well as cultural memories, family, and other forms of resistance, sustained the hope of freedom for African Americans through desperate times.[45]

Chapter 6

1829 David Walker publishes his *Walker's Appeal to the Colored Citizens of the World,* urging slaves to overthrow slavery

Slavery abolished in Mexico

1830 First national convention of African Americans held in Philadelphia

1831 Nat Turner slave revolt

William Lloyd Garrison begins publishing the *Liberator*

African American Maria W. Stewart delivers the first public lecture by a woman in the United States

1833 British Emancipation Act abolishes slavery in the British Empire

Integrated American Anti-Slavery Society established

1834 British West Indies slaveholders accept compensated emancipation

1837 White abolitionist newspaper editor Elijah P. Lovejoy killed by proslavery mob in Alton, Illinois

1838 Frederick Douglass escapes from slavery in Maryland

1839 Slave rebellion aboard the ship *Amistad.* Supreme Court decision in 1841 frees the surviving slaves, who are represented by former president John Quincy Adams, and thirty-five return to Africa

Antislavery Liberty Party formed in New York State

1841 Slaves aboard *Creole* revolt; bound from Virginia to Louisiana, they sail to freedom in Nassau

1842 Supreme Court, in *Prigg* v. *Pennsylvania,* rules that states may not be compelled to enforce the Fugitive Slave Law of 1793

1845 Frederick Douglass publishes *Narrative of the Life of Frederick Douglass*

1848 Discovery of gold at Sutter's Mill in California begins first gold rush

Frederick Douglass and Martin Delany publish the *North Star*

First Women's Rights Convention held at Seneca Falls, New York; Frederick Douglass seconds the motion for women's suffrage

Free-Soil Party formed, Martin Van Buren is the party's candidate for president, with the slogan "Free Soil, Free Labor, and Free Men"

1849 Harriet Tubman escapes from slavery in Maryland

Free People of Color
and the Fight against Slavery

*F*reedom for African Americans during the era of slavery was an ambiguous status between slavery and full citizenship. It was also precarious, especially in the South, where it generally depended on the sufferance of white authority.[1] There, in reaction to slave revolts and other perceived threats, advocating freedom for African Americans and organizing against slavery became progressively more difficult, even dangerous, during the nineteenth century. In the North, where black freedom was more secure, African American communities established organizations, the foundation for political action designed to broaden their own freedom and to secure the liberty of those enslaved in the South. Protest organizing in northern black communities was aided by African Americans' increasing independence from white control and oversight. More than 70 percent of blacks in Philadelphia and more than 80 percent in Boston lived in independent households by 1820. New York City had a smaller percentage that year, about 60 percent, due to New York State's gradual emancipation provision.[2] The state finally ended slavery completely on July 4 in 1827. African Americans celebrated with parades and festivals, and as the last slaves began to move out of the homes of former white masters, the number of independent black households grew. Many black families that had been torn apart by bondage were reunited, although poverty and the demand for live-in servants still meant that some blacks lived in white households. Yet, in New York as elsewhere, the early decades of the nineteenth century brought increasing numbers of independent black households and a growing black community committed not only to mutual support but also to the struggle for civil rights and black freedom.

In Boston in 1826 African Americans joined to form the Massachusetts General Colored Association, one of the first specifically antislavery black organizations. One of the group's founding members was David Walker, a free black man who came to Boston from North Carolina in the mid-1820s. Walker had never been a slave, but his life and travels in the South had made him intimately familiar with slavery's inhumanity. He described a slave owner forcing a son to whip his own mother to death, and another forcing a husband to beat his pregnant wife until she aborted their child.[3] In Boston, Walker became a community activist, working for abolition and racial justice. In 1827

Samuel Cornish and John Russwurm of New York gave black Americans a public voice when they founded *Freedom's Journal,* the nation's first African American newspaper, and Walker became its Boston agent.

The next year, in a militant speech before the Massachusetts General Colored Association, Walker called for the formation of black organizations to "protect, aid and assist each other to the utmost of our power," and advocated the use of "every scheme we think will have a tendency to facilitate our salvation."[4] In 1829 Walker expanded this message with his publication of *David Walker's Appeal to the Coloured Citizens of the World,* even sending it into the slave South. He condemned the hypocrisy of all those, especially Christians, who professed to love liberty yet supported slavery. He challenged the Jeffersonian thinking that called for freedom while profiting from human bondage and arguing that blacks were intellectually inferior, and he contended that slaves, inflamed by the same thirst for liberty that had moved American Revolutionary patriots, would be justified in revolting against their owners.[5] He saw education as a force for racial defense and uplift, believing it would produce revolutionaries. Southern slaveholders had vivid memories of earlier rebellions and Walker's *Appeal* exacerbated their fear.[6]

A few years later, in 1831, another strong antislavery voice came from Boston when William Lloyd Garrison began to publish his newspaper, the *Liberator.* Garrison, a white man, had good antislavery credentials. He had edited a political reform newspaper in Vermont, worked with Quaker activist Benjamin Lundy in Baltimore editing the *Genius of Universal Emancipation,* and had been jailed on a conviction of libel for accusing a New England shipowner of engaging in the illegal slave trade. Garrison spoke so passionately against slavery that many who had not met him assumed him to be black. Indeed, Garrison counted more blacks among his friends than did most white reformers of his day. He valued the opinions of his black associates and regularly sought their advice. When he was working out his positions on immediate emancipation and African colonization, he often did so with African American friends who criticized and helped him shape his ideas. James Forten and other blacks from Philadelphia provided a sounding board for some of Garrison's early fiery speeches. Speaking before black audiences in New York, New Haven, and Hartford helped him perfect his delivery, which a newspaper in 1830 had described as a bit stiff but admirable in "literary composition and 'philanthropic' concern." His speechmaking improved, and later that year, one enthusiastic observer said that when he spoke, people felt as though they had "heard the groans and viewed the lacerated bodies of the poor sufferers." With the power of an evangelical preacher, Garrison repeatedly announced, "I will not equivocate . . . I will not retreat a single inch—And I WILL BE HEARD." In his newspaper Garrison demanded both the abolition of slavery and the "improvement of the condition of the free people of color." It is no wonder that African Americans came to think of this most unusual white man as a "dearest friend."[7]

Garrison was so influential that those who subscribed to his ideas about immediate emancipation, anticolonization, and not participating in traditional political organizations came to be known as Garrisonians. Since he was a pacifist, Garrison had misgivings about the prospect of African American violence in opposition to slavery. Walker's call for a slave revolt put Garrison in a difficult position, but after some hesitation, he published portions of the *Appeal* in his newspaper. Rumor had it that Walker's southern agents had distributed his pamphlet in the South. In December of 1829 Walker sent thirty copies to Richmond, where they were sold for twelve cents or given away to those who could not afford the price. Many believed that black sailors carried copies south sewn into the linings of the clothing Walker sold in his secondhand clothing store. The *Appeal*'s publication in the *Liberator* gave it a wider circulation and a much higher visibility. In 1831 Nat Turner's deadly slave revolt in Virginia confirmed planters' fears that antislavery propaganda from the North was creating dangerous unrest among the slaves. State laws requiring the confinement of free black sailors when their ships were in port continued to be enforced in the South, despite the fact that the U.S. Supreme Court had declared South Carolina's Negro Seaman's Law unconstitutional in 1823.[8] In a further effort to protect their property, southern authorities put a price on Walker's head and offered substantial rewards for Garrison, his publisher, or any of the *Liberator*'s agents. The mayor of Savannah, Georgia, wrote to the mayor of Boston asking that Walker be arrested and that his writing be suppressed, but Walker's pamphlet had caused less controversy in the North than in the South, and Boston's mayor, unfamiliar with Walker and his writing, denied the request.[9]

The strength of southern animosity toward David Walker led many in the black community to suspect foul play when, later in 1831, he was found dead near the doorway of his clothing shop on Boston's Beacon Hill.[10] In 1835 William Lloyd Garrison, too, felt proslavery's wrath when he was attacked by antiabolitionist forces, seized, and dragged through Boston's streets at the end of a rope. Local blacks saved him in a daring wagon rescue, and city authorities placed him in protective custody. The violent opposition of southern slaveholders and their sympathizers did not deter the abolitionists, however. In 1832 Garrison and other abolitionists organized a meeting at the African Meeting House that established the New England Anti-Slavery Society. Several Boston blacks were among those signing the society's organizing documents. The Massachusetts General Colored Association became an auxiliary to this new society, and prominent black Bostonians John T. Hilton, Samuel Snowden, and Charles Lenox Remond assumed leadership positions. When, at Garrison's instigation, a national antislavery organization was formed in Philadelphia in 1833, seven black men were among the sixty delegates at the founding convention.[11] During the 1830s and 1840s abolitionists created a vast network of antislavery organizations that linked cities and towns in the North and Midwest, joined black communities in coordinated efforts, and tied black organizations to integrated groups. This organization was facilitated by the relatively high and rising black literacy that made pamphlets, newspapers, and handbills effective conduits of information in urban black communities. At midcentury the U.S. Census reported that nearly half of black adults there could read and write; by 1860 the majority were literate. Effective propaganda gained international support for the antislavery cause. Successful organizations also helped enslaved southern blacks escape to freedom.

In 1839 this network of antislavery organizations joined together to work for the freedom of escaped slaves in a celebrated international case. Fifty-three Africans had been captured in Africa and shipped to Cuba aboard a Spanish ship called the *Amistad,* despite the fact that in 1817 Spain had signed a treaty with England outlawing the Atlantic slave trade. Off Cuba the Africans killed the captain and some members of the crew, took over the ship, and attempted to return home. Eventually they were tricked by the crew into sailing into U.S. waters. They were captured, arrested, charged with murder, and imprisoned in Connecticut. The abolitionists went into action with a flurry of activity and publicity. They printed regular accounts in antislavery newspapers; visited the captives; and raised money for their defense, collecting donations at meetings, staging a play in New York, and commissioning and reproducing a portrait of the group's charismatic leader, Joseph Cinque. After sustained effort their case made its way to the U.S. Supreme Court, where former president John Quincy Adams and several prominent abolitionists defended the Africans. The court declared that the defendants had been kidnapped and set them free. In November 1841, finally, the thirty-five people who had survived this ordeal returned to Africa.[12]

Although antislavery societies brought black activists and white activists together, African Americans did not abandon all-black organizations. In 1829 an increase in Cincinnati's African American population had triggered white fears, resulting in a deadly assault on the city's black community. Despite a successful defense, many blacks were driven from the city, some to Canada. Cincinnati officials, bowing to local racist pressure, promised stricter enforcement of Ohio's exclusionary racial laws. Ohio had passed these laws earlier in the century in an attempt to limit black migration to the state. They required black migrants to register with the county, certifying that they were free, and to post a five-hundred-dollar bond to ensure that they would not become dependent on local charity. Anyone who knowingly hired or harbored fugitive slaves could be fined. Other western states also had restrictive laws: Illinois threatened bondage for any black migrant attempting to settle permanently in the state. Black migrants were barred from settling in Michigan, Indiana, Wisconsin, and Iowa. Oregon also prohibited blacks from owning land, and banned further black immigration when it became a state in 1859. In western states generally blacks were prohibited from voting, serving on juries, giving testimony in court cases involving whites, or attending public schools. Though these laws were irregularly enforced, they made African American freedom especially precarious in those states.[13]

In response to the Cincinnati riots and to attacks on black civil rights throughout the North, African Americans from nine states, including New York, Pennsylvania, Maryland, Delaware, and Virginia, met in Philadelphia in the first national convention of black leaders. The delegates meeting at the Mother Bethel Church chose the Philadelphian, Rev. Richard Allen, then seventy years old, to preside over the convention. The main topic on the agenda of this first meeting was the establishment of a Canadian settlement for refugees from American slavery, hostility, and discrimination. Delegates constituted themselves as the American Society of Free Persons of Colour, met annually for six years, then revived their national meetings again in the 1840s. Delegates came from local auxiliary societies organized to combat slavery and its ancillary effects on free black people.[14]

The conventions provided a national forum for African Americans and helped coordinate the actions of the local, state, and regional conventions and organizations of which they were an outgrowth. They also provided opportunities for black leaders to discuss and pass public resolutions on issues concerning their communities and to devise strategies for addressing them. The major concerns of these groups were opposition to slavery, the achievement and protection of civil rights, and the advancement of the race, especially through education and moral reform. The national conventions continued the determined opposition of most black organizations to the African settlement program of the American Colonization Society. Yet their support for Canadian settlements remained strong, especially after Canada abolished slavery in 1833 and refused to return fugitive slaves to the United States.[15]

Some African Americans also considered Haiti an appropriate place for possible settlement. As the first independent black nation in the Western Hemisphere, brought into existence by the defeat of French colonialism, Haiti was a symbol of black freedom and power. In the early 1820s Haitian president Jean-Pierre Boyer invited black Americans to settle in his country, offering free land, four months' provisions, and financial assistance. Haiti needed skilled farmers, and Boyer hoped that American blacks could form a stable rural population. Interest in Boyer's proposal was strong in black communities in the United States. Prince Saunders, a former teacher in Boston's black school, became a strong advocate of the project and worked with Haitian official

Jonathan Granville to recruit African Americans for an American-Haitian settlement. Granville toured New York, Philadelphia, Boston, and Baltimore, speaking to large and enthusiastic black audiences. With Saunders, Granville established the Haitian Emigration Society at a mass meeting in Philadelphia in 1824, and within a few weeks, 60 African Americans set sail from Philadelphia, 120 from New York, and 21 from Baltimore. During the next two years six thousand American blacks made the voyage to Haiti, and by the end of the decade, black communities in the United States had sent between eight and thirteen thousand emigrants.[16]

The venture was not entirely successful, however, and many African Americans returned within a few years. The Haitian government complained that these settlers were not willing to work the land but preferred to rent or sell their holdings and move into the cities. There the language and cultural differences between Catholic French-speaking Haitians and Protestant English-speaking African Americans created an uncomfortable urban coexistence. The most successful and longest-lasting settlement was located in an isolated section of the present-day Dominican Republic. There American blacks created an English-speaking enclave that retained its American identity well into the twentieth century. The reaction of the thousands of migrants who returned to the United States, however, for whom the French culture seemed too foreign, suggests the degree to which these blacks were American in their identity and cultural expectations. By this time almost all American blacks had been born in the United States, and most were several generations away from an African or Caribbean regional or cultural identification. This experience further strengthened the resolve of most American blacks to remain in the United States.

The plan of the American Colonization Society to settle blacks in Liberia was especially unpopular because most of the society's members were prominent slaveholders who, it was believed, simply wanted to remove free blacks from the country. Delegates who met in the national black conventions during the 1830s were particularly opposed to African colonization. In their broad program, they presented a united front—opposing colonization and slavery and supporting moral reform and racial uplift. Yet, the records of these conventions make it clear that free blacks had diverse opinions. All agreed on general aims but not always on the strategies for their accomplishment. Some favored separate all-black organizations and institutions as the major vehicles—advocating establishing all-black schools and encouraging blacks to patronize black businesses—believing that only black-controlled groups could properly speak for and serve the African American community. Others believed that true equality could only come through integrated facilities, organizations, and institutions. Some were committed to bringing about changes through the nonpolitical action of "moral suasion," holding fast to the Garrisonian approach of nonviolence and not participating in inevitably corrupt partisan politics. Others, especially by the 1840s, believed that African Americans would only gain their rights as Americans and have the power to force the society to abolish slavery by participating in politics and forging political alliances.

From the beginning, convention delegates were concerned with establishing the means for independent black achievement in order to escape the restrictions of racial discrimination. Austin Steward, a former slave and delegate from New York State, believed that farming could provide the independence that African Americans needed. To this end he supported the establishment of rural communities in Canada and moved his family to the Wilberforce Colony in Upper Canada for a time, to aid this enterprise. By the end of the 1840s there were such black settlements in Hamilton, Toronto, Chatham, Montreal, and other areas of eastern Canada, as well as a growing black community on Canada's West Coast. African Americans who found security in their new Canadian homes urged others to follow; some prospered in these new settlements. Mary Ann Shadd, daughter of a prominent Philadelphia black abolitionist family, opened a school for blacks in Windsor, just across the border from Detroit, in 1851. During the next decade she edited a newspaper, the *Provincial Freeman,* becoming the first black female newspaper editor in North America. She also published a guide to Canada for fugitives who had escaped from slavery in the United States, and became one of Canada's most effective and prominent abolitionist speakers. In 1856 she married Thomas J. Cary, a black businessman from Toronto. She was determined to remain in Canada herself and passionately urged others to emigrate. "Your national ship is rotten and sinking," she told American blacks. "Why not leave it?"[17]

Canada did seem a haven to many fugitive slaves whose freedom was insecure in the United States. This was true for Henry Bibb, another influential advocate of Canadian emigration. Bibb was a slave in Kentucky who made good his escape a number of times but was recaptured as he attempted to rescue his family. He was finally sold south to New Orleans and then into Texas and Indian Territory, where he became the slave of an Indian owner. In 1841 he escaped again, this time to Detroit, but by then he had given up any hope of rescuing his wife. She had been resold and had become a concubine of her new owner. In 1848 he married black abolitionist Mary Miles, and the couple was forced to flee to Canada when a new federal Fugitive Slave Law was passed in 1850. The Bibbs settled in Sandwich, Canada West (present-day Ontario), where she opened a school and he edited the *Voice of the Fugitive,* an antislavery weekly newspaper that advocated the emigration of American blacks to Canada. Through the efforts of the Bibbs, Mary Ann Shadd Cary, Austin Steward, and other black Americans who had come to see Canada as a land of freedom and opportunity, many Canadian black settlements were established

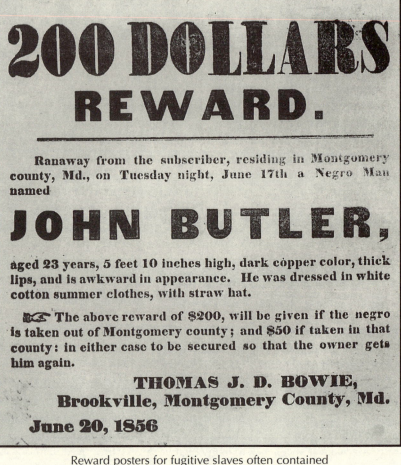

Reward posters for fugitive slaves often contained
detailed descriptions of runaways.

Mark E. Mitchell Collection of African American History.

in the three decades before the American Civil War ended slavery in the United
States.[18]

Although many African Americans came to believe that emigration was
their only route to security and independence, most were determined to
achieve full freedom in the United States. Richard Allen, for example, argued
that independence might also be achieved through practical training in the
mechanical trades. When a group of white abolitionists, including Garrison,
Lundy, and New York businessman Arthur Tappan, attended the second
national convention to propose the establishment of a manual labor school,
delegates received them enthusiastically. These schools, where students supported their education by learning and practicing trades, were popular insti-

tutions with reformers at the time. In fact the emphasis on the importance of black education for racial uplift was part of a general reform movement that linked black and white reformers in a commitment to antislavery, temperance, and other moral causes.

The convention endorsed the proposal for a racially integrated college and appointed editor Samuel Cornish to head fund-raising for the project. Integrationists also prevailed on decisions about the administration of the college, though it was agreed that African Americans should be in the majority on the board of trustees. When the residents of New Haven, Connecticut, the home of Yale University, learned that the new college was to be located in their city, they quickly organized in opposition. After a town meeting denounced the idea as promoting abolitionism and disorder, white mobs attacked blacks in New Haven and vandalized Tappan's home.[19] This hostile reaction discouraged the initiative for a college in New Haven, but black leaders remained interested in promoting education generally and in manual labor schools in particular. Especially as African Americans faced increased competition for low-level jobs from Irish immigrants in the 1840s and 1850s, there was heightened support for the establishment of educational institutions providing a combination of traditional and practical education.[20]

Although a black-controlled school of higher education was not established during this period, the cooperation between white abolitionists and black abolitionists did lead to the integration of a few institutions established and controlled by antislavery reformers. After 1830, such integrated schools as the Oneida Institute and New York Central College in New York State, and Oberlin Collegiate Institute in Ohio, educated a small but growing number of African American students. Oneida Institute, with a student body of just over one hundred, for example, under the presidency of white abolitionist Beriah Green and supported by the largesse of Arthur Tappan and his brother Lewis, educated fourteen black students between 1832 and 1844. Oberlin had educated one hundred African American students by the 1860s.[21]

Abolitionists' commitment to black education brought many people into the antislavery movement at a young age. In Cincinnati white abolitionist students from Lane Seminary taught black students, mixing lessons in reading and writing with moral and antislavery messages. In Boston black choirs and youth groups, such as the Juvenile Garrison Independent Society, participated in abolitionist programs and conventions.[22] It was common for whole families to be involved in the public programs held by black communities to protest slavery and racial discrimination. Walker Lewis of Boston was a founding member of the Massachusetts General Colored Association and a close associate of David Walker. Lewis's father, Thomas Lewis, had helped found Boston's African Society, an organization that in the early nineteenth century provided aid to African Americans in need and protested against slavery.

Thomas Lewis also helped establish the African Masonic Lodge in Boston, where David Walker was a member during the 1820s. By the 1840s, when Simpson H. Lewis joined the Boston Committee of Vigilance to protect fugitive slaves, three generations of the Lewis family had been active in antislavery and civil rights efforts. Both men and women in the Snowden family were also active in antislavery activity. Samuel Snowden was elected as a counselor to the New England Anti-Slavery Society in 1833, his two sons were part of a group that armed itself against slave catchers, and his daughters were members of the Boston Vigilance Committee.[23]

Women were critical to the antislavery movement in many ways. They held the bazaars and fairs that raised money, providing a major source of financial contributions. Women organized many auxiliaries to male groups, but they also participated in the meetings of the major integrated antislavery associations and were especially active in the moral reform movement. The Female Moral Reform Society, an interracial organization formed in New York in 1834, had sixty-one chapters in New England alone by 1841, and its bimonthly magazine was supported by three thousand subscribers.[24]

The campaign against slavery in the United States created organizations and networks that connected cities and regions, transcended generational divides, crossed racial divisions, and brought men and women together in coordinated and shared efforts. The crossing of so many boundaries often resulted in strong differences of opinion regarding strategy, and it was on the issue of all-black organizations that the black national convention movement floundered in 1835. A strong Philadelphia faction, led by William Whipper, believed that separate organizations undermined arguments for racial integration in American society. Other delegates, especially those from New York, argued that exclusively black groups, in addition to integrated groups, were necessary to fully represent the interests and views of African Americans. The 1835 convention, dominated by the Philadelphia delegation, formed the American Moral Reform Society, and subsequent meetings became embroiled in debates over this issue. The most extreme position was taken by Whipper, Robert Purvis, and other Garrisonians from Philadelphia who objected to any reference to race and opposed the designation of "free people of color" as unwarranted exclusivity. After years of contention the American Moral Reform Society discontinued its meetings in 1841. Although many black activists may have understood the philosophical principle of the moral reformers, most believed their position to be unrealistic and impractical. Samuel Cornish excoriated them for engaging in trivial debates that distracted them from more important endeavors. "They are quarrelling about trifles," he said, "while their enemies are robbing them of diamonds and of gold."[25] Although willing to work with white reformers, most African Americans believed it was important to maintain black organizations in order to be free from the constraints of integrated groups and the subtle prejudice and discrimination they suffered in them. Integrated organizations were more likely to accept gradualist positions and counsel patience, and, given the strength of northern prejudice toward interracial association, there was a greater danger of mob attacks on integrated meetings and economic reprisals on participants.

There were also benefits to working in the integrated antislavery movement, however. Through these groups African Americans asserted their right to equal participation in the society in a concrete way. They also gave black activists access to far greater financial resources and a much wider audience, and white reformers were educated by their contact with blacks. Within the first year of organizing, the integrated American Anti-Slavery Society had forty-seven local societies in ten northern and western states.[26] Although Garrison himself came from a modest background, some prominent white abolitionists—Gerrit Smith and the Tappans of New York, and Wendell Phillips of Massachusetts, for example—were wealthy men who could lend their names, political connections, social networks, and economic resources to the cause. The Tappans underwrote the educational efforts at Oneida Institute, and Smith was the primary supporter of New York Central College. With the assistance of black abolitionists James McCune Smith and Charles B. Ray, Gerrit Smith purchased and distributed more than three thousand land titles for farms near Lake Placid in upstate New York to African Americans from eastern cities. This created thousands of qualified black voters able to meet New York State's property requirement.[27] These were urban workers, cooks, waiters, coachmen, and barbers, ill prepared for farming. The land was poor, either low and swampy or rocky mountain slopes, and the winters were harsh, but the settlers established farms, raised sheep, and initiated a wool trade with Canadian towns. Many of them voted in state and national elections.[28]

Perhaps the greatest contribution of integrated abolition was that it enabled African Americans to speak to sympathetic white audiences. The American Anti-Slavery Society and its supporters published flurries of pamphlets, sermons, and newspapers, but their most effective agents were antislavery speakers. They crisscrossed the North, made forays into the West, and spoke to large gatherings in major cities and more intimate meetings in small villages. Both blacks and whites, men and women, became antislavery speakers, enduring the hardships of long periods away from home. They lived on subsistence wages and the kindness of supporters, collected money for the cause, encouraged local chapters, and often suffered vilification from hecklers and attacks and brickbats from hostile mobs. The most popular speakers by the early 1840s were African Americans who had been slaves, many of whom were still fugitives. For many whites attending these lectures, it was the first time they had heard a black speaker.

The first full-time paid black traveling abolitionist speaker was free-born Charles Lenox Remond, who was employed by the Massachusetts society in 1838. Yet, the best-known black American abolitionist was an escaped slave hired by the American Anti-Slavery Society in 1841. Born Frederick Bailey, a slave, on Maryland's Eastern Shore in 1818, Frederick Douglass grew up on the plantation of Edward Lloyd, former governor of Maryland and U.S. senator. With a hunger for knowledge encouraged by his grandmother, Douglass seized every opportunity to learn to read and write. From his young white playmates being tutored by a teacher from New England, from his owner's sister-in-law, who tutored him directly, and through his own efforts, Douglass acquired the beginnings of the education that he continued to expand throughout his life. When, as a young man, he was hired out in Baltimore, his curiosity about the world turned to a determination to secure his own freedom. At twenty, in the late summer of 1838, with the help of a free black woman named Anna and carrying identification papers borrowed from a black sailor, Douglass escaped.[29]

Traveling through Philadelphia and continuing northward, Douglass made his way to the New York home of underground railroad activist David Ruggles, where later Anna joined him and they were married. The couple moved farther north, settling in New Bedford, Massachusetts, where Douglass worked as a dock laborer. He became a lay preacher in the African Methodist Episcopal Zion church and attended local antislavery meetings, at which he occasionally told the story of his own bondage.[30] In August 1841 he attended an antislavery convention on Nantucket Island. White abolitionist William C. Coffin had heard him speak to a small gathering in New Bedford and asked him to give his personal testimony to the Nantucket meeting. Douglass was nervous standing before the crowd, but soon his powerful story captured and greatly moved the audience. William Lloyd Garrison and the other prominent abolitionists were so impressed that they offered him a position as an antislavery agent for the Massachusetts Anti-Slavery Society. Late that fall Douglass, Anna, and their two children moved to Lynn, Massachusetts, a Quaker community near Boston that was believed to be safe for a fugitive. Over the next two years Douglass gave antislavery speeches in more than sixty towns in New England and became an accomplished speaker whose power to affect and inspire his audience had few equals.[31]

As abolitionists continued formal organizing, less structured, more spontaneous activity carried on in secret liberated thousands of slaves from bondage. The modern technology of the steam locomotive provided the language for this underground railroad. Its safe houses were called stations, its operators were called conductors, and the fugitives were called passengers. Its function became legendary, and whites as well as blacks participated. Although some of its work was directed and financed by formally organized abolitionist societies, underground railroad activity extended far beyond the formal organizations. Its varied actions included everything from raids on southern plantations to desperate bids for freedom by individual slaves. Fugitive settlements, maroon communities, and blacks allied with the Seminole Indians of Florida struck from the cover of swamps and protective wilderness at the plantations of Georgia and South Carolina. Fugitives moved south as well as north. In the regions of the Deep South or the Southwest, fugitives fled toward Mexico, which had abolished slavery by the mid-1820s, or westward into the frontier territories.

In the southern interior, fugitives might seek temporary safety in deep woods, swamps, or mountains. In the Upper South, the North was the logical favored destination. The mythology of the underground railroad has emphasized the efforts of northern white abolitionists, mainly Quakers. While their support was important, the underground railroad radiated out from the South in all directions, and escape was generally a slave initiative. The initial hours and the first few miles, before a runaway reached the relative safety of free territory or a protective community, were the most critical. Generally unfamiliar with areas outside the immediate proximity of the plantation, fugitives were at a great disadvantage, easy prey for pursuers with tracking dogs or local patrols that routinely stopped blacks unescorted by whites. In this early phase fugitives were dependent on other slaves, friends, and family to shelter, feed, and guide them on their way. Later, in southern towns or in the North, contact with the free black community became increasingly significant, and along with it an increased possibility for contact with organized underground railroad activity.

James Williams escaped slavery in Virginia, headed north, and finally reached Carlisle, Pennsylvania, where he found a number of free blacks. When he inquired about employment, they surmised that he was a runaway from the South. "They knew that I was from Virginia, by my pronunciation of certain words [and] that I was probably a runaway slave," he recounted. He confided in these people, placing his fate in their hands in part because they were black. Later Williams explained that he was informed "that I need not be alarmed as they were friends, and would do all in their power to protect me." They sheltered him and "treated [him] with the utmost kindness." He was taken by wagon to Harrisburg to meet others, and from there he was taken to Philadelphia. To this point Williams had been cared for by strangers concerned for his safety. Only in Philadelphia did he contact the formally organized underground railroad.[32]

The Philadelphia Vigilant Association, formed in 1837, specialized in assisting fugitives and maintained contacts throughout the North. Through its resources Williams traveled to New York. But apparently Williams's master was so determined that he be recaptured that he had employed slave catchers, who

William Still

William Still was the son of former slaves. His father freed himself by self-purchase, but his mother escaped from slavery in 1807. In doing so, she was forced to leave her two sons behind. Fourteen years later, William was born free in New Jersey. As an adult, Still, one of the nation's most important abolitionists, lived in Philadelphia. He operated an elaborate network of safe houses and conductors, as part of the most extensive underground railroad system in the country.

In a letter written on August 8, 1850, from his office in Philadelphia, William Still described an astounding encounter with a man who called himself Peter Freedman from Alabama. Freedman sought information about his family, who had come north some years before, and as his story progressed, Still recognized much of the detail. "My feelings were unutterable," he explained. "I could see in the face of my newfound brother, the likeness of my mother."[*] Peter Freedman was William's brother left in slavery when his mother escaped. The brothers had never met.

"I told him I could tell him all about his kinfolk," William recalled, and the next day Peter was reunited with the family. Their father was dead by this time, but Peter met five brothers and three sisters that he had never known. "I shall not attempt to describe the feelings of my mother and the family on learning the fact that Peter was one of us," William wrote.[†] Slavery, a central social and economic feature of the South and a legal and political fact of American life, regularly created these and other hardships for families.

This family's struggle was not over, however. When Peter left Alabama, he had left behind a wife and children whom he was determined to free. Members of the underground railroad secured their escape to Indiana, but they were recaptured and returned to slavery. When Peter attempted to purchase their freedom, their master demanded the almost impossible sum of five thousand dollars. With the assistance of many of William's abolitionist friends, Peter began a lecture tour, telling his story and that of his enslaved family in order to raise money

William Still, abolitionist and underground railroad operative in Philadelphia. Photographs and Prints Division, Schomburg Center for Research in Black Culture, The New York Public Library, Astor, Lenox, and Tilden Foundations.

(continued)

for their freedom. It took four additional years of fund raising for Peter to gather the money, but in October 1854 he accomplished his goal.

Once free, Peter Still and his family settled on a ten-acre farm in Burlington, New Jersey, where they lived until Peter died of pneumonia in 1868. WIlliam Still continued his underground railroad activities and worked for civil rights in Philadelphia throughout the Civil War. During and after the war, he raised funds to assist former slaves who had gained their freedom in the South. He also served on Philadelphia's Board of Trade and helped establish a Young Men's Christian Association (YMCA) for the city's blacks. He lived into the twentieth century, dying in 1901. Many descendants of the Still family continue to live in southern New Jersey, where they hold regular family reunions.

---

*"William Still to James Miller McKim," Philadelphia, August 8, 1850, in Peter C. Ripley, Roy E. Finkenbine, Michael F. Hembree, and Donald Yacovone, eds., *The Black Abolitionist Papers*, vol. 4 (Chapel Hill: University of North Carolina Press, 1991), 53–58.
†Ibid.

searched for the fugitive as far north as Boston. When they were seen in New York, the New York Committee of Vigilance arranged for Williams to be sent to England. By this time the fugitive was under the protection of the formal underground, with international connections.[33]

Such black abolitionists as Jacob C. White and William Still in Philadelphia, David Ruggles in New York, and Leonard Grimes and Lewis Hayden in Boston, major figures in underground activities, represent the range of personal experiences that people brought to this dangerous and demanding work. The White family was important to much of Philadelphia's black abolitionist action. Jacob was a wealthy businessman and longtime activist, and his wife, Elizabeth, was a member of the Female Vigilance Committee. Jacob operated a free-produce store (selling products grown by free workers) and led a boycott of cotton, sugar, rice, tobacco, and other products grown by slaves. Their son, Jacob C. White, Jr., later continued this work. David Ruggles was born free in Connecticut and came to New York City as a teenager. After working in several businesses, he became an agent for the antislavery newspaper, the *Emancipator*, and for the American Anti-Slavery Society. Later he opened a bookstore specializing in antislavery publications. When a proslavery mob burned his store in 1835, Ruggles became an officer of the New York Committee of Vigilance, the chief arm of the city's antislavery underground. Over the next five years he and his associates facilitated the escape of more than six hundred fugitives, poor health finally forcing him to limit his underground work.[34]

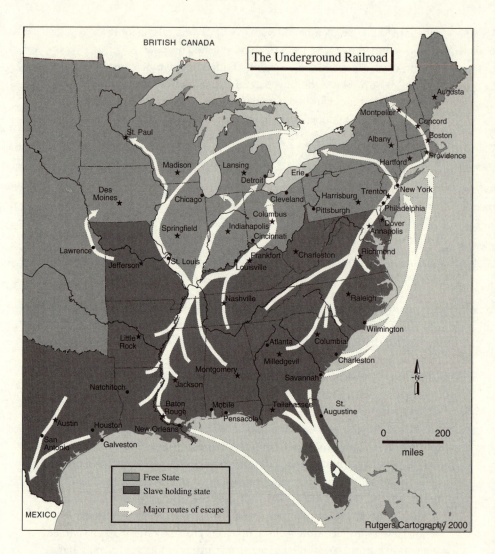

Leonard Andrew Grimes was born in northern Virginia in the small town of Leesburg in the early winter of 1815. He was free, and although his racially mixed heritage was readily apparent to many, he was light enough sometimes to be mistaken for a white person. As a young boy, he traveled to nearby Washington, D.C., where he worked first at a butcher shop and then for a druggist, before a slaveholder hired him to be a hack driver. In this employ, Grimes traveled through the South, where his observations led him to hate slavery and encouraged him to become active in the underground railroad. He saved his money and prospered in his business while using his wits, his money, and his horse-drawn hacks to assist fugitives to escape from bondage. After aiding one family that escaped to Canada from Virginia, Grimes was arrested in Richmond, found guilty of "stealing slaves," and sentenced to two years in prison. His prison term was hard on him both physically and emotionally, but after serving his time, he emerged, with his spirit intact and a powerful devotion to religion. He became a preacher and traveled north, settling first in New Bedford, where he ministered to a small congregation for two years. Then, in 1846, the Twelfth Baptist Church in Boston called Grimes to be its minister. From this pulpit he continued his abolitionist work, becoming a major leader of underground activity in the city. His church attracted so many runaways that it become known as the fugitive slave church.[35]

For most free blacks involvement in the underground railroad was a natural outcome of their personal relationships. Since nine of every ten African Americans were slaves, almost every free black person either had been a slave or had family members or friends in slavery. As one historian explained, "Practically every clump of Negro settlers in the free states was an underground depot by definition."[36] Fugitive slaves were some of those most directly involved in underground railroad activities, thereby risking their own recapture. Lewis Hayden was a fugitive from Kentucky who settled in Boston, opened a small clothing shop, and became active in antislavery and the underground. He often sheltered fugitives in his home and confronted slave catchers who attempted to capture people under his protection.[37] The story of Harriet Tubman, underground railroad conductor, is legendary. She was born into slavery on the Eastern Shore of Maryland, the property of one of the largest plantation owners in the region. At six years of age she was doing domestic work, and by her teens she worked full-time in the fields doing heavy labor. Her owner struck Harriet in the head while she was attempting to protect another slave from punishment. The blow left her severely injured, and thereafter she suffered short episodes of unconsciousness.

When her master died and it became clear that his slaves would be sold away from the area and possibly into the Deep South, she determined to escape. Failing to convince other slaves, even her own husband, to follow her, she set out alone and finally reached Philadelphia. There she found work as a domestic but soon determined to devote her life and the little money she was able to accumulate to freeing her family and other slaves. She was encouraged in this project by William Still, the leader of the underground railroad in Philadelphia. In late 1850 Tubman traveled to Baltimore on the first of many clandestine ventures into the South. This first trip was occasioned by word that her sister and her sister's two children were about to be sold and separated from their husband and father, a free black man on the Eastern Shore of Maryland. As the sale was about to commence, the husband broke into the room where the slaves were being held for auction, gathered up his

Harriet Tubman (*left*) and seven unidentified persons.

Photographs and Prints Division, Schomburg Center for Research in Black Culture,
The New York Public Library, Astor, Lenox, and Tilden Foundations.

family, and brought them to Baltimore, where Tubman waited to escort
them to freedom.

With forged papers and elaborate plans that included rescues on Saturday evening so as to delay the publication of advertisements for escaped slaves
until the Monday-morning newspapers, Tubman worked with free blacks and
white abolitionists. During the 1850s Tubman made at least twenty trips south
rescuing members of her family and other slaves, perhaps as many as three
hundred in all.[38] Although white abolitionists contributed much to the
movement, as white activist James G. Birney observed, "such matters [as direct
contact with and assistance of fugitives] are almost uniformly managed by the
colored people, I know nothing of them generally till they are past." Birney
understated the role of white reformers, but it was true, nevertheless, as
Cincinnati Quaker Levi Coffin remembered, that "fugitives often passed
through [town] generally stopping among the colored people."[39]

Even so, at its most organized levels the underground railroad was very
much an interracial enterprise. It was most formally organized and most interracial in the North, where the law and local sentiment were less hostile
toward antislavery activity, but some antislavery whites were willing to go
South, risking their freedom, even their lives, to assist fugitives. Calvin Fairbank and Delia Webster, students at Oberlin College, were arrested and jailed
for assisting fugitives (one of whom was Lewis Hayden) to escape from Ken-

tucky. Many of these fugitives worked to win their release, but Fairbank became so notorious for his actions that Kentucky finally sentenced him to fifteen years in prison, where he was tortured unmercifully.[40]

Jonathan Walker, a New England sea captain, was apprehended by authorities off the Florida coast in the summer of 1844 with fugitives whom he was attempting to transport to freedom in the Bahamas. His ship was captured, and he was arrested and taken to Pensacola. He was jailed, fined, whipped, and branded with a double S for "slave stealer." After seven months several of his friends, including a number of free blacks, secured his release from prison. Frederick Douglass praised Walker's actions, saying that abolitionists would make the double *S* a symbol for "slave-savior."[41]

Fugitives often sought the assistance of seamen who they thought were particularly willing to provide aid. With cosmopolitan knowledge and access to the means of long-distance travel, sailors could provide a fugitive with valuable services. After Frederick Douglass escaped slavery in Baltimore with false seaman's papers, another sailor in New York City facilitated his contact with the vigilance committee. The culture of seagoing men often encouraged defiance of shoreside social, legal, and even racial conventions. Perhaps it is too much to say that "there seemed to have been an entire absence of prejudice against the blacks as shipmates among the crew," as one nineteenth-century observer claimed, but historian William Jeffrey Bolster has documented the interracial comradeship on shipboard and the willingness of sailors, black and white, to assist fugitives. In the South sailors were always regarded with suspicion. One southern newspaper asserted that sailors actually kidnapped slaves who might otherwise be unwilling to leave the South.[42]

Seamen and riverboatmen were also crucial to the underground communication network that kept free blacks in the North in touch with friends and relatives in the slave South. In their regular trips up and down the Mississippi River or the Atlantic coast, these men often carried personal messages and antislavery literature and provided information to southern free blacks and slaves, breaking the isolation of southern society. Information about routes of travel, underground contacts in northern communities, and antislavery activities buoyed those held in bondage and helped to make escape a realistic aim.[43]

This communication network facilitated personal interaction on either side of the cotton curtain. When Henry Williams escaped from slavery in Louisiana during the 1830s, he left his wife behind. He settled in Cincinnati, where he was able to secure work and establish a new life in freedom. After several years Williams met and married a woman from a neighboring town. Members of his church who considered him already married were outraged. The congregation charged Williams with bigamy, and he was accused of having deserted his wife in slavery. The church demanded a signed release from her before it would sanction the new marriage. This posed a difficult and

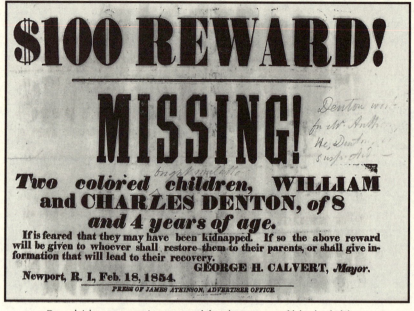

Broadside announcing reward for the return of black children
kidnapped and feared sold into slavery.
Graphics Division, Rhode Island Historical Society.

dangerous situation for an escaped slave, who might face reenslavement if he
returned to the South. The underground communication network provided
the answer to Williams's dilemma. He sent a message to his first wife by way
of a boatman who regularly traveled to southern port cities on the Mississippi
River. The boatman obtained her *X* and her enthusiastic expression of support for dissolving the marriage. The church was satisfied and recognized
Williams's new marriage.[44]

In addition to organized groups and extensive communication networks,
the underground railroad was sometimes specific, sometimes isolated, acts of
conscience that transcended political philosophy. The chief justice of the Ohio
Supreme Court, Joseph R. Swan, in his legal opinion supporting the constitutionality of the 1850 Fugitive Slave Law, explained, "As a citizen I would
not deliberately violate the Constitution or the law." Yet, if confronted by a
slave pleading for protection, the chief justice admitted, "I might momentarily
forget my allegiance to the law and the Constitution and give him covert [*sic*]
from those who were on his track."[45]

For African Americans the fight against slavery was both personal and
philosophical. It was about the liberty promised by the Revolution and the
Declaration of Independence, and the freedom denied to family and friends
bound in slavery. It was also about defending black people from an institu-

tion that by its very existence threatened the human rights of all African Americans. Resistance to slavery not only included overt physical confrontation with masters and overseers but also meant defeating slavery's attempt to control its victims and to hold them in debilitating isolation. The underground communication network was as much a part of antislavery activity as the underground railroad or formal abolitionist protest. In both formal and informal ways, blacks, often joined by progressive whites, engaged in a long-term agitation against slavery.

A call for a meeting in Buffalo, New York, in 1843 to reconvene the black national convention sparked a great deal of debate among black leaders. Their philosophical differences had become more public, their disagreements over strategy more strident, and meeting in New York State signaled a change that was partly generational, partly a reflection of changing political and social circumstances. All but one of the previous meetings had been held in Philadelphia, which, like Boston, was a stronghold of Garrisonian opinion. Many blacks had grown impatient with the tools of moral suasion, nonparticipation in politics, and nonviolence that had been so influential in the previous decade. Pacifism had always been a controversial philosophy among blacks. Many of their most loyal allies, including Quakers and William Lloyd Garrison, were pacifists, but few African Americans were committed to this belief. In 1837 a meeting of New York blacks had challenged the theory of nonviolence as impractical for "persons who are denied the protection of equitable law, and when their liberty is invaded and their lives endangered by avaricious kidnappers."[46] Samuel Cornish, editor of New York's *Colored American*, confessed that when faced with kidnappers or "a midnight incendiary with a lighted torch in his hand" he had trouble believing in the virtue of "using moral weapons."[47]

From the start it was clear that nonviolence would be a major point of contention at the 1843 meeting. Fearing acrimonious debate and conclusions they could not support, the Philadelphians opted not to attend. Samuel Davis of Buffalo, chair of the convention, opened the meeting by urging blacks not to wait for others to act on their behalf. Citing uprisings in Greece and Poland as illustrations of the need to strike for liberty, he asserted that "if we are not willing to rise up and assert our rightful claims, and plead our own cause, we have no reason to look for success."[48] On the second day Henry Highland Garnet took the podium and delivered a rousing speech, one of the most militant calls for slave uprisings since David Walker's *Appeal*. He argued that patience should be no virtue for black people and proposed a resolution urging African Americans to wait no longer for freedom and justice. The time for action had come, he declared, and for free blacks this meant the use of violence if necessary to defend their rights, their families, and the freedom of those who had been illegitimately held in bondage. For slaves this might mean open rebellion to secure freedom. "You cannot suffer greater cruelties than you have already. Rather die freemen," he urged, "than live to be slaves."[49]

Other New Yorkers echoed Garnet's sentiments and supported his call to action, but the Boston delegates and other Garrisonians dissented. Frederick Douglass and Charles Lenox Remond pointed out that openly encouraging slave rebellions provided an excuse for proslavery retaliation against both slaves and free blacks. They argued that it was reckless to jeopardize the entire abolitionist movement with such calls. Other delegates made counter-arguments, sentiment was closely divided, and the resolution failed by just one vote.[50]

A second issue—the wisdom of black involvement in partisan politics— also sharply divided black opinion. Garrison urged abolitionists not to participate in politics, arguing that party politics required compromises that would dilute antislavery principles and voting expressed tacit approval for the constitutional system that sanctioned slavery. Nevertheless many black abolitionists voted, and African Americans were powerful advocates for political reform even in states that prohibited black voting. In New York State the fact that there were property requirements for black voters but not for white voters made some African Americans more determined to participate in politics, if only to challenge this law.

In 1839 abolitionists from western New York had organized the Liberty Party, and antislavery hopes for political power were raised when the new party ran antislavery men for state and national offices. The Liberty Party nominated a former Kentucky slaveholder turned Ohio abolitionist, James G. Birney, for the presidency and attracted considerable black support. The *Colored American* endorsed the party's national slate, calling Birney "a better man in every possible respect to be President of the United States" than the current Democratic president Martin Van Buren or Whig candidate William Henry Harrison.[51] Black delegates attended the party's convention in 1840, but black support was equivocal. At the 1840 New York State convention of African Americans, a resolution endorsing the party was hotly debated before it was finally withdrawn.[52] Though strongly opposed to slavery, the Liberty Party attempted to broaden its appeal beyond antislavery circles by linking the evil of slavery with the injustice of poverty. "Pity not only the enslaved poor and the colored poor, but all poor," urged a broadside advertising its meeting in Peterboro, New York, in 1846.[53] Though some remained wary of any political party's ability to remain ardently antislavery, black support for the Liberty Party was substantial throughout the 1840s. Several blacks traveled the campaign circuit, combining stories of their slave experience with a partisan political message. In 1844 the minister and former slave Jermain Wesley Loguen agreed to merge fund-raising efforts for his church in Bath, New York, with tours on behalf of the Liberty Party. One contemporary recalled the effectiveness of Loguen's presentation in the small town of Cortland, maintaining that "no prayer ever made . . . melted the people like that." Liberty Party officials did remain committed to broadening the black franchise, not incidentally, increasing the number of their potential supporters. After his unsuccessful 1840 presidential candidacy, Birney wrote to Lewis Tappan suggesting a petition campaign to secure equal suffrage for blacks in New York State.[54] This was the context for abolitionist Gerrit Smith's distribution of farmland in upstate New York to black families, allowing more blacks to meet the property requirement for voting.[55]

The establishment of the Liberty Party seemed to many to indicate the growing power of the antislavery movement, but there were also ominous indications that slavery was expanding its territory and its power. In 1836 prominent slaveholders in northern Mexico rebelled against their government's restrictions on slavery and established the independent republic of Texas. In 1845 the United States annexed Texas as a slaveholding territory with the prospect of statehood. In his address to the Buffalo convention in 1843, Henry Garnet had anticipated just such an expansion of slaveholder influence, warning of the "propagators of American slavery spending their blood and treasure, that they may plant the black flag in the heart of Mexico and riot in the halls of Montezuma."[56] When President James K. Polk asked Congress to declare war against Mexico in 1846, Boston blacks denounced "any war which may be occasioned by the annexation of Texas, or . . . any other war . . . designed to strengthen or perpetuate slavery."[57] Douglass scolded Massachusetts, "the brightest of every other state," for becoming "the tool of Texas" when it offered men to fight and die in the unjust war, a war he saw as a hypocritical ruse to rob Mexico.[58] African Americans were alarmed that the slave power seemed strong enough to push the federal government into a proslavery war.

Meanwhile blacks in the late 1840s in northern cities worried about the wave of immigration that increased job competition among those at the bottom of the economic ladder. Economic competition threatened to create racial violence and provided potential converts for the antiabolitionist Democratic Party. As national political parties took up contentious issues directly related to the antislavery cause, and members of black communities felt under increasing political and economic attack, black abolitionists debated the most expeditious course of action. There were many disagreements over specific strategies, but all agreed that their responsibility to those still suffering under slavery and to those growing up in the limited northern freedom demanded their steadfast commitment to racial justice.

Chapter 7

1850 Congress passes major compromise legislation containing harsher federal Fugitive Slave Law, admitting California as a free state and outlawing the slave trade in the District of Columbia

1851 Mary Ann Shadd Cary publishes the newspaper *Provincial Freeman* in Ontario, Canada

1852 Harriet Beecher Stowe publishes *Uncle Tom's Cabin*

1854 Congress passes the Kansas-Nebraska Act; armed conflict erupts over the slave or free status of the future state of Kansas

African American singer Elizabeth Greenfield gives a command performance before Queen Victoria

Fugitive Anthony Burns is returned to slavery from Boston

Republican Party formed

1855 William C. Nell publishes *The Colored Patriots of the American Revolution*

1857 In the case of *Dred Scott* v. *Sanford,* the Supreme Court upholds the right of slavery to expand into the territories, refuses to free Scott, and denies black people the right to U.S. citizenship

1858 Senatorial election debates between Abraham Lincoln and Stephen A. Douglas in Illinois; Douglas wins election

1859 John Brown leads thirteen whites and five blacks in an abortive raid on Harpers Ferry, Virginia

1860 Abraham Lincoln elected president

U.S. population 31,443,790; black population 4,441,830 (14 percent)

1861–1865 Civil War; more than 180,000 African Americans serve in combat roles and 200,000 as support troops; twenty-four receive Congressional Medal of Honor

1862 Compensated emancipation pays slave owners for freeing their slaves in the District of Columbia

1863 Abraham Lincoln issues the Emancipation Proclamation

From Militancy to Civil War

B y the 1847 national black convention, debates were more pessimistic, more militant, and even more bellicose. Educate your sons in the "art of war," urged one resolution. Calls for patience and faith in rational debate were replaced by arguments favoring the use of violence to discourage slaveholding and the kidnapping of free blacks. The next year in Cleveland, the convention passed resolutions advocating women's rights and the right of violent self-defense. The delegates supported speakers who urged that additional committees of vigilance be formed "to measure arms with assailants without and invaders within."[1] Ohio blacks reinforced that message in 1849 when their meeting urged "the slave [to] leave [the plantation] immediately with his hoe on his shoulder" and made plans to publish five hundred copies of a volume pairing Walker's *Appeal* with Garnet's 1843 address.[2] Even Frederick Douglass, previously opposed to violence in the antislavery cause, could see justice in slaves' killing slaveholders. In the winter of 1849 Douglass asked, "Who dare say that the criminals deserve less than death at the hands of their long-abused chattels?"[3]

Events during the 1850s confirmed blacks' growing conviction that the federal government was unlikely to support the cause of freedom. The U.S. victory over Mexico brought large tracts of land under federal authority, again raising the inflammatory question of whether the new lands would be open to slavery. This issue had broad political consequences, since the common wisdom among northern white working men was that their labor was cheapened and their opportunities severely limited in regions that tolerated slavery. Although most white workers would not disturb slavery in the South, they were strongly opposed to allowing slavery in the western territories, fearing it would deprive white working people of access to the new lands that were the core of the American future. White southerners agreed that the nation's future lay in the western territories but asserted their right to bring slavery, an institution basic to their way of life, into that future. To forestall a clash between regions, Kentucky representative Henry Clay engineered a political compromise in Congress. California would be admitted as a free state, but the other southwestern territories taken from Mexico would be organized without a decision on slavery. For the antislavery forces the compromise promised the abolition of the slave trade in the nation's capital. For proslavery interests, the compromise offered the strictest fugitive slave law ever enacted, far stronger than the 1793 provision. This measure was so harsh that even President Millard Fillmore, who signed it into law in the fall of 1850, questioned its constitutionality.[4]

The Fugitive Slave Law of 1850 infuriated African Americans, who considered it definitive evidence that proslavery forces had taken over the federal government. This new law made it easier for slaveholders to retrieve runaways who sought asylum in the North. They were not even required to bring accused fugitives before a court but could take possession of their human property simply by presenting an affidavit drawn up by a southern court, with a physical description of the runaway, to any federal commissioner. Further, any bystander who refused to help recover a fugitive could be fined one thousand dollars and sentenced to up to six months in jail. This law not only struck down northern states' personal liberty laws, which prohibited the use of local and state officials or facilities in the capture of fugitives, but it even threatened the freedom of blacks who were legally free. Since alleged fugitives could not speak in their own defense, free blacks could more easily be kidnapped into slavery. Thus, even where abolitionists were strongest, no African American was beyond the reach of the slave power.[5]

Free blacks immediately swore to defy the new federal law. Meeting in Chicago only a few days after its passage, African Americans strongly denounced it. The city council in Chicago called it unconstitutional, deemed its supporters traitors, and refused to order city police to enforce it.[6] At Boston's Faneuil Hall abolitionists vowed that no fugitive would be taken from that city, and Frederick Douglass asserted that the streets "would be running red with blood" before the law could be enforced in Boston.[7] Pittsburgh blacks, stating their intention to make the recovery of fugitives in that city a costly proposition, bought one store's entire inventory of handguns and knives.[8] In Cazenovia, a town in the middle of New York State, abolitionists and fugitive slaves met defiantly in a "Fugitive Slave Convention" and called for slave rebellion. Anticipating a confrontation, leaders in Ohio and Massachusetts called for the formation of black military companies to be ready to take up arms against slavery.[9]

Despite such strong reactions, the federal government, prodded by southern political pressure, was determined to enforce the law. James Hamlet, who was arrested in New York City and taken to Baltimore, had the dubious distinction of being the first to be returned to slavery under its provisions. The New York abolitionists, who had been unable to prevent his capture, collected the eight hundred dollars demanded by Hamlet's master, bought his freedom, and returned him to the city. Others were not so fortunate and were returned to slavery from northern cities during the early 1850s. Many, even those who had lived in the North for several years, fled to Canada. Commu-

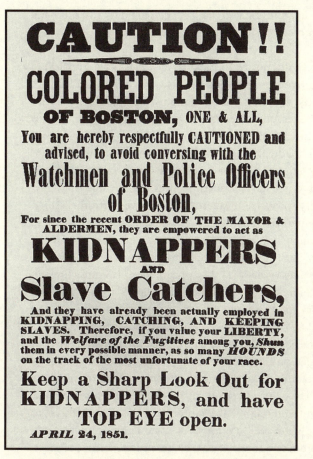

CAUTION!!

COLORED PEOPLE

OF BOSTON, ONE & ALL,

You are hereby respectfully CAUTIONED and advised, to avoid conversing with the

Watchmen and Police Officers of Boston,

For since the recent ORDER OF THE MAYOR & ALDERMEN, they are empowered to act as

KIDNAPPERS

AND

Slave Catchers,

And they have already been actually employed in KIDNAPPING, CATCHING, AND KEEPING SLAVES. Therefore, if you value your LIBERTY, and the *Welfare of the Fugitives* among you, *Shun* them in every possible manner, as so many *HOUNDS* on the track of the most unfortunate of your race.

Keep a Sharp Look Out for KIDNAPPERS, and have TOP EYE open.

APRIL 24, 1851.

Broadside warning of the presence of slave catchers in Boston.

Photographs and Prints Division, Library of Congress, Washington, D.C.

nities closest to the South felt this emigration most acutely. According to contemporary accounts, small towns in southern Pennsylvania were "almost deserted of black fellows, since they have heard of the new law. It is supposed that more than a hundred have left for Canada and other parts." The black population of Columbia, Pennsylvania, decreased by more than half in a matter of months.[10] One observer in Pittsburgh reported that "nearly all the waiters in the hotels have fled to Canada." According to his tally, "Sunday 30 fled; on Monday 40; on Tuesday 50; on Wednesday 30 and up to this time the number that has left will not fall short of 300."[11] Fugitive or free, blacks not well known in their local communities were especially vulnerable to capture or kidnapping.[12] Things were not much better farther north—in Buffalo one black church lost 130 members of its congregation, Rochester's black Baptist church lost 114 members, and Boston's Twelfth Baptist Church and Albany, New York's, Hamilton Street Church each lost one-third of its members to Canadian migration.[13] Shortly after the fugitive slave provision was signed into law, the

Anti-Slavery Society of Canada estimated that between four and five thousand African Americans had crossed the Canadian border, and many of them were free blacks.[14]

Most blacks, however, did not go to Canada. Free blacks were critical in the fight against the Fugitive Slave Law, and the historical record is filled with their defiance of authority, as they endangered themselves and their property in attempts to prevent the recapture of fugitives. Before the passage of the new law, William Craft and his wife, Ellen, had escaped slavery in Georgia. They had made their way to Philadelphia and then to Boston, using an ingenious disguise, with the light-complexioned Ellen posing as an ill young white man and the darker William as her slave attendant. After their escape they traveled widely as antislavery speakers, mesmerizing audiences with their story. While in Boston, the couple stayed with Lewis Hayden, the escaped slave and active abolitionist. Though one of the best-known centers of antislavery activity in the country, Boston was not beyond slavery's reach. In early November 1850 the *Liberator* warned of "the appearance of two prowling villains . . . from Macon, Georgia, for the purpose of seizing William and Ellen Craft, under the infernal Fugitive Slave Bill, and carrying them back to the hell of Slavery."[15]

Abolitionist pressure led to the temporary arrest of the slave hunters, but eventually they descended on Hayden's home intending to recover the fugitives. Hayden confronted the slave hunters on the front porch of his house where he had placed barrels of explosives. He made clear his intention to blow up the house and anyone who might enter rather than allow the fugitives to be taken back to slavery. Meanwhile a number of Boston's blacks met to consider their course of action, and it was the overwhelming sense of the meeting that the fugitives would not be taken without a fight. Yet, realizing it was only a matter of time before the federal government would prevail even in Boston, abolitionists raised funds to send the Crafts to England, where they were taken in by British abolitionists and remained safe from capture.[16]

In Springfield, Massachusetts, John Brown, a deeply religious—some said fanatical—white activist, organized the U.S. League of the Gileadites. This group of black men and women armed themselves and intended to act as a guerrilla force to defend fugitives and attack slavery. Defiant abolitionist action spread across the North, but federal officials grew more determined as resistance increased. When an integrated group of abolitionists successfully rescued a fugitive named Shadrach Minkins from a Boston courtroom, President Filmore ordered the prosecution of the rescuers. Eight Bostonians, four blacks and four whites, were arrested, but none was convicted. In Syracuse, New York, in a case that became known as the Jerry Rescue, William ("Jerry") McHenry, a fugitive from Missouri, was arrested, but abolitionists rescued him from authorities and delivered him to Canada.[17]

Resistance in many northern cities made enforcing the Fugitive Slave Law costly. In New York City two hundred policemen were required to guard a single chained fugitive and return him to slavery. An attempt to recapture a fugitive in Christiana, Pennsylvania, resulted in the "Battle of Christiana," which left one slaveholder dead and another injured.[18] The failed rescue of Anthony Burns, a fugitive from Virginia, in Boston in 1854 was one of the most dramatic and costly actions. Attempting to free Burns, several hundred abolitionists armed with stones, ax handles, guns, and knives attacked a federal courthouse and murdered a U.S. deputy marshal, and it took two military companies to quell the riot. Thousands of antislavery supporters came from the surrounding area to witness Burns's trial and return to slavery, proceedings that required more than two thousand police and military troops and cost the federal government one hundred thousand dollars.[19]

One attempt to recapture fugitives in Ohio was especially tragic. Margaret Garner was one of a group of seventeen fugitives from Kentucky, including her husband, her four children, and her husband's parents, who found sanctuary in Cincinnati in January 1856. Underground Railroad operatives were able to send nine of the fugitives on to Canada, but Garner and her family remained in Cincinnati while a relative attempted to arrange their passage. Before this could be accomplished, however, Kentucky slave hunters arrived, secured the assistance of the U.S. marshal, and surrounded the house where the fugitives had taken shelter. Although Garner's husband attempted to protect his family by firing on the slave hunters, capture seemed inevitable. Desperately determined not to allow herself and her children to be taken back into slavery, Garner killed her three-year-old, cutting her throat with a kitchen knife. Before her relatives could stop her, she had also severely injured two of her other children. Questioned later, Garner said that she had intended to kill all of her children and herself. "God did not appear to save us," she recounted calmly. "I did the best I could." Although state authorities indicted Garner for murder, federal law prevailed, and the court upheld the slaveholder's right to the return of his human property.[20]

The legal arguments of abolitionists, including Ohio governor Salmon P. Chase, could not prevent the fugitives' return to slavery. They were taken first to Kentucky, and then while en route farther south, their ship was involved in an accident. Garner and one of her remaining children fell overboard into the river; she was saved, but the child drowned. This final tragedy in the Garner case further inflamed northern opinion against the Fugitive Slave Law. The Ohio legislature, calling the law unconstitutional, ordered state officials to remove fugitives from the custody of federal authorities upon the state's issuance of a writ of habeas corpus.[21]

Attempts to enforce the Fugitive Slave Law heightened African American resistance, strengthened abolitionist resolve, and seemed to increase northern

Margaret Garner

In 1987 black writer Toni Morrison took the literary world by storm with a wrenching and haunting novel. *Beloved* was the story of Sethe, a fugitive slave woman who killed her baby rather than allow the child to grow up under slavery. The novel and the movie made from it were loosely based on an actual incident in 1856. Margaret Garner, her husband, their four children, and her in-laws escaped from slavery in Kentucky. It was winter, and they walked across the frozen Ohio River to the free state of Ohio. There they joined nine other fugitives from Kentucky and made their way to Cincinnati. Within sight of slaves across the river, Cincinnati was a virtual magnet for runaways. They were drawn there and to other towns on the north side of the river by the hope of safety within a free black community and aid from abolitionists. Nevertheless slave catchers trapped Garner and her children, but before they could seize her, she cut her baby girl's throat. Had she had time, Garner later said, she would have killed all of her children and herself. The prospective return of her children to slavery was too much for her to bear. The best efforts of Cincinnati abolitionists could not prevent her being returned to the South. Still, Garner was determined that she and her children would not be reenslaved. On a ship bound for their sale in the Deep South, she threw one child overboard and leaped in herself. Sailors pulled Garner from the water still alive, but the child drowned. Eventually she was sold in a New Orleans slave market.

One can hardly imagine a slavery so horrible that a mother would kill her children to save them from it. Defenders of slavery often claimed that slaves were contented. They contended that masters were benevolent, and they romanticized the master-slave relationship. The power of Margaret Garner's tragic story was not lost on the abolitionists. They told it again and again as heartbreaking proof of the inhumanity of slavery and the incredible lengths to which some would go to free themselves and those they loved from its grip.

Margaret Garner, escaped slave, killed her child rather than submit her children to slavery. Photographs and Prints Division, Library of Congress, Washington, D.C.

opposition to the inhumanity of keeping human beings in bondage. Highly publicized fugitive slave cases gave human form to what previously had been abstractions in the minds of many white northerners. Seeing some of these people returned to slavery evoked the sympathy of many formerly apathetic people, and the tragedies attending the enforcement of federal law galvanized the abolition movement. Harriet Beecher Stowe was a writer from a northern white abolitionist family whose sister urged her to use her literary talent to combat the Fugitive Slave Law. Stowe's 1852 novel *Uncle Tom's Cabin* caught the imagination and stirred the emotions of northern readers. Her melodramatic depiction of the plight of the fugitive and the horrors of slavery became the single most influential piece of antislavery literature in the century. Its authenticity was bolstered by consultation with people who had actually experienced slavery. Prominent among them was Frederick Douglass, whom Stowe admired and with whom she developed a close friendship. Douglass was effusive in his praise of Stowe's intelligence, philosophy, and character, and he called her novel *"the master book* of the nineteenth century."[22]

The moral discomfort the book caused in the North was not strong enough to unite northern whites in the antislavery cause. It and the Fugitive Slave Law did, however, convince many northerners that the expansion of slave power posed a threat to the civil rights of *all* Americans. *Uncle Tom's Cabin* sold out its first printing of five thousand copies in the first two days and sold three hundred thousand copies in the United States and two hundred thousand in England during the first year.[23] *The Times* of London reported on its wild popularity among the British. Lord Palmerston, who became British prime minister during the 1860s, claimed to have read the entire book three times, the only novel he had read in thirty years. This book's impact was so powerful that it influenced British authorities to keep the Canadian border open to people fleeing from slavery. Partly because of Stowe's novel and partly in response to the fugitive slave cases, many northerners who had supported slaveholders' property rights were forced to confront the morality of their position.

The novel was widely read even in the South. In Charleston, South Carolina, the stores could not keep it on their shelves, but reaction was decidedly negative. "I would have the review as hot as hellfire, blasting and searing the reputation of the vile wretch in petticoats who could write such a volume," the editor of the *Southern Literary Messenger* wrote to instruct his reviewer. In the two years after the publication of *Uncle Tom's Cabin,* southern authors wrote at least fifteen novels whose premise was that slavery was more benevolent than Stowe's depiction. Many argued that slavery compared favorably to the conditions of free labor in the North. Clearly Stowe's novel accentuated the growing rift between North and South, and it led President

Lincoln a decade later to address Stowe as "the little lady who wrote the book that made this great war."[24]

By the 1850s most of the South had become a closed society—a police state that barred dissent—where concurrence with slavery was the price of social acceptance and individual safety. Slavery was claimed to be a superior, more progressive, more humane system than free labor.[25] The abolitionist arguments that the South was controlled by proslavery forces bent on shaping national policies to their needs was made more credible by southern reactions to the rise of the antislavery movement in the North. White northern anxiety strengthened with each southern attempt to block the delivery of the U.S. mail for fear that it carried antislavery literature. Each act of violence meant to prohibit the public expression of antislavery ideas, and each reward for killing antislavery leaders offered or sanctioned by southern legislators, heightened northerners' concerns about their own rights. By the middle of the nineteenth century, northern support for the antislavery cause had broadened to include those "likely to be more concerned for the welfare of white men than they were for the rights of free black men and slaves."[26]

Sectional disputes erupted in violence as Congress began to organize the Kansas and Nebraska territories. Although the Missouri Compromise of 1820 had prohibited slavery in the territories held by the federal government north of the state of Missouri, the question was opened again in the 1850s. The discovery of gold in California in 1848 had spurred the desire for constructing a transcontinental railroad to the West Coast. When the U.S. Senate began to organize the territories in preparation for this construction, an agreement was struck between southern Democrats and the chair of the Committee on Territories, Illinois senator Stephen A. Douglas. In return for the southerners' support for a railroad route through Chicago in his home state, Douglas's bill left the issue of slavery's existence in the territories to the settlers, effectively rescinding the Missouri Compromise. The bill outraged African Americans. Many gathered in Philadelphia to denounce it, and all over the North abolitionists condemned Senator Douglas as a "sectional traitor." Angry antislavery supporters burned Douglas in effigy, and when he tried to explain the bill to a Chicago audience, he was hooted down. The Kansas-Nebraska Act was signed into law in the spring of 1854, and *Frederick Douglass' Paper* lamented the triumph of "the audacious villainy of the slave power" over "the most explicit and public pledges of both the great parties."[27]

The popular-sovereignty provision of the Kansas-Nebraska Act set the stage for a confrontation between antislavery and proslavery forces who rushed to settle Kansas. Planters sponsored proslavery emigrants from Missouri, who flooded into Kansas and were confronted by Free-Soilers from New England and New York. Frederick Douglass proposed raising funds to encourage black emigration to Kansas, but scarce resources discouraged such efforts. A large black migration would have been an especially risky project, since black settlers in the territory were often in mortal danger from proslavery forces. Free-Soil whites who took up residence in Kansas ultimately did battle with "border ruffians" from Missouri in bitter unrestrained conflicts that earned the territory the name "Bleeding Kansas." In 1856 warring forces killed some two hundred people. Despite his shocking execution of five proslavery men at Pottawatomie Creek, white abolitionist John Brown became a heroic figure in some antislavery circles for his battles against supporters of slavery.[28]

At the same time, in February 1854, a diverse group of abolitionists, Liberty Party people, Free-Soilers, and disaffected Whigs formed a new political party. They were joined by some northern Democrats appalled at the growing influence of southern planters within the Democratic Party. Within two years, this new Republican Party ran John C. Frémont as its first presidential candidate. Mainstream Republicans sought to keep the western territories free from slavery, and the party's slogan, "Free Labor, Free Soil, Free Men," was attractive to both African Americans and to land-hungry white workers. Yet the Republican plan was for slavery's containment within the borders of the South, not for its abolition. Especially troubling was the link between this Free-Soil stand and the philosophy of white supremacy, as Frederick Douglass noted in his 1856 essay, "The Unholy Alliance of Negro Hate and Anti-slavery."[29]

The pervasiveness of racism encouraged Republicans to filter their message through appeals to white racial chauvinism. Many of those attracted to the new party were also those who packed audiences in blackface minstrel shows. In these immensely popular performances by white men such as T. D. Rice, Dan Emmett, and Dan Bryant, working-class northern whites could measure their self-worth against caricatured degraded images of black people. Before the Civil War these performances by white actors who darkened their faces to assume stereotypical black styles became the embodiment of white ambivalence toward the interracial American culture. Many whites were attracted to black music, dance, and humor but feared and disdained black people. Appealing to this constituency while maintaining an antislavery stance was no simple proposition.[30] Thus the platform of the Republican convention in 1856 committed the party to freedom in Kansas but was silent on other issues of interest to African Americans, such as the Fugitive Slave Law, slavery in the District of Columbia, the interstate slave trade, and the abolition of slavery.

Most African Americans were more inclined to support the Liberty Party. It stood for abolition and civil rights for blacks, included several prominent African Americans in its leadership, and by 1855 was considering changing its name to the Radical Abolition Party. But the Liberty Party had no chance of electing candidates to office. The Republican Party was not an antislavery party, but it might at least be successful in limiting slavery's spread and curbing its power. Given the practical political choice between Republicans and Democrats, the "avowed supporters of the enslavement of [the] race," there really was no choice.[31] In Boston, African Americans, including Garrisonians, resolved to give Frémont their qualified support. As one speaker made clear, "We do not pledge ourselves to go further with the Republicans than the Republicans will go with us."[32] Before the November elections black meetings in Brooklyn, New York; throughout New York State; and in Ohio and Pennsylvania endorsed the Republican Party and its candidate, but their ambivalence was apparent. As one delegate from New York put it, "[W]e do not for a single moment endorse all the political tenets of that party."[33]

Even qualified political support from African Americans was a mixed blessing for the Republicans, and they came under harsh criticism from their opponents. Blacks, on the other hand, were encouraged when the Democrats attacked the party as "Black Republicans" and accused it of favoring radical abolitionists and race mixing. Republican candidates made a respectable showing in the election of 1856. Frémont lost to the Democratic presidential candidate, James Buchanan, by fewer than one-half million votes out of a total of four million cast.[34] Frederick Douglass took hope from these results. "We have turned Whigs and Democrats into Republicans," he wrote to abolitionist Gerrit Smith; "we can turn Republicans into Abolitionists."[35] Others, less optimistic about political change, concluded that "the peaceful annihilation of slavery [was] hopeless" and that the slaveholder's "execution only waits the finish of the training of his executioners."[36]

A Supreme Court case in the fall of 1857 made it even more difficult for African Americans to be optimistic about ending slavery and about their future. After a series of decisions and reversals in lower courts, a case involving a Virginia-born slave named Dred Scott reached the high court. Scott brought suit against his master, demanding freedom on the basis of their having lived in the free territories of Wisconsin and Illinois for a number of years. Scott had originally brought his case in Missouri, where other slaves had been successful in similar actions, but after winning his case initially, he lost on appeal, and the case moved to the Supreme Court. In his opinion in this case, southern-born Chief Justice Roger B. Taney went far beyond the simple decision. Taney declared that Congress had no authority to exclude slavery from the territories, essentially striking down the central plank in the Republican platform and finishing off the Missouri Compromise. Further, he stunned African Americans by attacking them directly, declaring that they were not and could not be American citizens and thus had no rights guaranteed under the U.S. Constitution—or, as Taney put it, "no rights which the white man was bound to respect."[37]

The Department of State, under Secretary Lewis Cass of Michigan, responded quickly and denied passports to blacks, a change in policy despite the department's insistence to the contrary. Defiantly the *Boston Daily Bee* pointed to several instances in which blacks previously had received passports. Protesting the Supreme Court's decision, the Massachusetts legislature instructed its secretary of state to issue passports to black citizens of the state. African Americans continued to exercise a right of citizenship by voting in five New England states and in New York (with property requirement restrictions). Many whites also denounced the court decision, and many state and federal officials expressed outrage at the obvious inequity.[38]

This federal assault on their rights led some blacks to reconsider emigration. In the summer of 1858 a group of blacks, led by Henry Highland Garnet, established the African Civilization Society to encourage settlement of American blacks in Liberia, which had become an independent West African nation in 1847. The society was not racially restricted and counted several white reformers as part of its membership, but unlike the earlier American Colonization Society, this was largely a black-controlled venture that condemned slavery and American hypocrisy and focused on expanding opportunities for black freedom and independence. It also reflected the desire of society members, many of whom were black ministers, to spread the faith among West Africans. But African colonization was not popular with many American blacks, some of whom reasoned that emigration to Canada or the West Indies was more practical for continuing the fight against slavery. James T. Holly, born free in Washington, D.C., returned from a visit to Haiti in the mid-1850s with glowing reports of the opportunities there for African Americans willing to take up residence. Perhaps aware of the earlier attempt at Haitian settlement, few American blacks agreed to emigrate there, but Canadian emigration continued.[39]

As the decade progressed, emigration seemed less likely, and the sequence of events encouraged African Americans to prepare themselves for military action. Boston blacks had petitioned the Massachusetts legislature in 1855 to charter a black military company, and when their request was denied, they had formed the Massasoit Guard without state sanction. In November 1857, after the Dred Scott decision was announced, the guard, armed and in full uniform, paraded through the streets of Boston.[40] At a meeting of Massachusetts African Americans in 1858, black lawyer Robert Morris called on his fellows to stand together against the federal attack: "If any man comes here to New Bedford and they try to take [any fugitive] away, you telegraph us in Boston, and we'll come down 300 strong, and stay with you; and we won't go until he's safe."[41] Cincinnati African Americans formed the Attucks Guards, named for Crispus Attucks, the black sailor who was the first to die in the American Revolution. African Americans in New York also called one of their units the Attucks Guards. Ohio blacks demanded that racial restrictions be removed from the state militia, and the Ohio convention of 1857 resolved that independent military companies should be established wherever blacks were denied places

FRANK·LESLIE'S
ILLUSTRATED
NEWSPAPER

No. 82.—VOL. IV.]   NEW YORK, SATURDAY, JUNE 27, 1857.   [Price 6 Cents.

ELIZA AND LIZZIE, CHILDREN OF DRED SCOTT.

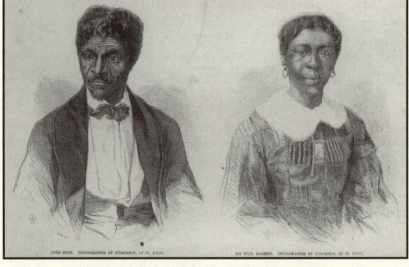

DRED SCOTT. PHOTOGRAPHED BY FITZGIBBON, OF ST. LOUIS.   HIS WIFE, HARRIET. PHOTOGRAPHED BY FITZGIBBON, OF ST. LOUIS.

Dred Scott, Harriet Scott, and their daughters,
newspaper article on the family, 1857.

in the state militia.[42] In cities and towns in the North, blacks anticipated war and readied themselves. "Captain" J. J. Simmons of the New York City unit prophesied that soon northern black military units would be called to march through the South with "a bible in one hand and a gun in the other."[43]

Through the spring and summer of 1858, a group of black abolitionists and white abolitionists met in the United States and Canada to discuss the feasibility of attacking slavery directly. John Brown, the leader of Kansas abolitionist guerrilla forces, devised a daring plan to strike against slavery in Virginia. With the financial backing of wealthy abolitionists from New England and New York, Brown gathered a band of eighteen men—thirteen whites and five blacks. As what had been plans for a small guerrilla action grew to plans for a full-scale assault, African Americans' doubts about the wisdom of the scheme also grew. Although Frederick Douglass had taken part in the early discussions, by the time of the raid he was convinced it was a noble folly. Later Douglass wrote that although he had prior knowledge of the raid, he had never intended to join it. "Let every man work for the abolition of slavery in his own way," he declared. "I would help all and hinder none."[44]

On October 16, 1859, Brown and his men raided the federal arsenal at Harpers Ferry, Virginia, in an effort to obtain weapons and ammunition to arm slaves on nearby plantations. With this expanded force, Brown intended to move against the slaveholders, freeing their slaves, and enlisting some of the slaves in a vast abolitionist army. Despite their doubts many blacks encouraged the mission and supported it. Of the twenty-one men who followed Brown to Harpers Ferry, five were African American: Shields Green, a fugitive slave from South Carolina; Osborne Anderson, a printer from Chatham, Canada; Lewis Sheridan Leary, from Oberlin, Ohio; Sheridan's nephew, John Copeland, a student at Oberlin College; and Dangerfield Newby, a freed slave from Virginia. Forty-four-year-old Newby, the oldest of the five, had personal reasons for participating in the raid. A fugitive himself, Newby hoped to free his wife, Harriet, and their six children, who were enslaved in Virginia near Harpers Ferry. Before the raid Harriet had written to him begging that he come for them. "If I thought I should never see you this earth would have no charms for me," she wrote. "[Come] this fall without fail."[45]

Newby never reached his family. John Brown and his raiders were trapped by federal troops under the command of Col. Robert E. Lee, and most of Brown's men, including Newby and Leary, were killed. Brown and four others, Copeland and Green among them, were captured, tried, convicted of treason, and sentenced to be hanged. Anderson escaped, while authorities sought other conspirators. A telegraph operator in Philadelphia warned Frederick Douglass three hours before delivering to the sheriff an order for Douglass's arrest. Douglass escaped to Canada and, near the end of November, sailed for England. Several of those identified as Brown's financial backers also fled to Canada.[46]

The raid on Harpers Ferry shocked the South and confirmed southern beliefs that only a strong proslavery federal government could protect slavery from abolitionist aggression. Among African Americans, John Brown was a hero. In a letter to his wife, Mary, a group of black women from New York called him "our honored and dearly-loved brother."[47] On the day of Brown's execution, blacks in Cincinnati, Pittsburgh, Philadelphia, and New York mourned his death. Three thousand gathered in Boston's Joy Street Church to hear the Reverend John Sella Martin, a former slave, condemn slavery and praise noble efforts to end that evil institution.[48] A solemn crowd in Detroit listened to a message on "Brown's Christian Fortitude" and his devotion to antislavery and heard the Brown Liberty Singers offer a musical selection entitled "Ode to Old Capt. John Brown."[49]

Reaction to John Brown's raid and his martyrdom reflected the growing conviction among abolitionists that only violence would bring an end to slavery. One black abolitionist from Boston, John Rock, expressed his certainty that "sooner or later, the clashing of arms will be heard in this country" and contended that "the black man's service will be needed . . . to strike a genuine blow for freedom [with a] power which white men 'will be bound to respect.'"[50] In early December 1859 broadsides called Canadian blacks to local meetings to consider ways to honor "Brown and his confederates . . . martyrs to the cause of Liberty," and Thomas Hamilton, editor of the *Weekly Anglo-African,* compared Brown's raid with Nat Turner's slave rebellion, the deadliest of nineteenth-century North America.[51]

By the end of the 1850s sectional considerations pervaded virtually every political decision in the United States, and sectional considerations involved slavery either directly or indirectly. Confrontations grew ever more bellicose, and violence reached even into the halls of Congress when a proslavery congressman from South Carolina attacked and beat Massachusetts senator Charles Sumner on the floor of the Senate chamber. Gun- and knife fights broke out in the House of Representatives, and one congressmen was killed by political rivals. In the presidential election year of 1860, sectional animosities split the Democratic Party between proslavery southerners who selected John C. Breckenridge of Kentucky as their standard bearer and northern Democrats who remained loyal to Stephen A. Douglas. Other southerners who refused to accept Breckenridge formed the Constitutional Union Party under the leadership of John Bell of Tennessee. Republicans nominated the politically moderate Abraham Lincoln as their presidential candidate.

African Americans continued to view Republicans as essentially the lesser of potential political evils. They found the Democratic proslavery position completely unacceptable, but they were also realistic about the shortcomings of the Republican Party. Blacks had observed the Republican rush to denounce John Brown and disassociate themselves from his raid. They had angrily noted Massachusetts Republican governor Nathaniel P. Banks's veto of legislation allowing blacks to enlist in the state militia. They knew that despite the black support that had helped elect Republican governor Edwin D. Morgan in New York, he had failed "to utter an anti-slavery sentence" during his annual message. Republicans had introduced a bill to repeal the Fugitive Slave Law, but it had failed when twelve Republicans voted against it and forty-three abstained. Further, in an effort to combat the "black Republican" label, some Republicans had declared themselves "a white man's party."[52]

Some black leaders argued that the Republicans' pretense of friendship was more dangerous to African American rights than the Democrats' animosity. John Rock asserted that Republicans "[aimed] to place white men and white labor against black men and black labor" and thus were "no better than" the Democrats.[53] Others considered Abraham Lincoln and his moderate wing of the Republican Party to be only Free-Soilers, not genuinely antislavery. Although Douglass and other black leaders expressed their misgivings, African Americans in New York, Brooklyn, Boston, and several other northern cities formed Republican clubs, and the vast majority of black voters cast their ballots for the victorious Lincoln.[54]

Lincoln's election precipitated a crisis. Before he could take office, South Carolina demanded that President Buchanan remove federal troops from the forts in Charleston Harbor and led the seven states of the Lower South (South Carolina, Mississippi, Florida, Alabama, Georgia, Louisiana, and Texas) in declaring their withdrawal from the United States. On February 4, 1861, representatives from all the seceding states—except Texas, whose delegates arrived later—met as a constitutional convention in Montgomery, Alabama, to define the political structure of the Confederate States of America. Lincoln reacted cautiously during his first days in office, trying to hold on to the slave states of the Upper South. In his inaugural address he firmly opposed the right of states to withdraw from the federal union but pledged that he would not interfere with slavery, the institution that was the foundation of Southern economic and social life. Attempted conciliation did not dissuade the states of the Confederacy, and war came on April 12, 1861, when Confederate batteries in Charleston Harbor opened fire on the federal Fort Sumter. Within days Lincoln issued a call for seventy-five thousand volunteers to put down the rebellion in South Carolina. Fearing a federal invasion that would threaten slavery, four states of the Upper South (Virginia, Arkansas, Tennessee, and North Carolina) withdrew from the United States, leaving Maryland, Delaware, Kentucky, and Missouri as the only slave states loyal to the U.S. government. Lincoln's increased need for federal troops was exacerbated by the fact that almost one-third of the nation's army officer corps, including important West Point–trained men, left to fight with the rebellion against the United

States. During the first year of the war the U.S. Army expanded from just over sixteen thousand men to more than seven hundred thousand. Blacks volunteered immediately, but the federal government refused them, and none of the new recruits was African American.[55]

African Americans in Washington, D.C., Pittsburgh, Boston, New York, and elsewhere, answered Lincoln's call. Through their military units and as individuals, they sent letters and petitions to the War Department expressing their eagerness to serve, but all their offers were rejected. Most whites and governmental officials, including Lincoln, questioned blacks' bravery. Many believed that ex-slaves in particular would be too submissive and cowardly to be good soldiers. One white corporal from a New York regiment bluntly summed up the general feeling among white recruits: "We don't want to fight side and side with the nigger. We think that we are too superior race for that."[56] Outraged black leaders pointed to the fact that black troops had served with distinction in the American Revolution and in the War of 1812. "Colored men were good enough . . . to help win American independence," Douglass noted angrily, "but they are not good enough to help preserve that independence against treason and rebellion." Why would the American government attempt to fight "rebels with only one hand?"[57]

Before the war many radical abolitionists had supported the idea of disunion, that is, withdrawing the free states from their union with slaveholders. Frederick Douglass had begun to reconsider when Lincoln's election had brought, as Douglass wrote, "at least an antislavery reputation to the Presidency." He was less hopeful, though, when Lincoln attempted to compromise with the South by proposing constitutional protections for slavery. "If the Union can only be maintained by new concessions to the slaveholders," Douglass had declared, "let the Union perish." Southern secession, however, changed abolition's prospects—southern slavery was no longer protected by the military might of the United States. Slave rebellion had a much better chance of success, and runaway slaves might be safe in free states.[58] Despite Abraham Lincoln's equivocation, African Americans agreed that the war ignited by the firing on Fort Sumter was "a war for and against slavery," and the United States could not win it without destroying slavery. Yet federal military commanders continued for two years to refuse the thousands of blacks who volunteered to be soldiers.[59]

The South recognized the value of black participation in the Confederate war effort. Slave labor produced most of the food for the troops, and the Confederacy impressed free blacks and slaves into service as laborers, teamsters, cooks, and servants to support southern troops. Despite their value to the southern war effort, however, U.S. commanders continued to return runaway slaves to their southern masters until Congress passed the Confiscation Act in August 1861. This act set Confederate slaves free once they came under

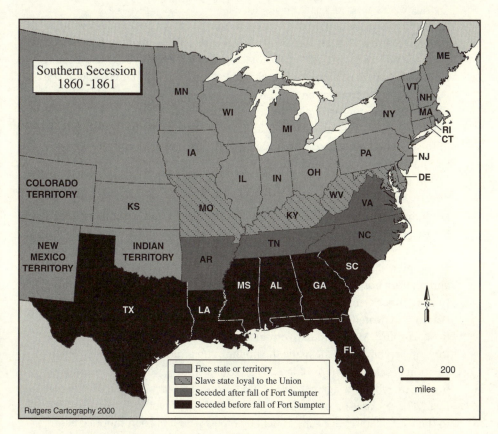

Southern Secession 1860-1861

Legend:
- Free state or territory
- Slave state loyal to the Union
- Seceded after fall of Fort Sumpter
- Seceded before fall of Fort Sumpter

0   200
miles

Rutgers Cartography 2000

the control of federal forces, but it did not free slaves who might escape from slaveholders in states such as Delaware and Maryland, which had remained loyal to the United States. African Americans were insulted by the government's refusing their service, and many, like Henry Cropper of the Philadelphia black military company, urged African Americans to maintain their dignity and self-respect by withdrawing their offer.[60]

Meanwhile the early years of the war brought enormous losses to the United States. At Shiloh, Tennessee, in April 1862, 63,000 United States troops fought the largest battle in American history and suffered more than thirteen thousand casualties. The United States lost sixteen thousand dead, wounded, or missing two months later, during the Seven Days Battle in Virginia, and more than fourteen thousand at the Second Battle of Manassas. By early summer 1862 it was clear that this would not be a short and relatively painless war. In the face of such losses, and with support for the Confederacy said to be building in Britain and Western Europe, Congress and the president decided to take desperate measures. In July Congress passed legislation allowing the president to enlist black troops should he deem it "necessary and proper for the suppression of this rebellion." By November the first black regiment had been raised, composed of ex-slaves in South Carolina who had been freed within U.S. lines. Thomas Wentworth Higginson, a white abolitionist who had participated in a daring attempt by blacks to rescue a fugitive slave in Boston before the war, was appointed to command these troops. By year's end the First South Carolina was engaged in combat along the Georgia-Florida border. Witnessing their courage and ability, Higginson wrote, "Nobody knows anything about these men who has not seen them in battle. . . . No officer in this regiment now doubts that the key to the successful prosecution of this war lies in the unlimited employment of black troops."[61]

In the summer of 1862, Lincoln had announced his intention to strike directly at slavery in the South, an attempt to redirect and rejuvenate the war effort, to enlist northern antislavery sentiment, and to make it more difficult for the British and Europeans to support the Confederacy. The president was true to form; Lincoln's timing and words were cautious: a U.S. victory would precede the public announcement, and he would pursue his political and military purpose with the least disruption for slaveholders in loyal states. In September Gen. George McClellan, commander of the U.S. Army of the Potomac, defeated Confederate forces under Robert E. Lee at Antietam Creek in Sharpsburg, Maryland. Lincoln moved swiftly, and five days after the victory, on September 22, he made the preliminary announcement of his Emancipation Proclamation. As of January 1, 1863, all slaves in areas controlled by people in rebellion against the United States would be declared "forever free." The declaration of freedom did not apply to slaves held by those loyal to the United States or to slaves held by rebels who had been subdued before January 1, 1863. Certainly a limited emancipation, but it reinforced Congress's abolition of slavery in the District of Columbia the previous April and seemed to be part of an abolitionist trend.

African Americans had waited anxiously for the promised New Year's proclamation. They were not confident of Lincoln's commitment. He had denounced slavery but had protected it to secure southern loyalty to the United States before the war. He had finally enlisted blacks into the military but had promised emancipation only to Confederate slaves. In August 1862 he had been the first American president to invite a delegation of African Americans to meet with him at the White House, but he had told them that black people were a burden on the nation and it would be better if they left the country and settled in Africa or the West Indies. Across the North, African Americans in small towns and large cities held mass meetings to await the proclamation. When it came they broke into wild celebration, greeting it with singing, dancing, prayers, lofty rhetoric, and plain speaking about family and friends still in slavery. Although it was a halfway measure, the Emancipation Proclamation transformed the war's purpose and made Lincoln the "Great Emancipator."[62]

The war's new moral purpose and the dedication and success of black soldiers influenced racial sentiment in the North. By late winter 1863, a second black unit from South Carolina, commanded by Col. James Montgomery, had been formed, and in March some of Montgomery's and Higginson's African American troops captured and occupied the Confederate stronghold of Jacksonville, Florida. Gen. David Hunter informed his superiors that his troops were "hardy, generous, temperate, strictly obedient, possessing remarkable aptitude for military training, and deeply imbued with that religious sentiment which made the soldiers of Oliver Cromwell invincible." He also wrote that he had detected the racist attitudes of many of the white soldiers who had come into contact with black troops "rapidly softening or fading out."[63] Newspapers challenged racial bigots with the "facts" of "good conduct and gallant deeds of the men they persecute and slander."[64] One white Illinois soldier who had voted Democratic before the war wrote to his wife, "So long as [my] flag is confronted by the hostile guns of slavery . . . I am as confirmed an abolitionist as ever was pelted with stale eggs." In the Eighty-sixth Indiana Regiment one officer reported that although many of his men had denounced what they called an "abolition war," by March 1863 they were expressing support for emancipation and for black combat troops. An Indiana sergeant who admitted that he did not like free blacks declared himself in favor of the Emancipation Proclamation if it would end the war. A poll of one Iowa regiment showed that only one-quarter of the white soldiers opposed the proclamation, while half favored it and the rest registered no opinion.[65]

There was still resistance to blacks' participation in the war, however. In Pennsylvania the governor refused to recruit them, and John Mercer Langston's offer to raise black troops in Ohio met an icy response from Governor David Tod. "Do you know[,] Mr. Langston," Tod asked, "that this is a white man's government; that white men are able to defend and protect it?" He continued, "When we want you colored men we will notify you."[66] Yet, now that Lincoln had committed the nation to the cause of freedom, and Congress had authorized raising black troops, there seemed reason for optimism. In January 1863 Governor John A. Andrew of Massachusetts was authorized to form the Fifty-fourth Massachusetts Volunteers, the first black military regiment recruited from the North. Governor Andrew, an abolitionist, placed Col. Robert Gould Shaw, a young man from a prominent white abolitionist family, at its head. He also appointed several black leaders, including Frederick Douglass, Charles Lenox Remond, Thomas Morris Chester, and Martin Delany, as recruiting agents, but the effort was slow at first. Many blacks were reluctant to join a force that had recently rejected their offers to serve. Chester presided over a meeting in Harrisburg, Pennsylvania, where blacks demanded a guarantee of fair treatment. If they were to serve, it must be with dignity and equality. Although most state and local officials accepted black military assistance only under the most dire circumstances, by April thirty or forty men a day were enlisting in the Massachusetts Fifty-fourth.[67]

African Americans who enlisted were refused positions as officers, and blacks in uniform risked being attacked and harassed by northern whites. A white gang and policemen attacked Cpl. John Ross in the streets of Washington, D.C., in the summer of 1863, and one police officer explained that he would shoot a "nigger recruit" as easily as he would a mad dog.[68] The greatest insult black soldiers faced, however, came from the Confederacy. In May the Confederate congress resolved that any black U.S. troops captured would be killed or enslaved, not treated as prisoners of war. White officers leading black troops were to be treated as criminals and might be executed. Chester gave up his recruiting efforts in disgust and left the United States for Britain in the fall of 1863, but African Americans continued to enlist despite the injustices they faced.

As an added insult, black troops were expected to serve for inferior pay. Initially the War Department pledged equal pay, and the first recruits enlisted with that understanding. But until 1864, when Congress actually authorized equal pay, black troops were paid at a rate less than half that paid to white soldiers. A white private was paid thirteen dollars per month plus a uniform allowance, and a regimental sergeant received twenty-one dollars per month plus allowances, while blacks at all noncommissioned ranks earned only ten dollars per month, from which three dollars were subtracted for uniforms. Black soldiers, their families, and many of their white officers complained bitterly, pointing out that soldiers could not provide for their families on this sub-standard pay. Black civilians employed by the military could earn as much as twenty-five dollars per month.[69] Some black soldiers' wives and children were forced into poorhouses while their men were defending the country. Some blacks refused to serve without full pay, some requested discharges so they could support their families, and others served without pay rather than accept inferior pay. For more than a year almost all of the Fifty-fourth Massachusetts refused to accept unequal pay. Protest was widespread, with black regiments from Michigan, Kansas, Rhode Island, and South Carolina joining in. The black women of Boston held fairs to raise money and gather supplies for soldiers' families. Black soldiers resented both the pay differential and the symbolic refusal to recognize their role as soldiers: it was about more than money. "To say we are not soldiers [even if they paid] us $20 would be injustice," wrote one black corporal from the Fifty-fourth Massachusetts, "for it would rob a whole race of their title to a manhood."[70] Pay inequities rooted in practicality and prejudice were not easy to change. One New Yorker expressed the prevailing sentiment, "[I]t is unjust in every way to the white soldier to put him

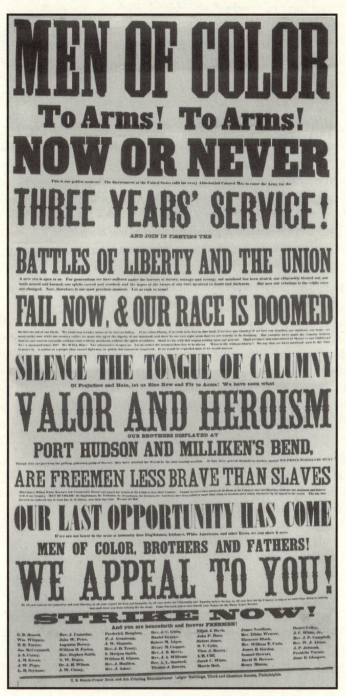

Broadside: "Men of Color to Arms."

on a level with the black."[71] Black protest met a swift military response. In the fall of 1863, when one company of the Third South Carolina Volunteers, led by Sgt. William Walker, refused to perform their duties until they were properly paid, the army charged the entire company with mutiny and executed Sergeant Walker.[72]

Although not admitted as soldiers, black women also served the war effort. *Provincial Freeman* editor Mary Ann Shadd Cary moved from Canada to Indiana during the war to help in black recruitment. Harriet Tubman, the best-known conductor on the underground railroad, expanded her activities to include spying for the government and bringing recruits to the army. In March 1863 she brought 750 black men out of slavery and into the federal forces. Thousands of other black women did everything from camp chores to taking up arms when circumstances warranted. Susie King, born a slave in Georgia, worked as a teacher of freed people and as a nurse during the war. She spent part of her time with her husband's unit, the First South Carolina Volunteers, doing the laundry and learning to handle a gun.[73]

Men, women, and children flocked to the Union lines to escape slavery as the U.S. Army moved through the South. Commanders quickly learned that black enlistees were far more willing to serve if the army guaranteed the protection of their families, and small shanty settlements of civilians sprang up on the fringes of military camps. The wives of black soldiers often did cooking and laundry for the officers, and although this allowed black women to be close to their husbands, it posed problems as well. White men in authority generally regarded black women as inferior and fair game for sexual exploitation. At one camp the harassment was so bad that a black soldier complained, "We have a set of officers here who apparently think that their commissions are license to debauch and mingle with deluded freedwomen, under cover of darkness."[74]

About 29,000 black sailors (about one-quarter of the navy) and more than 186,000 African American soldiers, in 166 black regiments, fought for the United States during the Civil War. One in every five black adult males in the entire country served in the U.S. forces, constituting one-tenth of the nation's military force. About half of those who served were former slaves. In battle black troops were often given the most dangerous jobs. Coupled with the Confederate treatment of captives, this resulted in a casualty rate roughly twice that of white troops. Despite their sacrifices and their service in previous wars, black troops were continually challenged to prove their courage and capability in battle. African Americans fought their first major Civil War battle at Port Hudson, Louisiana, in May 1863. The First and Third Louisiana regiments, a Native Guard composed of free, educated, affluent blacks from New Orleans, advanced under the command of black officers who gave orders in

Susie King

Susie King was born in 1848, the daughter of a domestic slave and the great-grandaughter of a slave midwife. She traced her lineage in America to her great-great-grandmother Dolly, five of whose children had fought in the Revolutionary War. Susie's grandmother took advantage of the family's favor with their master. He allowed her to take young Susie and her brother from the plantation to her home in Savannah. She supported them by doing odd jobs and laundry, and carrying on a trade between the farms and the city. Susie was fourteen when the Civil War began and her uncle took her to South Carolina's Sea Islands. There she saw northern soldiers, the first whites who did not treat her like a slave. Since she had attended school in Savannah, she was able to serve the army by teaching children and newly freed adults. Eventually she married Edward King, a former slave who was a sargeant in the U.S. First South Carolina Volunteers. She continued to work without pay as a laundress and as a nurse, ministering to white as well as black troops. She also handled weapons and learned to shoot, clean, and disassemble them.

For a time the regiment was stationed a mile from Fort Wagner, where in 1863 the black Fifty-fourth Massachusetts Regiment had lost more than 250 men. King visited the former Confederate fort, then under federal control, and watched U.S. guns shelling Charleston. As she remembered the gruesome sight, there were "many skulls lying about. Some thought they were the skulls of our boys; others thought they were the enemies'."* When the regiment entered Savannah in early 1865, King remained there, running a school until her husband's death the following year. She alternately operated her school and worked for a white Savannah family until she secured her husband's military pension. King eventually moved to Boston, married Russell Taylor, and organized a relief organization for Civil War veterans. In 1902 Susie King published her memoir, illustrating the varied and important roles that black women played in the Civil War and in the black community.

Susie King Taylor, Civil War nurse. Photographs and Prints Division, Schomburg Center for Research in Black Culture, The New York Public Library, Astor, Lenox, and Tilden Foundations.

*Dorothy Sterling, Speak Out in Thunder Tones (Garden City, N.Y.: Doubleday & Company, Inc., 1973), 355.

Charge of the Fifty-fourth Massachusetts Colored Regiment
on Fort Wagner, South Carolina, July 1863.
Mark E. Mitchell Collection of African American History.

both English and French. Seven successive charges on Confederate fortifications left one of five black soldiers dead or wounded. The siege by white and
black regiments lasted for forty-eight days, and the United States lost nearly
ten thousand men. Witnesses were effusive in their praise of the black troops.
"No regiment behaved better than they did," reported one white officer.
"Nobly indeed, they have acquitted themselves," read the *New York Times,* and
poet George H. Boker commemorated their heroism with a verse distributed
in English and German.[75]

About the same time, two regiments of African Americans beat back a Confederate attack at Milliken's Bend on the Mississippi River near Vicksburg. At
one point, 840 black soldiers and 160 white soldiers defended the U.S. position against almost two thousand Confederates. The Confederate advance
pushed U.S. forces to the edge of the river, and Confederates summarily executed captured black troops. Finally, with the arrival of a gunboat, the U.S.
forces made a desperate stand, with soldiers using their rifles as clubs in
hand-to-hand combat. Even the defeated Confederates praised this predom-
inately black force, and one U.S. officer declared that, "[b]y their coolness and
determination in battle," blacks had moved themselves into "high standing

Sergeant
W. H. Carney,
Company C,
Fifty-fourth
Massachusetts
Colored Regiment,
winner of the
Congressional
Medal of Honor.

Photographs and Prints
Division, Schomburg
Center for Research
in Black Culture,
The New York Public
Library, Astor, Lenox,
and Tilden Foundations.

as soldiers."[76] Finally that summer, the famous assault by the Fifty-Fourth Mass-achusetts at Fort Wagner in Charleston Harbor brought further proof of black valor. They suffered enormous losses in this futile attack on the Con-federate stronghold, but they fought with courage and skill. Leading the charge, Colonel Shaw fell on the ramparts and was killed. For his part in the attack, Sgt. William H. Carney received the Congressional Medal of Honor, and the *New York Tribune* praised the Fifty-fourth's performance in this "test of black troops." The *Tribune*—its editor apparently ignorant of the black sol-diers who had fought in that famous Revolutionary War battle—compared the bravery of the Fifty-fourth at Fort Wagner to the courage of white troops at the Battle of Bunker Hill. By the end of the summer of 1863, Abraham Lin-coln was convinced of the value of enlisting black troops and urged Gen. Ulysses S. Grant to increase enlistments, saying, "I believe [they are] a resource which, if vigorously applied now, will soon close the contest." Finally the fed-eral government had acceded to black demands that African Americans be relied on to strike a blow for freedom.[77]

Chapter 8

1865 President Abraham Lincoln assassinated; Vice President Andrew Johnson,
a Democrat, succeeds him

Slavery abolished by the Thirteenth Amendment to the Constitution

Congress establishes the Bureau of Refugees, Freedmen,
and Abandoned Lands

1866 Congress passes Civil Rights Bill over President Andrew Johnson's veto

1868 President Johnson impeached by U.S. House of Representatives, but Senate
fails to muster votes needed to remove him

1868 Fourteenth Amendment to Constitution ratified, removing racial restrictions
to U.S. citizenship

John W. Menard of Louisiana becomes first African American
elected to Congress

1870 Hiram Rhoades Revels becomes the first African American U.S. senator, elected
to fill the Mississippi seat of former Confederate president Jefferson Davis

Fifteenth Amendment to the Constitution removes racial restrictions on voting

1872 Most ex-Confederates pardoned by U.S. General Amnesty Act

1875 Congress passes Civil Rights Bill guaranteeing equal access to public
accommodations regardless of race

1877 African American Henry O. Flipper graduates from West Point

Last occupying federal troops withdrawn from the South

1880 Thousands of black "exodusters" migrate from the South to Kansas

1883 U.S. Supreme Court declares Civil Rights Law of 1875 unconstitutional

1884 Moses Fleetwood Walker becomes first African American in major league
baseball, playing for Toledo

1886 Colored Farmers' Alliance organized in Texas

1889 Ida B. Wells-Barnett becomes editor of the *Memphis Free Speech,* platform
for her antilynching campaign

1893 African American surgeon Daniel Hale Williams performs the world's first
successful heart operation in Chicago

1895 Booker T. Washington delivers his "Atlanta Compromise" speech
at the Cotton States and International Exposition

1896 In *Plessy* v. *Ferguson,* U.S. Supreme Court declares "separate but equal"
public facilities to be constitutional

From Reconstruction to Jim Crow

*I*n 1864 Thomas Morris Chester returned from Britain, where he had been an advocate for the Union cause on the antislavery lecture circuit. He became a reporter for the *Philadelphia Press* and covered the war, adding his powerful voice to others demanding fair and equal treatment for African American soldiers. Such black newspapers as the African Methodist Episcopal (AME) Church's *Christian Recorder* and New York's *Anglo-African* had reported on the war from its beginning, but Chester's accounts in the *Press,* a white newspaper, reached a much wider audience. Chester was born in 1834 in Harrisburg, Pennsylvania's capital. His mother had been born in slavery in Virginia and had eventually escaped from her owner in Baltimore, Maryland. His father, an oysterman and restaurateur in Harrisburg, was active in antislavery activities and was the local agent for William Lloyd Garrison's *Liberator.* Thomas Chester's life was marked by his dogged determination to gain an education. While attending Allegheny Institute, later Avery College, in Pittsburgh, Pennsylvania, he broke with his parents' politics and allied himself with the African colonizationists. This was not a popular stand with many African Americans, who condemned colonization as a "vicious" and "nefarious" plot to "drain the country of the most enlightened part of our colored brethren." Even in the 1850s colonization was controversial, and although he argued that emigration to Africa was a practical alternative to racial injustice in America, Chester was ambivalent, and his relationship with the colonizationists was a stormy one. Nevertheless he emigrated to Liberia, working as a teacher and a newspaper editor there during the next ten years. He returned to the United States, however, for extended visits to represent the colonization society in Boston and Philadelphia.[1]

The promise of black military involvement in the war persuaded Chester to remain in the United States. He led Harrisburg blacks in demanding full citizenship rights in return for service, was a recruiter for the Fifty-fifth Massachusetts Regiment in the spring of 1863, and became the captain of a state militia company formed to defend the city from possible Confederate attack. Disturbed by the limits the government placed on African Americans' participation in the war and by their unequal pay, Chester set off for Britain late that year in the vain hope of finding a way to finance his training in law. Upon his return to the United States in 1864, he took the influential and danger-ous position as war correspondent. From Virginia and North Carolina he wrote candid and dramatic accounts of the black troops. He provided abundant evi-dence of their courage and honor in battle and reminded his readers that black fighting men suffered special hardships. Except in a few special cases in which black doctors and ministers became officers late in the war, African Americans remained restricted to the enlisted ranks. They endured racial injustice, even from their own white officers. Chester's reports condemned those "wrongs which . . . exhibit a disgraceful depth of depravity, practiced by dishonest men, in the name of the Government."[2]

Perhaps Chester's news stories contributed to a change in public senti-ment and influenced federal legislators: in June 1864 Congress finally passed a law equalizing pay, arms, equipment, and medical services for black troops, though the new pay rate was made retroactive only to January 1, 1864. Black troops still faced special hazards, however. Southern commanders took few black prisoners and executed many of those they did take. At Fort Pillow, Ten-nessee, in the spring of 1864, Confederate forces commanded by Gen. Nathan Bedford Forrest murdered hundreds of captured U.S. troops, about half of whom were African Americans. Reportedly Forrest, whose short temper was well known to his men, was angered by the fort's refusal to surrender to his supe-rior numbers and further incensed by the taunts of black soldiers. The Con-federates, with more than twice as many men, overran the garrison and then conducted a bloody massacre. Although some Confederate soldiers were reluctant to indulge in the carnage, Forrest "ordered [the captured U.S. troops] shot down like dogs. . . . Kill the last damned one of them," Forrest reportedly demanded, and his men complied, clubbing the wounded to death, burning some alive, and nailing others to walls. Many of the victims ran into the river in a vain attempt to escape, but they were shot, "their heads presenting 'beautiful' targets." At one point the killing was so furious that even Forrest seemed to have had second thoughts, as one of his men wrote that "if General Forrest had not run between our men and the Yanks with his pis-tol and sabre drawn not a man would have been spared." Later Forrest observed that "the river was dyed with the blood of the slaughtered for 200 yards." Chester called the Confederate atrocities at Fort Pillow "evidence of Southern barbarism and inhumanity," and northern newspapers carried out-raged headlines of the "Fort Pillow Massacre." The *New York Tribune* referred to Forrest, who had been a slave trader before the war and would be one of the organizers of the Ku Klux Klan after it, as "BUTCHER FORREST." Less than a week after the massacre, twelve hundred black troops in Memphis fell to their knees to take a solemn oath of revenge. "Remember Fort Pillow!" became their rallying cry.[3]

By the summer of 1864 the tide of the war had turned. U.S. military victories in Atlanta and in Virginia's Shenandoah Valley made the Democrats' contention that the war should be abandoned less convincing, and northern acceptance of the Emancipation Proclamation and federal recruitment policies contributed to Lincoln's reelection that fall. Eighty percent of the federal army voted for him, and those African Americans who could vote gave him their overwhelming support.[4] By the time Abraham Lincoln delivered his second inaugural address in January, the conflict was almost over. Confederate desertions were high and increasing; southern soldiers were low on ammunition, food, shoes, and other vital supplies. They were losing the hope of victory, and some wives and other family members suffering hardships at home encouraged their men to desert.[5] Many poor southern whites questioned the disproportionate sacrifices they were making in what they began to consider a rich man's struggle to maintain a rich man's privilege.

A desperate situation called for desperate measures, and Confederate officers, with the support of their commander, Robert E. Lee, proposed the recruitment of slaves into the southern military. As Richmond was increasingly threatened by U.S. troops, Virginia's governor lobbied for the conscription of black soldiers. One staunch slavery supporter contended that all the slaveholders he knew would support giving freedom to slaves who would fight in the military. A bill to that effect was hotly debated in the Confederate Congress, and reaction was intense. Although enlisted men generally supported the measure, one southern soldier spoke for many. He wrote to his mother saying that he was considering deserting the Confederate army because "I did not volunteer my services to fight for a free Negroes country but to fight for a free white mans country & I do not think I love my country well enough to fight with black soldiers." Nevertheless, the bill authorizing the recruitment of three hundred thousand slaves to serve the South narrowly passed and became law in the Confederacy on March 13, 1865, three weeks before the war's end. Ironically the slaveholders who had claimed that slaves did not desire freedom offered slaves freedom in return for their fighting in the war to maintain slavery.

In the end the Confederate recruitment of blacks was a failure. According to one contemporary account, only about twenty Richmond blacks volunteered, and a regiment was raised in Tennessee, but the war was over before black Confederate troops went into combat. Even if slaves had fought, they would obviously have been fighting for their own freedom, not to preserve the system of slavery.[6]

The Confederate capital at Richmond fell in early April 1865 to a U.S. force including five thousand black infantrymen and eighteen hundred black cavalrymen. In Boston, Frederick Douglass told an audience gathered at

Faneuil Hall that the occupation of Richmond meant "the fall of the rebellion" and the start of "the upbuilding of liberty through the Southern States."[7] Most African Americans agreed, especially the southern blacks, roughly 40 percent of the region's population. As Jefferson Davis and his political entourage withdrew, Richmond's whites were near panic. One Richmonder captured their mood on the night of the evacuation: "We walked the streets like lost spirits til nearly daybreak."[8] Robert Lumpkin, a well-known local slave dealer, tried to remove his slave property before the U.S. troops arrived. Unsuccessful, he returned his slaves to the holding pens known locally as Lumpkin's jail. There he spent the night with a black woman who was his slave, the mother of his two children, and soon to be his wife.[9]

Although conditions were changing rapidly and black hopes were high, indignities remained. African American troops had led the advance on Richmond, but their white commanders ordered them halted to allow white troops to overtake them and enter the city first. "History will show," wrote the editor of Philadelphia's *Christian Recorder,* "that [the black troops] were in the suburbs of Richmond long before the white soldiers, and but for the untimely and unfair order to halt, would have triumphantly planted their banner first upon the battlements of the capital of 'ye greate confederacie.'" Black soldiers deeply resented being denied the opportunity to lead the conquering forces into the Confederate capital. They understood the symbolism of being first to "tear down Jeff. Davis' nest."[10] Nonetheless black soldiers, some of whom were former Virginia slaves coming home to liberate their people, took great pride in being part of the occupying force. Garland White had escaped from slavery in Virginia and settled in Ohio before the war. On his return as chaplain with the Twenty-eighth U.S. Colored Troops, he addressed the large crowd, "one huge sea [of] black faces" filling the street. Thomas Morris Chester noted the enthusiasm and pride of the city's blacks as they watched African American soldiers march through the streets of Richmond. Amid much congratulatory handshaking and backslapping, they sang out boldly, "Richmond town is burning down, High diddle diddle inctum inctum ah." Black women, and some white women too, raided Confederate food supplies, seizing flour, coffee, sugar, and whatever they could find. President Lincoln, a consummate practitioner of symbolic expression, walked the streets of Richmond a few days later. After greeting black soldiers and civilians, he entered the Confederate White House and sat in Jefferson Davis's chair.[11]

Lincoln returned to Washington on April 9, and on that same day, the southern forces under Robert E. Lee surrendered to Gen. U. S. Grant at Appomattox Court House. By the time of their surrender, the Confederate forces had lost more than a quarter of a million men to death from combat, accident, or disease. The southern economy was devastated, its money was worthless, and its slave property was lost. U.S. forces lost 360,000, and 37,000 of these dead were black men. Two days after Lee's surrender, Lincoln made a public speech outlining the pressing postwar and postemancipation problems that faced the United States government and the American people. He spoke of molding a new government in the South from the "disorganized and discordant elements" of "Jefferson Davis's fugitive government," and of providing the vote to literate blacks and black veterans. Among those listening to Lincoln's speech was John Wilkes Booth, an actor, southerner, and a believer in the southern cause. Booth was furious at the Confederacy's defeat, and doubly furious that Lincoln now seemed to embrace the Radical Republican stand on race. "That means nigger citizenship," Booth believed, and he told a friend, "That is the last speech [Lincoln] will ever make."[12]

That was no idle threat. On the evening of April 14, the Lincolns were watching a play at Ford's Theater in Washington when Booth suddenly appeared at the rear of the presidential box, aimed, and shot the president. Abraham Lincoln died at 7:22 the next morning, the first president in American history to be killed by an assassin. Most black people felt Lincoln's death as a personal loss. Even though the Emancipation Proclamation had been more a military and political document than a humanitarian act, it had great symbolic significance, and former slaves had come to consider Lincoln their friend and ally. The Twenty-second Regiment of African American troops took their stations along Pennsylvania Avenue as the president's funeral procession moved from the White House to the Capitol. African Americans lined the railroad tracks as the funeral train returned Lincoln's body to his hometown of Springfield, Illinois. Soon after the funeral, the Twenty-second Regiment joined the search for Booth. Frederick Douglass recalled the tragedy "as a personal as well as a national calamity; on account of the race to which I belong and the deep interest which that good man ever took in its elevation."[13]

Lincoln had led the nation through its greatest crisis. He had come to appreciate the value of blacks' service during the war, had publicly acknowledged their role in winning the war, and had even cautiously suggested in private to the governor of Louisiana that in some of the states "the very intelligent [newly freed blacks] and especially those who fought gallantly in our ranks" might be enfranchised.[14] Lincoln was certainly not an unequivocal supporter of African American civil rights, but this did represent a change from his stand in the 1850s, when he had questioned the federal government's power to secure emancipation, and from his willingness in 1860 to support the constitutional protection of southern slavery. It is impossible to know what Lincoln's postwar policies might have been. He had not totally abandoned the colonizationist alternative, but he had proved himself able to learn from experience and to take advantage of changing conditions. Furthermore, he seemed open to arguments for racial justice, something that could not be said of his successor, Vice President Andrew Johnson, a former Democrat from Tennessee. Johnson's presidency was short-lived and highly contentious, coming as it did at this critical moment for African Americans and the nation.

The most immediate problems facing the nation were food and labor shortages in the South. Mounting numbers of freed people were walking off plantations with little more than what they wore or could carry. Many white southern workers and small farmers had been ruined by the war; their jobs were gone and their farms were destroyed. The sheer magnitude of human need threatened to overwhelm the resources of the U.S. Army and the federal government. Initially during the war, private groups had taken on much of the relief work, feeding, clothing, counseling, and providing education to freed people and poor whites. Many black soldiers, too, learned to read and write in schools established by these private charities in the occupied South. One of the most successful social aid projects, the Port Royal Experiment, was begun early in the war on islands off the coast of South Carolina and Georgia. In November 1861, planters fled, U.S. troops occupied the islands, and ten thousand slaves on 195 plantations were suddenly free. Beginning the following spring, thousands of abolitionist teachers, missionaries, medical professionals, and legal advisers came from New England, New York, and Pennsylvania to aid the freed people.[15]

Many former slaves enthusiastically welcomed those who traveled south to assist their transition from slavery to freedom. Medical needs and a thirst for education brought freedmen of all ages flocking to the northern reformers, who established hospitals, welfare centers, and schools. Slaves had been denied access to learning, and in most places in the South it had been illegal for them to acquire even a rudimentary education. Now that slavery was over, many blacks were determined to get an education, considering learning a symbol of freedom. Parents wanted to learn to read and write, and they sought more extensive instruction for their children. The large numbers of enthusiastic students gratified and overwhelmed the teachers. Many conservative southern whites found the prospect of education for former slaves both ridiculous and disturbing. As throngs of African Americans of all ages flocked to the schoolhouse, one white man in Louisiana remarked, "I have seen many an absurdity in my lifetime, but this is the climax of absurdities." Others feared that educated blacks might challenge the traditional system of white supremacy. They were right to be concerned, for African Americans generally saw acquiring an education as both a racial responsibility and a means to racial equality. "I'm going to school now to try to learn something which I hope will enable me to be of some use to my race," explained one young black man in Augusta, Georgia. "The Lord has sent us books and teachers," he continued. "We must not hesitate a moment, but go on and learn all we can."[16]

Freed people found black teachers especially inspiring. Charlotte Forten, the twenty-five-year-old granddaughter of James Forten, the black abolitionist and wealthy Philadelphia sailmaker, was among the zealous reformers who took their first tentative steps toward postwar Reconstruction at Port Royal. Forten taught school, nursed wounded soldiers, counseled freed people on legal and political matters, and played the piano for their entertainment. Some, such as Laura Towne, fervent white Garrisonian from Philadelphia, became part of the community. Reformers continued to serve sea island blacks for almost forty years. Their devotion saved lives and educated thousands, and their letters to northern friends and colleagues gained enthusiastic support and assistance for their work. Their efforts also encouraged public backing, which came in March 1865 when Congress established the Bureau of Refugees, Freedmen, and Abandoned Lands—known simply as the Freedmen's Bureau—and placed it in the War Department.

The Freedmen's Bureau expanded the work of private charities both programmatically and geographically, opening local offices to extend aid to former slaves and to white war refugees throughout the South. The Freedmen's Bureau issued 13 million food rations of cornmeal, flour, and sugar during its first fifteen months. It oversaw thousands of schools and helped former slaves negotiate labor contracts, legalize marriages, and become taxpayers, voters, business operators, and landowners. Freedmen's Bureau officials took complaints from former slaves who were victimized by former slaveholders, negotiated with whites, and tried to resolve community and family conflicts among blacks.[17]

With limited resources and unreliable political support, the Freedmen's Bureau attempted to reconstruct the social system as well as the southern economic and political system. This involved many difficulties and uncertainties. Most black people had definite ideas about the meaning of freedom, and at least in the short run, it meant being freed from the place they had been bound to by slavery. Some planters lamented the "disloyalty" of their former slaves, whom they saw as "deserting" the plantation when their labor was desperately needed. Some U.S. Army officers observed that multitudes of black people were wandering the roads as "vagabonds," confirming white fears that freed slaves would become an idle, vagrant people who would only work if compelled. In reality many people went in search of family and friends who had been sold away from them during the years of slavery. Former slaves walked hundreds of miles, following rumors that loved ones resided in some distant place, hoping to reunite their families. Under these circumstances the Freedmen's

Bureau was under great pressure from southern planters and northern textile manufacturers to stabilize the southern work force, reverse the flow of former slaves from plantations to southern cities, and rebuild the agricultural system. Thus, bureau officials expended a great deal of effort persuading former slaves to sign labor contracts with planters.

Many freed people asserted their right to possess the lands they had worked as slaves. At war's end there were a few politicians and military men, such as Gen. Rufus Saxton, head of the Freedmen's Bureau in South Carolina, Georgia, and Florida, who urged that freed people be provided with small farms carved from the tens of thousands of acres Confederate planters had abandoned. This would have established an independent class of African Americans and the foundation for a black southern economy less dependent on the largesse of the federal government or southern white patronage. Blacks understood how important land ownership was. As one former slave from Mississippi confided, "[A]ll I wants is to git to own fo' or five acres [of] land [that] I can build me a little house on and call my home."[18] "Gib us our own land and we take care ourselves;" one freedman explained, "but without land, de ole massas can hire us or starve us, as dey please." A popular song, sung to escaping slaves by Harriet Tubman during the Civil War, expressed the expectations of former slaves. "Come along! Come along! Don't be alarmed, Uncle Sam is rich enough to give you all a farm."[19] National wealth notwithstanding, none but the most radical Republicans considered permanently redistributing confiscated Confederate land to former slaves. Senator Charles Sumner proposed legislation to provide homesteads to freed people, but even his colleague from the same state, fellow radical Henry Wilson, would not support it. Wilson argued that passing the measure would show special favor to blacks, to which Sumner replied that slavery had already placed blacks in a uniquely unfavorable position. In the House of Representatives, Pennsylvania's Thaddeus Stevens introduced a bill calling for the distribution of forty acres of confiscated land to freed people, but there too most members opposed it.[20] The strength of southern opposition to which Congress acquiesced extended even to selling land to African Americans, as reported by Whitelaw Reid shortly after the war:

> The feeling against any ownership of the soil by Negroes is so strong [among whites] that the man who should sell small tracts to them would be in actual personal danger. Every effort will be made to prevent Negroes from acquiring land; even the renting of small tracts to them is held to be unpatriotic and unworthy of a good citizen.[21]

Andrew Johnson, the new president, was even more resistant than Congress to the idea of redistributing land to blacks. Johnson had controlled the

process of reconstruction in the months immediately after Lincoln's assassination and had shown himself willing to concede power to the defeated Confederates. Former slaveholders asserted their authority over former slaves with
special laws called black codes, which restricted blacks' movements, their economic and political opportunities, and their civil rights. Racially discriminatory
vagrancy laws reduced black workers to near-slave conditions. Congress was
so outraged by the apparent attempt to continue old relationships under new
names that moderate Republicans united with radicals to wrest control from
the president and institute their more liberal congressional reconstruction,
sometimes called Radical Reconstruction. Before the war educating slaves had
been illegal, and even free blacks had played almost no role in southern politics. Now Radical Reconstruction extended education for blacks, protected
black voting rights, and encouraged blacks to hold political office. Yet most
African Americans remained landless, and the few blacks who had been
settled on confiscated land soon found themselves dispossessed. Hopes that
the government would deliver forty acres and a mule were dashed against hard
political reality. Congress voted to return almost all Confederate land to
prewar owners, leaving the economic power structure of the South largely
intact. There were temporary political gains, but without the provision of land
to freed people, emancipation could bring no fundamental or lasting economic
change.[22]

One of the most significant and longest-lasting efforts during these years
was the establishment of a number of black colleges in the South. Some
schools, notably Howard University in Washington, D.C., begun in 1867, were
founded with the aid of the federal government and received some public support, but the vast majority were formed by northern missionary groups.
Starting with Fisk University in Nashville in 1866, and Morgan College in Baltimore and Morehouse College in Atlanta the following year, black higher education was off to an impressive start. By 1895 there were forty colleges
educating a predominantly black student body. These colleges were the intellectual centers of southern black life, and their graduates became the teachers of generations of African American leaders.[23]

Once in control, in 1867, the Republican Congress divided the former Confederacy into five military districts and declared black suffrage to be one important precondition for reinstating the rights of southern states in the federal
union. Initially the southern state governments under Reconstruction were
dominated by an alliance of northern migrants and southern loyalists. Most
white southerners disdainfully called these northerners "carpetbaggers" and
derided the loyalists by calling them "scalawags." With black voters providing a solid base, this Republican alliance controlled southern state governments
for nearly a generation. African Americans were generally well represented at

the state conventions that drew up new constitutions removing race as an obstacle to voting. They constituted a majority of the eligible voters in South Carolina, Florida, Mississippi, and Louisiana and exercised their greatest political power in these states. In South Carolina blacks made up more than 60 percent of the delegates to the postwar constitutional convention, and fifty-seven of them had been slaves. This convention, which also included twenty-seven southern whites, adopted a remarkably progressive constitution in 1868. It abolished racial discrimination in voting, schools, and the militia, and abolished dueling, property requirements for voting or officeholding, and imprisonment for debt. This constitution established the state's first free public school system with regular support and reformed the courts by providing for elected rather than appointed judges. Women also gained rights under its provisions, as a married woman's property could no longer be sold to satisfy her husband's debts, and it instituted South Carolina's first divorce law.[24]

There were also important changes at the federal level during Reconstruction, as Congress passed and the states ratified amendments to the nation's Constitution. The Thirteenth Amendment (1865) prohibited slavery, the Fourteenth Amendment (passed 1866; ratified 1868) nullified the Dred Scott decision by banning the use of race as a bar to citizenship, and the Fifteenth Amendment (passed 1869; ratified 1870) prohibited the use of race to deny the right to vote. The provision of citizenship rights to African Americans was unpopular with President Johnson, with northern Democrats, and particularly with whites in the southern states. These amendments helped Republicans build and sustain their political power in the South. They also escalated the conflict over the control of Reconstruction policy between Congress and Johnson that resulted in the impeachment and near removal of the president in 1868.

Later that year John W. Menard from Louisiana, where nearly 50 percent of the population was black, became the first African American elected to the U.S. House of Representatives. However, the House Committee on Elections ruled that, though Menard had been fairly elected, Congress was not yet ready to admit an African American. Menard, whose parents were French Creoles, addressed the House, eloquently defending his right to serve, but the House refused to seat him. In South Carolina, where almost 60 percent of the population was African American, blacks held state and local offices from lieutenant governor, secretary of state, treasurer, and speaker of the state house to county sheriff and court clerk. In 1869 the University of South Carolina was opened to all races, and two African Americans were elected to its board of trustees. The next year the state sent its first African American, Joseph H. Rainey, to the U.S. House of Representatives. Within a year, Rainey was joined by four other blacks from Alabama, Florida, and South Carolina. When the

African Americans in the Forty-first and Forty-second
Congress of the United States, 1872.

Photographs and Prints Division, Schomburg Center for Research in Black Culture,
The New York Public Library, Astor, Lenox, and Tilden Foundations.

South Carolina General Assembly met in the fall of 1872, African Americans
took their places as president pro tem of the senate and speaker of the house.
Although no state elected a black governor, Louisiana's lieutenant governor,
P.B.S. Pinchback, formerly denied his seat in the U.S. Senate, served as acting governor after the corrupt white governor was removed from office.

Although hundreds of African Americans were elected to state and local
offices in the South, they never controlled any state government. Yet the
promise held by the dramatic political changes going on in the South drew
many African Americans. Some who had moved north before the war returned,
and many who had been born in the North went south to work, teach, and
share in the new political power. Jonathan J. Wright, for example, had been
born in Pennsylvania, had studied law, and had been the first African American admitted to the bar in that state. The opportunity to work for the Freedmen's Bureau attracted him to South Carolina. There he became a member
of the postwar constitutional convention and, a few years later, was elected

to the bench of the state supreme court, where he served until 1877.[25] African Americans were powerful in the Republican Party in the South and held high positions in state and regional governments. Voters elected black men to offices at all levels, from local sheriff to representative in the national Congress, and blacks were in office from the late 1860s throughout the nineteenth century. More than six hundred served in state legislatures, and by the beginning of the twentieth century, twenty had served in the House of Representatives and two had served in the Senate.

Although most southern blacks were illiterate at the end of the war, most black political leaders were educated. They were former soldiers, abolitionists, businessmen, ministers, lawyers, and teachers. Some were self-taught, like Oscar J. Dunn, who was born a slave in Louisiana and became lieutenant governor of the state. Others had considerably more formal education, like Francis Louis Cardozo, who was educated in Europe at the University of Glasgow and the London School of Theology. Cardozo returned to his native South Carolina in 1865 to head Avery Institute, the area's largest black educational institution. He was also a member of the convention that drew up the state's progressive post–Civil War constitution and served as secretary of state from 1868 to 1872 and state treasurer from 1872 to 1877. Jonathan Gibbs, who graduated from Dartmouth College and Princeton Theological Seminary, was Florida secretary of state from 1868 to 1872 and later was state superintendent of education. The educational accomplishments of many African American officeholders contradicted the claims of white southerners that illiterate blacks controlled the South. Some blacks made the point that most of the African Americans who served at the national level had more formal education than President Andrew Johnson. Working through the Republican Party and political associations such as the Union League, black leaders and their constituents transformed southern politics, at least for a time.

Although voting was limited to men, black women were a powerful presence in Reconstruction politics. Before the war both enslaved and free women had been active participants in black family, work, and community life. Now that freedom had finally come, they continued to be active. White women sometimes attended political conventions and rallies, sitting quietly at the rear of the room or observing from the gallery, but black women were known actually to take the floor and participate in the debate. White Republicans in Charleston, South Carolina, became so exasperated that they once asked their black colleagues to "leave their wives at their firesides."[26] Despite such protests black women continued to play important roles in community decision making and participated in every phase of politics but voting. Black Republican organizers traveled the South during the 1860s speaking to blacks at churches and other community gatherings and urging the men to vote and

Hiram Rhoades Revels

Born free in 1822 in Fayetteville, North Carolina, during the height of slavery, Hiram Revels left the South to be educated at a Quaker seminary in Indiana and at Knox College in Illinois. After graduation he became a minister in the African Methodist Episcopal Church, serving congregations in the midwestern and border states. When the Civil War broke out, he helped recruit black troops for the U.S. Army in Maryland and Missouri. He joined the Republican Party and served on the city council in Natchez and in the Mississippi state senate in the late 1860s. In 1870 Revels was elected to fill the seat recently vacated by former Confederate president Jefferson Davis in the U.S. Senate, becoming the first African American to serve in that body. Mississippi Democrats were furious at the election of a black man to represent their state, calling him "a thousand dollar darky." Referring to the cost of the war, one northern writer argued that Revels was "a three thousand million Darky," adding, "I hear in his voice the thunders of [Confederate defeats at] Donelson, and Shiloh, and Vicksburg, and Gettysburg and in his footsteps the tread of mightier armies than Napoleon marshalled for the conquest of Europe." Senator Simon Cameron of Pennsylvania recalled ironically that he had once warned Davis that through the justice of God "a Negro some day will come and occupy your seat." The Senate gallery was filled when Senator Revels came forward to take his oath of office. The *Philadelphia Press* reported, "Never since the birth of the republic has such an audience been assembled under one roof . . . the greatest and the least American citizens."*

With Revels formally placed in the Senate, that body set about bringing Mississippi back into the United States as a full partner in the union. After serving in the Senate, Revels returned to Mississippi, at first to minister to an African Methodist Episcopal church and then to serve as the president of two black schools, Alcorn Agricultural and Mining College and the newly formed Mississippi State College for Negroes. By the end of his life in 1901, Revels had turned conservative, even supporting the Democratic Party and the white supremacist White League. Perhaps the violent end of Reconstruction led him to be afraid for African Americans who continued to resist the inhumane and murderous force of the Ku Klux Klan and other terrorist groups.

Hiram Revels, U.S. senator from Mississippi. Mark E. Mitchell Collection of African American History.

*Lerone Bennett, Jr., *Black Power U.S.A.: The Human Side of Reconstruction, 1867–1877* (Chicago: Johnson Publishing Company, Inc., 1967), 213–214.

the women to see that they did.[27] In many places "the voting," as blacks often called it, was a festive occasion, a family day on which women accompanied men to the polling places, where they shared picnic lunches. The female presence was not just symbolic. One observer in South Carolina reported that black women "appear to have assumed a role more in keeping with their 'place' as they, like the ancient Greek women of Lysistrata, reportedly applied the sanctions of the bedroom to whip male political defectors into conformity with self-interest."[28] In rural Mississippi, women threatened similar sanctions. In other places women employed more direct methods of controlling black male votes. One black woman in South Carolina attacked her husband with an ax after she learned that he had sold his vote to the Democratic candidate.[29]

African American participation in southern politics was a revolutionary change, but it was only part of the change brought about by emancipation. Deviations from southern traditions governing everyday racial interactions angered and frightened Southern whites. Many blacks had decided, as one former slave in Georgia put it, to take "no more foolishness off white folks," and they were incensed when whites tried to continue the old racial conventions designed to reinforce status distinctions. Addressing a black man as "boy" and a black woman as "girl" or either as "nigger" was likely to lead to a confrontation. In Helena, Arkansas, when an elderly former slave addressed a white man on the street as "Mr. Powell," Powell followed the prewar convention and replied, "Howdy, uncle." The black man angrily assured him that they were not related and demanded, "Call me Mister."[30]

Black political power in the Reconstruction South could not force changes in land policies needed for long-term economic and social transformation. Most blacks were without land, so the best they could manage was to work for white landholders who had little cash but offered shares of the crop in return for their labor. Although sharecropping could conceivably have offered an approximation of the family farm, it most often led to debt peonage. White landholders used both legal and illegal means to bind black sharecroppers to the land through real or contrived indebtedness. Impecunious sharecroppers were forced to rely on credit advanced against the next year's crop to purchase farming supplies. The seed, tools, and teams of mules or horses were purchased on credit, as were the food, clothing, and other necessities that families needed to sustain themselves. The farmers secured credit either at stores the landholder operated on his land or at independent local stores. In either case expenses were generally manipulated to the sharecroppers' disadvantage. At the end of the year, when profits were figured and debts were settled, sharecroppers were likely to find themselves in debt. Their debts grew each year, and there was no authority to whom they could appeal. "They said figures didn't lie," reported one Arkansas sharecropper. "You know how that was. You dassent dispute a [white] man's word then."[31] Sharecropping offered some independence compared to the slave gang-labor system, but the shift in power was limited. Former slaves understood very well that they were farming the white man's land and were forced to play by the white man's rules. Looking back over his life as a sharecropper, eighty-year-old Henry Blacke explained, "No matter how good accounts you kept, you had to go by [the white landowners'] account, and—now brother, I'm telling you the truth about this—it has been that way a long time."[32] Even during the late 1860s and 1870s, when Republicans held political power, southern Democrats often had so much white popular support that U.S. troops could not protect blacks' legal rights.

The organization of political terrorist groups also made it extremely difficult to enforce black civil rights laws. There were many groups such as the Knights of the White Camellia or the Pale Faces, but the most notorious was the Ku Klux Klan, initially formed as a social group in Pulaski, Tennessee (on Christmas Eve) in 1866. These groups attempted to impose social, economic, and political control on former slaves and their allies by intimidating voters and enforcing the southern racial etiquette. They punished black sharecroppers for questioning white landlords, besieged black businesses for being too competitive, attacked black students for displaying too much intelligence, and assaulted white people for encouraging black aspirations. Few white southerners accepted full emancipation; most refused to acknowledge black people as citizens and continued to treat them as property, albeit property at large. White "[m]en who are honorable in their dealings with their white neighbors will cheat a Negro without feeling a single twinge of their honor," reported one Freedmen's Bureau official.[33] Such whites believed that their version of southern civilization must be protected by punishing any black person who showed signs of contesting their control.

Punishment ran the gamut from individual beatings and whippings to massacre. African Americans understood that "to kill a Negro [white southerners] do not deem murder; to debauch a Negro woman they do not think fornication; to take the property away from a Negro they do not consider robbery."[34] As one black soldier in Mississippi reported to the Freedmen's Bureau, "houses have been tourn down from the heades of women and Children," and none dared complain for fear of their lives. "Report came to [Vicksburg, Mississippi] this morning," he wrote, "that two colored women was found dead side the Jackson road with their throats cut lying side by side."[35] The Klan targeted the churches and their ministers for bolstering black spirits and the schools and teachers for educating black children. Before the war white southerners had considered African Americans who could read and write dangerous, and educating them had generally been prohibited. Rates of literacy among southern whites, themselves, were low. Particularly to poor illiterate whites, a black person with a superior education seemed to be a violation of the natural social order. Education, many argued, would create false pride, raise unrealistic aspirations, and spoil blacks for the work for which they were destined. "The cook, that must read the daily newspaper," one white educator warned, "will spoil your beef and your bread." Underlying these fears was the threat of social equality and the belief that black men might demand access to white women as the badge of their equality. Southern white women had become the embodiment of southern civilization. The slave system had given white men virtually free access to black women. In the aftermath of emancipation, southern white men envisioned a postrevolutionary society where black men asserted the same privileges. This was the nightmare that gave rise to extreme fantasies of racial menace and could bring even law-abiding white people to justify the most grisly violence.[36]

Between midnight and one o'clock in the morning in May in the early 1870s the Klan descended on the home of Elias Hill, a black minister severely crippled by rheumatism in both arms and legs. They beat his brother's wife and forced her to show them where Hill was sleeping. They dragged him from his bed, took him to the front yard, and accused him of encouraging "black men to ravish all the white women" in the town. While he protested his innocence, the night riders beat him with their fists and whips, put a gun to his head, and threatened to kill him. After the beating their real purpose became clear—they demanded that Hill place an ad in the newspaper "to renounce all republicanism and never vote." They threatened to return and kill him if he did not stop preaching republicanism.[37]

Although the Klan drew its footsoldiers from the ranks of poor white southerners, the southern planter aristocracy encouraged, condoned, and sometimes controlled their actions. Democratic leader Wade Hampton of South Carolina explained to his political colleagues that illegal action, even murder, in defense of racial domination was completely acceptable. "Every Democrat must feel honor bound to control the vote of at least one Negro," he argued. Then he elucidated, "Never threaten a man individually. If he deserves to be threatened, the necessities of the times require that he should be killed."[38] This kind of rhetoric encouraged terrorist groups' violent action. In 1876 President U. S. Grant charged that "murders and massacres of innocent men" because of their political opinions had become so frequent as to be familiar. An undetermined number of blacks in Aiken County, South Carolina (estimates ranged from 15 to 125), were killed trying to vote, and in Hamburg, South Carolina, whites assaulted black voters in a "cruel, bloodthirsty, wanton, and unprovoked" attack.[39] The pattern was the same in Louisiana, Mississippi, and everywhere Republicans were strong. In Kentucky alone more than one hundred blacks were lynched in the first decade after the war.

This Klan violence was not simply randomly directed at African Americans. It was political terrorism designed to restore southern Democratic power. On occasion Klan leaders seemed willing to endorse black political action if it supported the Democrats. In Memphis the Klan encouraged and agreed to protect sixty-five African Americans who established the Colored Democratic Club in the summer of 1868. Not many blacks were willing to support the Democrats, however, and Klan attacks on Republicans, regardless of race, increased so that in 1870 Congress passed the first of a series of Enforcement Acts authorizing the use of federal troops to control Klan violence. In 1871 Congress launched an extensive investigation of the Klan, and in a series of federal trials in Mississippi, South Carolina, and North Carolina, hundreds of whites—some of whom were doctors, lawyers, ministers, college professors, and other professionals—were arrested and indicted. Congress also passed a limited-term law that forced much of the Klan's activities underground, but with the support of the South's most influential citizens, the Klan continued its terrorism throughout the late nineteenth century.[40]

African Americans did not submit meekly to Klan violence. Black judges issued arrest warrants, and black sheriffs jailed white terrorists. Confrontations between black soldiers or returning veterans and whites were common. Black troops arrested the white chief of police in Wilmington, North Carolina, when he refused to surrender his weapon as ordered. Black soldiers in Victoria, Texas, retaliated for the murder of a black civilian by lynching the white killer, and black soldiers in South Carolina shot a Confederate veteran who had stabbed a black sergeant for refusing to leave a railroad car in which white women were seated. Many black veterans retained their military weapons, and some formed militia units to protect their communities. Southern whites made various attempts to disarm the black community, especially where black militia units most actively resisted attacks. Often white Republican officials acceded to white petitions to gain the cooperation of prominent local citizens. Disarming these units left black communities much more vulnerable to terrorist attack.[41]

Though some historians have speculated that blacks were unwilling or unable to defend themselves, there is strong evidence to the contrary.[42] African Americans were most vulnerable and white terrorists were most active in areas of the South where blacks were a minority or just barely a majority. The Klan and other groups were far less active where there were large majority-black populations. Even where they were most vulnerable, however, blacks did not submit to intimidation quietly. In 1868 Charles Caldwell, a black Mississippi politician who was wounded by a white man, shot and killed his assailant. Such confrontations were common, but Caldwell's acquittal by an all-white jury on the grounds of self-defense was unusual.[43]

Historical suggestions of a general black acquiescence to intimidation were more propaganda than reality, but those who resisted were likely to pay a heavy price. On Christmas Day almost a decade after his acquittal, Caldwell was shot dead by a white gang. By the mid-1870s terrorist tactics were returning Democrats to power, and there were fewer and fewer protections for southern African Americans. Leaders continued to urge resistance throughout the century. Writing anonymously in an 1885 New York newspaper, one black Kentuckian counted the number of blacks killed by white attacks. "We cannot stand it any longer," he contended. "We should kill as well as be killed." But African Americans in the South understood the impracticality of armed confrontation with the whites and the dwindling prospects for justice. A political compromise between Republicans and Democrats in the winter of 1877 brought Republican Rutherford B. Hayes into the White House in return for business investment in the South, the withdrawal of the few remaining U.S. occupying troops, and the tacit understanding that southern blacks would be left to the mercy of southern Democrats.[44]

By the late 1870s the rapprochement between the political parties, the disarming of the local black militia, and the reassertion of white control over black labor had nearly ended black political influence. Supreme Court decisions in a series of cases from 1873 to 1883 removed federal protection for almost all black civil rights in the South, leaving terrorists free rein. To make matters worse, in the middle of the national economic depression of 1873, the privately operated Freedmen's Savings Bank failed. The bank had been incorporated by Congress in 1865 to provide financial services and encourage thrift among the freedman, but the speculation of its directors made it one of many institutions to succumb to the economic crisis. It closed its doors in 1874, depriving its depositors—individual blacks, black churches, and black benevolent societies—of most of their hard-earned savings. Bank customers were paid a fraction of their deposits, and these poor people who had trusted their meager accounts to what had seemed to be an institution backed by the federal government lost faith in banks and their government for many generations.[45]

In the face of economic hardship, diminishing opportunities, and mounting racial violence, many former slaves decided to leave the South. In Louisiana political activist and former U.S. soldier Henry Adams expressed the feelings of many southern blacks. "This is a horrible part of the country," he lamented. African Americans could not find justice or enjoy the basic rights of citizenship in a society still controlled by whites who had never accepted the demise of slavery.[46] Frustration and pessimism over conditions in the South again led some African Americans to consider African emigration. In the spring of 1878, more than two hundred people departed for Liberia from Charleston, South Carolina, on the ship *Azor*, chartered by the black-owned Liberian Exo-

Handbill,
Lexington, Kentucky,
1877.
Kansas Historical
Society.

dus Joint Stock Steamship Company. Although their motives are difficult to assess, there were some for whom emigration was a matter of racial pride and nationalism. One such emigrationist was Bishop Henry McNeal Turner of the African Methodist Episcopal Church. He experienced the disappointment and disillusionment of postwar reconstruction in Georgia, became convinced that America offered no future for black people, and hoped that two or three million African Americans would establish a humane and just society in the land of their ancestors.[47]

However, though conditions were dismal, most African Americans, like other generations before them, were unable or unwilling to leave the United States. Most remained in the rural South, and those who migrated went to southern cities or to the North. A considerable number dreamed of attaining independence and self-sufficiency by becoming landholders in the West. Some struck out for New Mexico, Arizona, or Colorado. Groups left North Carolina and Mississippi for Nebraska, and a large number moved to Kansas. Henry Adams claimed that ninety-eight thousand black people had enrolled their names with him to express their intention to migrate to the West.[48] "Exodusters," as they were called, led by such men as Adams and former slave Benjamin "Pap" Singleton, moved their families from the Deep South westward into Kansas in 1879 and 1880. Singleton's real estate company promised affordable land to those who would move west to claim it, enticing several thousand to relocate. Life in Kansas was hard, but many found greater freedom there than they had known in the South. The first group of Exodusters arrived in April 1879, traveling up the Missouri River by steamboat to Wyandotte in eastern Kansas. These were poor people, dressed in patched, tattered clothes, with little money, a few of them sick and unable to go to work immediately. By that fall they had been joined by fifteen thousand others, and the Kansas governor promised a delegation of one hundred that they would receive justice and aid.[49]

Former abolitionists established a Freedmen's Relief Association to provide food and medical supplies, and Kansas's whites seemed willing to provide jobs and homes. Other aid came from as far away as Chicago and New England. Many black women found jobs cooking and doing laundry in town, while the men secured homesteads outside town and built homes. Men who could not secure land found jobs on farms, in coal mines, or on the railroad. Within a few years blacks had purchased more than twenty thousand acres of land and built the new black towns of Dunlap, Singleton, and Nicodemus. Unable to build homes during harsh weather, settlers spent their first winter in dugout shelters. Although Nicodemus is the only one of these formerly all-black towns still in existence, for a time they were home to hundreds of settlers. Eventually crop failures, lack of water, and damage from winds so strong that they blew away seeds and full-grown plants forced many to move to urban black communities in Kansas City and Topeka. Although life in the West was generally better than in the South, there was also discrimination, and blacks' precarious lives depended on the ebb and flow of whites' fears and tolerance. Denver residents refused to rent to blacks or give them jobs, and some communities like Lincoln, Nebraska, expelled black migrants.[50]

Hundreds of African Americans went West with the cattle drives from Texas to the new settlements of the region. Britton Johnson was a former slave who became a black cowboy and made his reputation as an Indian fighter on the Texas frontier. The cowboy Nat Love was said to have won the title "Deadwood Dick" in a roping contest. Stagecoach Mary Fields, born a slave in Tennessee, became famous driving freight wagons in Montana. James Beckwourth, one of the best-known black fur trappers and mountain men, was, for a time, a tribal leader of the Crow Indians. Beckwourth opened a pass through the mountains into California that bears his name. Black gunfighters and outlaws, such as Babe Fisher and Ned Huddleston, alias the Black Fox, disrupted town life, while the black troops of the U.S. Ninth and Tenth Cavalries, whom Native Americans respectfully called Buffalo Soldiers, attempted to keep the peace. On both sides of the law, blacks exercised a power that challenged assumptions about white supremacy. In an effort to preserve the lives of its citizens, one frontier town passed an ordinance making it a crime to insult or otherwise assault Cherokee Bill, a black gunfighter known to confront and kill those who molested him. Bill, whose skill with a weapon was notorious, was eventually hanged for murder. On the western frontier, race was sometimes subordinated to the need for cooperation and comradeship. On cattle drives, among the mountain men, and even in some frontier towns, blacks and whites often found an easy association generally not possible in the South or the East.[51]

Southern Democratic politicians built a new structure of racial control to replace slavery. In the state legislatures and the courts, southern conser-

Nat Love, the black cowboy also known as "Deadwood Dick."

William L. Katz, Blacks in the West Photograph Collection, Schomburg Center for Research in Black Culture, The New York Public Library, Astor, Lenox, and Tilden Foundations.

vatives set about abrogating black political rights and reversing even the limited social and economic progress made during Reconstruction. By the early 1880s Supreme Court decisions that declared federal civil rights laws unconstitutional left the responsibility for protecting black rights to the states. This effectively thwarted the Thirteenth, Fourteenth, and Fifteenth Amendments to the Constitution, as southern states refused to recognize black civil rights. A new state constitution for Mississippi, adopted in 1890, contained complicated restrictions, including a poll tax and a literacy test, specifically designed to limit or eliminate black voting. So as not to deprive illiterate whites of the vote, the law provided that those who could not pass the literacy test might still vote if their grandfather had voted before 1866. This "grandfather clause" effectively denied blacks, most of whom had been slaves before that time, the voting rights that the Fifteenth Amendment was designed to guarantee.

Cover of *Harper's Weekly,* the Buffalo Soldiers.

Mark E. Mitchell Collection of African American History.

In the 1896 case of *Plessy* v. *Ferguson,* the Supreme Court helped shape social and economic inequality in the postwar South by supporting laws that sustained a far-reaching system of racial segregation. Justice John Marshall Harlan, the lone dissenting voice on the Court, observed, "[T]he judgment rendered this day will, in time, prove to be quite as pernicious as the decision made by the tribunal in the Dred Scott case." Gradually other southern states adopted the Mississippi plan for disenfranchising blacks and instituted racially discriminatory laws.[52] These were referred to as Jim Crow laws, taking their name from the mid-nineteenth-century minstrel characterization performed in blackface by Thomas "Daddy" Rice, a white comedian who portrayed a stereotypical ignorant, helpless African American. These state and local laws separated the races in public transportation and accommodations, in public education, and in virtually every public phase of life from the trivial to the significant. Some of the old pre–Civil War patterns remained, as African Americans still performed intimate services for the white middle class and elites, cooking their food, cleaning their houses, and caring for their children. Blacks often lived conveniently near whites, and they did much of the manual labor in fields and factories owned and operated by whites. But Jim Crow laws enforced inequality and demanded greater racial separation than had generally existed during slavery. Eventually all southern drinking fountains, public parks, swimming pools, hospitals, restaurants, movie theaters, and phone booths were segregated by race. Courtrooms even had separate Bibles for swearing in members of different races. Segregationists drew on so-called experts in the biological sciences to lend support to the theories of black inferiority concretized in the laws. By the early twentieth century racial discrimination and segregation were the law of the South.

Reconstruction, begun with such promise for African Americans, ended in disappointment as opportunities for southern blacks constricted, Republican power waned, and constitutional guarantees vanished under the power of Supreme Court rulings. Debt bound many sharecroppers to the land almost as tightly as slavery had gripped slaves before the war. A few black politicians remained in office, even in the U.S. Congress, into the twentieth century, but by the 1890s the reversal of interracial progress was clear. As the nation turned its attention to the more northern concerns of industrialization, urbanization, and European immigration, the South was increasingly free to develop its own policies on race, and southern blacks found themselves isolated in poverty and oppression. For most African Americans freedom remained—in the words of poet Langston Hughes a generation later—"a dream deferred."

Chapter 9

1898	Spanish-American War; four black army regiments serve
1899	W.E.B. Du Bois publishes *The Philadelphia Negro,* pathbreaking study of an African American community
	Composer-pianist Scott Joplin releases "Maple Leaf Rag"
1900	U.S. population 75,994,575; black population 8,833,994 (12 percent)
	"Lift Every Voice and Sing," composed by James Weldon Johnson and J. Rosamond Johnson and called the black national anthem, first sung at a celebration of Abraham Lincoln's birthday
1903	W.E.B. Du Bois publishes *The Souls of Black Folk,* opposing Booker T. Washington's accommodationist stance
1904	African Americans compete in Olympic Games for first time; George Poage wins a bronze medal in the four-hundred-meter hurdles
1905	Black leaders, including W.E.B. Du Bois and William Monroe Trotter, establish the Niagara Movement
	Chicago Defender inaugural issue published; the newspaper becomes major information source for southern blacks considering moving north
1908	Jack Johnson becomes the first black heavyweight boxing champion, defeating Tommy Burns
1909	The integrated National Association for the Advancement of Colored People (NAACP) founded as the successor to the black Niagara Movement
1910	Madame Walker (born Sarah Breedlove) establishes the Madame C.J. Walker Manufacturing Company in Indianapolis, Indiana
1911	National Urban League established to address racial problems in employment, health, and social welfare
1915	Association for the Study of Negro Life and History established in Chicago
1916	Marcus Garvey establishes Universal Negro Improvement Association (UNIA) to promote African emigration and racial pride
	First issue of *Journal of Negro History* published
1917	Ten thousand blacks participate in a silent march down Fifth Avenue, New York City, to protest lynching
1917–1918	American involvement in World War I includes service by about four hundred thousand African Americans
1919	The Red Summer: Whites kill and wound African Americans and destroy their property in twenty-six riots around the nation

Populism, Industrial Unions, and the Politics of Race

*I*n late January 1890, T. Thomas Fortune, editor of the *New York Age*, addressed the national convention of the Afro-American League, meeting in New York City. He urged blacks to join together to face the rising tide of support for white supremacy in America. There must be black-owned banks; agricultural, mechanical, and business schools; as well as academic and professional colleges, he contended. African Americans must establish special bureaus to provide shelter, employment, and protection for migrants and form a committee to lobby the federal government for the restoration of black civil rights. Black people must accomplish this and more to deal with "an abnormal condition" threatening every African American in the nation.[1]

Their loss of political and civil rights by the end of the nineteenth century left blacks few options. Many turned to the potential power of their labor, especially in the South, where African Americans were a large proportion of the work force, believing that achieving economic independence was a practical route to racial progress. After the Civil War, as soon as they were free, blacks in urban areas began to demand better working conditions and better wages. Workers at tobacco factories in Richmond and Manchester, Virginia, for example, pointed out that free black workers were earning half as much in 1865 as they had made when they were hired out as slaves.[2] John Mercer Langston's keynote address to the first Colored National Labor Convention in Washington, D.C., in 1869 underscored the importance of black wages, noting that the black population of about four and a quarter million people contained three million workers.[3] Black labor had built the South. Leaders knew that black labor, given opportunity, could assure the progress of the race, but serious impediments had restricted black progress. Before the war slaves had worked in both skilled and unskilled positions in farming, construction, and in the region's fledgling industries, but freed people faced severe discrimination. Only a small number of African Americans managed to remain in skilled positions after the war. They were generally relegated to the worst jobs and paid the lowest wages. When hired, they were usually segregated from white workers, but often they were not hired at all. Many postwar industrialists built cotton mills in southern mountain regions where the work force was predominantly white rather than in the cotton-growing regions where the

Fisk Jubilee Singers, 1882. The Fisk singers traveled the nation
as ambassadors for black higher education, raising money
for the university and needy students.
Photographic Collection, Moorland Springarn Library, Howard University.

greatest number of black workers lived. In industries like tobacco and iron manufacturing, technological development in the prewar South had been retarded by the availability of cheap labor. After the war labor was further cheapened by racial antagonisms. Employers fought unionization by racially segregating workers and threatening whites with replacement by blacks. The cities offered some opportunities for the skilled laborers and teachers who were the foundation of the small black middle class, but the vast majority of African Americans were agricultural workers. Therefore the fortunes of the race had depended greatly on farmers' prospects for advancement.

The postwar period brought some hopeful social and political changes. As businessmen promoting railroads and industry joined the old plantation aristocracy, the shared agricultural interests that formerly held whites together fractured along class lines. The desperately poor farmers, both whites and blacks, suffering from severe economic depressions, formed cooperative alliances as an alternative to the mounting indebtedness that threatened to make them sharecroppers instead of independent farmers. Joining together, they hoped to pay lower prices for supplies and services and get higher prices for their crops. They created parallel political organizations—whites in the Southern Farmers' Alliance and blacks in the Colored Farmers' National Alliance and Cooperative Union. By about 1890 the black farmers' organization reported more than one million members in twelve southern states. A few years later Alliance movement organizers claimed to have reached more than two million families in forty-three states.[4] Although the Alliance organizations worked together on some issues, a strike of cotton pickers in 1891 angered some members of the white Alliance who employed black farm laborers.

The most radical of the Alliance organizations identified with northern industrial workers and saw themselves in common cause with such labor unions as the Knights of Labor against oppression by capitalist bankers and corporations. The issues raised at a Texas meeting in 1886 clearly expressed Alliance class consciousness and echoed the positions of the Knights of Labor, asking for regulated railroad rates, high taxes on speculators' land, and inflated currency. In their own words their aim was to establish laws to gain "freedom from the onerous and shameful abuses that the industrial classes [were] suffering at the hands of arrogant capitalists and powerful corporations."[5] Unable to interest the major political parties in their legislative agenda, the Alliance ran its own candidates for local and national offices in Texas and Georgia and finally formed a new national People's Party, or Populist Party, in 1890 in Topeka, Kansas. In the same year white Farmers' Alliance officers proposed a joint meeting with organized black farmers, and these interracial meetings laid the foundation for their cooperative support of the Populist movement.

Interracial cooperation was never easy, especially in the South. Blacks remained tied to the Republican Party, considered the "Party of Lincoln," and Democrats continually reminded white workers that their race was more significant than their economic condition. But blacks did hold office in the Populist organization, were featured speakers at rallies, and formed their own Populist political clubs. In 1892 ninety-two blacks were delegates to the national convention in St. Louis, where Populist leader Ignatius Donnelly electrified the crowd. Arguing that there was only one important division in America, between the rich and the poor, Donnelly predicted that a Populist victory would erase the color line. The meeting erupted in wild enthusiasm, but blacks and southern white Populists understood that their cooperation was fraught with peril in the South. In order to attract the diminished numbers of black voters while not alienating white voters, the movement played down the interracial aspects of the party. Georgia congressman Tom Watson, running as a Populist in 1892, was one of the few white politicians to address black voters in public. "There is no reason why the black man should not understand that the law that hurts me, as a farmer, hurts him, as a farmer" (or a share-cropper or a mechanic), Watson argued. Black and white could work together, he said, so long as all understood that "self-interest rules."[6]

One writer, calling himself "Hayseeder" and claiming to have been "born under a Democratic roof, rocked in a Democratic cradle [and] sung to sleep with a Democratic lullaby," published a statement in one Populist newspaper arguing that blacks had as much right to participate in politics as did whites, and that Populists should encourage them to do so. Another predicted the imminent demise of the Democratic Party despite its attempts to survive by using race to divide the Populists. Although these statements indicated sentiment in favor of political cooperation, race remained a powerful social divider, and Tom Watson was quick to deny any belief in interracial organization. "It is best for your race and my race that we dwell apart in our private affairs," he explained to a gathering of blacks and whites. Race was clearly a dangerous issue in the South; H. S. Doyle, a black minister, was threatened with lynching for promoting the Populist cause. Although two thousand white men indicated their willingness to protect Watson and Doyle, Democratic-supported intimidation menaced the Populist Party as it had the Republicans at the height of Reconstruction.[7]

The Populist Party gained a partial success in the election of 1892. It won more than a million votes and elected Populist governors in Kansas and Colorado, but white animosity continued to handicap its efforts in the South. The party did poorly in the Upper South, winning few votes or offices in Virginia, West Virginia, Tennessee, or Kentucky. In the Lower South there were some close elections in Georgia, Alabama, and Texas, but Democrats remained dominant. The party, with a visible black component, continued to attract votes throughout the 1890s. When James Weaver, the Populist presidential candidate in 1894, appeared in a parade in North Carolina's capital city of Raleigh, 350 men, both blacks and whites, accompanied him on horseback.

Populist stands on issues such as the party's condemnation of the convict-lease system, continued to be popular among blacks. African Americans were the most likely victims of the system, which provided prisoners as near-slave labor for prominent white politicians, planters, and businessmen. The absence of jails in the South after the Civil War had prompted the states to offer convict labor to private contractors in return for a fee and their provision of food, clothing, and housing for the prisoners. This system made cheap labor available for lumbering, mining, agriculture, and railroad building throughout the South. The available labor supply had been greatly increased by the passage of measures such as Mississippi's 1876 "pig law," under which the theft of any property, including farm animals, valued at ten dollars or more became grand larceny, punishable by up to five years in state prison. Many southern businessmen became rich literally working these convicts to death. The historian David Oshinsky noted that "not a single leased convict ever lived long enough to serve a sentence of 10 years or more." He suggested that conditions under the convict-lease system in Mississippi's notorious Parchman prison farm and in other southern prisons during the late nineteenth and the early twentieth centuries may actually have been "worse than slavery."[8]

While Republicans turned away from black allies, Populists maintained interracial alliances and nominated African Americans for political and party offices. Successful black politician and lawyer George H. White, for example, a former slave who had served as a Republican in the North Carolina legislature and twice was elected to the U.S. House of Representatives, switched his political allegiance to the Populist Party in the mid-1890s. By the end of the century, though, the Populists were struggling. Reactionaries were intimidating and killing blacks and racially progressive whites in an attempt to maintain the power of the white southern separatists, and failure seemed inevitable. As southern Democrats redoubled their efforts to prevent blacks from voting, successful politicians, some of them former Populist allies, abandoned black supporters. Tom Watson blamed African Americans for the party's demise. He made venomous public statements and had become notorious as anti-Catholic, anti-Semitic, and bitterly racist by the time of his death in 1922. The Ku Klux Klan honored Watson by sending an eight-foot-high cross of roses to his funeral. The failure of both the Republican Party and the Populist movement demonstrated the power of racial division in the South. White rural and urban workers were willing to sacrifice their own economic interests to the principle of white supremacy.

Widespread racial violence reinforced this principle. An alarming number of lynchings occurred in the South—85 in 1890 and 113 in 1891. When Thomas Moss, Calvin McDowell, and Henry Stewart established their People's Grocery Company, outside Memphis, Tennessee, whites accused them of conspiring to monopolize black patronage and invaded the black community. Blacks armed to defend themselves, and police responded by arresting Moss, McDowell, and Stewart for inciting a riot. In March 1892 a white mob removed the three from jail, took them outside of town, and shot and then hanged them. Ida B. Wells, Moss's friend and black editor of the *Memphis Free Speech and Headlight,* published the shocking story. She argued that it refuted the claim by some whites that lynching was necessary to protect white women from black rapists, since these prominent businessmen had not even been charged with attacking white women. About Moss she wrote, "A finer, cleaner man than he never walked the streets of Memphis." The lynching of these three upstanding black men, she continued, was simply an "excuse to get rid of Negroes who were acquiring wealth and property and thus keep the race terrorized." Wells's continued investigation of other lynchings and urging blacks to leave Memphis brought increasing white hostility and finally the destruction of her newspaper office. Wells moved to New York City, where she joined T. Thomas Fortune and Jerome B. Peterson, owners and editors of the *New York Age,* and continued her crusade from the pages of that newspaper. Lynching rose to an all-time high of 161 in 1892. Many of these lynchings were public affairs that attracted huge crowds of onlookers who traveled long distances to view the spectacle. Ten thousand people assembled to watch the lynching of Henry Smith in Paris, Texas, in 1893. A special train was chartered for the occasion, which took on a carnival atmosphere as families shared picnic lunches. Some people began to fear a race war in the country, and in 1900 black congressman George White introduced the first federal antilynching bill, but Congress refused to vote on it.[9]

Racial ideology thwarted most possibilities for cooperative organization among workers and weakened the position of American labor well into the twentieth century. In 1881 skilled workers organized the American Federation of Labor (AFL), the largest, most successful labor organization of the period, and though they claimed to be open to all, few African Americans were ever admitted. By 1900, for example, only one thousand of the more than twenty-two thousand black carpenters were unionized. Jeremiah Grandison and other blacks attending the first meeting warned that management could use black workers as strikebreakers if they were excluded from the union. Indeed, the use of black workers as replacements was one factor in what labor historians have characterized as "the collapse of the union movement" after the white workers affiliated with the AFL struck Andrew Carnegie's Homestead Mill in Pittsburgh, Pennsylvania, in 1892.[10] Homestead hired three hundred heavily armed guards to protect the strikebreakers from angry union men, and management broke the strike after six months of hostilities and considerable violence. In the segregated system of labor organization that pitted workers against one another, white unionized workers often resorted to violence to drive black nonunion workers out of jobs. When white firemen on the Georgia Railroad refused to integrate their organization, black firemen were forced to take jobs with the company for lower pay. The company then cut its labor costs by hiring African Americans, and they constituted more than 40 percent of its firemen by 1909. The white union went on strike when the company replaced a fired white worker with an African American, and the strike quickly became a racial confrontation. White workers claimed that blacks were taking their jobs, but blacks thought it hypocritical for the union to exclude them and then complain when they competed with union members for jobs. The long, bitter strike was punctuated by violence, and although the Georgia Railroad continued to hire black firemen, black workers suffered from their reputation as strikebreakers who would undercut white wages.[11]

A few exceptional unions organized both black workers and white workers. The United Mine Workers of America (UMW), in an industry with a large proportion of black workers, organized industrywide rather than within specific crafts like most AFL affiliates. This relatively progressive union employed black recruiters, and by 1900, its twenty thousand black miners constituted 25 percent of the membership. Richard L. Davis was largely responsible for the UMW's success in recruiting black members. Davis argued that black miners could find real opportunities within the union, and he pressured white union leaders to open high-level positions to blacks. Despite Davis's organizing success, the UMW was no safe haven for black labor. When mine owners banned him from work, Davis's white union friends abandoned him, and he could find no employment with the UMW. He died in 1900 at the age of thirty-five, discouraged and unemployed. That same year Samuel Gompers took over the AFL. Under his leadership, the organization, pressured by its southern affiliates, moved away from the effort to organize black workers. The rare integrated unions notwithstanding, generally the best that black labor could expect from the AFL was sporadic and indirect support. Within a few years of his rise to power, Gompers argued that blacks were "unorganizable."[12]

Though African Americans were denied full economic and political participation, in early 1898 the country once again called on them to discharge the responsibilities of citizenship. Hostilities with Spain began in February, after the battleship *Maine* exploded and sank in Havana harbor, taking 266 American lives. The sensationalized newspaper accounts that followed blamed Spain and fueled demands for revenge. Stirred by calls to "Remember the *Maine!*" the public demanded that the United States invade Cuba, and Congress responded with a declaration of war. President William McKinley, unlike Washington and Lincoln before him, immediately commissioned blacks for service. He appointed one hundred black army officers to facilitate the raising of black troops, and advised blacks to "be patient, be progressive, [and] be determined." However, he did little to reward their patriotism. When four regiments of black Buffalo Soldiers embarked for Cuba, they traveled on the same ships as white troops but were segregated and confined below-decks. They fought in separate units and led Theodore Roosevelt's famed Rough Riders in their charge up San Juan Hill. Gen. John "Black Jack" Pershing, commander of the Tenth Cavalry, clearly exaggerated when he observed: "White regiments, black regiments, regulars and rough Riders, representing the young manhood of the North and South, fought shoulder to shoulder, unmindful of whether commanded by an ex-Confederate or not, and mindful only of their common duty as Americans."[13] Yet, it is remarkable that black troops and white troops served together at all in Cuba, given the segregation and racial hostilities at home, where 101 African Americans were lynched in 1898.[14]

African Americans were very aware of the contradictions posed by black participation in the Spanish-American War. Black lawyer Charles Baylor from Providence, Rhode Island, pointed out the irony that black Americans were fighting black Cubans for a nation in which all blacks were relegated to Jim Crow cars on southern trains. A new group, the National Negro Anti-Imperialist League, organized black resistance to American expansion, and opposition increased after American soldiers occupied the Philippines. Howard University professor Kelly Miller warned African Americans that "the bitter pill of imperialism may be sugar-coated to the taste, but the Negro swallows it to his own political damnation."[15] Opposition leaders saw racism implicated in American imperialism against colored people abroad. As Americans used biological theories of white supremacy to justify racial injustice at home, so they claimed expansion into Latin America and the Pacific as a part of the "white man's burden," a paternalistic mission to bring the blessings of white civilization to supposedly unfortunate and inferior colored peoples abroad.

Black responses to segregation, labor union policies, and racial violence in the late nineteenth and early twentieth centuries formed a broad spectrum, with two prominent African Americans coming to represent its opposite poles. Booker T. Washington, the most powerful of all southern black public figures of this period, was born a slave in Virginia and rose to national prominence as an educator and political leader. He was educated at Hampton Institute in Virginia, a school begun for freed people by northern religious philanthropists. Hampton's philosophy combined work, study, and self-help, and that training became the foundation of Washington's racial strategy. In 1881 Booker T. Washington became the president of the predominantly black Tuskegee Institute in Alabama, and he and his students literally built the school from the ground up. Tuskegee's faculty taught the students the importance of thrift, hard work, self-reliance, and, most important, trades for making a living. Basic carpentry, farming techniques, and the principles of small business headed the curriculum. Washington was a practical man who was propelled to national prominence by a speech he gave to a mainly white audience at the 1895 Cotton States and International Exposition in Atlanta, Georgia, in which he declared that it was necessary for African Americans to accept the developing southern system of racial segregation.

In this Atlanta Compromise speech, as it became known, Washington announced blacks' willingness to provide the labor that the South needed. Don't turn to foreign immigrant labor, he urged his listeners, but "cast down your bucket where you are, among eight millions of Negroes . . . whose fidelity and love you have tested . . . who have, without strikes and labor wars,

From Booker T. Washington's speech at the Atlanta Cotton States and International Exposition, September 18, 1895

. . . A ship lost at sea for many days suddenly sighted a friendly vessel. From the mast of the unfortunate vessel was seen a signal, "Water, water; we die of thirst!" The answer from the friendly vessel at once came back, "Cast down your bucket where you are." A second time the signal, "Water, water; send us water!" ran up from the distressed vessel, and was answered, "Cast down your bucket where you are." The captain of the distressed vessel, at last heeding the injunction, cast down his bucket, and it came up full of fresh, sparkling water from the mouth of the Amazon River. To those of my race who depend on bettering their condition in a foreign land or who underestimate the importance of cultivating friendly relations with the Southern white man, who is their next-door neighbour, I would say: "Cast down your bucket where you are"—cast it down in making friends in every manly way of the people of all races by whom we are surrounded.

Cast it down in agriculture, mechanics, in commerce, in domestic service, and in the professions. And in this connection it is well to bear in mind that whatever other sins the South may be called to bear, when it comes to business, pure and simple, it is in the South that the Negro is given a man's chance in the commercial world, and in nothing is this Exposition more eloquent than in emphasizing this chance. Our greatest danger is that in the great leap from slavery to freedom we may overlook the fact that the masses of us are to live by the productions of our hands, and fail to keep in mind that we shall prosper in proportion as we learn to dignify and glorify common labour and put brains and skill into the common occupations of life; shall prosper in proportion as we learn to draw the line between the superficial and the substantial, the ornamental gewgaws of life and the useful. No race can prosper till it learns that there is as much dignity in tilling a field as in writing a poem. It is at the bottom of life we must begin, and not at the top. Nor should we permit our grievances to overshadow our opportunities.

To those of the white race. . . . I would repeat what I say to my own race, "Cast down your bucket where you are." Cast it down among the eight millions of Negroes whose habits you know, whose fidelity and love you have tested in days when to have proved treacherous meant the ruin of your firesides. Cast down your bucket among these people who have, without strikes and labour wars, tilled your fields, cleared your forests, builded your railroads and cities, and brought forth treasures from the bowels of the earth. . . . While doing this, you can be sure in the future, as in the past, that you and your families will be surrounded by the most patient, faithful,

(continued)

(continued)

law-abiding, and unresentful people that the world has seen . . . in our humble way, we shall stand by you with a devotion that no foreigner can approach, ready to lay down our lives, if need be, in defence of yours, interlacing our industrial, commercial, civil, and religious life with yours in a way that shall make the interests of both races one. In all things that are purely social we can be as separate as the fingers, yet one as the hand in all things essential to mutual progress. . . .

The wisest among my race understand that the agitation of questions of social equality is the extremest folly, and that progress in the enjoyment of all the privileges that will come to us must be the result of severe and constant struggle rather than of artificial forcing. . . . It is important and right all privileges of the law be ours, but it is vastly more important that we be prepared for the exercises of these privileges. The opportunity to earn a dollar in a factory just now is worth infinitely more than the opportunity to spend a dollar in an opera-house.

. . . far above and beyond material benefits will be that higher good, that, let us pray God, will come, in a blotting out of sectional differences and racial animosities and suspicions, in a determination to administer absolute justice, in a willing obedience among all classes to the mandates of law. This, this, coupled with our material prosperity, will bring into our beloved South a new heaven and a new earth.

———

Booker T. Washington, *Up from Slavery* (Boston, 1901), 217–227.

tilled your fields, cleared your forests, [built] your railroads and cities," all in the most respectful manner. He assured white skeptics that blacks were "unresentful people" willing to be socially separate and eager to work together with whites for "all things essential to mutual progress," accepting second-class citizenship in exchange for jobs. "The wisest among my race understand that the agitation of questions of social equality is the extremest folly," he contended. Thus white southerners should be willing to look with paternalistic favor on African Americans whose prosperity, Washington believed, depended on their learning to "dignify and glorify common labour."[16] Washington had gauged his white audience correctly. He had told them what most whites wanted to believe, and they anointed him national spokesman for his people. African Americans' responses were more complex. Many believed that Washington's "submissive philosophy" signaled "an invitation to further [white] aggression."[17] Black educator John Hope called Washington's remarks cowardly, and castigated him for giving whites the hope that African Americans might accept economic security as a substitute for full citizenship. Black novelist Charles Chesnutt was critical of Washington's popularity with many blacks. "It is not a pleasing spectacle to see the robbed applaud the robber," he observed sharply.[18]

Reflecting Washington's increasing status, however, in the fall of 1901, President Theodore Roosevelt invited him to dinner at the White House to discuss the state of race relations. Although Lincoln had met in the White House with Frederick Douglass and others during the Civil War, southerners were incensed that President Roosevelt would actually sit down to eat with a black man. Initially the president angrily defended his actions in a letter, saying, "I shall have him to dine just as often as I please." Still, Roosevelt confided to a friend that inviting Washington to dinner at the White House had been a mistake. He understood that his action seemed to send an unacceptable message, approving of social equality, in this Jim Crow era. Many whites

Booker T. Washington's meal with President Theodore Roosevelt
at the White House brought strong reaction from southern segregationists
who saw the act as an insult to the South.
Photographs and Prints Division, Library of Congress, Washington, D.C.

insisted on referring to the meal as a luncheon, apparently seeing a midday meal as less objectionable. To calm his critics, the president let it be known that there had been no women present, thus avoiding the intimation of interracial sexual impropriety. Furthermore, the meal had been served informally on trays in an office, not in a dining room.[19]

Hoping the furor would die down, Roosevelt told friends he was certain his southern policy was right, but he further angered southerners by supporting the appointment of Minnie Cox, a black woman, as postmistress in Indianola, Mississippi. Nonetheless the president did not support racial equality. He supported the "Lily-white" Republicans, as the southern wing of his party was called, and even supported some of the southern Democrats' white supremacy programs.

The best-known and most formidable opponent of Booker T. Washington's strategy was Dr. William E. Burghart [W.E.B.] Du Bois. Born in New England, raised in a largely white community, and educated for most of his early life in white schools, Du Bois went south for the first time as an undergraduate to attend Fisk University, a black school in Nashville, Tennessee. He found the racial attitudes and violent traditions of the South shocking. After graduating from Fisk, Du Bois went to Harvard University, where he received an M.A. and a Ph.D., and then to the University of Berlin. In contrast to Washington, who placed his faith in manual training and accepted the necessity of working within the southern system of segregation, Du Bois brought social-science methods to bear on the nation's racial problem. He was committed to racial progress through the achievement of political and social equality. Du Bois became a professor at the University of Pennsylvania and in 1899 published *The Philadelphia Negro*, a study documenting the poverty and discrimination that limited the opportunities of that city's blacks. After moving to Atlanta University, the black intellectual center of the South, he initiated a remarkable set of intellectual gatherings that became known as the Atlanta Conferences and edited the resulting scholarly studies of black social and economic issues.[20]

Du Bois attacked Booker T. Washington directly in his book, *The Souls of Black Folk*, published in 1903. He agreed with Washington that blacks must be thrifty, patient, and learn practical skills that prepared them for employment, but he abhorred any intimation that they should abandon claims to full citizenship, ignore violence and injustice, or accept a socially inferior status. Moreover Du Bois placed his hope for racial progress in leadership by the best educated, intellectually trained African Americans. He envisioned this "Talented Tenth" as a living argument for racial justice in the United States, a group that carried the responsibility for uplifting their brothers and sisters. In the summer of 1905 Du Bois put his plan into action and convened a meeting to establish a permanent national organization for racial progress. Twenty-nine black business and professional men gathered in Niagara Falls, Canada, meeting just over the border so that they might find acceptable accommodations with fewer racial restrictions than in the United States. Taking its name from this meeting place, their organization became known as the Niagara Movement. The following year the group met at Harpers Ferry, West Virginia. There they trod barefoot across the ground hallowed by the sacrifice of John Brown and his band and dedicated themselves to a grassroots campaign: "We will not be satisfied to take one jot or tittle less than our full manhood rights," they pledged, "[and will] never cease to protest and assail the ears of America." To implement their plan, they formed local chapters, initiated court actions, and filed petitions with all levels of government, protesting the abuse of civil rights.[21]

Many regions of the South experienced a renewed wave of racial violence during the first decade of the twentieth century, and Du Bois's organization of the Niagara Movement aroused Booker T. Washington's fears that demands for racial equality would further inflame southern racists. Washington's attacks added to the internal disputes, northern indifference, and southern hostility that plagued the fledgling civil rights movement. Perhaps he believed that further appeasement of white racism might help shield southern blacks. In 1903 he seemed to argue that Africans benefited from the slave experience: "When the Negro went into slavery he was without anything which might properly be called language; when he came out of slavery he was able to speak the English tongue . . . when he entered slavery he had little working knowledge of agriculture, mechanics, or household duties; when he emerged . . . he was almost the entire dependence in a large section of our country for agricultural, mechanical and domestic labor." A few years later he added a characterization of blacks' African background likely to infuriate Du Bois. In Africa, Washington contended, the ancestors of former slaves had been "barbarous" with "a childish way of looking at and explaining the world"; in slavery, he noted, they had become Christians.[22]

This interpretation of slavery was, of course, exactly what promoters of the Old South wanted to believe, and it had special force coming from a prominent black leader, but if Washington hoped that his words might help curb racial violence, he was greatly mistaken. Race riots and lynchings of black people continued at an alarming pace throughout these years. Some of the worst racial violence occurred in Atlanta, Georgia. It was there that a middle-class boy of thirteen named Walter White came to the realize what it meant to be black in the American South. Politicians and the press in Atlanta had inflamed white anger over the question of black voting, and in response, one evening in late September 1906, a white mob moved through the black community, killing and burning at random. Walter's father took his mother and sister to the rear of their house, out of the line of fire. His father then stationed him at one of the front windows with the instruction, "Son, don't shoot until the first man puts his foot on the lawn and then—don't you miss!" The mob stopped short of their home after a number of black men opened fire, forcing it to retreat, but before the violence was over, the police had joined the mob, and ten black men and women had been killed and sixty others wounded. During the Atlanta massacre, Walter White discovered that, though he had white skin and light eyes and hair, when white men hunted black people, they sought him out too. "I was a Negro," he noted, "a human being with an invisible pigmentation which marked me as a person to be hunted, hanged, abused, discriminated against, [and] kept in poverty and ignorance." African Americans suffered all that, White believed, so that white people might feel superior. Atlanta's was only one of many riots that summer. In Abraham Lincoln's hometown of Springfield, Illinois, a white mob rampaged for six days, beating and killing African Americans and forcing hundreds of people from the city.[23]

During his 1905 tour through the South, Theodore Roosevelt had made no comment about the disenfranchisement of blacks, the fifty-seven lynchings that year, or the seventy-five lynchings the year before. In 1906 Roosevelt took drastic action against African American troops stationed at Fort Brown in Brownsville, Texas. The black soldiers, veterans of the Spanish-American War, were accused of attacking the town, killing one white civilian and wounding another. Individual soldiers could not be identified, however, nor was it clear that those involved had been black soldiers. Reaction to this incident occurred in the context of white outrage at rumors circulated earlier that a black man, believed to be a soldier, had assaulted a white woman in the town. The story was confused. The woman in question was supposedly either pushed to the ground or perhaps only patted on the head and spoken to disrespectfully. Whatever the truth, white townspeople assumed that black soldiers were to blame for the raid and the assault and demanded retribution. An army investigation could not determine which black soldiers, if any, were involved but assumed that all were implicated. With little regard for the obvious discrimination, the danger that black soldiers regularly faced in the South, or the unit's unblemished record, a military court quickly found them guilty. Booker T. Washington wrote to Roosevelt, explaining that he had important information about the case. The president ignored his message, however, and ordered the whole three companies of black soldiers, including five recipients of the Congressional Medal of Honor, dishonorably discharged. Any faith that blacks had had in Roosevelt or the Republican Party waned thereafter. White supremacy set the tone of American politics during the early decades of the twentieth century. African Americans saw Theodore Roosevelt, who believed that blacks were "altogether inferior to whites," as a man of his time.[24]

Presidents who followed Roosevelt were little better, and sometimes worse, on racial issues. The White House and Congress refused to move against lynching or to protect civil rights in the South, and it was common for high-level government officials pubicly to express racist beliefs. In 1909 Republican president Howard Taft told a group of black North Carolina college students that "your race is meant to be a race of farmers, first, last, and always."[25] There were, however, small numbers of white people who remained allied with blacks against racial injustice and violence. In 1909 white social workers Mary White Ovington and Jane Addams and a German Jewish newspaper reporter named William English Walling joined black educators Mary Church Terrell, Mary McLeod Bethune, and Du Bois to discuss ways to counter the racism that threatened to overwhelm black progress. The next year other reformers joined this group, and they formed the integrated National Association for the Advancement of Colored People (NAACP), the successor to the Niagara Movement. The NAACP soon became the nation's staunchest defender of civil rights. It attacked Jim Crow laws in the courts, and its magazine, the *Crisis*, celebrated the achievements of African Americans, exposed racial injustice, and promoted such political action as lobbying for a federal anti-lynching law. A short time later, another interracial organization, the National Urban League, was formed. The Urban League, which focused on employment and socioeconomic issues in urban communities, had ties to Booker T. Washington and his supporters. By 1910, however, persistent racial violence was eroding Washington's followers' belief in economic and social progress through the paternalistic race relations of a segregated South. In an article published just before his death in 1915, Washington himself acknowledged the futility of compromising black constitutional rights.

Although the South was the region most likely to deny civil rights to blacks, the notion of white supremacy was pandemic in American society. The unflattering popular stereotypes and caricatures of blacks that had been standard in nineteenth-century minstrel shows found their way into print and graphic advertisements, continued to shape popular music, and helped mold motion pictures, the newest twentieth-century entertainment. Black faces with exaggeratedly stereotypical features decorated the packaging of food, soap, and other household products. Popular songs were filled with negative references, and black actors were cast in insulting and demeaning roles on the American stage. In order to work black minstrels were often forced to wear blackface during their performances, an accommodation to white fantasies about the nature and uniformity of blackness. During this era white audiences were enamored of "coon songs" with titles like "All Coons Look Alike to Me" and "New Coon in Town." Even though they found these songs very offensive, black musicians and singers performed them for whites. Success in the white theater generally meant conforming to white expectations, and even the 1898 musical written and produced by blacks, the first to play on Broadway, was entitled *A Trip to Coontown*.[26]

Some black artists and forms of popular entertainment were not forced to conform to negative stereotypes. Popular culture within black society was dynamic, and its music, based in African-influenced slave songs and work songs of the eighteenth and nineteenth centuries, had broad appeal. In the fields of the rural South, on the docks of port towns and coastal cities, in small town churches and urban barbershops as well as in formal schools of music, black performers learned and honed their skills. Gussie Davis's music, songs such as "Down Poverty Row," "In the Baggage Car Ahead," and the prizewinning "Send Back the Picture and the Ring" earned him praise as one of the ten best songwriters in the nation, and remained popular even after his death at the end of the century. Madame M. Sissieretta, the "black Patti," whose powerful soprano voice had entertained President Benjamin Harrison in the White House, toured with a vaudeville company and was one of several black musical stars in America and abroad during the Gay Nineties. The twentieth century opened to the sounds of a new music called ragtime, popularized by piano player Scott Joplin. Joplin was born in Texas and made his reputation as the "King of Ragtime" in St. Louis, Sedalia, and Kansas City, Missouri; publishing "The Maple Leaf Rag," his first hit song, in 1899. Joplin was the first of many black ragtime performers, such as Ferdinand Joseph "Jelly Roll" Morton, who played in New Orleans and Chicago, and James Hubert "Eubie" Blake, who played on the East Coast from Baltimore to New York City, thrilling blacks and whites in segregated audiences.[27]

The travels of black musicians and the spreading popularity of their music reflected the migration of African Americans from the rural South to northern cities and western towns. The movement of people first to the southern cities during the 1880s and 1890s and from there to the North and West became the first wave of the Great Migration just before World War I. In 1900 more than 90 percent of all African Americans lived in the South, and these more than eight million people comprised one-third of the region's population. Violence, agricultural mechanization that reduced the value of labor, and infestations of the cotton-destroying boll weevil drove more than two million blacks from the southern countryside during the first decades of the twentieth century. In 1916 floods in the Mississippi Delta destroyed much of the cotton crop, forcing thousands of black cotton workers off the land. Southern blacks settled in Chicago, Philadelphia, and New York City; and by 1920 these three cities were the home of more than one in every four black north-

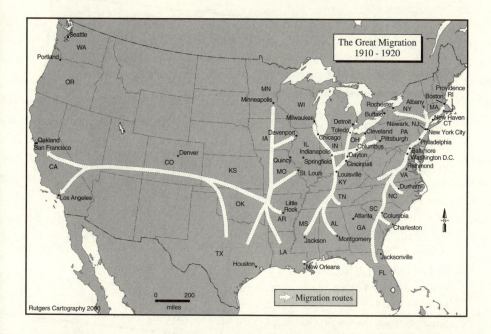

erners. Though blacks were still only 2 percent of the total northern population in 1920, their continued migration was encouraged by the editorials of Robert S. Abbott in the *Chicago Defender*. Abbott assured southern blacks that they would find freedom and jobs in the North, and his exaggerated descriptions of opportunities contributed to the rapid growth of the black communities there. Between 1910 and 1920 Chicago's black population increased from just over 44,000 to more than 109,000 and New York's from nearly 92,000 to more than 152,000. There was comparable growth in smaller cities, like Cleveland, Ohio; Pittsburgh, Pennsylvania; and Gary, Indiana. Detroit's black population increased from under 6,000 people to almost 41,000 during the decade.[28]

The enormous number of African American migrants during these years transformed these cities and invigorated northern urban cultural life. Like other immigrant groups, blacks tended to cluster together for mutual support, but prejudice and racial restrictions also forced them into racially segregated neighborhoods. Black northern urban ghettos were taking form for the first time in American history. However, African Americans in the North enjoyed greater freedom than did their southern counterparts. They were less vulnerable to white violence, had better educational opportunities, the vote, and greater possibilities for political organization. Their concentration provided a consumer market for black businesses, clients for black professionals, and the potential for economic power. While most African Americans in the North

Henry Ossian Flipper

Henry O. Flipper

Henry Ossian Flipper began his life in 1856, as a Georgia slave. During the Civil War, his father, Festus, was able to save enough money to buy the family's freedom, and in 1865, the Flippers moved to Atlanta. After the Civil War the children were educated in a missionary school established for blacks in Atlanta. Henry attended Atlanta University before being admitted to the United States Military Academy at West Point in 1873. Flipper joined James W. Smith, the academy's first African American student, who entered in 1870. Life at West Point had been very hard for Smith. He had been ostracized and abused for the entire three years of his stay, and in the end, he was dismissed before he could graduate. Flipper hoped his treatment might be different, since at first several of the white cadets seemed quite cordial toward him, but soon, their attitudes cooled considerably. "In less than a month they learned to call me 'nigger,' and ceased altogether to visit me," he recalled. Flipper soon found himself isolated, cursed, and despised. He faced constant harassment, what he called "little tortures—the sneer, the shrug of the shoulder, the epithet, the effort to avoid, to disdain, to ignore." Professors were no more supportive than the white cadets, and most expected Flipper's stay to be a short one. From the very beginning, it was clear to him that white cadets were determined to force him out. Newspapers speculated on how long he could survive, and though predictions varied, all agreed "that Flipper will never be allowed to graduate."*

In June 1877, however, Henry Flipper graduated fiftieth in his class of seventy-five, becoming the academy's first African American graduate. He was commissioned a lieutenant and assigned to the Tenth Cavalry, called the Buffalo Soldiers. After all he had suffered to become an officer, his military career was short lived. While serving at Fort Davis, Texas, Flipper was charged with embezzlement.

Henry O. Flipper, the first black graduate of West Point Military Academy. Photographs and Prints Division, Schomburg Center for Research in Black Culture, The New York Public Library, Astor, Lenox, and Tilden Foundations.

(continued)

Cleared of that charge, he was found guilty of conduct unbecoming an officer. Apparently he had gone riding in the company of a young white woman. Although that information did not appear in the formal charge, Flipper felt certain that the incident was the foundation for his conviction. In 1882 he was discharged from the army.

Flipper became a mining engineer in Mexico and the American Southwest and was later hired by the U.S. Department of Justice. His knowledge of Spanish and Mexican land law made him a valuable asset. He served in several capacities with the federal government, from translator for a Senate subcommittee on Mexican affairs, to assistant to President Warren G. Harding's secretary of the interior. During the 1920s he also worked with a major U.S. oil company in Venezuela before retiring to Atlanta. He never stopped trying to clear his name. He wrote an autobiography about his years at the academy and in the military, but despite his efforts, when he died of a heart attack in 1940, he was still under the cloud of his dishonorable discharge. Not until 1976 did the Army reverse its earlier decision and grant Flipper an honorable discharge. Ironically, the following year, West Point honored him by installing his likeness at the academy.

----

*Henry Ossian Flipper, *The Colored Cadet at West Point* (New York: Homer Lee & Co., 1878), 15, 120, 135.

were still poor, higher wages in northern industries circulated more cash in the community than was ever possible in the South. There was more social freedom too. Northern whites did not expect blacks to address them as "sir" and "ma'am," to step from the curb to allow whites to pass, to sit in segregated places on public transportation, or to use segregated public facilities. True, northern customs excluded almost all blacks from elite restaurants, hotels, and private clubs, but everyday life in the North lacked the embarrassment and inconvenience typical of the Jim Crow South. As one migrant explained, unlike in the South, a black woman in Chicago was not committed to buying a hat by simply trying it on.[29]

The Great Migration to the North significantly changed African American life and culture, as former agricultural laborers found work in urban factories. Blacks filled more than five hundred thousand factory jobs in 1910 and more than double that number by the end of the "roaring twenties." In 1917 the United States entered the widening war in Europe. As the need for soldiers drained away northern factory workers and World War I cut off the supply of European immigrant workers, the need for industrial labor drew tens of thousands of southern blacks northward. Male migrants found jobs in steel

COLORED MAN IS NO SLACKER

African American men leave their families to march off to World War I,
called the war to end all war.
Mark E. Mitchell Collection of African American History.

mills, meat-packinghouses, railroad yards, and shipyards, while female migrants
worked as domestics in white middle-class homes and as service staff in
hotels. Although labor-saving household technology replaced some servants,
as white domestics found opportunities in expanding factory and office
work, opportunities for black domestics increased. The proportion of black
female domestics doubled, reaching 20 percent by 1920. Relegated by dis-

crimination and poverty to the bottom of the labor force, black women had few choices. In Chicago for example, 90 percent of black women worked as domestics or laundresses.[30]

The already considerable pressure on black women to take paid employment increased as 370,000 black men served in World War I. Formerly denied factory work, thousands of black women entered industrial plants, where they were employed manufacturing consumer goods and the hardware of war. They earned wages considerably higher than they had as southern farmworkers or northern domestics. As a woman in Chicago making three dollars a day in a railroad yard explained, "The colored women like this work [because] we make more money . . . and we do not have to work as hard as at housework," which had required fifteen- or sixteen-hour days, six days a week. Even though many women found that "they expect more from a colored girl if she is to keep her job," factory work offered African American women, especially those with children, irresistible advantages—more money and more time to spend with their families.[31]

Of the black men in military service in World War I, more than two hundred thousand fought in France and elsewhere in Europe. Four black regiments—the 369th, 370th, 371st, and 372nd—received the Croix de Guerre for valor. The 372nd received special honor for enduring 191 days under fire without ceding a foot of ground. Despite blacks' demonstrated military proficiency and bravery, white American soldiers constantly insulted and harassed them abroad, establishing an American Jim Crow system in France insofar as they could. As one black soldier put it, "There was extreme concern lest the Negro soldiers be on too friendly terms with the French people."[32] White Americans were especially incensed when French people did not seem to share their racial prejudices. Some white commanders prohibited black soldiers from walking or talking with Frenchwomen, and the white military police enforced the order. General Pershing's office sent special orders containing "Secret Information Concerning the Black American Troops" to French military leaders, warning against allowing their soldiers to treat black troops as equals. They "must not eat with them, must not shake hands or seek to talk or meet with them outside the requirements of military service," the order commanded. The French were also cautioned against "commend[ing] too highly the [black] American troops, especially in the presence of [white] Americans," and were advised against "spoiling the Negroes."[33]

The war lasted less than eighteen months after the United States entered, but experience abroad changed the lives of thousands of black soldiers, despite the restrictive military orders. For many their time in Europe and their association with Europeans was their first taste of racial equality. Having risked their lives for democracy abroad, some returned willing to do the same at home.

Black Soldiers in the U.S. Army in World War I

By order of the American army in Europe during World War I, black soldiers of the Ninety-second Division were forbidden to speak to French women.

Another official order was issued by the headquarters of General Pershing on August 7, 1918. Headed "To the French Military Mission Stationed with the American Army—Secret Information Concerning the Black American Troops," it concluded:

1. We must prevent the rise of any pronounced degree of intimacy between French officers and black officers. We may be courteous and amiable with the last, but we cannot deal with them on the same plane as with the white American officer without deeply wounding the latter. *We must not eat with them, must not shake hands or seek to talk or meet with them outside of the requirements of military service.*

2. We must not commend too highly the [Negro] American troops, particularly in the presence of [white] Americans. . . .

3. Make a point of keeping the native cantonment population from "spoiling" the Negroes. *[White] Americans become greatly incensed at any public expression of intimacy between white women and black men.*

Lerone Bennett, Jr., *Before the Mayflower* (New York: Penguin Books, 1988), 348–349.

In an editorial for *The Crisis,* Du Bois called America "a shameful land" that lynched, disenfranchised, stole from, encouraged ignorance among, and then insulted its black citizens. He announced: "We return from fighting. We return fighting." There was a "New Negro" returning to America; a young, militant, northern, urban African American was coming of age. Fearful of the precipitous rise in the number of African Americans in northern cities and alarmed by the determined attitude of blacks returning from the war, many white Americans resorted once again to racial violence.[34]

Mobs particularly targeted African American soldiers in uniform who had recently returned from military duty. In East St. Louis, Illinois, in the summer of 1917, labor protest erupted into a full-scale race riot, as white union members attacked black workers. They burned black neighborhoods, inflicting heavy property damage and leaving hundreds dead and injured. In Chicago minor racial confrontations broke out that summer. When rumors circulated that white gangs were arming themselves, blacks readied arms in response. Street fights between groups of whites—self-styled "athletic clubs"—

World War I poster of black troops carrying the flag of freedom
into Germany as the spirit of Abraham Lincoln looks on.

and groups of blacks were frequent, and any African American who dared venture into white neighborhoods risked attack. There was a riot in Texas that year and others in Pennsylvania in 1918, but the two summers proved to be only the prelude to more extensive urban violence.

During the summer of 1919, thousands of people flocked to the beaches of Lake Michigan, seeking relief from Chicago's heat. Although there were no laws or signs to divide them, black bathers and white bathers were separated from each other by invisible lines of convention and social pressure. African Americans had unsuccessfully challenged this custom many times before the hot day in July when seventeen-year-old Eugene Williams, floating on a railroad tie, drifted across the racial boundary. Confrontations between whites and blacks escalated. The white mob targeted Williams, stoning him until he finally lost his hold and drowned. Shocked and irate, blacks demanded that police arrest the culprits. When the police instead arrested a black man for disorderly conduct, violence escalated quickly. In the ensuing confrontation the police took the side of the white crowd and attempted to drive black people from the beach. Fighting spilled over into the streets, police sometimes joining the white mob to attack blacks, and before the night was over, two people had been killed and fifty injured. During the next six days blacks and whites fought pitched battles in the city streets. African Americans on their way home from work were dragged from streetcars and beaten. Gangs of armed white teenagers roamed black neighborhoods firing into homes and shooting at anyone they found on the street. Twenty-three blacks and fifteen whites were killed, and more than five hundred people in all were injured before rain and the state militia brought the violence under control.

During that bloody "red summer" there were twenty-six riots in cities including Omaha, Nebraska; Washington, D.C.; Longview, Texas; and Knoxville, Tennessee. White mobs attacked and killed African Americans and destroyed their property, and many black communities armed for self-defense. In 1921, when Tulsa police arrested a black man and charged him with attacking a white woman, word spread that the prisoner was about to be lynched. Determined to prevent a lynching, blacks, many of them war veterans, armed themselves, and gathered at the county courthouse. As the Tulsa police attempted to disperse the crowd, someone fired shots. In what Tulsa blacks called a "race war," "white thugs" invaded African American neighborhoods, and black defenders fought them from house to house. The white mob torched entire sections of the black community and killed black people indiscriminately. Wilhelmina Guess Howell was a young girl when the riot broke out. She remembered that the whites burned her father's law office and killed her uncle, Dr. A. C. Jackson, a respected surgeon. Ironically the family had recently come to Tulsa to escape racial violence in Memphis, Tennessee, where her grandfather had narrowly escaped a lynch mob.[35]

The Tulsa police proved so ineffective against the growing mob that the mayor was finally forced to call for state assistance. Before the riot ended, more than sixty blacks and at least twenty-five whites were killed, and the black section of the downtown area was burned to the ground. The Oklahoma National Guard detained more than six thousand blacks. Though African Americans could not prevent white attacks, they did exact a price. Black poet Claude McKay expressed their determination:

> If we must die, O let us nobly die. . . .
> Though far outnumbered let us show us brave
> And for their thousand blows deal one death-blow!
> What though before us lies the open grave?
> Like men we'll face the murderous, cowardly pack,
> Pressed to the wall, dying, but fighting back![36]

In the early twentieth century, migration, the organization of political power in urban black communities in the North, the war experience, and the small but vocal interracial civil rights movement combined to create a different black America. When the Ku Klux Klan moved north during the 1920s, racial attacks continued, but they met a new Negro: more urban, more militant, and politically and economically more powerful.

Chapter 10

1919   Eighteenth Amendment to the Constitution ratified; Prohibition begins in 1920

1920   League of Nations founded; U.S. Senate votes against joining

Gandhi leads India's struggle for independence

Nineteenth Amendment to the Constitution grants the vote to women

National Negro Baseball League founded

1921   Whites attack black community in Tulsa, Oklahoma; sixty blacks killed

1925   A. Philip Randolph organizes Brotherhood of Sleeping Car Porters

1926   Poet Langston Hughes publishes *The Weary Blues* to critical acclaim

First Negro History Week (later Black History Month) celebrated

1927   Edward Kennedy "Duke" Ellington and his band open at the Cotton Club in Harlem, New York City

Supreme Court, in *Nixon* v. *Herndon,* strikes down white-only primary elections

1928   Oscar DePriest of Chicago becomes first African American elected to Congress since Reconstruction and the first ever from a northern state

The Harlem Renaissance between the Wars

R ichard Wright was one of the nation's greatest twentieth-century novelists. His stories laid bare the harsh realities of race in the United States. Wright's life followed a common pattern. He was born in the Deep South, near Natchez, Mississippi, and moved briefly to Memphis, Tennessee, farther north, before settling in Chicago, leaving the South behind him. He was still a teenager in the mid-1920s, when he reached Chicago, where for one socialized in southern segregation he found surprising freedom. Even in relatively cosmopolitan Memphis, he had been unable to obtain a library card because African Americans were not allowed to handle books used by white patrons. Taking a job washing dishes in a Chicago café, he marveled at the cordiality of the white workers, especially the waitresses, who did not shrink from contact with him as they went about their work. Shortly after his arrival he passed an examination and secured a sixty-five-cent-an-hour job at the Central Post Office, earning twice his café salary and much more than he had ever received in the South. His new prosperity was relatively short-lived, since he was not physically strong enough to keep the job, but he was able to help his mother and siblings migrate to Chicago. Though times were never easy for the family, with everyone working they were able to sustain themselves.[1]

White southerners had a mixed reaction to the migration of thousands of African Americans to the North. At first some approved, believing that reducing the southern black population might end what they called the "Negro Problem." Others agreed, noting that the mechanization of farming and destruction by the boll weevil had reduced the need for black labor. Yet many thought it was dangerous for the South to lose so many workers. They recognized the truth of Booker T. Washington's comment that the southern economy was based on "the Negro and the mule." In some areas where labor shortages were acute, whites discouraged black migration. Their methods ranged from publishing newspaper articles warning blacks of dangers in the North and advising them to remain among "friends" in the South, to threats of arrest by local sheriffs who tore up their train tickets. The southern white press gave considerable attention to African Americans who returned from the North with reports of unfavorable conditions there for blacks, promoting them as counselors for their people.[2] Even some influential black southern leaders, a few concerned that mass migration might reduce their constituency, urged African Americans to remain in the South. "You are farmers; stick to your job," urged the *Negro Farmer and Messenger,* Tuskegee University's journal. Booker T. Washington wrote that he had never "seen any part of the world where it seemed to me the masses of Negro People would be better off than right here in these southern states."[3]

Efforts to persuade blacks to remain in the South were countered by accounts of success provided by friends and relatives who had already migrated north. Such northern black newspapers as the *Chicago Defender* reported on employment possibilities and opportunities for a life as respected citizens. These reports may have been as exaggerated as those they sought to counter, but they confirmed the hopes of thousands of blacks. Young migrants like Richard Wright not only found greater economic opportunities in Chicago, they encountered a complex political and intellectual world. Members of a group of black bohemian scholars on Chicago's South Side drew his attention and encouraged his interest in writing. He also discovered a controversial political and cultural organization with astounding strength. Called the Universal Negro Improvement Association (UNIA), it had claimed an international following of more than one million people in thirty-eight countries by 1920. The association had been established just before the First World War by a black nationalist named Marcus Garvey, who had come to the United States from his native Jamaica. In 1920 Garvey led a parade of fifty thousand African Americans through Harlem in a show of support of the UNIA and convened a national convention with twenty-five thousand delegates in Madison Square Garden. Formed as a black-owned corporation, owning and operating a chain of businesses, groceries, hotels, restaurants, laundries, small factories, and a shipping company called the Black Star Line, this multimillion-dollar corporation was both an impressive capitalist venture and a cultural movement expressing racial pride and the rhetoric of social protest. The charismatic Garvey used elaborate ceremony and costuming, appealing to African Americans with denunciations of racial discrimination and his arguments that they need not be confined by the restrictions and degradation of white supremacy. He urged blacks on to greater achievements and bigger dreams, and exhorted them to raise themselves to their "rightful" status as an exceptional people with a homeland in Africa. He spoke with a power and determination that few could ignore, even those who cared nothing for his message: "If Europe is for the Europeans, then Africa shall be for the black people of the world, we say it; we mean it," and commanding, "Up you mighty race, you can accomplish what you will."[4]

Ida B. Wells-Barnett, journalist and civil rights activist.

Photographs and Prints Division, Schomburg Center for Research in Black Culture, The New York Public Library, Astor, Lenox, and Tilden Foundations.

The success of Garvey's message was part of a long tradition among African Americans, a tradition carried on by generations of black people whose frustration and despair convinced them that they had no future in America. Like those in the early nineteenth century who signed on with Paul Cuffe for the voyage to Sierra Leone, those in the 1850s who migrated to the newly independent Liberia under the auspices of the American Colonization Society, or the followers of Bishop Henry McNeil Turner just a generation before, many Garveyites looked to Africa as an ancestral homeland where they dreamed of finding the freedom that the United States would not grant to them.

Ida B. Wells-Barnett was a strong supporter of Marcus Garvey for another reason. She believed his message helped create the racial consciousness and racial solidarity necessary for concerted social action. As if to confirm her belief, the United States Secret Service considered her a dangerous radical for her support of Garvey.[5]

As had been true with other African emigration movements, not all African Americans believed that their freedom could be found in Africa. Richard Wright was one of them. By the time Wright arrived in Chicago, Garvey had been convicted of mail fraud for selling stock in a Black Star Line ship that he had not actually purchased. Garvey had been jailed in 1923 and was deported in 1927. Nevertheless his hope of building a home for all black people in West Africa still enlivened the dreams of many black Americans, and his followers continued to operate a busy office in the city. Wright was greatly suspicious of the entire black nationalist movement, seeing the Garveyites as "romantic rebels, bearers of the impossible dream. . . . Blacks were people of the West," he argued, "and would forever be until they either merged with the West or perished."[6] Nor was W.E.B. Du Bois persuaded by Garvey's black nationalism. Although he had addressed a London meeting of the Pan-African Congress in 1900, Du Bois's commitment was to international solidarity and equal rights, not mass emigration. Calling Garvey an untutored demagogue and a fraud, Du Bois characterized the movement as a naive wrongheaded venture that had cost black people no less than a million dollars. His description of one of UNIA's ceremonies revealed his disdain for Garvey, whom he portrayed as a buffoon:

> It was upon the tenth of August, in High Harlem of Manhattan Island, where a hundred thousand Negroes live. There was a long, low, unfinished church basement, roofed over. A little, fat black man,ugly, but with intelligent eyes and big head, was seated on a plank platform beside a "throne," dressed in a military uniform of the gayest mid-Victorian type, heavy with gold lace, epaulets, plume, and sword. Beside him were "potentates," and before him knelt a succession of several colored gentlemen. These in the presence of a thousand or more applauding dark spectators were duly "knighted" and raised to the "peerage" as knight-commanders and dukes of Uganda and the Niger.[7]

To Du Bois, Garvey represented one of "two grave temptations" black Americans had survived during the early decades of the century. Booker T. Washington had attracted a substantial following by preaching: "Let politics alone, keep your place, work hard, and do not complain." Garvey had appealed to masses of African Americans by counseling: "Give up! Surrender! The struggle is useless; back to Africa and fight the white world."[8]

Garvey's movement and black reaction to it had a complex history, complicated by issues of class, color, ethnicity, and educational background. In Garvey's native Jamaica, color and class combined in ways that carried great social significance. Mixed-race people constituted a distinct class, economically and socially more privileged than darker Jamaicans. Garvey came from the stratum of black Jamaicans that generally constituted the laboring class. After working for a time in England and France, he had returned to Jamaica

Marcus Garvey, speaking to a convention of African Americans
called to draw up a "Constitution for Negro Rights."
Photographs and Prints Division, Library of Congress, Washington, D.C.

and attempted to establish an industrial college open to lower-class blacks, usually excluded from higher education, modeling the school on Booker T. Washington's Tuskegee. The Jamaican class system colored reactions to Garvey's plan. The mayor of Kingston (the capital), the governor of the island, and other influential whites were supportive; mulattoes were opposed; and black Jamaicans seemed indifferent. "I was openly hated and persecuted," Garvey recalled, and he blamed the mulatto elite for trying to dissociate themselves from the island's black population.[9] UNIA's emphasis on racial pride and solidarity owed much to Garvey's experiences at the bottom of Jamaica's class/color system.

On his arrival in the United States in the spring of 1916, Garvey set up his headquarters in Harlem and then traveled through thirty-eight states observing the condition of African Americans and talking to community leaders. Although he had contacted Booker T. Washington before coming to the United States, Garvey was unable to consult the one black leader who had influenced him most. Washington died before they could meet. In his travels Garvey became convinced that black American leaders "had no program [for the improvement of racial conditions], but were mere opportunists who were living off their so-called leadership while the poor were groping in the dark."[10] He thought that too many of these leaders, particularly those in the NAACP, were too willing to rely on white philanthropists and other white allies. He condemned light-skinned leaders as the "mulatto establishment" and singled out Du Bois for special attack, calling him "purely and simply a white man's nigger."[11]

The class contempt evident in Du Bois's depiction of Garvey's movement confirmed Garvey's preconceptions about mulatto leaders. He found Du Bois's description of him as a man with "no thorough education and a very hazy idea of the technic of civilization" particularly insulting. Contending that African Americans of light complexion were "surprise[d] and disgust[ed] . . . when Garvey launched his Jamaican color scheme," Du Bois argued that Garvey had little understanding of color in the United States. Though Du Bois was an elitist who undoubtedly underplayed color consciousness among African Americans, he was right that Garvey greatly overestimated the divisiveness of shades of color in African American life. Du Bois observed that in the United States "colored folk as white as the whitest came to describe themselves as Negroes."[12]

Garvey had correctly read the rise in racial pride and willingness for independent black action during the 1920s. His message was directed at the masses of black people, and his greatest popularity was among the less educated northern urban working class. His movement benefited from the migration to northern cities, as many blacks now working for wages possessed the cash to purchase shares in his stock ventures. Garvey's militant language also had more appeal in the urban North among people emboldened by the rise of northern black political power. His UNIA was only one facet of the cultural revolution under way in urban America.

The war experience and the growing militancy of the younger generation of blacks stimulated a wide range of new cultural and political activities. In the postwar years professional sports became an increasingly popular and lucrative American pastime. Although some black baseball teams had been formed as early as the late nineteenth century, and promoters had even talked of forming national leagues that would include both black and white teams, by 1920 black athletes were excluded from baseball's major leagues. In February of that year Andrew "Rube" Foster, the owner of a local black team, the Chicago American Giants, organized the National Negro Baseball League. Initially eight teams fielded the best black players in the country. Flamboyant showmen as well as talented athletes who developed a style of play based on surprise, speed, and strategies not seen in the white leagues, these early black teams were barnstormers, paid by the game. The hit-and-run bunt and frequent base-stealing were the stock in trade of Negro League play. The original eight teams were all midwestern, but within a few years, black professional baseball spread to the South and East. The Indianapolis Clowns were joined by such teams as the Newark Eagles and the Birmingham Black Barons. In the fall of 1924 they sponsored the first "Colored World Series" in Kansas City, Missouri, with the Kansas City Monarchs and Philadelphia's Hilldale Club vying for the championship. Forty-five thousand fans, almost all black, watched the Monarchs win in a ten-game series, five games to four with one tie. At a time when most Americans rarely traveled long distances, the Negro League players traveled throughout the country, to the Caribbean and into Latin America, delighting fans wherever they went. The money was better outside the United States, and the players faced less discrimination. At home, especially in the South, traveling teams had trouble finding places to stay or restaurants that would serve them, and there was always the threat of attacks by whites who disapproved of black men playing professional baseball. In Mexico, on the other hand, one player reported, "we live in the best hotels, we eat in the best restaurants and can go anyplace we care to." Since black professional baseball was played almost entirely before African Americans, however, it was, as one author observed, "an empire built on poverty." Its success depended on ingenuity and innovation.[13]

Double headers were a common way to draw more fans and increase revenue. In 1930 the Kansas City Monarchs became the first team to play night baseball under electric lights. For all their disadvantages, these players were among the best in the country, and when baseball was finally integrated in the late 1940s, the major league teams recruited thirty-six of the Negro League players. On occasions when black teams faced white teams in exhibition games, African American players proved their skill by defeating the white teams most of the time. These were more than athletic victories. They were evidence of their prowess and worth, countering the insults by white science that justified segregation and held them at the bottom of society with assumptions of black biological inferiority. So, too, were other black athletic victories, as when DeHart Hubbard won the broad jump at the Paris Olympic games in 1924, becoming the first black American gold medal winner, or when the all-black New York Renaissance (the Rens) won the World Basketball Championship by defeating the Boston Celtics in 1932.

There were other expressions of racial pride and self-assertion, especially in the North. Black intellectuals, writers, artists, and musicians achieved prominence in America, as well as Europe. By 1926 the Harvard-educated black historian Carter G. Woodson and his Association for the Study of Negro Life and History established Negro History Week to celebrate black accomplishments and contributions. This was the era of the "New Negro," defined by the black writer Alain Locke as an African American proud of black accomplishments. Although the outpouring of intellectual and cultural expression was widespread, it was generally known as the Harlem Renaissance, taking its name from one dynamic black community in New York City. Economic prosperity during the 1920s helped fuel this phenomenon. Extra cash allowed urban upper- and middle-class whites to hire black domestics, to expand the manufacturing work force, and to support an expanding entertainment industry. White patrons flocked to nightclubs and dance halls to hear the new sound of jazz, music with rough rural origins, becoming progressively more sophisticated in New York, Chicago, Detroit, and Kansas City. In 1918 W. C. Handy presented a "jass [sic] and blues concert" in New York's Selwyn Theater. A few years later, the popular music called jazz was electrifying America and the world.[14] Jazz came out of the South with the people who created it, incorporating the improvisational qualities of blues and southern folk music, the call and response traditions of the African and southern African American religious music, and the syncopation and piano instrumentation of ragtime. These combined with the techniques of classic New Orleans brass bands and Afro-Caribbean dance traditions to produce music with a new rhythmic style. The separate contributory musics continued to extend and influence jazz, which developed differently in various regions of the country. In Chicago, where southern migrants came from the Mississippi Delta, Memphis, and New Orleans, jazz had a distinctly Dixieland sound, as exemplified by King Oliver's Creole Jazz Band and the New Orleans Original Band,

King Oliver's Band with Louis "Satchmo" Armstrong on trumpet (*rear*)
and Lil Hardin on piano.
The Hogan Jazz Archives, Howard-Tilton Memorial Library, Tulane University.

directed by William Manuel "Bill" Johnson. In 1922 an extraordinary cornet
player, Daniel Louis "Satchmo" Armstrong, arrived from New Orleans to add
a sixth piece to Oliver's quintet. Armstrong had played in the New Orleans
clubs and on Mississippi riverboats. After 1915 the black dance bands featured
on riverboats entertained a white clientele six nights a week and integrated
crowds on Monday nights.[15]

In New York City big band jazz developed under the leadership of Fletcher
Henderson, whose ten-piece orchestra was playing regularly at Club Alabam
on Forty-fourth Street by 1923. After the mid-twenties, his group expanded
to sixteen players, making Chicago's New Orleans style of improvisation difficult and encouraging the arranged compositions that became known as New
York's big band sound. In 1927 Edward Kennedy "Duke" Ellington, a young
migrant from Washington, D.C., took a job playing at Harlem's new Cotton
Club and became the master of arrangements. With more instruments to coordinate, big bands often required more memorization and practice, since
many arrangements were not written down. Bands such as those led by Cab
Calloway, Jimmie Lunceford, and Chick Webb became known for their New

York jazz, and the form soon migrated westward to Chicago, Dallas, Tulsa, Denver, and San Francisco. By the middle of the 1930s, one of the most famous big bands was formed in Kansas City by jazz pianist William "Count" Basie, who had joined Bennie Moten's big band there in the 1920s.

African American music drew whites uptown to the Harlem clubs and ballrooms; the Cotton Club, Small's Paradise, the Roseland Ballroom, and the other hotspots of Harlem became fashionable for "slumming," as excursions by whites into these exotic districts were called. On any night one might find millionaires and politicians rubbing shoulders with visiting European royalty and enjoying the music of Duke Ellington or dancing the black bottom and the Charleston at the Cotton Club. Ironically, African Americans found their own opportunities to see black performances restricted, even in Harlem or on Chicago's South Side. Except on designated evenings and in early-morning jam sessions, gaudy nightspots such as New York's Connie's Inn admitted African Americans only as performers and employees. W. C. Handy, composer of "St. Louis Blues," was denied entry to the Cotton Club, even on the night they celebrated his music. As white comedian Jimmy Durante explained, "The chances of a war are less if there's no mixing."[16] There were a few exceptions—the black-owned Small's Paradise and the black-managed Savoy Ballroom had an interracial clientele. The Savoy, one of the earliest and largest dance halls, boasted two bandstands where large integrated orchestras played dance music for as many as four thousand people at a time, who "danced nightly under the colored spotlights and the watchful eyes of tuxedo-clad bouncers to the music of bands led by such famous musicians as Benny Goodman, Tommy Dorsey, Louis Armstrong, Chick Webb, Count Basie and Cab Calloway."[17]

The success of African American music also took performers to New York's Broadway, the most important entertainment street in the world. In 1921 *Shuffle Along* catapulted its young star, Florence Mills, to fame; all of New York and much of the nation was singing its hit song, "I'm Just Wild about Harry." After this hit, black casts achieved recognition with such musicals as *Green Pastures, Porgy,* and *Chocolate Dandies.* In 1923 *Liza, Running Wild* came to Broadway and introduced the nation to the Charleston, which became the most popular dance of the era. The unforgettably rich bass-baritone voice of Paul Robeson started him along the road to international acclaim when he sang at New York's Greenwich Village Theater in 1925. In 1929 he was featured in the Broadway hit *Show Boat.*[18]

Nearly all the jazz instrumentalists were men, but women were popular singers with the bands, and many became known to the public through their recordings. African American women blazed their own trail in the world of popular music with the more sophisticated sound of urban blues,

Elizabeth Taylor Greenfield, one of the most popular performers of the mid–nineteenth century, became known as the Black Swan. Her singing style inspired many black female singers of the 1920s.

Photographs and Prints Division, Schomburg Center for Research in Black Culture, The New York Public Library, Astor, Lenox, and Tilden Foundations.

the gritty southern rural music shaped by poverty and oppression, or a blend of the two. Their songs told stories of betrayal, abuse, love gone wrong, and their own special brand of revenge. Their song titles were descriptive, "Weeping Woman Blues" or "Send Me to the 'Lectric Chair." Their singing styles ranged from something akin to the popular white music of the day to a unique "low-down blues" sound that sometimes grated on the ears of the unschooled public. Ethel Waters was mistress of a sophisticated sound that attracted both whites and middle-class blacks. She was one of the first blues artists to record for the Black Swan label, a company established in New York by Harry Pace and named in honor of the famous nineteenth-century singer Elizabeth Taylor Greenfield, called the "Black Swan." Waters established the company's reputation with such songs as "Down Home Blues" and "Oh Daddy." In addition to her success singing with jazz bands, she also became a star on the Broadway stage and in film. Her records sold so well that, for the first time, white record companies took note of the lucrative consumer market among blacks.[19]

Josephine Baker (1906–1975)

She was a sensation in Europe and around the world. First and foremost a dancer, she was also a singer, Broadway actress, and movie star. In Paris they called her "La Baker" and the Black Venus of France. In North Africa many knew her as Princesse Tam-Tam, taking the name from the title of the 1935 movie she filmed there. She appeared in the Ziegfield Follies, several film productions, and in stage plays. She was one of the most remarkable musical artists of the twentieth century.

Born Josephine Freda MacDonald in St. Louis, she practically grew up on stage. A great success in the chorus line of the black musical *Shuffle Along*, which burst onto the New York stage in 1921, she was then only fifteen years old. Her exotic beauty and talent stunned the white audiences that flocked to Harlem's most popular nightclubs to see her dance. In some ways a product of the Harlem Renaissance and the changing gender roles of the 1920s, Baker helped popularize the short dresses, high kicks, and erotic behavior that symbolized the new liberated woman. Famous artists painted and sculpted her, and Ernest Hemingway called her the most beautiful woman he had ever seen. Josephine Baker was too restricted by the America set aside for African Americans, and in 1925 she went to Paris. Freed from the racial limitations imposed on black performers in the United States, Baker became an international superstar. French fashion designers inspired by her stage costumes developed a new look for European women. In the United States, she once complained, "they would make me sing mammy songs." In Europe she sometimes played on racial stereotypes that saw her as "*La Sauvage*," but she never suffered the abuse in Europe faced by even the most popular black stars in the United States. She was never completely comfortable on her few American tours, never feeling fully appreciated by white American audiences.

When war broke out in Europe, Baker used her fame to support the Allied effort. She entertained for American troops stationed in North

Josephine Baker, international star, dancer, singer, and actress. Prints and Photographs Division, Library of Congress, Washington, D.C.

(continued)

Africa, worked with the Red Cross in Belgium, and joined the Resistance in France. After the war the French government awarded her the Legion of Honor. In the United States, she remained controversial. Even African Americans were uncomfortable with some of the statements she made, statements open to interpretation as anti-American, but her reputation was restored for blacks after she became a strong supporter of the civil rights movement during the 1950s. In 1963 she flew to the United States specifically to take part in the March on Washington. Like so many African Americans of her day, she was swept up in the movement that changed all of the United States. Some blacks resented her impatience with the notion of black power during the late 1960s; nevertheless, she remained a legendary figure in black America. The dancer died in 1975 after a performance in Paris, as she had always wanted to: "Breathless, spent, at the end of a dance."*

---

*Kariamu Welsh Asante, "Josephine Baker," in Darlene Clark Hine, ed., *Black Women in America: An Historical Encyclopedia,* vol. 1, 75–78; quote, 78.

Gertrude "Ma" Rainey, who toured for years with various southern show bands, was the queen of the traveling blues. The travel theme in blues music was most often the domain of male singers, but Rainey broke into their circle with songs like "Leaving This Morning," "Walking Blues," "Runaway Blues," and "Traveling Blues." Her songs spoke of racial oppression, "Chain Gang Blues," or of its effects, "Dead Drunk Blues," or of the hardships of rural life in the South, "Bo-Weevil Blues." She was a sensation among southern blacks but also found a white audience, particularly after she started recording in the early 1920s. Her records combined a country blues style with urban blues, and she became known as the "Mother of the Blues."

Like Ma Rainey, Bessie Smith combined the rural southern blues singing style with the sophistication of the city. A native of Chattanooga, Tennessee, she came north and took the music scene by storm. She did it with an earthy voice and words that matched the mood of the time—open and direct, full of expression, and bespeaking greater freedom for women. In her version of "I'm Wild about That Thing" she sang, "If you want to satisfy my soul, come on and rock me with a steady roll." Bessie Smith's gritty and explicit blues sound was too much for Black Swan Records and its blue-ribbon board of black directors, which included W.E.B. Du Bois. The firm rejected Bessie Smith's audition in favor of the popular music sound of Ethel Waters. It is likely that Smith's rejection had more to do with the discomfort her singing style caused the black elites at Black Swan Records than the quality of her performance.

Although jazz and blues musicians achieved great popularity, African Americans did not universally acclaim them. This was especially true of those like Smith, who—for black elite longtime residents of northern cities—seemed to personify the most disturbing characteristics of the black southern newcomers. Generations of northern middle-class blacks had wrapped themselves in a cloak of respectability to shield themselves from white intolerance, and they were more likely to approve of black successes in more classical forms of music in the 1930s. They favored internationally trained soprano Caterina Jarboro's performance with the Chicago Opera Company or Katherine Dunham's lead in the West Indian ballet *La Guiablesse*. In contrast, the new southern migrants, and the jazz that migrated with them, made many northern middle-class blacks uncomfortable. "A lot of them were good people," commented one longtime Pittsburgh resident, "but along with them were a lot of roustabouts who had no good intentions at all." These people, he contended, abused the freedom they found and "changed the whole picture of Duquesne [a suburb of Pittsburgh]." Many feared that the migrants and the music that seemed undignified and immoral would confirm the worst racial stereotypes.

Jazzman Benny Carter's mother disapproved of his playing in Harlem's clubs. "I think it was a bit appalling to her that I was making a living like that," he recalled.[20] As one of Bessie Smith's biographers argued, "[S]uccessful blacks disliked Bessie because they felt her behavior endangered their own image of themselves. The crudity of her language, and the unpredictability of her mood, made her seem like a part of the street life they wanted to forget."[21] Poet Langston Hughes was one of the few black intellectuals who took jazz and blues seriously. He wished aloud for the "blare of Negro Jazz bands and the bellowing voice of Bessie Smith singing Blues [to] penetrate the closed ears of the colored near-intellectuals until they listen and perhaps understand." Yet, even some of the other entertainers found Bessie Smith's style discomfiting. As New York entertainer Alberta Hunter explained, "[M]y background was poor, but it was humble . . . but Bessie, hers was a little too fantastic," and "[W]e never associated with Bessie." Hunter belonged to a more genteel social group, "I can't stand a rough woman," she explained.[22] Despite the reservations of black elites or some of her fellow performers, Smith's career was a smashing success. In 1923 she made her first recording with Columbia Records, "Down Hearted Blues." It sold one million copies within a year and by 1924 Bessie Smith, "Empress of the Blues," was the highest-paid black person in America.[23]

The reluctance of some African Americans to embrace jazz was particularly restrictive for musicians from proper black middle-class families. Lil Hardin and her parents moved to Chicago from Memphis in the summer of 1918 when she was twenty years old. Hardin was one of the best jazz pianists in Chicago during the 1920s. Schooled in classical music, she so impressed the management at Jones's Music Store in Chicago with her sightreading ability that they gave her a job paying three dollars a week demonstrating music for its customers. When she moved from this to playing jazz in a prominent Chicago club, she told her parents that she was playing in a dance studio because she knew they would not approve of her entertaining at the DeLuxe Café, a local nightclub that her father called "a regular sporting house." In this new job her salary jumped to an amazing twenty-seven dollars weekly, plus as much as twenty dollars a night in tips. When her parents found out the truth, they allowed her to keep her job but insisted that her mother escort her to and from work every night. It caused a family uproar when Lil joined King Oliver's band and married Louis Armstrong because, as a friend commented, "Lil's mother thought she was too good for Louis."[24]

Class and regional tensions apparent in music were exacerbated by differences in color. Shade of skin color had significance in the social structure of all African Americans, but historically, it was much more important in the South than in the North, particularly in the Lower South. The strong influence of rigidly color conscious Caribbean and Latin American societies through the early settlers of New Orleans, Charleston, and other southern port cities encouraged an aristocracy of light color. Mixed-race people in the South could often trace their white heritage to a local family or even a specific person, often the former slave master. Under the desperate circumstances of slavery or rigid segregation in the South, African Americans valued the aid and protection of white relatives who might be willing to intercede for them. Mulattoes in the Deep South were more likely to have been fathered by a wealthy slaveholder than those in the Upper South, where white fathers were likely to have been less affluent and less influential yeoman farmers. To maintain the privileges of family connections, especially in the Deep South, mulattoes often separated themselves from darker African Americans, even from those to whom they were related. Southern migrants sometimes transplanted the color-exclusive societies in the South, like the "blue vein societies" of rural Mississippi, to northern cities. Such elite associations as the Nassau Society and the Manasseh Club in Chicago gave their members social standing and helped them secure better jobs.[25]

Color differences divided musicians as well, and mixed-race musicians from New Orleans and other areas in the Deep South brought their color prejudices north with them. Jelly Roll Morton, a mulatto from New Orleans, shunned darker blacks, a behavior said to be "typical of New Orleans Creoles."[26] King Oliver, Louis Armstrong, Lil Hardin, Baby Dodds, and other dark-skinned jazz musicians suffered slights and sometimes taunts from their lighter colleagues. "Hi, Blondie," Morton once shouted sarcastically as King Oliver was playing a cornet solo. Although Oliver was quick with self-deprecating wit, as one scholar observed, he was "deeply hurt by [the] prejudice in jazz against dark skin."[27]

Several black writers were critical of the color hierarchy within black society, arguing that an oppressed and struggling people could ill afford such divisiveness. Wallace Thurman's *The Blacker the Berry* was a blunt discussion of skin color among African Americans, and Nella Larsen was outspoken about class and color in her novellas *Quicksand* and *Passing*. Black intellectuals, artists, and writers, however, most often focused their attention on the issues of racial injustice and the racism faced by African Americans of all shades of color. Writer and anthropologist Zora Neale Hurston exposed the twin evils of racism and sexism in *Their Eyes Were Watching God* and other novels. Such writers as Langston Hughes and Claude McKay examined the lives of common black people struggling to cope with the urban experience. Hughes later explained his intention: "All of us know that the gay and sparkling life of the so-called Negro Renaissance of the 20s was not so gay and sparkling beneath the surface as it looked."[28] Performing or discussing their work in the coffeehouses on Chicago's South Side, the salons of Harlem, or the cafés of Paris, where many sojourned during the twenties, these writers became popular with blacks, white intellectuals, and white philanthropists. On weekend nights or Sunday afternoons, Harlem's Hobby Horse bookstore, for example, was enlivened by debates about race, philosophy, politics, and economics. In poems, essays, and novels, black writers exposed the pain and suffering that was the underside of the glamour and achievement of the Harlem Renaissance.

The black sections of most cities during this period were crowded and racially segregated. Poor people filled their overpriced dwellings with friends and relatives, migrants unable to find housing outside the circumscribed black community. Underemployment and limited job opportunities kept wages low, while limited housing kept rents high. In 1919 the Eighteenth Amendment to the U.S. Constitution made the manufacture, sale, or transportation of alcohol illegal, and almost immediately an illicit trade in alcohol began. From small shabby "speakeasies" to swank private clubs for the upper class, almost anyone could find a drink accompanied by entertainment, prostitution, gambling, and often the best jazz in town. Crime was common everywhere during Prohibition, but it was rampant in black neighborhoods. White criminals generally controlled the large-scale operations, while African Americans filled the jails. There were almost three times as many black prisoners as could be expected based on their proportion of the population. "Negroes are more likely to be arrested on suspicion than white persons," remarked one Chicago judge. Harlem's black underworld was populated with small-time bootleggers, racketeers, and petty hustlers with nicknames like Prophet Martin, the barefoot seer; Black Herman, the mysterious herbalist; Battling Siki, the boxing champion from Senegal; and Casper Holstein, who ran one of the most lucrative numbers and betting rackets in the city. In Chicago during the early twentieth century, John "Mushmouth" Johnson ran gambling and prostitution rackets, and by the 1920s many blacks had become part of the criminal establishment. After whites realized how much money could be made in black communities, black crime bosses often found themselves in competition with such white gangsters as Al Capone in Chicago or Dutch Shultz in New York. A few black criminals had a status and power that approximated that of big-time white racketeers. Dan Jackson operated a bootlegging and gambling syndicate, but Chicago blacks were fond of recalling that he also provided coal to heat the homes of the poor and loans or gifts that helped them pay their rent. A college graduate who contributed to community charities and to the NAACP, Jackson sat on the Chicago Republican Party committee that selected political candidates and served on the state commerce commission.[29]

During this era, crime and politics were closely related. Al Capone, for example, was both a major figure in Chicago crime and a powerful member of the political establishment. African Americans who had been barred from politics in the South were eager to participate in northern urban political life. As among whites, urban black political support was organized by hierarchical political associations called machines. These machines delivered votes in return for community services and individual favors. Political machines included gangsters like Dan Jackson and such reputable figures as Oscar DePriest, one of the most powerful black politicians in Chicago. DePriest had been born in Alabama and migrated to Kansas as part of the Exoduster movement. After he moved to Chicago in the late nineteenth century, DePriest became a loyal Republican, turning out the black vote for local and state politicians. He was rewarded with the party's support, and in 1928 he became the first black person to be elected to the U.S. Congress from a northern district, Illinois's First Congressional District. Growing middle-class black communities in Chicago, New York, Detroit, Philadelphia, and other northern cities provided a political base for the black politicians who served as Republican Party officials and on city councils. From these positions they organized and rewarded black professionals and businessmen with political favors, maximizing their local political influence.

Black political influence did not extend to the national level, however. After Republican Warren G. Harding was elected president in 1920, the NAACP mounted protests aimed at getting him to speak out against racial discrimination, disenfranchisement, lynching, and other racial violence. Harding made no statement, nor did his Justice Department investigate the Klan or other terrorist groups. As an antilynching bill failed in Congress, Harding's contribution to the debate was to call on all Americans to stand against social equality for the races and to oppose what he called "racial amalgamation."[30] Harding died in office in 1923 and was succeeded by Calvin Coolidge, but the new president was no better on racial issues. Any support for racial justice would have hurt the Republican Party's efforts to wrest the South from the Democrats, their major goal during those years. The Democratic Party was so solidly southern that it would not condemn Klan activities, giving African Americans few attractive choices. Although the Progressives ran Robert La Follette in 1924 as a third-party presidential candidate, even they refused to mention any major racial issues at their national convention.[31] Rising racial intolerance expanded the ranks of the Ku Klux Klan to more than two million members, growing even in urban areas in the North. This new Klan, formed during the 1910s but patterned after terrorist groups in the Reconstruction South, drew supporters from the Midwest and Southwest as well as the South, and added anti-Catholic and anti-immigrant sentiments to its traditional antiblack attitudes. A rise of intolerance marked not only Klan activity but growing conservatism in the federal government. In 1924 Congress passed and the president signed into law the National Origins Act, which provided quotas favoring northern European immigration. This measure limited Italian and Jewish immigration by cutting the numbers of southern and eastern Europeans who could immigrate to the U.S. and insured that very few Africans, Latin Americans, or Asians would be able to immigrate.

In celebration and assertion of their strength and popularity, forty to fifty thousand men, women, and children in full Klan regalia paraded down Pennsylvania Avenue in Washington, D.C., one day in the summer of 1925. Three horsemen "garbed in the ghostly vestments of the Klan" led, followed by marchers who clogged the street for three hours and forty minutes. The *Washington Evening Star* newspaper dubbed the procession a "colorful march" and noted that the marchers carried a "great display of American flags." The *Baltimore Afro-American* reported that a small group of blacks watched the marchers from curbside, with a larger group assembled near the National Archives at Seventh Street and Pennsylvania Avenue. Years later one African American recalled, "We were ready to fight if they broke ranks. We didn't know anything about nonviolence in those days." President Calvin Coolidge was conveniently out of town for the weekend.[32]

By the time Herbert Hoover, the third Republican of the decade, entered the White House in 1928, it was clear that the party of Lincoln held little hope

More than one thousand African Americans were lynched
in the United States during the first third of the twentieth century.
After each reported lynching, this flag was flown outside
the office of the NAACP in New York City.
Photographs and Prints Division, Library of Congress, Washington, D.C.

for African Americans. Indeed, Chief Justice of the Supreme Court William Howard Taft believed that Hoover planned to abandon the party's African American constituency by implementing a strategy "to break up the solid [S]outh and to drive the [N]egro out of Republican politics."[33] Hoover reflected this aim when he appointed no blacks to federal office, placed pro-segregationist southerners in key posts, and nominated North Carolina segregationist John J. Parker to the Supreme Court. "Participation of the Negro in politics," Parker had said, was "a source of evil and danger to both races."[34] Outraged by Parker's racism, the NAACP mounted a protest, and in the spring of 1930, the U.S. Senate refused to confirm his nomination.

The politics of the 1920s mirrored the contradictions of popular culture. Racism permeated the culture—minstrelsy and blackface performances remained fashionable in white America, and amusement parks included the popular "Hit the Coon" ball-toss game. D. W. Griffith's motion picture *The Birth of a Nation,* produced in 1915 and later praised by President Woodrow Wilson, remained one of America's most popular films during the 1920s, despite the NAACP's protest over its blatantly racist caricatures and the glorification of the Ku Klux Klan. In 1927, in *The Jazz Singer,* the first sound film, Al Jolson, a Russian Jewish immigrant, portrayed a rabbi's son who performed as a blackface minstrel. He delighted audiences with his rendition of the film's final song, "Mammy." The next year *Amos 'n' Andy* began its syndicated radio broadcasts with two white actors feigning "black accents" to caricature two black southern migrants.[35] Although blacks had little power to influence the way they were portrayed in films made by whites, they did challenge caricatured images. They protested racial stereotypes and produced their own movies to counter them. The first black film was *The Railroad Porter,* a comedy directed by the black filmmaker Bill Foster in 1912, but *Birthright,* made in 1918, was the first black full-length film. It became the first of more than thirty films made by the Oscar Micheaux Corporation, a black-owned firm that produced the popular 1925 *Body and Soul,* starring Paul Robeson. During the 1920s other African American groups, such as the Lincoln Motion Picture Company, began making movies about black life, providing more alternatives to mainstream stereotypes.

As the 1920s ended African Americans could look back on the decade with mixed feelings. Sharecroppers continued to suffer extreme poverty and inequality in the rural South, convicts provided cheap leased labor, and segregation defined social and political life. But jobs in the North offered hope, and local northern urban politics promised changes that might come from increased power. As African Americans raised by parents born in freedom made their way north—though they had not escaped all the beliefs, customs, and restrictions of slave days—they were prepared to demand recognition. More and more black Americans settled in northern cities, and the waves of protest, music, art, and literature became a tide of cultural expression. The artists, writers, and musicians of the Harlem Renaissance retained their roots in African heritage and African American life. Their move to the urban North gave their work a new sophistication and allowed them to create a new cultural conversation with the literary and artistic traditions of Western society. To the world Harlem came to symbolize the creative energy of African Americans. The writers of the Harlem Renaissance gave voice to the culture created by the painful black experience in America, passionately expressing the spirit of the African American people. James Weldon Johnson, one of those writers, understood that this artistic expression was grounded in the lives of the people:

This was the era in which was achieved the Harlem of story and song; the era in which Harlem's fame for exotic flavor and colorful sensuousness was spread to all parts of the world; when Harlem was made known as the scene of laughter, singing, dancing, and primitive passions, as the center of the new Negro literature and art. . . . The picturesque Harlem was real, but it was the writers who discovered its artistic values and, in giving literary expression to them, actually created the Harlem that caught the world's imagination.[36]

Chapter 11

1929 October 28 stock market crash begins the Great Depression

1932 Franklin Delano Roosevelt elected president

1933 Adolf Hitler gains dictatorial powers in Germany

1934 First live show staged at Apollo Theater in Harlem

1935 Mary McLeod Bethune founds National Council of Negro Women

1936 Jesse Owens wins four gold medals at Berlin Olympics; black athletes win thirteen Olympic medals

1937 Joe Louis becomes the heavyweight boxing champion of the world, defeating James J. Braddock

1939 Singer Marian Anderson performs at the Lincoln Memorial before an audience of seventy-five thousand after being denied the use of DAR's Constitution Hall

1940 Benjamin Oliver Davis, Sr., becomes the first black general in the regular army

1941 First U.S. Army pilot training program initiated at Tuskegee, Alabama

Japan bombs Pearl Harbor; United States enters World War II

President Roosevelt issues Executive Order 8802, prohibiting racial discrimination in war industries

1942 James Farmer organizes Congress of Racial Equality (CORE) at University of Chicago

1943 Race riots in Detroit, Mobile, Los Angeles, and Harlem

1944 Adam Clayton Powell, Jr., elected to Congress from New York City

1945 World War II ends; more than one million African Americans served in the armed forces during the war

United Nations formed

John H. Johnson begins publishing *Ebony* magazine

Depression and War

L ouis Banks came to Chicago with his family from a cotton farm in Arkansas in search of a better life. At fourteen he got a job as a cook's helper on the lake boats and dreamed of becoming a chef, but that was in 1929. In that year, the stock market collapse marked the beginning of the Great Depression. Although relatively few workers were directly affected by the drop in stock prices, within a few months industrial production nationwide had fallen by half, and thousands of unemployed workers took to the roads and the rails in search of jobs. Banks was one of them. As he recalled:

> 1929 was pretty hard. I hoboed, I bummed, I begged for a nickel to get somethin' to eat. . . . When I was hoboing, I would lay on the side of the tracks and wait until I could see the train comin'. I would always carry a bottle of water in my pocket and . . . a piece of bread . . . so I wouldn't starve on the way. I would ride all day and all night long . . . atop a boxcar and went to Los Angeles, four days and four nights.[1]

The unemployment rate rose from 3 percent in 1929 to 25 percent by 1933. A pool of fewer than two million unemployed workers in 1929 expanded to more than 13 million in four years. The depression hit hardest in agriculture, unskilled manufacturing jobs, the construction industry, mining, lumbering, and domestic service—the sectors of the economy in which black workers were concentrated. In fact, many areas employing African Americans had been in recession during the general prosperity of the 1920s, creating economic hardship for those workers long before the stock market crash. In the middle of the depression, a severe drought in the midsection of the country exacerbated the problems of farmers. Black families who had sought new opportunities in the West joined the trek of farmers from Oklahoma who had abandoned their farms and struck out for California in search of work. The depression brought added suffering to blacks already living with the hardships of lower wages, uncertain employment, and few financial reserves. As white unemployment grew, discrimination mounted, and so African Americans lost their jobs at a much higher rate than whites and remained out of work longer. Half the African American workers in Cleveland, and almost two-thirds in Detroit and St. Louis were out of work by the end of 1930. In Chicago, where blacks represented about 8 percent of the labor force, they were 22 percent of the unemployed. The median annual black family income in Harlem dropped by nearly half between 1929 and 1932. Though blacks were earning much less than whites, the average rent in Harlem remained from twelve to thirty dollars a month higher than in other parts of Manhattan. This was part of the cost of segregation to black residents with limited housing choices.[2]

By 1932, in Philadelphia, where more than half of the African Americans were unemployed, on Chicago's South Side, or in any black community in the country, the desperation was apparent. The sidewalks were filled with furniture bearing witness to the eviction of families unable to pay the rent. In many cities and in the countryside, black women and children scavenged for food and for material with which to construct makeshift housing. Men walked the streets in the middle of the day searching for any kind of job. Without work and without money, many men and some women took to the rails. They begged for food, sometimes exchanging food for odd jobs, camped near the railroad tracks, and rode illegally on freight trains. Crossing and recrossing the country in search of employment, they became known as tramps or hoboes, and their encampments were called Hoovervilles in criticism of President Herbert Hoover.

African Americans fortunate enough to keep their jobs during the depression generally faced poor working conditions they had little power to change. Black women employed as domestics put in long days, leaving their homes in the early hours of the morning in order to reach the kitchens of white employers in time to prepare breakfast. "I leave home quarter of 7 every morning," reported one black domestic in a letter to the NAACP. "I finish 9:30 P.M. When I get home it is 10 o'clock."[3] Although many domestics had one day a week off from work, this woman described working every day. She was among the lucky ones who lived at home, since domestics who lived away from their families in their employers' homes were always on call. Domestic workers earned very little money for these long hours, with scant time off for their families, even by the standards of the day. Mabel Brady of Philadelphia recalled, "My mother and grandmother and [other black women she knew] worked for a dollar and a quarter a day."[4] Other black women without steady jobs stood on street corners each morning hoping to be chosen for day work by the white people who cruised black neighborhoods, looking for domestic help. Years later writer Paule Marshall remembered that her mother and her friends in Brooklyn often waited from morning into the early afternoon on a corner called "the slave market."[5]

Black workers were generally paid lower wages than white workers doing the same jobs. Most employers did not admit to wage discrimination, but one Philadelphia laundry openly advertised for black women at nine to ten dollars weekly and for white women workers at tweve dollars (even tweve dollars was not enough to support a single woman). The racial differential between wages was even greater for men, although the men made more than women. As a result black family income averaged about half of white family income. The depression brought a drop in income for all American families, but while it reduced white family income by as much as 50 percent, it lowered the black family's already meager income by 75 percent or more.[6]

Meanwhile black businesses, often precarious, began to close almost immediately after the crash, collapsing at a higher rate than their white-owned counterparts. Financial institutions closed throughout the nation; the losses in black-owned banks were often the paltry resources of those who could least afford the misfortune. Jesse Binga's Binga State Bank in Chicago failed in the summer of 1930. The relatively substantial resources of Harlem's Nail & Parker Realty were not enough to support the firm, and the proprietor was forced to put his collection of black artist Henry Ossawa Tanner's paintings on the market.[7] Most black-owned businesses were groceries, funeral homes, laundries, barber shops, and beauty parlors, small local concerns which depended on their immediate community. As the unemployment rate increased and the living standard deteriorated, more businesses struggled and bankruptcies increased.

In dire circumstances, people shared what little they had. Families and friends shared housing when some could not pay their rents. People paid a modest admission fee to attend house parties, called rent parties, that helped the host collect enough money to pay the landlord and avoid eviction. In some cities militant "flying squadrons" of young men threatened landlords and defied police, rushing to reinstate families in the apartments from which they had been evicted. Protesting the high rents blacks often paid, they sometimes planted themselves on the furniture of the evicted and sang defiantly, "We Shall Not Be Moved." As Louis Banks remembered it, on the road even color didn't matter: " 'cause everybody was poor. . . . We used to take a big pot and cook food, cabbage, meat and beans all together. We all set together, we made a tent. Twenty-five or thirty would be out on the side of the rail, white and colored."[8]

African Americans relied on family members and on the black community. "People who would now be considered below the poverty line on any statistical chart," recalled one North Carolinian, "had enough sense of self, of human worth, to enjoy sharing what they had with others. The meal was the tie that binds."[9]

Most turned to their traditional source of aid—the black church. From large churches like the Abyssinian Baptist Church in Harlem to storefront churches in Chicago or Detroit, black ministers and congregations provided both spiritual and practical assistance. Religious leaders like Father Divine and Daddy Grace were more than ministers; many led direct-action movements.

They operated restaurants, grocery stores, and cleaning services that provided work for some and food, clothing, and loans for others. The Father Divine Movement was begun on Long Island near New York City by a black minister from Georgia named George Baker. Although the vast majority of his disciples were African Americans, during the 1920s and 1930s, he gradually attracted an interracial following numbering in the tens of thousands to his pacifistic communal religious cult. Believers considered him to be the personification of God; hence the appellation Father Divine. After his movement began to attract large numbers of adherents to his house on Long Island, Father Divine was arrested and tried for maintaining a public nuisance. The judge sentenced him to a year in prison and fined him five hundred dollars, and when the judge died of a heart attack three days later, it was taken by Father Divine's followers as Divine's retribution. Word spread that Father Divine had commented, "I hated to do it." On appeal, on the grounds that the judge had made prejudicial statements, particularly about the interracial character of the movement, the verdict was reversed and Father Divine's popularity soared. Divine kingdoms, as his installations were called, spread across the Midwest, to the West Coast and to Washington, D.C. During the depression his kingdoms rented rooms for one dollar a week, served meals for ten and fifteen cents, solicited jobs for followers, investigated and protested discrimination and segregation, and advocated government ownership and operation of idle factories.[10]

Charles Emmanuel "Sweet Daddy" Grace, with his long hair and red-, white-, and blue-painted fingernails, was even more flamboyant than Father Divine. A native of the Cape Verde Islands, Daddy Grace mixed religion and capitalism to establish a multimillion-dollar empire of real estate and retail business that supported his Washington, D.C.–based church, the United House of Prayer. Although he never claimed to be divine, many of his followers saw him as such. Daddy Grace and Father Divine were the most prominent of the charismatic religious leaders who rose to power through the mutual aid organizations in black urban society during the depression. This movement sought to fill gaps in government programs, blending religion with protest and welfare benefits, ministering to both physical and spiritual needs.[11]

In 1930 an African American peddler working among the poor in Detroit began one of the most enduring charismatic religious movements. His name was W. D. Fard, and he taught his followers that they were from the Muslim "lost-found tribe of Shabazz." He preached a disciplined religion that exhorted blacks to glory in their African heritage and blamed their degraded condition and the evils of the world on whites. Fard disappeared in 1934, but he left behind an institutional framework for the militant political and religious movement that became the Nation of Islam, also known as the Black Muslims. For the next four decades this movement was led by Elijah Muhammad, Fard's chief lieutenant, who claimed that Fard had been the incarnation of Allah and that he, Muhammad, was his prophet. Under his leadership the Nation of Islam began building temples and schools and an extensive network aimed at economic self-sufficiency composed of farms, groceries, restaurants, and apartment houses.[12]

A short time into the depression, the always economically precarious southern sharecroppers were devastated. Two-thirds received no cash from their labor, either breaking even or falling farther into debt each year. Most were reduced to foraging or seeking charity in order to survive. Before long, black workers found even the least desirable jobs reserved for unemployed whites. Vigilantes killed ten black railroad workers in Louisiana in an effort to force blacks from their jobs. White workers in Milwaukee demanded that railroad officials fire black workers. Some cities passed ordinances forbidding the employment of blacks or severely limiting their employment. By 1935, 87 percent of blacks in Norfolk, Virginia, depended on relief services for survival. In Atlanta more than 66 percent of the city's African Americans were on relief.[13]

Economic need was so widespread that whites and blacks joined to form the Bonus Expeditionary Force, comprised of more than twenty thousand unemployed World War I veterans, and marched on Washington in the spring and summer of 1932. They held government bonus certificates for future payment, but they demanded that the government pay immediately, since they and their families were so desperate for money. These men, some accompanied by their families, set up a makeshift camp in Anacostia, on the shores of the Potomac River just east of the Capitol building, and vowed to remain until Congress acted. For these men common hardship had apparently softened rigid racial divisions, as black reporter Roy Wilkins wrote, some blacks had their own tents, but some black veterans and white veterans shared tents. "There was no residential segregation," he observed, citing the example of "the Chicago group [that] had several hundred Negroes in it and they worked, ate, slept, and played with their white comrades."[14] They also suffered the government's retribution together. After a bill to pay the veterans passed the House but failed in the Senate, President Herbert Hoover ordered the army to remove the bonus marchers from their camp. By the time their eviction was complete, two veterans and one eleven-week-old baby were dead, one eight-year-old boy had been partly blinded from tear gas, and thousands of people had been injured.[15]

There was also interracial cooperation among southern tenant farmers who supported one another's strikes. In Arkansas in July 1934, after concluding that organizing separately in the past had weakened the position of both whites and blacks, they established the Southern Tenant Farmers' Union. The argument for unity was strong as they faced starvation, and by the following spring, ten thousand people had joined this Socialist union. Socialists and

A meeting of the Southern Tenant Farmers' Union
in a Muskogee, Oklahoma, schoolroom, May 1939.
Photographs and Prints Division, Library of Congress, Washington, D.C.

Communists were in the forefront of interracial organizing across the nation during the depression, often championing black rights against economic and political injustice. It was the American Communist Party that provided legal aid to nine young black men who were falsely accused of raping two white women on a freight train in a famous case in Scottsboro, Alabama, in 1931.[16] In Alabama black sharecropper Nate Shaw joined the Communist Alabama Sharecropper Union in the early 1930s, as he said, because "I heard about it bein' a organization for the poor class of people—that's just what I wanted to get into." Talk circulated in Shaw's neighborhood that the union organizers would arm the sharecroppers so that they could protect themselves from the landholders and the local authorities who were their agents. Shaw himself recalled chasing deputy sheriffs from his home, with a ".32 Smith and Wesson." Like many poor, illiterate sharecroppers in the South, Shaw did not understand all the political philosophy of the organization that he came to call a "soviet union," but he was certain that he "was man enough to favor its methods" and goals. He believed the organization deserved his loyalty because, unlike the "democratic system" he saw around him, which victimized poor people of all races and used race to justify injustice, the union "was workin' for right."[17]

Other African Americans understood very well. Communist organizers, such as Hosea Hudson and Angelo Herndon in Birmingham, saw racial injustice in America as part of a larger class struggle. Herndon, a coal miner and the son of a coal miner, had experienced the discrimination and segregation that forced black workers into the most difficult, most dangerous jobs and the powerlessness of sudden pay cuts at a mine in Lexington, Kentucky. In 1930 he attended a meeting of the Unemployment Council in Birmingham where he first met members of the Communist Party. Their message of interracial struggle for workers' rights greatly impressed him. Later Herndon recounted the impact of his new awareness:

> All my life I'd been sweated and stepped on and Jim-Crowed. I lay on my belly in the mines for a few dollars a week, and saw my pay stolen and slashed, and my buddies killed. I lived in the worst section of town, and rode behind the "Colored" signs on the streetcars, as though there was something disgusting about me. . . . I had always detested it, but I had never known that anything could be done about it. [Finding interracial organizations working for equality and workers' rights] was like all of a sudden turning a corner on a dirty, old street and finding yourself facing a broad, shining highway.[18]

Members of the Washington Communist Society at a planning meeting for a White House demonstration, March 1930.

Photographs and Prints Division, Library of Congress, Washington, D.C.

When the state of Georgia closed relief offices in 1932, Herndon led an interracial protest march of unemployed people to the courthouse in Atlanta to "show that there was starvation in the city." He was arrested under an old law passed to punish slave insurrection. The prosecutor at his trial in 1933 demanded the death penalty for his actions and for his membership in the Communist Party. Herndon was convicted but given a lesser sentence of eighteen to twenty years in prison. Benjamin J. Davis, his black lawyer, who later became a New York City Councilman and a national leader of the American Communist Party, initiated a worldwide campaign protesting Herndon's imprisonment. Finally, in 1936, after three years in prison, Herndon won his freedom.[19]

Although many people shared Herndon's belief in the necessity for interracial unity in the struggle for economic justice, the best that most could hope for was segregated programs that might relieve some of their suffering. These hopes were encouraged when Franklin Delano Roosevelt, the first Democratic president since Woodrow Wilson, entered the White House. Although most African Americans who could vote remained loyal to the party of Abraham Lincoln and voted Republican during the 1920s, the Republican strategy to attract southern white voters gradually changed blacks' allegiance. In the presidential election of 1928, Republican Herbert Hoover carried at least seven southern states. Significantly Democrat Alfred E. Smith showed more interest in African American welfare than did most Republicans. President Hoover did nothing to inspire black loyalty, a fact that encouraged many to vote Democratic in the next presidential election. For many African Americans the change in political allegiance was difficult, but the black weekly *Pittsburgh Courier* advised, "My friends, go turn Lincoln's picture to the wall . . . that debt has been paid in full."[20] In 1932 about one in four black voters in northern cities cast their ballots for Roosevelt, and the percentage increased substantially when he was elected to a second term in 1934. The visible support for black causes of first lady Eleanor Roosevelt, and her personal friendship with several African Americans, including educator Mary McLeod Bethune, drew black people to the Democratic Party in increasing numbers. African Americans appreciated the symbolism that marked a new era when the Roosevelts invited black actress Etta Moten to sing for a dinner party at the White House in 1934. That same year Chicago blacks sent Arthur L. Mitchell to Congress, the first African American ever elected on a Democratic Party ticket.[21]

President Roosevelt also impressed many people when he sought out blacks in government jobs to be his advisers on racial matters, a group dubbed his "Black Brain Trust." His consultation with such prominent blacks as the Interior Department's Robert C. Weaver; lawyer William H. Hastie; Ralph J. Bunche, who was later the U.S. representative to the United Nations; and Mary McLeod Bethune, led many African Americans to regard him as their friend in the White House. The early depression years, with rising unemployment and business failures, had convinced the new president that state resources could no longer provide the assistance that people needed, and that the federal government must be more active in moderating the effects of the economic downturn. Within weeks of taking office, Roosevelt ended the banking crisis and pushed Congress to institute a fiscally conservative program that would cut the salaries of federal workers, reduce veterans' pensions, and balance the federal budget. In 1933 he established the Agricultural Adjustment Act (declared unconstitutional in 1937) to assist farmers and support crop prices, and the National Recovery Act (declared unconstitutional in 1935), which aided industrial recovery, recognized the rights of organized labor, and established minimum wage levels and maximum hours of work. These were the first of many innovative measures creating an array of programs, including the National Recovery Administration (NRA), Agricultural Adjustment Administration (AAA), Works Progress Administration (WPA), Tennessee Valley Authority (TVA), Civilian Conservation Corps (CCC), and Federal Emergency Relief Administration (FERA), all aimed at ameliorating the nation's unprecedented economic disaster. Many African Americans wrote to Roosevelt to encourage him to use the power of his office to relieve the people's suffering and to strike down racial discrimination. A representative of the National Association of Colored Women wrote to him in 1933, saying, "[P]olitically, you realize that many of us are your friends and supporters." She urged him to encourage the southern states to save money by discontinuing the duplication of services and resources required to maintain the Jim Crow system, and closed her letter with a sentiment many blacks shared: "Mr. Roosevelt, we believe in you. You have expedited reconstruction and have given hope to despairing millions."[22]

These millions pinned their hopes on Roosevelt's efforts to relieve unemployment, provide relief, and rebuild the economy. Under the broad programs of Roosevelt's New Deal, Democrats created the structure for the modern welfare system. By the mid-1930s the president had appointed forty-five African Americans to serve in its agencies. Through the force of his personality and his effective use of the modern medium of radio, Roosevelt bolstered Americans' spirits and strengthened their wills. Although Roosevelt's programs were very popular at first, blacks quickly found that all of them failed to protect blacks from the racial biases of discriminatory employers, agency officials, and local white authorities. When the federal government paid farm owners to lower production and stabilize prices, those owners fired black farm workers. White employers often refused to hire black workers at the new minimum wage levels, arguing that they were not as productive as white workers. One elderly black Mississippian with a family of eight was denied welfare assistance even though he had not been able to find steady work for three and one-half years. When he asked why he had been refused, he was threatened with arrest for "pressing the relief agency for assistance." In South Carolina black workers complained to the NAACP that they were not paid equal wages and that they were charged for relief that was supposed to be given to the poor for free. When they complained to local officials, they were fired from their jobs.[23]

Though the New Deal administration maintained racial segregation, especially in the South, blacks did derive some benefit from its jobs programs. The Civilian Conservation Corps (CCC) provided work for blacks, although they worked in segregated groups. The CCC took young men to military-style camps for training and then furnished them "healthy, outdoor labor" performing public service jobs, building parks, dams, and other public structures, and doing general conservation work. The federal government paid them a small salary, part of which was sent to their families. As one black CCC worker described his introduction to the program in New Jersey, "colored boys fell out in the rear . . . and stood in line until after the white boys had been registered and taken to their tents." The camps were well equipped with books, magazines, a radio, a piano, and a small store, but the "separation of the colored from the white was complete and rigidly maintained" even in the North. Nonetheless, one black CCC worker advised, "as a job and an experience, for a man who has no work, I can heartily recommend it."[24] Some African Americans found jobs with the Works Progress Administration, a New Deal program that employed artists, musicians, writers, and scholars who created public art, provided cultural entertainment, recorded the historical experiences of Americans, and improved public education. Jazz bands presented free public concerts, scholars recorded the memories of former slaves, and artists painted murals depicting the history, aspirations, and everyday lives of their communities.

Though depression-era opportunities were important, most African Americans understood the need for long-term political solutions to their economic problems, and black organizations pressured the Roosevelt administration, Congress, and private businesses to treat black workers fairly. In the winter of 1936 more than eight hundred African Americans, representing at least five hundred organizations, gathered in Chicago to organize a national jobs campaign. They formed the National Negro Congress and chose A. Philip Randolph as their president. Randolph had founded the black union called the Brotherhood of Sleeping Car Porters and Maids in 1925, and had won a few wage agreements for his workers. The brotherhood achieved a major success in 1937 in negotiations with the Pullman Company, resulting in wage increases for eight thousand black workers.[25] The National Negro Congress set up chapters in local communities and worked on behalf of the poor and unemployed with mass meetings and direct action. In the South activists established the interracial Southern Conference on Human Welfare in an effort to improve economic and social conditions for the southern poor. Under the protection of the National Recovery Act, the emerging new national labor movement was more racially inclusive than any since the Knights of Labor in the previous century. The Congress of Industrial Organizations (CIO) was formed in 1938 under the leadership of John L. Lewis, head of the United Mine Workers of America. The NAACP and the Urban League praised the CIO for its egalitarian policies and its efforts to organize black workers.[26]

Meanwhile blacks in northern cities organized picketing, boycotts, and protest marches against white owners of businesses dependent on black customers who refused to employ black workers. In Harlem the Coordinating Committee for Employment carried on a massive campaign to pressure large department stores, public utilities, insurance companies, banks, and the bus company to hire blacks. "Three hundred and fifty thousand consumers are not anything to sneeze at and if anyone dares to sneeze, we are killing him with the worst cold he ever had," declared future congressman Adam Clayton Powell, Jr., minister of the Abyssinian Baptist Church. In the spring of 1938 Powell reported that because of economic pressure "The Gas and Electric Company has seen the light," and "Negroes can work at Ovington's, Wanamaker's, Macy's and Bloomingdale's" in Manhattan. That same year the New York Uptown Chamber of Commerce and the Greater New York Coordinating Committee for Employment agreed to hire black workers for one-third of all new executive, clerical, and sales jobs in retail stores. Effective campaigns were also waged in Chicago; Philadelphia; Boston; Newark, New Jersey; and many other cities.[27]

These victories helped, but by the end of Roosevelt's second term in the late 1930s, unemployment was still extremely high, especially for African Americans. New Deal programs favored whites, and the president seemed willing to sacrifice African American rights to his own political interests. When Walter White approached Roosevelt about support for a federal antilynching law, the president refused. "If I come out for the anti-lynching bill now," Roosevelt told him, southern congressmen "will block every bill I ask Congress to pass to keep America from collapsing. I just can't take that risk."[28] White had risked a great deal, even though he was not identifiably black, gathering information about lynchings and the terrorist activities of the Ku Klux Klan. Working as an investigator for the NAACP, he had attended meetings where white terrorists planned their activities. Roosevelt's response was a bitter personal disappointment for Walter White. As a child he had witnessed the attacks on blacks in the Atlanta riot of 1906, and his white skin, light hair, and blue eyes had offered no protection when he and his family huddled inside their home, armed and ready to defend themselves against the mob.

The frustrations of African Americans sometimes erupted into violence during the depression. In March 1935, unable to get jobs, lacking food, and with little hope for improved living conditions, ten thousand blacks rioted in Harlem. This riot was unlike earlier American riots when whites had invaded black neighborhoods, killing people and destroying property. Angered by rumors of white police brutality in Harlem, this time African Americans attacked property owned by white merchants in black areas. Three blacks were killed before seven hundred policemen quelled the rioting. Black resentment remained, however, at the end of the 1930s. There was too little relief to meet the community's needs, black unemployment remained high, racial discrimination continued, and Congress threatened to cut some the most important New Deal social programs.[29]

Sensitive to the manifestations of racism at home and abroad, African Americans warily watched developments in Europe. Many had been distressed by the rise of Adolf Hitler in Germany—they were familiar with the consequences of theories of racial superiority. During the 1920s and 1930s, African Americans in France had found remarkable racial tolerance and freedom, but blacks in Germany had not been as free, even under the liberal Weimar Republic. Though aspects of American culture were fashionable with Germans, and jazz was especially popular among young people, in Germany, unlike France, black musicians were generally marginalized. Nazis disdained jazz as a product of African culture or, as one described it, "nigger noise." Their disdain was also related to the fact that most German jazz musicians were Jews. Nazis drew on the theories of German Social Darwinians, which stereotyped Africans and their descendants. Hitler equated black and Jewish inferiority and established a special Gestapo task force to root out jazz music and musicians as part of his campaign of anti-Semitism. These developments alarmed African Americans; as one maintained, "[A]ny individual who becomes a world menace on a doctrine of racial prejudice, bigotry, and oppression of minorities . . . is our concern." Kelly Miller, a black educator and writer, drew direct parallels between Nazism and American racial terrorism in an article entitled, "The German Ku Klux."[30] Their kinship was underlined when the Klan in Westchester, New York, openly supported the German Nazi Party in 1934. In New York, Father Divine mounted a campaign against racism at home and abroad by condemning the persecution of the Scottsboro boys in Alabama and demanding an end to the "mistreatment of Jews in Germany and all other countries." W.E.B. Du Bois condemned the rise of Nazi power and equated the persecution of Jews with the evils of American racism. In 1935 Mary McLeod Bethune mobilized the power of black women to fight against racism and discrimination against women when she organized the National Council of Negro Women.[31]

African Americans protested Italy's invasion of Ethiopia in 1935 and collected money and medical supplies to assist the African victims. On Chicago's South Side, white workers joined black writers and intellectuals to march in demonstrations against Mussolini and Italian fascism. In New York, NAACP leaders Walter White and W.E.B. Du Bois spoke to a crowd of nine thousand at a "Hands Off Ethiopia" rally in Madison Square Garden sponsored by the American League against War and Fascism. A few months later, a "People's March for Peace" drew fifteen thousand marchers.[32] Italy's move into Ethiopia created some tensions between blacks and Italian Americans, but they were often united by opposition to fascism. Black Communists in Harlem organized antifascist rallies, and a member of the Universal Negro Improvement Association addressed a receptive audience at the Italian Workers Club. He delivered a fiery message, and then "there was this burst of applause, [and] they gave him money" for the work of his organization.[33]

Considering racism to be a global problem, African Americans believed that a strike against racism abroad was a strike against racism at home. In this context the 1936 Olympic Games in Berlin took on great symbolic significance. They provided direct competition between Germany's so-called Aryan athletes and black athletes, whom Hitler had declared to be mentally and physically inferior. As Hitler watched, Jesse Owens, an African American from Danville, Alabama, set new track records as he won four of the seven gold medals earned by blacks. Shaken by this challenge to his racial beliefs, Hitler congratulated the German winners but left the stadium without recognizing the blacks. Race continued to be a major, though often unspoken, factor in athletic contests. In 1936, when German boxer Max Schmeling knocked out African American Joe Louis, Hitler and hundreds of white Americans sent messages of congratulations to Schmeling. The following year Louis, nicknamed the Brown Bomber, became heavyweight champion of the world by defeating James J. Braddock. In 1938 he faced Schmeling once again. As news of Nazi death camps in the service of Hitler's "final solution" seeped out of Germany, African Americans were fiercely jubilant when Joe Louis knocked out Max Schmeling in the first round. The singer Lena Horne recalled black reactions: "Joe was the one invincible Negro, the one who stood up to the white man and beat him down with his fists. He in a sense carried so many of our hopes, maybe even dreams of vengeance."[34]

In 1939 Russia formed a nonaggression pact with Hitler. In response the American Communist Party softened its opposition to Nazi Germany. Those African Americans who had been attracted to the American Communist Party as one way of directly attacking racism and discrimination were disillusioned and angry. The party's civil rights and labor movement work had great appeal for African Americans. Thousands of blacks had attended Communist rallies, but comparatively few had actually joined the party. In Harlem, for example, thousands of blacks attended marches and rallies on behalf of the party's legal defense of the Scottsboro boys, yet only eighty-seven Harlem residents were party members.[35] A. Philip Randolph, a socialist who had worked with the Communist labor effort, was one of the leaders who denounced the party and worked to exclude it from civil rights activity. As the most powerful black labor leader in the country, Randolph warned African Americans not to be fooled by Communist propaganda, arguing that Stalin was no better than Hitler. As one journalist characterized the situation by 1939, "Communism made a bid for the Negro with promises of abundant home relief, but their promises failed, and since they could not offer Russia, or Siberia, Garveyism has taken the lead again."[36]

By 1940 the war needs of European allies had stimulated American industry. Factories began to hire new workers. Since Jim Crow employment and wage policies kept blacks at a disadvantage, however, black workers benefited little from the rising employment rate and increased wages. Early in 1941 A. Philip Randolph met with the president to demand equal employment for blacks in industries working under federal government defense contracts. He threatened to lead one hundred thousand African Americans in a march on Washington, D.C., if action was not taken by July 1. After a great deal of tension, finally, on June 21, 1941, Franklin Roosevelt issued Executive Order 8802, forbidding discrimination based on race, creed, color, or national origin in the employment of workers for defense industries with federal contracts. The government also established a Committee on Fair Employment Practices to oversee the implementation of the order. Roosevelt's actions immediately opened thousands of steady, well-paying jobs to black workers. This action encouraged a new surge of migration from the South that brought more than five hundred thousand southern blacks to the North by 1945.

In Europe in the late summer of 1939, Hitler's forces moved into Poland. By the following spring, they had swept through Denmark, Norway, Belgium, and the Netherlands. By early summer 1940 the Third Reich controlled Paris and most of the French countryside. Within the next year Hitler mounted an air offensive against England, and in the early summer 1941 he violated the nonaggression pact with Russia and moved against the Soviet Union. African Americans followed these developments avidly and hotly debated America's isolationist stand. In 1940 Max Yergan, president of the National Negro Congress, asserted that although "there are, among our group, those who, in their justifiable hatred of Hitler and Hitlerism, feel it to be our country's duty to send military aid to Britain," African Americans should not support any imperialist power. "Aghast at the horrors of the regimes of Hitler and Mussolini," he denounced "their inhuman, brutal persecution of the Jewish people." He argued, however, that the nation should not cast its lot with "Great Britain, France and the other imperialist countries" that had colonized and continued to oppress the peoples of Africa.[37] Fighting for democracy at home, he contended, should be the African Americans' primary concern.

The debates raging among black Americans and white Americans over whether the nation should enter the war were overtaken by events on December 7, 1941. Dorie Miller was assigned as a mess attendant, the only position open to blacks in the navy, aboard the USS *Arizona* anchored in Pearl Harbor, Hawaii, on that Sunday morning. An amateur boxing champion from Waco, Texas, he was born Doris Miller. When his commanding officer refused to have a man named Doris aboard ship, Miller changed it to Dorie. In the confusion and panic of the Japanese surprise aerial attack on Pearl Harbor and the adjacent Hickam Air Field, Dorie Miller dropped the laundry he was gathering, climbed to the deck, and pulled the wounded captain to safety. He seized a machine gun and fired at the attacking planes, shooting down at least four, before he was ordered to leave the sinking ship. For his "distinguished devotion to duty, extraordinary courage, and disregard for his own personal safety," Miller received the Navy Cross, becoming the first U.S. World War II hero. His actions eventually helped open other ranks in the navy to African Americans.

The Japanese bombing of Pearl Harbor brought the United States into the war, increasing the demand for labor as the country's manufacturing industries went on a full wartime footing. As men entered the military, more and more women were drawn into industrial work, and white women who had pushed African Americans out of domestic work during the depths of the depression left those jobs for more lucrative manufacturing employment. Many black women moved back into domestic work. By 1944 they constituted 60 percent of the country's private household workers.[38] Roosevelt's executive order prohibiting discrimination in war industries did help some black women get factory jobs, employment that offered better pay and was generally less physically demanding than domestic work. The main disadvantage of these jobs was the factory managers' tendency to assign black women the most dangerous, most noxious tasks. A study by the federal Women's Bureau of the Department of Labor found that black women were routinely employed in the "dope rooms" in aircraft plants, where the glue fumes were nauseating and hazardous, and in plants where ore dust heated by blast furnaces filled the air.[39]

As the United States entered the war, the NAACP called on all African Americans to support the war effort. In the next four years three million black men registered for service, four thousand black women served in the army, and almost a half million African Americans served abroad, most of them in Europe and North Africa. By war's end nearly one million blacks had served in the armed forces. Despite the mortal danger of war, military service brought the security of steady work for many African Americans who had faced economic uncertainty and despair throughout the depression. "When the war

UNCROWNED
CHAMPION
©

Joe Louis
before he won the
heavyweight boxing
championship
by defeating
James J. Braddock
on June 22, 1937.

Photographs and
Prints Division,
Library of Congress,
Washington, D.C.

came, I was so glad when I got in the army, recalled Louis Banks, "I knew I was safe. . . . I had money comin', I had food comin', and I had a lot of gang around me. I knew on the streets or hoboing, I might be killed any time."[40]

Though their desperate need for work offered some motivation, blacks also shared the nation's patriotic fervor, even though they continued to meet racial discrimination in the service. They were rejected from the military at a rate five times greater than that of whites. The War Department explained that this was mainly the result of a lack of education, but the NAACP found racial bias in the grading of tests administered to potential draftees. While white recruits were required to achieve a score of 15 on the Army Intelligence Test, blacks needed a score of 39 in order to be inducted. Black men and women were not integrated into the military but served in all-black units. Black women made up 10 percent of the Women's Army Corps (WAC), but it was late in the war before they were enlisted in the navy. African Americans and civil rights organizations continually protested discrimination in the armed forces. Judge William H. Hastie resigned as civilian assistant to the secretary of war to protest the effort by the new Army Air Corps to keep blacks from becoming pilots.[41]

Black recruits suffered the indignities of Jim Crow at southern military training camps, especially when they were off duty in the civilian community. A black chaplain recalled the constant blatant racial bias black troops faced, explaining that while stationed in Virginia, he was not allowed to share the officers' barracks with the white officers, even though half the barracks was unoccupied. Instead the army drew up plans to build a special colored officers' barracks in which he alone would be housed. The base construction officer even suggested that the chaplain might want to select the site for the new structure. "I immediately discovered the South more vigorously engaged in fighting the Civil War," the chaplain commented, "than in training soldiers to resist Hitler."[42]

Private Nellie Holliday became absent without leave from her WAC unit in Florence, South Carolina, because of the complex effects of racism. She was black but so light in complexion that the army placed her in a white unit despite her protest. Her commanding officer refused to transfer her because she was more white than black, arguing that "the social standing of the negro was so low that I would not want to be associated with them." The women in her unit assumed that she was white, and she noted that her assignments were better than those she would have received as a black WAC. She disliked most of her white colleagues, and there were other disadvantages as well. Under the segregated system her more discernibly black family could not visit her, nor could her boyfriend, who had been in service abroad for almost three years. Frustrated by her inability to persuade her commander to let her be part of a black unit, she finally ran away from her post.[43]

Racial discrimination was omnipresent on military bases and in the surrounding areas. Tensions were exacerbated by the War Department's belief that white southerners were particularly well suited to be officers in charge of black units because they had experience with and understood blacks. Violence was especially common around southern military installations. In 1941 white civilians shot twenty-eight African Americans in Alexandria, Louisiana. When white soldiers and civilians fought with black soldiers in North Carolina, a black private and a white military policemen were killed. These were the first of many violent incidents that continued throughout the war, as black soldiers resisted discriminatory treatment. At Freedman Field in Indiana, one hundred black officers were arrested and held in the military stockade for attempting to integrate the base's all-white officers club. Jackie Robinson, a black army lieutenant from California who had been a star in football, basketball, track, and baseball at UCLA, was excluded from the amateur military

Benjamin Oliver Davis, Sr. (1880–1970)

Benjamin O. Davis was born and raised in Washington, D.C. He served in the Spanish-American War, a lieutenant in the Eighth U.S. Volunteer Infantry. After the war he joined the regular army and became an officer by passing a competitive examination. Serving in a variety of positions from military attaché to instructor with the Ohio National Guard, Davis became professor of military science at Tuskegee Institute during the early 1920s and again during the 1930s. In 1940 President Franklin D. Roosevelt appointed him brigadier general, the first African American to receive that rank. During World War II General Davis assisted the inspector general and investigated race relations in the military and attempted to encourage the army, segregated at the time, toward a more progressive racial policy. He was a member of the Committee on Negro Troop Policy, formed to deal with racial problems in the U.S. armed forces. When German attacks demanded more fighting men than white units could supply, Davis submitted a plan to integrate black combat troops into formerly all-white forces. Despite the objections of Gen. Dwight Eisenhower, a few black platoons were integrated into white units in Europe years before President Harry Truman officially integrated the U.S. armed forces in 1948.

Meanwhile General Davis's son, Benjamin Oliver Davis, Jr., was among the black pilots taken into the new Army Air Corps in 1941. Benjamin Davis, Jr., who commanded the first class of African American student pilots at Tuskegee Institute, was awarded the rank of major and placed in command of the Ninety-ninth Pursuit Squadron, the first black air unit. The success of the Ninety-ninth in combat missions over North Africa, and that of subsequent black air units, convinced many in the Army's high command that black men made good pilots.

The Davises, father and son, became symbols of black achievement and role models for African Americans during and after World War II. Benjamin Davis, Sr., retired just before the armed forces were integrated, while Benjamin Davis, Jr., became an important part of the new integrated U.S. Air Force. Like his father, Benjamin Davis, Jr., went on to become a general, eventually outranking his father when he became the first African American lieutenant general in 1965.

Benjamin O. Davis, Sr., the first African American to hold the rank of brigadier general in the U.S. Army. Appointed by President Franklin D. Roosevelt in 1940. Photographs and Prints Division, Library of Congress, Washington, D.C.

baseball team because of his race. In 1944 at Fort Hood, Texas, he refused to follow the driver's instructions to sit in the rear of a bus, even when confronted by the military police and the base provost marshal. Robinson was arrested and court-martialed, though eventually acquitted.[44]

Black newspapers were highly critical of racist government policies. They continually protested the segregation and unfair treatment of black troops, prompting the Justice Department to consider charging them with sedition. When government pressure made it difficult for them to publish, the NAACP interceded and helped to establish guidelines for criticism of the government.[45] The black press printed news of discrimination throughout the war, but it also covered the valor of black troops in Europe, North Africa, and the Pacific. African American military units were visible in every theater of the war. The black press was alert to examples of distinguished service and valor. Readers were informed of the progress in Normandy of the 761st Tank Battalion, the first black tank unit ever to fight in the American armed forces. They learned that the commander of a white airborne unit sent a letter of appreciation to the 969th Negro Field Artillery Battalion for "gallant support" at the Battle of the Bulge. They knew that the first blacks admitted to the Marine Corps won distinction in the invasion of Saipan, and that African American engineers built bridges and fortifications in India, Burma, and China. They celebrated the valor of the airmen trained in Tuskegee's pilot school, eighty-eight of whom won the Distinguished Flying Cross in air combat over Africa and Europe. The eight hundred black pilots who won medals and awards for valor in the war were a source of great pride among African Americans. Gen. Benjamin O. Davis, the highest ranking African American officer, who won a Silver Star, a Distinguished Flying Cross, a Legion of Merit, and an Air Medal with four Oak Leaf Clusters, was a hero.

The African American press recounted the tales of black bravery in battle to give recognition to black men and women in the military and to inspire the black population at home, but they also had another purpose. White soldiers, white officers, and the white American public, seemingly unaware of African American service in the Revolutionary War, the War of 1812, the Civil War, the Spanish-American War, and World War I, watched black troops closely for any sign that they were unfit for combat. Gen. George S. Patton's admonition to black troops in France that "everyone has their eyes on you. . . . Don't let them down" must have struck the soldiers as bitterly ironic, given the long history of black military service to the nation and the discrimination they still faced.[46] African Americans had courageously fought fascism abroad, bringing freedom and democracy to millions in other parts of the world. They returned demanding freedom and equality at home.

1946   In *Morgan* v. *Commonwealth of Virginia,* Supreme Court declares segregation in interstate bus travel unconstitutional

1947   CORE freedom riders test the ban on segregation with southern bus trip, called the Journey of Reconciliation

John Hope Franklin publishes *From Slavery to Freedom*

Jackie Robinson joins the Brooklyn Dodgers, breaking the color line in major league baseball

1948   President Harry Truman ends segregation in the U.S. armed forces

1949   Apartheid established in South Africa

1950   U.S. population 150,697,361; black population 15,042,286 (10 percent)

1950–1953   Korean War; Americans serve in integrated military units for the first time since the Revolutionary War

1952   No reported lynchings for the first time since 1882

1954   In *Brown* v. *Board of Education of Topeka,* Supreme Court declares public school segregation unconstitutional, saying separate is "inherently unequal"

White Citzens Council formed in Mississippi to resist racial integration

1955   The Montgomery Freedom Association, led by Martin Luther King, Jr., begins bus boycott in Alabama

1957   Black students, protected by federal troops, attempt to integrate Central High School in Little Rock, Arkansas

Congress passes Civil Rights Act of 1957 to form Civil Rights Commission and Civil Rights Divison of the Justice Department

Althea Gibson becomes the first African American to win the Wimbledon tennis championship and the U.S. Open championship

1959   Cuban revolution; Fidel Castro becomes premier

Berry Gordy, Jr., founds Motown Record Company

1960   Student Nonviolent Coordinating Committee (SNCC) organized in Raleigh, North Carolina

Students sit in at Woolworth lunch counter, Greensboro, North Carolina, protesting segregation

Presidential candidates John F. Kennedy and Richard M. Nixon hold televised debate; Kennedy, a Roman Catholic, is elected

1961   Integrated group of Freedom Riders attacked and beaten in Alabama

U.S.–sponsored Bay of Pigs invasion of Cuba fails

Soviet Union constructs Berlin Wall, dividing East Berlin from West Berlin

1962   Cuban missile crisis

James Meredith becomes the first black student to enroll at the University of Mississippi

The Postwar Civil Rights Movement

*A*he Allied Powers invaded Europe on June 6, 1944. Within the year Hitler committed suicide, and Germany surrendered unconditionally. The end of the war in Europe was a joyous occasion, made more so by the prospect of swift victories in Asia and the Pacific as well. It had been a difficult war, the Allies had incurred heavy losses, and black families had experienced more than their share of death and injury. Although the military was racially segregated, the army was sometimes forced to use black troops temporarily to replace casualties in depleted white units. In such circumstances some whites had their stereotypes challenged by the experience, and once again, officers testified to the bravery of African Americans. After Americans repelled the German attack in the Battle of the Bulge, Gen. Buck Lanham told the black troops who joined his forces, "I have never seen any soldiers who have performed better in combat than you."[1]

The African Americans among the first Allied troops to liberate Jewish prisoners at Dachau and other concentration camps were deeply aware of racism and its consequences but were sometimes puzzled by the fact that Jews had been the primary target of Nazi genocide. Paul Parks remembered confronting the horror of the camps with their wretched, skeletal survivors. "Why Jews?" he asked. "It doesn't make sense. Why were they killed?" One of the camp inmates explained that Jews were killed simply because they were Jews. On reflection Parks understood "because [he had] seen people lynched just because they were black." Pondering racial violence, Parks and many African Americans made the connection "between the history of [their] people in America and [what] happened to the Jews in Europe."[2]

Before the United States entered the war, some African Americans had questioned the wisdom of fighting on behalf of a country that would not grant them full rights of citizenship. Black journalist George Schuyler expressed what many felt. "Our war is not with Hitler in Europe, but against Hitler in America," he wrote. "Our war is not to defend democracy, but to get a democracy we have never had."[3] Nevertheless they did fight, and returning home after enduring the hardships of war, they were even more determined to gain the rights to which they were entitled. After the end of fighting in Europe and before the end of the war, on April 12, 1945, President Franklin D. Roosevelt had a sudden stroke and died, just five months after his election to an unprecedented fourth term of office. Through the force of his personality and his intimate style of leadership, Roosevelt had brought the nation through depression and war. African Americans felt they had lost a sympathetic ally. "Negro America has suffered its greatest loss since Abraham Lincoln," announced the *Chicago Defender*. The vice president who assumed the presidency was Harry S. Truman, a man from the Jim Crow state of Missouri. His immediate appointment of James Byrnes, a segregationist from South Carolina, as his close adviser confirmed progressives' fears that he would follow FDR just as the reactionary Andrew Johnson had followed Abraham Lincoln. Yet, African Americans were hopeful when the new president promised to pursue policies to insure returning black soldiers "a full and equal role in the postwar employment picture."[4]

Shortly after Roosevelt's death, a conference was convened in San Francisco to establish the United Nations, a new organization dedicated to the proposition that international conflicts could be resolved peacefully. The conclusion of World War II promised to rearrange the colonial holdings of nations as well. African Americans were among those who hoped that the United Nations could help bring freedom to colonized people in Africa and throughout the world. Ralph Bunche, the State Department's acting chief of the Division of Dependent Territories and a member of Roosevelt's informal black cabinet, was part of the official U.S. staff. African American observers included Walter White and W.E.B. Du Bois of the NAACP and Mary McLeod Bethune of the National Council of Negro Women. The black press followed the deliberations avidly, focusing on the place accorded colonized peoples in the discussions and expressions of support for human rights. Du Bois and White protested strenuously when the United States and many of its European allies voted down the Chinese-Russian proposal that the UN Charter guarantee independence to colonies. The preamble to the charter did speak to the aspirations of minorities, however, with its proclamation of "faith in fundamental human rights, in the dignity and worth of the human person, in the equal rights of men and women and of nations large and small." Blacks dared to hope that the charter's declaration of "universal respect for, and observance of, human rights and fundamental freedoms for all without distinction to race, language, or religion" would be applied to blacks in the United States as well as to colonized peoples and oppressed minorities in less powerful nations.[5]

As the United Nations took shape in San Francisco, the continuing war demonstrated the need for an organization dedicated to peace. Allied forces blanketed Japanese cities with the type of saturation bombing that had devastated Dresden and other German cities. In Tokyo eighty thousand people died in one night. But it was the final acts of the war that changed warfare forever and lent the greatest urgency to the establishment of the United

Nations. On August 6, 1945, the United States dropped a new, secretly developed atomic bomb of unimaginable power on the Japanese city of Hiroshima. This single bomb killed one hundred thousand civilians, injured tens of thousands, and left countless others mortally ill. Three days later, an American plane dropped another atomic bomb on the city of Nagasaki, killing an additional fifty thousand people. The war ended within days; Japan surrendered unconditionally, and millions of American soldiers returned home.[6]

At the end of World War II, the world faced the terrors of the nuclear age, and Americans faced postwar economic uncertainty. The defeat of racism abroad and the employment of unprecedented numbers of African Americans in war industry heightened expectations in black communities. There were other hopeful signs for advancing the fight for freedom at home. During the war the NAACP had won important victories in the Supreme Court—legal decisions that forced southern states to attempt to implement the nineteenth-century judicial mandate that racially separate schools and other facilities must be equal. In reality the separate facilities open to blacks were almost never equal, and it was clear that maintaining a more equal southern Jim Crow system would require a massive financial commitment. The Court had also supported black political rights with its ruling in 1944 that the southern Democratic Party could not declare itself a private club in order to close its primary elections to black voters.[7]

African Americans recognized that the war against Hitler and the Axis powers had changed the international context of race relations. In 1947 the NAACP issued a "Statement on the Denial of Human Rights to Minorities in the Case of Citizens of Negro Descent in the U.S.A., and an Appeal to the United Nations for Redress." Although opponents argued that the UN had no jurisdiction in domestic concerns, its influence was particularly clear in a Supreme Court ruling in 1948 striking down the Alien Land Law, which barred Japanese immigrants from owning or leasing land. Not only was this law declared unconstitutional, but the Court decided that it violated the UN Charter of Human Rights and Freedom and was "an unhappy facsimile, a disheartening reminder, of the racial policy pursued by those forces of evil whose destruction recently necessitated a devastating war."[8] American race relations had become an international concern, with lynchings drawing the world's attention during the 1940s and 1950s. As the post–World War II Cold War with Russia cast the United States as the champion of the free world, American racial discrimination became an international embarrassment. The incongruities were clear in 1948 when the United Nations appointed Dr. Ralph Bunche, the grandson of a slave, as the mediator in negotiations between Arabs and Jews in the Middle East. Two years later he received the Nobel Peace Prize. As late as the 1960s Secretary of State Dean Rusk made the government's continuing problem explicit: "The biggest burden we [as a nation] carry on our backs in our foreign relations," he observed, "is the problem of racial discrimination here at home."[9]

Wartime experiences and new freedoms made it more difficult to suppress black anger at injustice. In his autobiographical essays published in the 1950s, novelist James Baldwin recalled his encounters with the Jim Crow customs of transplanted southerners when he worked at a defense plant in central New Jersey. Baldwin was born in New York City in 1924 and grew up in Harlem. His grandmother had been born in Louisiana during the time of slavery, and his father had migrated after World War I from New Orleans to New York, where he worked primarily as an impecunious minister, eventually struggling to support a wife and nine children. Baldwin's teachers recognized him as a student of exceptional promise. He began writing early in life, and he was trying to establish himself as an author when he worked at the defense plant for a year during the war. His experiences with discrimination there in virtually all areas of his daily life introduced him to the rage that was an integral part of being black in the United States. In a moving account of his run-in with a white waitress in the last of a series of restaurants where he was refused service, Baldwin described how he hurled a pitcher of water at her, breaking the mirror on the wall behind her, and was pursued by the police as he ran for his life. The anger Baldwin discovered in himself frightened him, and when he returned home, he found a similar anger in the residents of Harlem. As he described the mood in Harlem, and in all of black America:

> I had never before known it to be so violently still. Racial tensions throughout this country were exacerbated during the early years of the war, partly because the labor market brought together hundreds of thousands of ill-prepared people and partly because Negro soldiers, regardless of where they were born, received their military training in the south. What happened in defense plants and army camps had repercussions, naturally, in every Negro ghetto.[10]

Wartime discrimination touched African Americans from all walks of life. As Baldwin observed, "[O]n each face there seemed to be the same strange, bitter shadow." Some black spokesmen vowed revenge for the dangers faced by black soldiers at the hands of their own countrymen as they prepared to face the perils of war. After the war James Baldwin fled the racial tensions of America and lived in France for ten years, while he developed his literary voice as a leading chronicler of the American racial dilemma.[11]

In 1946 President Truman, aware of postwar racial tensions, issued an executive order creating a Presidential Commission on Civil Rights to study the federal role in civil rights protection. Under the threat of a mass protest led by A. Philip Randolph, in 1948 he banned segregation and discrimination in

Lorraine Vivian Hansberry (1930–1965)

Lorraine Hansberry was born in Chicago when that city was a hub of African American culture and music. Both her parents were educated and politically active, and Lorraine was influenced by their respect for learning and their commitment to civil rights. After high school she enrolled in the University of Wisconsin, becoming the first black student to live in her dormitory. She became active in politics, and in 1950 she moved to Harlem, took a job with the liberal newspaper *Freedom,* and two years later became its associate editor. Hansberry wrote many impressive stories and articles for the press, but her most important contribution as a writer was her play, originally named *The Crystal Stair.* The play about a black family's struggle to survive in the harsh, racially restrictive world of post–World War II Chicago drew on the experiences of people she had known on Chicago's South Side. Inspired by Langston Hughes's poem that described black people's deferred dreams drying up like "a raisin in the sun," Hansberry renamed her play. When it opened in New York in 1959, the critics were wildly enthusiastic, praising the writing and its realistic mixture of anger and control. *Raisin in the Sun,* starring Sidney Poitier and Claudia McNeil, received the New York Drama Critics Circle Award, the first play by a black playwright to receive such an honor. In 1961 Columbia Pictures released the movie version of her play.

The play and movie reached a wide audience and helped expand support and sympathy for the growing civil rights movement. Hansberry's fame allowed her to carry forward her parents' civil rights work. She raised funds for the Student Nonviolent Coordinating Committee. She also worked to abolish the House Un-American Activities Committee, which had used investigations, allegations, and innuendo to destroy the careers of many people in politics, academia, and the arts during the 1950s. Hansberry's political and literary career was cut short by her death from cancer in 1965 at age thirty-four, but her courage and involvement had inspired many in the arts to lend their aid and celebrity to the civil rights cause.

Lorraine Hansberry, playwright and author of the 1959 play Raisin in the Sun. *She was the first African American to receive the Critics Circle Award. Photographs and Prints Division, National Archives.*

the American armed forces.[12] Racial issues greatly influenced national politics during the presidential election of 1948. President Truman's liberal stand on civil rights alienated the southern wing of the Democratic Party, and southerners split off to form the States' Rights Party, running South Carolina Senator Strom Thurmond as their presidential candidate. The Republican Party also took a stand on civil rights, calling for legislation against lynching and supporting the abolition of impediments to black voting rights. The Progressive Party, led by Henry A. Wallace, vice president in Roosevelt's second administration and former secretary of agriculture, endorsed the idea of a presidential proclamation to end segregation and discrimination in the military and other federal employment. The candidate of the American Communist Party ran on a platform that included all of these measures, plus outlawing the Ku Klux Klan and a federal recommitment to the Thirteenth, Fourteenth and Fifteenth (Reconstruction) Amendments to the U.S. Constitution. Truman won one of the closest elections in American history by using an anti-Communist stance to position himself as a centrist. He attacked the Communist Party and branded the Progressives as Communists. He attracted a substantial number of black votes by separating himself from the States' Rights advocates and playing on black suspicions about Republicans going back to the 1920s. The campaigns and Truman's victory appeared to make civil rights and racial equality part of the nation's agenda.[13]

Truman continued Roosevelt's policies by appointing African Americans to leadership positions. He nominated black civil rights lawyer William Hastie as the first African American to sit on the U.S. Circuit Court of Appeals and named Edward Dudley as U.S. ambassador to the West African nation of Liberia. Truman also sent Secretary of State Dean Rusk to New York City to offer Ralph Bunche the position of assistant secretary of state. In addition to his experience in international affairs, Bunche was a distinguished scholar. Born in 1904 in Detroit, Michigan, and raised in Los Angeles, California, where he graduated from UCLA, he received a Ph.D. in government and international relations from Harvard University, and subsequently served on the faculty of Howard University in Washington, D.C. He had also done research on colonialism in Africa for the Office of Strategic Services during the war, and had served at the Library of Congress and in the State Department. Knowing the discrimination he and his family would face in this southern city, Bunche was reluctant to return to Washington. One small indignity he remembered from their former residence there exemplified for him the continual racial slights African Americans faced in the South. When the family dog died, Bunche had made arrangements for the dog's burial and found that racial segregation was so strict that even the pet cemetery was segregated according to the race of the pet owner. Unwilling to live again under this system, he turned down Truman's offer and instead accepted the appointment by the

United Nations Security Council as mediator in Palestine. Ralph Bunche eventually became deputy secretary-general of the United Nations, a position he held until his death in 1971.[14]

While the federal government was making only slow progress on bringing African Americans into leadership positions, recognizing black civil rights, and integrating some institutions under its jurisdiction, there had been significant changes in a few areas of society during and immediately after the war. Up to this time team sports were generally segregated. African Americans had played professional baseball in all-black leagues since the nineteenth century. There were rumors that some African Americans played for major league teams by passing themselves off as Cubans, Mexicans, or American Indians, and that the great Babe Ruth had some African ancestry. In the idiosyncratic American racial classification, nationality could sometimes override racial heritage. In one case in 1911 major league baseball accepted two Cuban players of relatively dark complexion as "genuine Caucasians" after they traveled to Havana, certifying their Cuban ethnicity. In an experiment calculated to improve game attendance and increase profits, baseball manager Branch Rickey brought the outstanding college athlete and military veteran Jackie Robinson to the minor leagues and, finally in 1947, to his major league team, the Brooklyn Dodgers.[15] Robinson's race was unmistakable, as was his playing ability. The only doubt was about his ability to control his temper when people in the stands hurled racial insults and sometimes solid objects at him, and players used dirty tricks to frustrate and even injure him during the games. In 1949 Robinson was named Most Valuable Player with the highest batting average in the National League. All over the United States black people identified with him and considered this a great opportunity and a breakthrough for integration, despite the hardships and the injustice of his situation.[16]

Though Jackie Robinson's was the most celebrated case, there were other advances for African Americans in sports, business, and other employment during the postwar period. In 1946 professional football signed the first four black players of the modern era, and in 1950 Chuck Cooper and Nat "Sweetwater" Clifton became the first black players in the National Basketball Association. The next year Sugar Ray Robinson became middleweight boxing champion of the world following up on his welterweight title in 1946 and in 1956 Floyd Paterson won the heavyweight championship. Althea Gibson became the first black player to win a major national tennis championship, taking singles titles at the French Open in 1956 and at Wimbledon and the U.S. Open in 1957. In 1958 she won a second Wimbledon singles title. Blacks slowly gained ground in the business end of entertainment as Atlanta's WERD, the first black-owned radio station, began broadcasting in 1949. In 1958 choreographer Alvin Ailey formed his Alvin Ailey American Dance Theater in New York, and the next year Berry Gordy, Jr., founded the Motown Record

Company in Detroit. During these postwar years African Americans saw wider economic opportunities as New Jersey, Connecticut, Massachusetts, New York, and Rhode Island took important steps to outlaw racial discrimination in employment, and the federal government prohibited racial discrimination in the federal civil service.

Federal sponsorship during the Great Depression and World War II contributed to the growing recognition of black music and musical performers and their increasing integration into American popular culture. In World War I, black infantry units had organized bands, some of which became known in the United States and abroad for their talent; in World War II, the opportunities to perform under government initiative were greatly expanded. The military organized bands and glee clubs and hired touring musical groups, accomplished concert artists, and popular singers and bands to entertain the troops. These performers introduced many Americans and many people in other parts of the world to the African American musical heritage and increased the already considerable influence of black musical styles on European-derived American music. According to the historian Eileen Southern, the rest of the world gradually came to see jazz as "the only true American music" during this period.[17]

In the 1940s a Harlem nightclub called Minton's Playhouse became the center for the early morning jam sessions that developed a new experimental style of jazz that came to be known as bebop, or simply bop. Some of the musicians who played together in these sessions were pianist Thelonious Monk, trumpeter Dizzy Gillespie, saxophonist Charley Parker, and drummer Max Roach. The new music reached a wider audience when the bands of Earl "Fatha" Hines and Billy Eckstine began to play it, and by the time it moved downtown in the mid-1940s, integrated bands played in small New York clubs. Bop was one of many different styles of jazz that developed as musicians experimented and reacted to earlier forms. The establishment of the first jazz festival in Newport, Rhode Island, in 1954, followed by others in the United States and in Europe, testified to the popularity and respectability attained by this once-underground music rooted in African American culture. In another indication of the integration of music during the postwar period, music recorded for black communities, formerly called "race" music, began to be called rhythm and blues. This music crossed the racial divide during the 1950s, first popularized among white teenagers by white singers such as Elvis Presley and Bill Haley, and then with records by such black artists as Willie Mae Thornton, James Brown, Sam Cooke, Aretha Franklin, Ray Charles, and Little Richard played on formerly exclusively white radio stations.[18]

Integration was not limited to popular music. Slowly during this period, accomplished classical musicians such as Paul Robeson, Dorothy Maynor, Todd Duncan, and Marian Anderson achieved recognition on the concert stage.

Anderson's career is especially illustrative of these changes. Born in 1902 in Philadelphia, Pennsylvania, Anderson began singing in her church, studied music, appeared with the internationally acclaimed singer Roland Hayes while still in her early teens, and won a contest sponsored by the New York Philharmonic in 1924. She achieved more widespread recognition for her talents in Europe where she performed for two years, first appearing in Berlin in 1933. She stunned listeners at a recital in Salzburg in 1935. The conductor Arturo Toscanini, who was in the audience, proclaimed hers a voice that "comes once in a hundred years." Despite her European triumph, the Daughters of the American Revolution would not allow her to sing in their Constitution Hall in Washington in 1939 because she was black. Her exclusion, however, so outraged the public and Eleanor Roosevelt that the Roosevelt administration arranged for Anderson to sing at an outdoor concert in front of the Lincoln Memorial. Seventy-five thousand people came to hear her on Easter Sunday morning. In 1955 Marian Anderson became the first African American to perform with New York City's Metropolitan Opera Company.[19]

The prospects for overcoming legal barriers to racial integration were advanced during the 1940s by NAACP victories in a series of cases that chipped away at Jim Crow education and finally directly took on the separate-but-equal doctrine. This campaign, headed by NAACP lawyer Thurgood Marshall, culminated in 1954 with a Supreme Court ruling against legalized segregation in the case *Brown* v. *the Board of Education of Topeka, Kansas.* With the *Brown* decision the Supreme Court reversed the nineteenth-century ruling that laws separating the races in public facilities were not forbidden by the Constitution so long as the facilities were equal. The Brown case focused specifically on schools, but the arguments that segregation carried detrimental social and psychological consequences and deprived racial minorities of their rights could clearly be applied to other public facilities.

Though southern state and city authorities immediately promised to comply with the court's ruling, equivocal statements by President Dwight Eisenhower encouraged opposition. Eisenhower declared that although he would not tolerate resistance to desegregation, he was not convinced that the federal government should play an active role in such a controversial issue. He desegregated schools and public facilities under federal control, including District of Columbia schools, but did little to discourage growing southern resistance. In Mansfield, Texas, the governor dispatched Texas Rangers to prevent the integration of a high school. In Humphreys County, Mississippi, where blacks outnumbered whites two to one, the Reverend George W. Lee was murdered for attempting to register African American voters. The White Citizens Council of Mississippi organized economic pressure. Those who registered to vote or supported school integration risked losing their jobs and being denied credit. The NAACP set up a twenty-thousand-dollar fund to assist

Thurgood Marshall, civil rights lawyer. Appointed as the
first African American to sit on the U.S. Supreme Court
by President Lyndon B. Johnson in 1967.

Photographs and Prints Division, Library of Congress, Washington, D.C.

the black Mississippians targeted by these tactics, but white terrorism reduced
the number of African American registered voters from twenty-two thousand
to eight thousand within a year. The president still remained silent even when
there were bombings in Tennessee and Alabama.[20]

In the summer of 1955 a sensational case focused the nation's attention
on the struggle. Whites murdered and mutilated Emmett Till—a fourteen-year-
old black boy from Chicago who was visiting relatives near Money, Mississippi—allegedly for speaking disrespectfully to a white woman. Strong
evidence pointed to the woman's husband and his half-brother, and they were
arrested and charged with kidnapping and murder, but the all-white jury
found them not guilty. The murder of Emmett Till received broad coverage
in the national and international press. Almost every black newspaper and
magazine and most of the white news media ran long, detailed stories.
Charles Diggs, a black congressman from Michigan, traveled to Mississippi

for the trial, explaining that the picture of Till's mutilated body that appeared in *Jet* magazine moved him to see Mississippi justice for himself. A black reporter noted that having Diggs there made a great impression in a place where almost no one had ever seen a black congressman.[21] Till's funeral in Chicago, covered by the *Chicago Defender,* attracted thousands of mourners. "The Emmett Till case was one that shook the foundations of Mississippi, both black and white," recalled one civil rights worker. "With the white community because . . . it had become nationally publicized, with us blacks because it said that even a child was not safe from racism, bigotry, and death."[22]

The nation may have been horrified, but the Justice Department was unmoved and claimed that it was Mississippi's responsibility to protect those within its jurisdiction. Eisenhower did not respond to a telegram from Till's grieving mother. Roy Wilkins of the NAACP expressed the frustration of many people when he said of the former commander of Allied forces in Europe during World War II, "Eisenhower was a fine general and a good, decent man; but if he had fought World War II the way he fought for civil rights, we would all be speaking German today."[23] Congress seemed equally paralyzed. Adam Clayton Powell, Jr., made an unsuccessful attempt to deny federal aid to segregated schools and segregated public housing projects. While the president and Congress hesitated, 101 southern congressmen signed the "Southern Manifesto," vowing to resist integration.

Local civil rights efforts, often aided by the national resources of the NAACP, continued in the South. A year and a half after the *Brown* decision, activists waged a pivotal campaign in Montgomery, Alabama, the first capital city of the former Confederacy. Montgomery maintained the rigid system of public segregation typical of many southern cities at the time. "All of the restaurants were segregated, the hotels and motels . . . even in the public courthouse, blacks could not drink water except from the fountain labeled 'Colored' . . . [and] colored people had to use the same restroom, male and female. And the janitor never would clean up the restroom for the colored people."[24] The Women's Political Council, led by Jo Ann Robinson, had directed much of the civil rights struggle in Montgomery for years. They had succeeded in getting local department stores to use the titles Mr., Miss, or Mrs. when corresponding with black customers, and had tried to get the city to integrate the water fountains and hire black police officers. Their most ambitious undertaking began on the chilly afternoon of December 1, 1955, when Rosa Parks, a black seamstress, boarded a city bus and sat in the colored section. Black passengers were legally required to give up their seats and move farther back when the front section of the bus filled with whites, but on this particular day Parks was tired, frustrated, and determined not to comply when a white male passenger demanded her seat. She again refused when a black man offered her his seat in an attempt to defuse the increasing

Rosa Parks, arrested for refusing to give up her seat on a Montgomery, Alabama, city bus in 1955. Her action became the catalyst for the Montgomery bus boycott, which first brought Martin Luther King to national attention. She is shown here at the 1963 March on Washington.
Gelman Library Photographic Collection, George Washington University.

tension. Neither the bus driver nor a local policeman could change her mind, and she was arrested.

The news of Ms. Parks's arrest spread through the black community within minutes. One of her friends called E. D. Nixon's wife, who then telephoned him at his office. Nixon, a labor activist and leader of the local NAACP, had been searching for the right case to challenge segregated seating on the Montgomery buses. For a year he and other NAACP officers had discussed a boycott as one possible means of forcing integration. Others had been arrested for protesting segregated seating, but each case had problems that could have been exploited in court by a clever prosecutor. Rosa Parks was different. Known and loved in the community—a good Christian, churchgoing woman, secretary of the local chapter of the NAACP, and a veteran of that summer's desegregation workshops at the Highlander Folk School in Tennessee—she was perfect. Nixon posted her bond and appealed to her to allow the case to serve as a challenge to the city's segregation law. "We can break this situation on the bus with your case," he asserted. She agreed after discussing the proposition with her husband and her mother.[25] Immediately after Parks's arrest Robinson and the Women's Political Council distributed flyers in the community to organize a one-day black boycott of the buses for December 5. It was so successful that leaders formed the Montgomery Improvement Association to continue the boycott, and Nixon approached a young minister named Martin Luther King, Jr., to be their spokesman. King initially demurred, noting that he had come to Montgomery and the Dexter Avenue Baptist Church only a little more than a year before, was only twenty-six, and was still working on his doctorate. When Nixon persisted King said he would think it over. "I called him back," Nixon recalled, "and he said, 'Yeah, Brother Nixon, I'll go along with it.'" Confident but relieved, Nixon replied, "I'm glad of that, Reverend King, because I talked to eighteen other people, [and] I told them to meet at your church at three o'clock."[26]

Martin Luther King, Jr., was recognized as an accomplished orator even then. He came by it naturally as the son and grandson of Baptist ministers in Atlanta, Georgia, who devoted their lives to the church and to the pursuit of civil rights. Born into a rural sharecropping family, Martin Luther King, Sr., made his way to Atlanta and eventually followed his father-in-law into the pulpit of the Ebenezer Baptist Church. His life was actively and passionately committed to racial equality. Martin Luther King, Jr., was educated at Morehouse College in Atlanta and Crozer Theological Seminary in Pennsylvania, and received his doctorate from Boston University. In 1953 he married Coretta Scott, a woman from Alabama he had met while she was a student at Boston's New England Conservatory of Music. He returned with her to the South to begin his ministry at the Dexter Avenue Baptist Church in Montgomery, a church with a well-educated middle-class congregation.[27]

King was elected president of the Montgomery Improvement Association, launching his career as a leader of militant nonviolence in the fight for African American rights. The blacks of Montgomery carpooled and walked, and the community, inspired by the courage of its leaders and the oratory of Martin Luther King, maintained its nonviolent protest for 381 days despite white threats and violent attacks. The boycott brought national attention to local leaders such as King, Nixon, Robinson, and the Reverend Ralph Abernathy, and drew in national activist Bayard Rustin, who connected their protest to Gandhian nonviolent activism.[28] Ninety percent of Montgomery's African Americans boycotted the buses, ending debates about whether blacks had the resolve and determination successfully to confront the southern Jim Crow system. By the time the boycott ended in 1956, when the Supreme Court declared that the buses should be integrated, the aims of the protesters had become broader and more radical. At first they had requested only that bus drivers in Montgomery be more courteous to black passengers, that the company hire more black drivers, and that the line between black and white seating be more flexible. In the end they demanded the complete integration of the bus system. Heartened by their success, a group of activist ministers, led by King, established the Southern Christian Leadership Council (SCLC) to continue their attack on southern segregation.[29]

The growing availability of television in American society during the 1950s gave new, more powerful media coverage to the events in Montgomery and to subsequent civil rights action. Most young middle-class whites in the North were growing up in residentially segregated communities. The development of urban ghettos after World War I and the growth of white suburbs after World War II had created two essentially separate societies. Crossover music, the development of rock 'n' roll from its beginnings in rhythm and blues, and such early TV personalities as singers Nat "King" Cole and Eartha Kitt had given young white Americans glimpses of contemporary black culture. News coverage of civil rights demonstrations, however, brought black Americans and the violence of southern racism into American living rooms with a new immediacy and a kind of distant intimacy. Many young viewers were inspired by the courage of the demonstrators and the moral force of Martin Luther King as he urged his followers to speak truth to power.

Although racism was a national phenomenon, it was most blatant and most deadly in the South, and television's detailed coverage of southern atrocities encouraged the rest of the nation to identify southern society as the locus of its racial ills. The South reacted defensively, with politicians drawing on southerners' perceptions of their beleaguered history to gain political support in a stand against integration. Governor Orval Faubus of Arkansas, who had won a closely contested election, stopped school integration in Little Rock, the state's capital city. The school board had quickly announced its intention to integrate the public schools after the *Brown* decision, but white opposition grew as the time for integration approached. Daisy Bates, editor of the black *Arkansas State Press* and president of the Arkansas NAACP, had led a cooperative venture bringing the school board together with the black community to devise an integration plan. They worked for three years to arrive at a plan that would bring only nine black students into Little Rock's Central High School and hoped for a mild statement of support from the governor.

At first Faubus seemed willing to go along, but in the end he seized the political advantage and stood firmly against integration. Claiming to be motivated by a desire to protect the black students from dangerous "well-armed groups who didn't proclaim their intentions publicly and kept them well concealed," Faubus called out the national guard to block integration. In the fall of 1957, Americans watched on national television as guardsmen with rifles

Daisy Bates (*center*) and eight of the nine students who integrated
Central High School in Little Rock, Arkansas, in 1957.
Photographs and Prints Division, National Archives.

at the ready and fixed bayonets prevented a fifteen-year-old girl from entering Little Rock's Central High School.[30] A federal judge ordered the immediate
enrollment of all nine black students, but Governor Faubus refused to allow
it. In a meeting with the president, Eisenhower believed Faubus agreed that
the national guard would protect the students instead of blocking their path.
But the governor changed his mind and withdrew the guard, leaving the black
students exposed to the attacks of a mob gathered outside the school. Finally,
after a public outcry, Eisenhower acted. He federalized the Arkansas National
Guard and sent twelve hundred paratroopers to oversee integration at Central High School.[31]

Enrollment was only the first step in the integration struggle for the students who entered Central. Thelma Wair remembered a teacher who took every opportunity to demonstrate her disdain for black students and integration, refusing to seat any students behind Wair even though it meant leaving seats vacant. Ernest Green recalled "white kids following us, continuously calling us niggers." Angered by constant harassment, Minniejean Brown finally dumped a bowl of chili on the head of one of her tormenters. The white students were shocked into silence when the all-black lunchroom staff gave her a standing ovation. Like Jackie Robinson and other African Americans who broke the color line, these students were expected to take abuse stoically without retaliating. Brown was suspended for violating this expectation and finally finished her high school education in New York.[32] Ernest Green, the only black senior in a class of more than six hundred, graduated in the spring of 1958 but was not allowed to participate in any of the celebrations for graduating seniors. He remembered that at the graduation ceremonies "there were a lot of claps for the students," but when his name was called there was only an "eerie silence."[33]

Three months after Green's graduation, and one year after Central High was integrated, Governor Faubus closed all of Little Rock's high schools rather than integrate them. Some municipalities in Virginia and elsewhere in the South followed his example, but public opinion polls by the end of the 1950s indicated that compromise was possible, especially in the border states of the Upper South. Even though most whites did not favor total active resistance, the advantage gained by opposing integration was too great for some southern politicians to resist.[34] Faubus's extreme actions garnered him great political capital. A Gallup poll in 1958 named him one of the ten most admired men in the world, along with such people as President Eisenhower, Winston Churchill, Albert Schweitzer, and Dr. Jonas Salk. Another southern politician bluntly acknowledged learning the advantage of "playing the race card." George Wallace ran for the governorship of Alabama in 1958, refused to speak at a Ku Klux Klan rally, and lost to a candidate supported by the Klan. Wallace learned a lesson that guided his future political career: "They out-niggered me that time," he recalled. "They'll never do it again."[35]

Aware that southern intransigence made their struggle costly but encouraged by federal successes, civil rights proponents continued the direct action campaign. On February 1, 1960, 4 students from the all-black North Carolina Agricultural & Technical College, inspired by the students in Little Rock, sat down at a lunch counter in Greensboro's Woolworth variety store and ordered cups of coffee. "The people started to look at us," remembered Joe McNeil. The blacks who worked in the store "looked at us with disbelief . . . concerned for our safety." The students were not served and soon left, but when they returned the next day there were 15. They were not served, and on the third day there were 150 students. At one point the demonstration included most of the North Carolina A&T football team, and eventually at least one thousand people participated. Whites insulted, harassed, and violently attacked the demonstrators, but the protest spread quickly, and within days, there were sit-ins in at least fifteen places across the South, including the nearby cities of Durham and Winston-Salem in the first week.[36] Within a month one thousand students from all-black Alabama State marched on the state Capitol to protest segregation and racial injustice. The Alabama Board of Education retaliated by expelling nine of the protesters, and in Montgomery, police arrested thirty-five protesters. Police used tear gas to disperse student protesters in Tallahassee, Florida, and a sit-in in Chattanooga, Tennessee, became a race riot when whites attacked the protesters. By the end of 1960, 75,000 students, both blacks and whites, had staged sit-ins in seventy-five cities and towns, and 3,600 had been arrested. Two thousand had been jailed in northern cities for forming sympathy picket lines at local branches of national chain stores with Jim Crow practices in the South.[37]

As these spontaneous, locally organized, student-led demonstrations spread, veteran civil rights organizer Ella Baker decided they could be even more effective with coordination and direction. Baker had worked to establish NAACP chapters in the South during the 1940s and was the executive director of the Southern Christian Leadership Conference at the time. At a meeting Baker convened at Shaw University in Raleigh, North Carolina, in April 1960, King and other SCLC leaders anticipated that the students would form a youth branch of their organization, but Baker understood the students' wish to remain independent. Indeed, she herself had chafed under the sometimes imperious direction of the ministers who were the primary leadership of the SCLC, men who were accustomed to exalted positions and deference in their churches, especially from female parishioners. She encouraged the students to establish a more democratic form of leadership, to share their experiences, and to arrive at a consensus plan for future action. "I think her participation as a person some years older than we were," wrote one of the students, "could really serve as a model of how older people can give energy and help to younger people and at the same time not take over and tell them what to do."[38]

The meeting was attended by more than 120 students from fifty-six southern black colleges and high schools, including schools in the District of Columbia. Representatives from northern student and reform groups and a few southern white students also attended. Leaders included Marion Barry, a graduate student at Fisk University in Nashville, Tennessee; Diane Nash, who had grown up in Chicago, also a student at Fisk; John Lewis, a ministerial student at the American Baptist Theological Seminary in Nashville; and Julian Bond, from Morehouse College in Atlanta. Martin Luther King addressed the gathering and urged the students to form a permanent organization, recruit activists willing to march on the South, pack the jails, and force the federal government to enforce the law. He also exhorted them to dedicate themselves to the techniques of nonviolence. The students responded favorably to King, but James Lawson inspired them. An experienced practitioner of nonviolent protest, Lawson had been jailed for refusing to serve in the military during the Korean War, had studied Gandhi's techniques in India, and had recently been expelled from Vanderbilt Theological Seminary in Tennessee for participating in sit-ins. In 1960 he was southern field secretary of the nonviolent pacifist protest group called the Fellowship of Reconciliation (FOR), a position Bayard Rustin had held in the 1940s. FOR had worked during the 1930s and 1940s on projects for racial justice and had trained many of the civil rights leaders active in the 1950s and 1960s. Guided by Baker and Lawson, the students gathered in Raleigh formed the Student Nonviolent Coordinating Committee (SNCC), one of the most important organizations of the modern civil rights era.[39]

Direct action continued during the presidential election year of 1960. Martin Luther King joined students protesting and vowing, "Jail, no bail," at Rich's Department Store in Atlanta, was arrested with thirty-five others, and was sentenced to four weeks' hard labor on a Georgia chain gang for violating probation. It was a very severe sentence, and blacks were certain that King's life would be in great danger inside a Georgia prison. Many African Americans were surprised and touched when presidential candidate and U.S. Senator John Kennedy called Coretta Scott King to express his sympathy and support for her husband. The call impressed and reassured Mrs. King, who was pregnant at the time with the couple's third child. "If there is anything I can do to be of help," Kennedy had said, "I want you to please feel free to call on me."[40] Within hours the senator's younger brother and campaign manager, Robert, called the governor of Georgia and arranged for King to be released the following day. African American people voted overwhelmingly for Kennedy that fall in the closest presidential election in American history. More than 70 percent of blacks voted for him as he defeated his rival, Richard Nixon, by less than ⅔ of 1 percent of the popular vote. As CORE leader James Farmer recalled, blacks did not support John Kennedy blindly: "Many of us felt that [his] commitment to civil rights was political, that it was a device to get him elected."[41]

Civil rights activists tested the Kennedy administration's willingness to protect civil rights and enforce federal law in the spring of 1961. That year the Supreme Court had extended a 1946 ruling against racial discrimination on interstate trains and buses to cover terminal facilities, and SNCC and CORE decided to test compliance with federal regulations. In May, inspired by the "Journey of Reconciliation" that had tested the integration of interstate buses fourteen years earlier, seven blacks and six whites spent one week training for nonviolence and then boarded two buses in Washington, D.C., bound for Atlanta. In the tradition of nonviolent protest, the group had informed relevant authorities at the FBI, the White House, the Interstate Commerce Commission, and the bus companies of their plans. White activists sat in the back of the bus while blacks sat in the front, planning to refuse to move to the rear if asked. One group rode a Greyhound bus and the other rode a Trailways bus; both rolled through Virginia without incident. In Charlotte, North Carolina, one rider was arrested for attempting to get a shoeshine and haircut at a whites-only barbershop, but the following day, his case was dismissed. In Rock Hill, South Carolina, whites beat and kicked John Lewis of SNCC and Albert Bigelow, a white pacifist from Connecticut, when they tried to enter the terminal's whites-only waiting room. In Anniston, Alabama, white attackers burned the Greyhound bus and beat its riders. An hour later the Trailways bus arrived and a group of white men boarded it, beat the blacks seated in the front, and forced them to the backseats. Two white riders, CORE's James Peck, a participant in the original "Journey of Reconciliation," and retired college professor Walter Bergman, were seated in the rear of the bus. When they came forward to protest the beatings, the attackers clubbed them. The crushing blows Bergman received left him permanently paralyzed. In Birmingham another mob met the bus and beat the riders; this time Peck's head injury from a beating with metal pipes required fifty-three stitches.[42]

The freedom riders stopped in Birmingham, and the police who had been notified in advance were nowhere to be seen when Klansmen attacked. Later Police Chief Bull Connor explained that since it was Mother's Day, Sunday, May 14, when the freedom riders arrived, most of his force was not at work. Although J. Edgar Hoover's FBI had advance information about the mob's plans and also knew that members of the Birmingham police department belonged to the Ku Klux Klan, they failed to inform anyone in the Justice Department. Governor John Patterson of Alabama expressed the sentiments of many state and federal authorities when he declared, "I thought that the Freedom Riders should stay home and mind their own business and let us try to work out our problems down here in some legal way." President Kennedy attempted to phone the governor, who had supported him during the presidential campaign, to discuss protecting the freedom riders while they exercised their legal rights. The governor would not take his call; aides informed the White House that the governor had gone fishing.[43]

After these attacks no bus driver would agree to take the riders out of Birmingham, and they were forced to fly from Birmingham to New Orleans. Although the first freedom ride was over, Diane Nash, a Fisk University student active in SNCC, was determined that the freedom riders would not be defeated by violence. She recruited a group of eight blacks and two whites from Nashville to continue the ride to Montgomery. "We were informed we should be willing to accept death," recalled a twenty-year-old Fisk student

Letter from the Birmingham Jail

The response of the Reverend Martin Luther King, Jr., to an open letter signed by eight highly placed Alabama clergymen decrying civil rights demonstrations in their state.

April 16, 1963

MY DEAR FELLOW CLERGYMEN:

While confined here in the Birmingham City Jail, I came across your recent statement calling our present activities "unwise and untimely." Seldom do I pause to answer criticism of my work and ideas. . . . But since I feel that you are men of genuine goodwill and that your criticisms are sincerely set forth, I want to try to answer your statement in what I hope will be patient and reasonable terms. . . .

In any nonviolent campaign there are four basic steps: collection of the facts to determine whether injustices exist; negotiation; self-purification; and direct action. We have gone through all these steps in Birmingham. There can be no gainsaying the fact that racial injustice engulfs this community. Birmingham is probably the most thoroughly segregated city in the United States. Its ugly record of brutality is widely known. Negroes have experienced grossly unjust treatment in the courts. There have been more unsolved bombings of Negro homes and churches in Birmingham than in any other city in the nation. These are the hard, brutal facts of the case. On the basis of these conditions, Negro leaders sought to negotiate with the city fathers. But the latter consistently refused to engage in good-faith negotiation. . . . Nonviolent direct action seeks to create such a crisis and foster such a tension that a community which has constantly refused to negotiate is forced to confront the issue. It seeks so to dramatize the issue that it can no longer be ignored. . . . We know through painful experience that freedom is never voluntarily given by the oppressor; it must be demanded by the oppressed. Frankly, I have yet to engage in a direct-action campaign that was "well timed" in the view of those who have not suffered unduly from the disease of segregation. For years now I have heard the word "Wait!" It rings in the ear of every Negro with piercing familiarity. This "Wait" has almost always meant "Never." . . . We have waited for more than 340 years for our constitutional and God-given rights. The nations of Asia and Africa are moving with jetlike speed toward gaining political independence, but we still creep at horse-and-buggy pace toward gaining a cup of coffee at a lunch counter. Perhaps it is easy for those who have never felt the stinging darts of segregation to say "Wait." But when you have seen vicious mobs lynch your mothers and fathers at will and drown your sisters and brothers at whim; when you have seen hate-filled policemen curse, kick, and

(continued)

even kill your black brothers and sisters; when you see the vast majority of your twenty million Negro brothers smothering in an airtight cage of poverty in the midst of an affluent society; when you suddenly find your tongue twisted and your speech stammering as you seek to explain to your six-year-old daughter why she can't go to the public amusement park that has just been advertised on television, and see tears welling up in her eyes when she is told that Funtown is closed to colored children, and see ominous clouds of inferiority beginning to form in her little mental sky, and see her beginning to distort her little personality by developing an unconscious bitterness toward white people; when you have to concoct an answer for a five-year-old son who is asking: "Daddy, why do white people treat colored people so mean?"; when you take a cross-country drive and find it necessary to sleep night after night in the uncomfortable corners of your automobile because no motel will accept you; when you are humiliated day in and day out by nagging signs reading "white" and "colored"; when your first name becomes "nigger," your middle name becomes "boy" (however old you are) and your last name becomes "John," and your wife and mother are never given the respected title "Mrs."; when you are harried by day and haunted by night by the fact that you are a Negro, living constantly at tiptoe stance, never quite knowing what to expect next, and are plagued with inner fears and outer resentments; when you are forever fighting a degenerating sense of "nobodiness"—then you will understand why we find it difficult to wait. There comes a time when the cup of endurance runs over, and men are no longer willing to be plunged into the abyss of despair. I hope, sirs, you can understand our legitimate and unavoidable impatience.

You express a great deal of anxiety over our willingness to break laws. . . . One may well ask: "How can you advocate breaking some laws and obeying others?" . . . The answer lies in the fact that there are two types of laws: just and unjust. . . . One has not only a legal but a moral responsibility to obey just laws. Conversely, one has a moral responsibility to disobey unjust laws. . . . One who breaks an unjust law must do so openly, lovingly and with a willingness to accept the penalty. I submit that an individual who breaks a law that conscience tells him is unjust, and who willingly accepts the penalty of imprisonment in order to arouse the conscience of the community over its injustice, is in reality expressing the highest respect for law. . . .

I hope the church as a whole will meet the challenge of this decisive hour. But even if the church does not come to the aid of justice, I have no despair about the future. . . . We will reach the goal of freedom in Birmingham and all over the nation, because the goal of America is freedom. Abused and scorned though we may be, our destiny is tied up with America's destiny. Before the pilgrims landed at Plymouth, we were here. Before

(continued)

(continued)

the pen of Jefferson etched the majestic words of the Declaration of Independence across the pages of history, we were here. For more than two centuries our forebears labored in this country without wages; they made cotton king; they built the homes of their masters while suffering gross injustice and shameful humiliation—and yet out of a bottomless vitality they continued to thrive and develop. If the inexpressible cruelties of slavery could not stop us, the opposition we now face will surely fail. We will win our freedom because the sacred heritage of our nation and the eternal will of God are embodied in our echoing demands. . . . Let us all hope that the dark clouds of racial prejudice will soon pass away and the deep fog of misunderstanding will be lifted from our fear-drenched communities, and in some not too distant tomorrow the radiant stars of love and brotherhood will shine over our great nation with all their scintillating beauty.

Yours for the cause of Peace and Brotherhood,

MARTIN LUTHER KING, JR.

Martin Luther King, Jr., *Why We Can't Wait* (New York: Harper & Row, Publishers, Inc., 1964), 76–95. Reprinted by Arrangement with the Heirs to the Estate of Martin Luther King, Jr., c/o Writers House, Inc. as agent for the proprietor. Copyright 1963 by Martin Luther King, Jr., copyright renewed 1991 by Coretta Scott King.

who was a member of the group.[44] Governor Patterson accused these freedom riders of being Communists and had them arrested, taken 120 miles by police car, and released on the highway at the Tennessee state line. The freedom riders then telephoned other civil rights workers, who took them back to the Birmingham bus station. They attempted to board a bus bound for Montgomery, but the bus driver was afraid for his life and refused to take them.

Meanwhile the governor told federal officials that his popularity had skyrocketed since he had outspokenly opposed the freedom riders and civil rights. He vowed that should the federal government send troops into his state to enforce desegregation laws, there would be "warfare." When the federal government did not back down, Patterson finally relented and declared that the state of Alabama would not tolerate "rabble-rousers and outside agitators" but would protect the freedom riders. Within a few days, under the protection of the police, a bus carrying freedom riders left Birmingham for Montgomery.[45] The police disappeared when the bus reached Montgomery, where hundreds of jeering whites awaited the buses. The mob grew to nearly a thousand and beat the riders savagely before the head of Alabama's State Police pulled his pistol and threatened to shoot the rioters if they did not stop. Media coverage of this freedom ride was intense, and special television broadcasts from the scene horrified the nation. The White House sent federal marshals to Montgomery to protect the civil rights workers hospitalized from their beatings, and Martin Luther King came to rally support for the freedom ride movement. "Alabama will have to learn to face the fact that we are determined to be free," he told those assembled at the First Baptist Church.[46] King readied the gathering to face the mob outside, but Governor Patterson, pressured by Attorney General Robert Kennedy, declared martial law and sent Alabama state troopers to escort the people safely from the church. Two days later the freedom rides continued, and two buses, protected by almost seven hundred U.S. marshals, hundreds of national guardsmen, and helicopters, left Montgomery for Jackson, Mississippi. Riders arrived in Jackson unhindered, entered the whites-only waiting room, and were promptly arrested and taken to jail. In court, the prosecutor's case was simple, and his statement charging the freedom riders with trespassing was brief. The judge turned his back to the proceedings while a civil rights lawyer presented the defense. After the defense the judge turned back to the court and sentenced the freedom riders to sixty days in Mississippi's notorious maximum-security Parchman Penitentiary. Undeterred, hundreds of freedom riders went to the South that summer, were arrested, refused to accept bail, and went to jail. Finally, in response to Robert Kennedy's request, the Interstate Commerce Commission issued a set of rules implementing the Supreme Court's ruling outlawing segregation in interstate bus terminals.[47]

Civil rights demonstrators continued to pressure the government to guarantee black rights, but the Kennedy administration's response was slow and cautious. Television continued to bring scenes of violent southern reactions into American homes. African Americans were outraged, and white Americans outside the South were shocked by the sight of mobs beating civil rights workers, and dismayed by the apparent collusion of southern police officers. Some white southerners, too, were embarrassed and appalled. Cities and towns where confrontations took place became notorious, as did many southern officials, such as Mississippi's governor Ross Barnett, who was convicted of civil contempt for attempting to stop the integration of the University of Mississippi. As the nation's attention focused on the civil rights movement in the South, Kennedy took a few symbolic steps. He appointed Thurgood Marshall to the U.S. Circuit Court of Appeals in 1961 and issued an executive order prohibiting racial discrimination in federally financed housing in 1962.[48]

Pressure on the government increased as demonstrations spread to the North. In the early 1960s authorities arrested seven whites and four blacks protesting school segregation during an all-night sit-in at the city hall in

Englewood, New Jersey. Students at the University of Chicago demonstrated against discrimination in off-campus housing, three thousand black students in Boston boycotted schools to protest de facto segregation, and marches in Cairo, Illinois, protested segregation in swimming pools, skating rinks, and other public facilities. Violence escalated in the South. Eight black churches were burned or bombed in Georgia during a two-week period in 1962.[49]

Civil rights forces led by SCLC began a concerted attack on segregation in Birmingham, Alabama, in April 1963, targeting downtown department stores that refused to serve blacks at their lunch counters. They planned to mount an economic boycott and nonviolent demonstrations that would result in demonstrators being arrested and jailed, thereby bringing economic pressure on the businesses and media attention to the cause. However, most stores closed their lunch counters to avoid confrontation, and the relatively small number of people arrested received little attention. Martin Luther King himself then joined the demonstrations, was arrested, refused bail, and was placed in solitary confinement. In jail King penned a letter on newspaper borders and scraps of paper explaining his mission and castigating the local clergy for inaction and smuggled it out of the jail. Running low on funds, organizers escalated their confrontations in the face of a new Alabama ban on demonstrations. After much debate, they agreed to let schoolchildren march, and on May 2 hundreds of singing youngsters, taken away by paddy wagons and school buses, filled the city and county jails to overflowing. The controversial children's crusade continued the following day, as a thousand more demonstrators faced high-pressure fire hoses and police dogs. Energized by the children's bravery and appalled by the police reaction, activists and the press flocked to Birmingham, thousands of supporters filled the churches, the rising tide of arrests became a flood, and a fairgrounds became a makeshift open-air prison camp. Growing demonstrations increased the pressure on downtown businesses and made nonviolence difficult to maintain, as rock-throwing bystanders clashed with police and firemen. One week after the children first marched out of the churches, leaders announced a desegregation agreement. The agreement did not end violent confrontations in Birmingham. The next day bombs that exploded at the parsonage of A. D. King and at a motel used by organizers prompted rioting. But the campaign raised the visibility of the movement in the United States and abroad, enlisted the president in its resolution, and fired the conscience of the nation.[50]

In June 1963 National Guard troops were required to protect two black students enrolling at the University of Alabama over the outspoken objection of Gov. George C. Wallace. That day President John Kennedy addressed the nation, proclaiming segregation morally wrong and calling for Congress to

Medgar Evers,
Mississippi field
secretary of the
NAACP,
assassinated 1963.

Photographs and
Prints Division,
National Archives.

act against it. One day later NAACP field secretary Medgar Evers was murdered
in the driveway of his home in Jackson, Mississippi. On the day of Evers's
funeral, President Kennedy sent Congress a bill prohibiting discrimination in
public accommodations and authorizing the U.S. attorney general to enforce
the Fourteenth and Fifteenth Amendments to the Constitution. Legal strategies and nonviolent protest had advanced the cause of freedom, and each
advance carried a cost.[51]

1963 President Kennedy sends federal troops to Birmingham, Alabama, to protect demonstrators from white rioters; Martin Luther King, Jr., arrested and jailed

Some 250,000 join March on Washington; Martin Luther King, Jr., delivers "I Have a Dream" speech at Lincoln Memorial

NAACP field secretary Medgar Evers murdered at his home in Jackson, Mississippi

Four black girls attending Sunday school killed by bomb in Birmingham, Alabama

President John F. Kennedy assassinated

1964 President Lyndon B. Johnson signs Civil Rights Act of 1964, prohibiting racial discrimination in public accommodations, employment, and education

Martin Luther King, Jr., receives Nobel Peace Prize

Malcolm X breaks with Black Muslim Elijah Muhammad and forms Organization of Afro-American Unity

Three civil rights workers murdered in Philadelphia, Mississippi

Gulf of Tonkin incident; U.S. military involvement in Vietnam War escalates

1965 Malcolm X assassinated at a rally in the Audubon Ballroom in New York City

Major race riots in Watts area of Los Angeles

Julian Bond denied seat in Georgia legislature; Supreme Court orders him seated the following year

1966 Black Panther Party founded in Oakland, California

SNCC's Stokely Carmichael popularizes the call for "Black Power"

1967 More than forty race riots occur during the summer months

Thurgood Marshall is the first African American appointed to Supreme Court

1968 Martin Luther King, Jr., assassinated

Presidential candidate Robert F. Kennedy, brother of the slain president, is assassinated

Richard M. Nixon elected president, promising to end Vietnam War

1969 Hundreds of thousands participate in urban demonstrations against the Vietnam War

Chicago Eight, militant young civil rights and antiwar activists, including Black Panther Bobby Seale, indicted in connection with riots outside the 1968 Democratic convention in Chicago

1970 Toni Morrison publishes her first novel, *The Bluest Eye*

From Civil Rights
to Black Power

*I*n 1963 LeRoi Jones, a black activist and writer from Newark, New Jersey, published *Blues People,* a study of black music and its relationship to the historical experience of African Americans. Black actor Sidney Poitier won an Oscar for his role in the movie *Lilies of the Field,* Alvin Ailey's American Dance Theater of Harlem was attracting attention among both whites and blacks, and Chubby Checker had black teenagers and white teenagers dancing the "twist." Black historian John Hope Franklin published the *Emancipation Proclamation* to commemorate the 100th anniversary of Abraham Lincoln's declaration, and in August, the largest protest march to that time in American history brought more than 250,000 people to Washington to demonstrate for civil rights.[1] Initially Bayard Rustin had called for the protest to culminate in a sit-in at the Capitol demanding prompt passage of the president's civil rights bill. The Kennedy administration, however, feared violence and pressed for less confrontational action. Roy Wilkins of the NAACP and Whitney Young of the National Urban League agreed to a compromise, a march bringing together massive numbers of whites and blacks in a show of solidarity. Martin Luther King and the other moderate leaders assured the president that the march would be nonviolent. Many SNCC members felt the protest would be too limited and subdued, but after some debate, they decided to take part. SNCC hoped to raise a more militant voice, but the march organizers maintained tight control and insisted on overseeing the proposed speeches. SNCC chairman John Lewis was disturbed to find his speech censored; its most inflammatory passages with words like "masses" and "revolution" had been removed. The march was a great show of unity with television pictures showing blacks and whites holding hands and singing protest songs. Martin Luther King inspired the nation with his "I Have a Dream" speech and quickly became the internationally recognized embodiment of the civil rights movement. A Gallup poll showed that 72 percent of blacks favored demonstrations. Only 21 percent of whites thought they helped the civil rights cause.[2]

The tensions in organizing the march, however, revealed the strains in the civil rights community, manifested in disagreements between the young militants of SNCC and the more moderate leaders of SCLC and the NAACP.[3]

Many younger activists were growing impatient with the gradualist approach and becoming more interested in forms of political and cultural nationalism. Separatist strategies and cultural nationalism had a long history in black America, including the philosophies of such leaders as Martin Delany in the mid–nineteenth century and Marcus Garvey in the early twentieth. A new proponent of nationalism had recently gained African Americans' attention. Malcolm X had been born Malcolm Little, in Omaha, Nebraska, in 1925. His father, J. Early Little, was a Baptist preacher from Georgia who became an organizer for Garvey's Universal Negro Improvement Association. After the family moved to Michigan, his father was killed by white supremacists, leaving his mother, who was also a Garveyite, to support the family. His mother struggled unsuccessfully to hold the family together, finally breaking under the emotional strain; the children became wards of the state. Malcolm, an unusually bright child, excelled in school until discouraged by a white teacher who admonished him to recognize his place and learn a trade rather than aspire to a profession in law. He did neither, but as "Detroit Red" he turned instead to a life of hustling and petty crime in Boston and New York. Before he was twenty-one years old he was convicted of burglary and was sentenced to prison. In prison Malcolm educated himself, reading the dictionary and books on law and black history. He also converted to the beliefs of Elijah Muhammad's Nation of Islam, or Black Muslims. He selected the letter X as a surname to symbolize the loss of his African family name in slavery, and after his release he became a Black Muslim minister. Although Malcolm X was always careful to acknowledge the primacy of Elijah Muhammad, he was a very charismatic speaker and became the Muslims' best known and most popular proponent.[4] Malcolm X was critical of the 1963 March on Washington and accused black leaders of acquiescing to white pressure and turning a black-run protest into a "Chump's March." He ridiculed the march as the "Farce on Washington . . . subsidized by white liberals and stage-managed by President Kennedy."[5] Malcolm's harsh criticism compounded SNCC leaders' uneasy sense that their radical protest had been muted to please the Kennedy administration.

In contrast to the display of unity in the march, racial violence continued, and even seemed to escalate in the South. James Baldwin's extended essay, entitled *The Fire Next Time*, published that year, predicted that more and more deadly violence would result from America's racial tensions. His prediction proved accurate. In September, less than a month after the Washington march, a bomb killed four young black girls while they attended Sunday School in Birmingham's Sixteenth Street Baptist Church. Then, in late November 1963, President John F. Kennedy was shot and killed while he rode in a motorcade in Dallas, Texas. Americans were stunned by the assassination of the president, and some believed it a continuation of a century of southern violence,

Martin Luther King and Malcolm X
before a press conference, March 1964.
Photographs and Prints Division, Library of Congress, Washington, D.C.

recently manifest in the killing of civil rights workers. Malcolm X asserted that the murder of the young president was the natural consequence of American toleration of racial violence and said it was "the chickens come home to roost." He charged that "the hate in white men had not stopped with the killing of defenseless black people" but had finally "struck down this country's Chief of State." Martin Luther King seemed to agree. "In the life of Negro civil-rights leaders," he observed, "the whine of the bullet from ambush, the roar of the bomb have all too often broken the night's silence."[6]

When Vice President Lyndon Baines Johnson ascended to the presidency, he proposed that Congress pass Kennedy's civil rights bill immediately as a memorial to the fallen president. The bill cleared both houses over the objections of southern legislators. On July 2, 1964, Johnson signed the far-reaching bill into law. It outlawed discrimination in public accommodations, withheld federal money from states and local agencies or organizations that discriminated, banned discrimination in employment and in labor unions, and established an Equal Employment Opportunity Commission. It also provided financial assistance to school districts' efforts to desegregate.[7] That summer civil rights groups increased their efforts to register black voters in the Deep South, where there was a high proportion of African Americans in the population and a high level of white resistance to their advancement. Organizers trained white students and black students, sending between seven and nine hundred to rural Mississippi to work in interracial groups developing grassroots organizations to register voters.[8] Movement workers believed that the presence of northern white students would bring national media attention to their efforts, thereby offering some protection to civil rights workers and the black citizens attempting to vote. They called their project in 1964 the Mississippi Freedom Summer.

In 1964 Mississippi was America's poorest state, with the highest rate of illiteracy and the most violently racist reputation. African Americans constituted 42 percent of the state's population and were the majority in more than one-third of the counties. Black income was less than one-third the level of white income, and fewer than one in twenty eligible black Mississippians were registered voters. Mississippi followed the general southern pattern in the extreme. The state had the longest history of comprehensive segregation laws, having been the first to develop a Jim Crow system in 1890, a system often called the Mississippi Plan. Robert Moses, a young African American member of SNCC, understood that the voter registration project in Mississippi would require a major federal law enforcement presence. Efforts earlier in the 1960s had already cost black lives. He had seen the publicity that one hundred white student workers from the North had brought the movement in 1963. He concluded that bringing in more white northern college students that summer would increase the publicity and enhance their chances of getting federal protection.[9]

Robert Moses had been born in 1935 in Harlem, grew up in a poor household, and gained admission to an elite public high school with a high score on a citywide exam. While a college student, he worked at Quaker-sponsored summer camps in Europe and Japan. He graduated from college, received a master's degree from Harvard University, taught mathematics in a Harlem high school, and in 1959, joined Bayard Rustin to help organize a demonstration for integrated schools. Moses worked with SCLC in the Deep South during the summer of 1960 and the following summer joined the staff of SNCC and began organizing voters. In 1964 he was the program director for a Mississippi consortium of civil rights groups called the Council of Federated Organizations (COFO). Addressing an interracial group of three hundred student volunteers assembled for training in Oxford, Ohio, he was brutally blunt. "If we can go and come back alive, then that is something," he told them. Within a few days events in Mississippi bore out his remarks. "Yesterday, three of our people left Meridian, Mississippi, to investigate a church bombing in Neshoba County. They have not come back, and we haven't any word from them," he informed a subsequent group. Six weeks later they learned that three volunteers from the first group were dead. The bodies of African American James Chaney, a native of Meridian, Mississippi; twenty-year-old Andrew Goodman, from Queens College in New York; and Michael Schwerner, from Brooklyn; both white, had been found near Philadelphia, Mississippi.[10]

Despite these deaths, and despite the fact that terrorists bombed at least thirty buildings and burned thirty-five churches, attacked and beat at least eighty civil rights workers, shot thirty-five others, and murdered six people that summer, the FBI refused to provide any "special protection" for the voter registration project volunteers.[11] Many COFO volunteers in Mississippi that summer became convinced that nonviolence had practical limitations for civil rights work in the rural South, and most of the SNCC workers began to carry guns. In Louisiana a group of blacks armed themselves, called themselves the Deacons for Defense and Justice, and provided security for CORE workers. Such tactics violated the principles of nonviolent SCLC leaders, and they and young SNCC militants debated the continued viability of nonviolent strategies in the Deep South.[12]

To dramatize the potential power of black voters, civil rights forces staged a challenge to Mississippi's all-white delegation to the Democratic National Convention in 1964 by forming the Mississippi Freedom Democratic Party (MFDP), open to all regardless of race. During the fall of 1963 Robert Moses had conceived the idea of a "freedom vote," and in the summer of 1964, the MFDP enrolled almost 80,000 African Americans and elected forty-four

Fannie Lou Hamer
(1917–1977)

Fannie Lou Hamer was the youngest of twenty children born to a Mississippi Delta sharecropping family. She began to work chopping and picking cotton when she was six and dropped out of elementary school to help support the family. When she was an adult, the plantation owner hired her as the record and timekeeper, a position from which she sometimes argued for fairness toward the workers. Inspired by SNCC workers' appeals for black voter registration, Hamer joined a group journeying to the county seat in 1962. She "failed" the literacy test, yet she and the others risked dire consequences just for trying to register. Refusing to withdraw her application, she was fired from her job. After passing the test the next year, she was harrassed by the police, night riders shot into a house she was visiting, her husband lost his job, and the family was forced out of their sharecroppers' cabin.

Hamer then began a career with the civil rights movement, teaching citizenship courses for the SCLC, becoming a field secretary for SNCC, organizing and training people for summer voter registration drives, and helping to found the Mississippi Freedom Democratic Party. Her televised testimony before the Credentials Committee of the 1964 Democratic Party Convention riveted the nation with her eloquent account of the brutal beating she and other women had received in a Mississippi county jail and the threats to her life and livelihood for trying to exercise her rights. The MFDP's challenge to the Mississippi delegation failed, but they did win the promise of fairer representation in 1968.

The bravery of Fannie Lou Hamer and thousands of other ordinary African Americans helped to end legal segregation and the denial of black voting rights in the South. She explained her strength and courage in attempting to create a better life for poor blacks by explaining that she had been "just sick and tired of being sick and tired." In the early 1970s Ruleville, Mississippi, celebrated Fannie Lou Hamer Day in her honor, and when she died of cancer in 1977, the Mississippi legislature passed a resolution recognizing her service to the state.

Fannie Lou Hamer speaking at the Democratic National Convention in Atlantic City, New Jersey, in August 1964. Photographs and Prints Division, Library of Congress, Washington, D.C.

delegates and twenty-two alternates to the national Democratic convention in Atlantic City, New Jersey.[13] Arguing that their delegation was the only one from Mississippi that was democratically chosen, MFDP representatives asked to be seated as the official delegation from their state. Fannie Lou Hamer, an uneducated sharecropper, was spokeswoman for the group. Hamer was permanently injured from being beaten while attempting to register to vote. She spoke eloquently about conditions in Mississippi's Delta and the hardships and dangers she and her delegation had undergone just to attend the convention. Many conventioneers and many in the national television audience were moved by her words, but in the end party regulars offered the delegation only two at-large seats with full voting rights. Senator Hubert Humphrey, a liberal from Minnesota who was hoping to be Lyndon Johnson's vice-presidential candidate, offered this compromise. When he tried to explain that it was politically impossible to replace the regular Mississippi delegation with the MFDP delegation, Hamer retorted, "Mr. Humphrey, do you mean to tell me that your position is more important than Mississippi's four hundred thousand black lives?"[14]

Roy Wilkins, Bayard Rustin, Martin Luther King, and James Farmer of CORE discussed the conflict with Democratic Party leaders. Although they believed the MFDP's position to be morally right, under intense pressure from Johnson, they finally agreed to advise MFDP delegates to accept the compromise. They hoped for a later pledge that no delegation selected in racially exclusive elections would be seated at future conventions. Hamer and the rest of the MFDP delegation felt abandoned by their "false friends." They refused to accept the compromise and staged a sit-in at the convention, taking the seats of the white Mississippi delegates.[15] Finally forced out, they left for Mississippi, angry and discouraged by the betrayal of their formerly trusted allies. SNCC leaders were profoundly disillusioned with American politics and with the moderate civil rights movement. "After Atlantic City," one wrote, "our struggle was not for civil rights, but for liberation." Malcolm X expressed their frustration: "We *need* a Mau Mau," he told a gathering of MFDP and SNCC workers. "If [white Americans] don't want to deal with the Mississippi Freedom Democratic Party, then we'll give them something else to deal with."[16]

There were more ominous signs of anger and frustration in 1964, after a decade of civil rights marches, sit-ins, freedom rides, and demonstrations. African Americans rioted in Harlem in July, reacting to the suspicious killing of a fifteen-year-old black boy by an off-duty police officer. Rioting also occurred in Brooklyn and Rochester, New York; Jersey City and Patterson, New Jersey; Philadelphia and Chicago, each outbreak triggered by an encounter between blacks and the police.[17]

African Americans were impatient at the lack of progress, but they were also proud of the gains that had been made. NAACP lawyer Constance Baker Motley became the first black woman elected to the New York State Senate; U.S. ambassador to Finland Carl Rowan became head of the U.S. Information Agency and the first African American to sit on the National Security Council. Tennis player Arthur Ashe, Jr., was the first African American named to the American Davis Cup Team and represented the United States in international competition. In 1962 U.S. Air Force veteran James Meredith, protected by federal troops, become the first African American to enroll at the University of Mississippi. This protection continued until 1963, when he became the first black graduate of that university. In that same year Martin Luther King, who had been named "Man of the Year" by *Time* magazine, won the Nobel Peace Prize.

Ninety-five percent of black voters cast their votes for the Democrats, contributing to Johnson's sweeping victory over Barry Goldwater in November's presidential election. Goldwater and Republican conservatives had blatantly courted the southern racist vote, but for many African Americans, this was an ambiguous triumph. Though the president expanded his welfare program, called the War on Poverty, and established an Office of Economic Opportunity, progress remained painfully slow. Legal segregation had been outlawed, but racial discrimination was pervasive, and southern whites seemed largely unrepentant. Despite the courage and sacrifice of volunteers, only relatively few blacks had braved the danger of injury and death to register to vote in the Deep South. Compared to the 60 to 70 percent of northern blacks who were registered voters in 1964, just over one-third of eligible blacks were registered in the entire South. In some states in the Deep South the percentage was even lower: 22 percent in Alabama and under 7 percent in Mississippi. Nationally, Alabama governor George Wallace, enemy of civil rights for African Americans, received surprising support outside the South in the Democratic presidential primary. News reporters had begun to describe a "white backlash" to civil rights gains.[18] Even some of the most liberal whites counseled patience, appearing perplexed as well as angered by black militancy.

Immediately after President Johnson signed the Voting Rights Act in August 1965, the civil rights movement began to place greater emphasis on gaining black political and economic power. According to the historian James Cone, at first Martin Luther King saw this law as the culmination of his work for civil rights. Then, only five days after Johnson signed the bill, African Americans rioted in Los Angeles, burning many of the buildings and looting many of the stores in Watts, a black working-class area of the city. This was the most extensive rioting since the post–World War II era—thirty-four people were killed (mainly black men killed by the police), more than one thousand were injured, nearly four thousand were arrested, and hundreds of buildings were destroyed. The Watts riot received international news coverage and consumed the nation's attention. Many whites asked why blacks would burn their own homes. California governor Ronald Reagan dismissed the riot as the work of criminals, "lawbreakers and mad dogs." But the grossly substandard housing that was burned was not owned by the occupants, and looting targeted establishments that overcharged the confined community. Younger and poorer blacks were more likely to join rioting than older, middle-class blacks. Though ambivalent about the violence, most black people understood the causes of the riots and refused to condemn them totally.[19] King's conversations with African Americans in Watts after the rioting subsided strengthened his growing conviction that the civil rights movement had paid too little attention to pressing economic issues. He described the riots as "a class revolt of underprivileged against privileged," asserting that ghetto residents had been "bypassed by the progress of the past decade." Outlawing segregation in schools and public facilities and obliterating legal impediments to voting in the South did not address the racial discrimination that left so many northern blacks poor and powerless.[20]

Martin Luther King and Malcolm X symbolized the opposite ends of black political thought, but there had been subtle changes in their philosophies. Malcolm X had been estranged from Elijah Muhammad and the Nation of Islam for several months. Muhammad had suspended Malcolm for violating his directive not to comment on Kennedy's assassination in 1963 with his reference to the "chickens coming home to roost." The strain between them worsened when Malcolm's suspicions that Muhammad had violated the religion's strict moral precepts were confirmed. Muhammad and some Muslim ministers believed Malcolm X had grown too political, too confrontational, and too powerful, eclipsing Muhammad himself as a spokesman for the organization. The ministers plotted to discredit him with Elijah Muhammad and remove him from a position of influence. Malcolm publicly broke with Muhammad and the Nation of Islam in the spring of 1964 and established a new Muslim organization called the Muslim Mosque Incorporated. "Now that I have more independence-of-action, I intend to use a more flexible approach toward working with others to get a solution to this [race] problem," he announced. Some scholars believe that at this point, "Malcolm decided to enter the civil rights movement as a supporter of blacks everywhere who were fighting against segregation." He continued to urge blacks to defend themselves when attacked and argued that they should form rifle clubs to safeguard life and property. The civil rights leadership disagreed with Malcolm's apparent call for defensive violence and his predictions of racial warfare, but King cautioned against taking him too literally, believing that there might be some common ground for discussion.[21]

Possibilities for cooperation improved in 1964 after Malcolm completed a pilgrimage to Mecca and to newly independent African nations. In the Holy City he discovered that interracial harmony was possible and found Elijah Muhammad's antiwhite teachings contradicted by orthodox Islam. This "spiritual rebirth" forced him to completely revise his thinking about white people.[22] He wrote to James Farmer of CORE, "I have just visited the Holy City of Mecca and witnessed pilgrims of all colors, from every part of the earth, displaying a spirit of unity and brotherhood like I've never witnessed during my entire life in America. It is truly a wonderful sight to behold."[23] After that trip, in an amazing display of personal growth, Malcolm X accepted King's invitation to meet and talk about a common approach to the struggle. He formed the Organization of Afro-American Unity to "lift the whole freedom struggle from civil rights to the level of human rights, and also to work with any other organization and any other leader toward that end."[24] In subsequent speeches Malcolm X was highly critical of American foreign policy, contending that it oppressed many of the peoples of Africa, especially in the Congo. He argued that the United States should be charged in the United Nations with human rights violations. He was outspoken in his criticism of Elijah Muhammad and the Nation of Islam, advocating instead what he called the "true Islam." In mid-February 1965, Muslims bombed Malcolm's New York home, and on February 21, at least three of Muhammad's followers assassinated Malcolm X as he addressed a rally in New York's Audubon Ballroom. That summer, as Malcolm had predicted, violence erupted in Watts, followed by increased violence in more cities the following year.[25]

A few months before the rioting in Watts, King and other SCLC leaders had held a retreat in northern Virginia to discuss a possible northern civil rights campaign. They had agreed on a nonviolent protest against racism in education, housing, and employment either in New York City or in Chicago. While they discussed a northern foray, there were signs of trouble in the civil rights community. Lax supervision of volunteers in an expensive southern voter registration campaign had garnered criticism from community members and from resentful SNCC volunteers who had been working in those communities for years. Serious conflicts had also surfaced between SCLC and the NAACP in Mississippi, and all dissensions were exacerbated by continuing and escalating financial problems. As SCLC expanded its work, King's role gradually changed. He covered an increasingly larger territory and was called on to provide inspiration to movement workers and bring attention to their efforts. However, facing increasing exhaustion, he was forced to rely more and more on his lieutenants for day-to-day strategy and oversight. Despite these difficulties, in January 1966, Martin Luther King and his wife, Coretta Scott King, demonstrated their commitment to the daunting northern initiative by moving their family into an apartment in the South Side slum of Chicago. The railroad flat had been renovated, but a government official who visited that summer remembered it as a "typical ratty third-floor walk-up."[26] In Chicago, King brought the spotlight of the publicity that always attended him to the already established, though intermittent, efforts of local community organizations attacking de facto segregation in the city's schools.

Meanwhile, early in the summer of 1966, James Meredith and a few friends began a 220-mile march from Memphis, Tennessee, to Jackson, Mississippi. They characterized it as a demonstration that Mississippi blacks had overcome their fear, hoping their action would encourage blacks to vote in a primary election. On the second day Meredith was ambushed and wounded by an unemployed white man. Civil rights leaders decided to continue his march nonetheless. Recent changes in leadership had brought the more militant representatives of a younger generation to the head of two civil rights organizations. Stokely Carmichael, chairman of SNCC, and Floyd McKissick, head of CORE, joined the older leaders, Martin Luther King, Roy Wilkins, and Whitney Young. As they discussed the conditions under which the march would continue, the growing rift between organizations became clear. Carmichael and Cleveland Sellers from SNCC were convinced that this should be primarily a local black-led effort, though they also wanted to include Louisiana's Deacons for Defense and Justice. The young leaders of SNCC had lived on subsistence wages and under constant threat, having concentrated their voter registration efforts in rural Mississippi, probably the most dangerous part of the country for black people. Over time they had committed themselves to the principles of grassroots leadership and local empowerment. Carmichael and Sellers argued strongly that the Deacons should be included in the march, that there should be no national call for participants, and that whites should not be in leadership positions, though they agreed not to exclude whites from the march. The most contentious issue was the participation of the Deacons for Defense. King finally agreed with SNCC on the assurance that the marchers would be nonviolent. Wilkins and Young responded to the decision and to Carmichael's provocative verbal attacks by angrily leaving the meeting and dropping out of the march.[27]

As the march and its accompanying voter registration rallies moved deeper into Mississippi, police protection diminished, while white counterdemonstrators became more confrontational and vociferous. Periodically along the route, marchers were attacked by onlookers and sometimes by police. In Greenwood, while King was away for a brief visit to his operation in Chicago, Stokely Carmichael was arrested and jailed. After his release on bail that evening, he publicly expressed his anger and frustration, and his rhetoric electrified the crowd. Blacks had given their lives, even black children had been attacked by southern policemen with dogs and clubs and cattle prods. Nonviolence and going to jail, he said, were not working. "This is the twenty-seventh time I have been arrested—and I ain't going to jail no more!" Blacks had been saying "freedom" for six years without success. It was time for a change, he announced: "[W]hat we gonna start saying now is 'Black Power.'" The crowd repeated the slogan over and over in unison as the refrain to Carmichael's question, "What do we want?" The young leaders of SNCC had been strongly influenced by Malcolm X and his black nationalist message of racial pride. They had been discussing the issues of black power among themselves for some time and had tried out the message at smaller public meetings during the march. The following evening in Greenwood, when cries of "Freedom now!" were drowned out by demands for "Black Power!" even Carmichael was shocked by the vehemence of the crowd's response.[28]

The black power slogan was open to many interpretations. Some whites saw it as a call for race war, particularly in the context of mounting urban violence. The link between the call for black power and Malcolm X's call for a black revolution added credibility to that interpretation. Malcolm had used humor to ridicule the civil rights movement characterized by some as a "Negro revolution." If it was a revolution, he said, which he seriously doubted, he considered it a trivial revolution interested only in: "a desegregated lunch counter, a desegregated theater, a desegregated park, a desegregated public toilet, . . . [but] going to the toilet with white people is not a revolution. . . . Revolution is hostile, revolution knows no compromise, revolution overturns and destroys everything in its way."[29] Malcolm had charged that the ineffectiveness of the nonviolent revolution resulted from the pusillanimous leadership of "so-called Negroes" like Roy Wilkins and Martin Luther King. Early on he had attacked King as a "traitor to his race" and "religious Uncle Tom." He contended that liberal whites who financed much of the civil rights movement were hypocrites seeking to manipulate the civil rights leaders as their puppets. Nonviolence, Malcolm had argued, encouraged whites to believe that they could attack blacks without fear of retaliation. "I'm against anybody who tells black people to be nonviolent while nobody's telling white people to be nonviolent," he said. African Americans should speak to attackers in their own language. "If the language is a shotgun, get a shotgun. But don't waste time talking the wrong language." Malcolm's words rang true to many young blacks frustrated and impatient with the nonviolent approach and ready to embrace a militant black movement in which they controlled the agenda.[30]

Many white college students in the civil rights movement interpreted this shift toward black power as a signal for separatist organizing. David Dawley remembered SNCC's stance on the Meredith march in 1966:

> We left the march a couple of days later. Basically we had come for a few days. We had to return to finals. We were not unhappy to leave the march. When we came, we had felt wanted. We felt needed. When we left, we didn't feel wanted . . . there was a sense that this was a time when blacks had the right to define the movement. . . . And the strategy coming out of Black Power from SNCC was that blacks should organize with blacks and whites should organize with whites. . . . So we moved on to work with whites on issues that we felt we should work with. In the next year that was not civil rights, that was Vietnam.[31]

Lerone Bennett, Jr., editor of *Ebony* magazine, wrote approvingly that the idea of black power "was in the heads and hearts of long-suffering men who had paid an enormous price for minuscule gains." Most of the more traditional black leaders, including Roy Wilkins, Andrew Young, A. Philip Randolph, and Bayard Rustin, were horrified by the slogan. Wilkins said it was "the father of hate and the mother of violence," and argued that "black power [meant] black death." The generational divide was clear—Roger Wilkins, a nephew of Roy Wilkins, remembered black power as an affirmation of black humanity in the face of racism's psychological destructiveness:

> [M]ost white people didn't understand what was happening when Stokely Carmichael started talking about black power, when people began saying that black was beautiful, when black kids in the movement began telling whites to go work on the racism in their own communities. . . . But Stokely and the other young intellectuals in the movement knew . . . they were purging themselves of all of that self-hate, asserting a human validity that did not derive from whites and pointing out that the black experience on this continent and in Africa was profound, honorable and a source of pride.[32]

Martin Luther King's response to black power was mixed. He understood its appeal, empathized with the motivation of many who took up the slogan, but worried about its separatist and violent connotations. King believed that Malcolm X's harsh language, calling whites "devils" and the common enemy of all black people, was dangerous to the progress of civil rights, and was afraid that demands for black power were likely to arouse whites' fears and diminish their support for the movement. He tried to interpret that language in a way that would be acceptable, remarking on the need for increased political and economic power to build a better life for all Americans. Yet King remained uneasy about the dissension and the potential for violent reactions by civil rights activists.[33] It seemed to him that violent revolution by African Americans, who were at that time only 10 percent of the American population, would be mass suicide. "Thus, in purely practical as well as moral terms, the American Negro has no alternative to nonviolence," he told author Alex Haley in an interview for *Playboy* magazine.[34]

The revolution seemed imminent to many Americans as Huey Newton and Bobby Seale organized the Black Panther Party in Oakland, California, in September 1966. College students and veterans of anti-poverty-program work in Oakland, California, Newton and Seale had been inspired by their study of black history, their reading of Frantz Fanon's writing on liberation struggles in Africa, the speeches and death of Malcolm X, and the courage of SNCC workers in their southern campaigns. These influences combined with a socialist perspective on economic inequality in the United States and a streetwise conception of what the black community needed to create an organization dedicated to the realization of black power.[35]

The Panthers advocated and engaged in community service and promoted armed self-defense for black ghetto residents. They started a newspaper and instituted a breakfast program for poor children. They also established a strict code of conduct, emphasizing responsibility to the poor black community for their members, and distributed copies of their ten-point program in urban ghettos. Their aims and beliefs included restitution from the government for generations of slave labor, self-determination for black communities, full employment, housing, and education in black history. They believed blacks to be essentially a colonized people within the United States and considered the police to be an occupying force. As a consequence their demands included an exemption from military service, trials by juries of peers from the local community, freedom for incarcerated black people, and an end to police brutality and oppression. The final summary point expressed their desire for a plebiscite supervised by the United Nations to determine the political destiny of black America, and stated, "We want land, bread, housing, education, clothing, justice, and peace." The declaration of beliefs ended with a long quotation taken from the Declaration of Independence regarding the commitment to equality and the need for revolution. Newton and Seale recruited hundreds of new members. The Panthers openly carried guns, legal under California law, as they said, to protect African Americans from violations of their rights by the police. The policemen in urban ghettos considered it an act of aggression for gun-toting Black Panthers to monitor their actions. Armed confrontations between the Panthers and police occurred in a number of cities.[36]

Black Panther Party
Platform and Program

What We Want
What We Believe

1. *We want freedom. We want power to determine the destiny of our Black Community.*

   We believe that black people will not be free until we are able to determine our destiny.

2. *We want full employment for our people.*

   We believe that the federal government is responsible and obligated to give every man employment or a guaranteed income. We believe that if white American businessmen will not give full employment, then the means of production should be taken from the businessmen and placed in the community so that the people of the community can organize and employ all of its people and give a high standard of living.

3. *We want an end to the robbery by the capitalist of our Black Community.*

   We believe that this racist government has robbed us and now we are demanding the overdue debt of forty acres and two mules. Forty acres and two mules was promised 100 years ago as restitution for slave labor and mass murder of black people. We will accept the payment in currency which will be distributed to our many communities. The Germans are now aiding the Jews in Israel for the genocide of the Jewish people. The Germans murdered six million Jews. The American racist has taken part in the slaughter of over fifty million black people; therefore, we feel that this a modest demand that we make.

4. *We want decent housing, fit for shelter of human beings.*

   We believe that if the white landlords will not give decent housing to our black community, then the housing and the land should be made into cooperatives so that our community, with government aid, can build and make decent housing for its people.

5. *We want education for our people that exposes the true nature of this decadent American society. We want education that teaches us our true history and our role in the present-day society.*

   We believe in an educational system that will give to our people a knowledge of self. If a man does not have knowledge of himself and his position in society and the world, then he has little chance to relate to anything else.

(continued)

6. *We want all black men to be exempt from military service.*

   We believe that black people should not be forced to fight in the military service to defend a racist government that does not protect us. We will not fight and kill other people of color in the world who, like black people, are being victimized by the white racist government of America. We will protect ourselves from the force and violence of the racist police and the racist military, by whatever means necessary.

7. *We want an immediate end to POLICE BRUTALITY and MURDER of black people.*

   We believe we can end police brutality in our black community by organizing black self-defense groups that are dedicated to defending our black community from racist police oppression and brutality. The Second Amendment to the Constitution of the United States gives a right to bear arms. We therefore believe that all black people should arm themselves for self-defense.

8. *We want freedom for all black men held in federal, state, county, and city prisons and jails.*

   We believe that all black people should be released from the many jails and prisons because they have not received a fair and impartial trial.

9. *We want all black people when brought to trial to be tried in court by a jury of their peer group or people from their black communities, as defined by the Constitutuion of the United States.*

   We believe that the courts should follow the United States Constitution so that black people will receive fair trials. The Fourteenth Amendment of the U.S. Constitution gives a man a right to be tried by his peer group. A peer is a person from a similar economic, social, religious, geographical, environmental, historical, and racial background. To do this the court will be forced to select a jury from the black community from which the black defendant came. We have been and are being tried by all-white juries that have no understanding of the "average reasoning man" of the black community.

10. *We want land, bread, housing, education, clothing, justice, and peace. And as our major political objective, a United Nations–supervised plebiscite to be held throughout the black colony in which only black colonial subjects will be allowed to participate, for the purpose of determining the will of black people as to their national destiny.*

    When, in the course of human events, it becomes necessary for one people to dissolve the political bands which have connected them with another . . .

Bobby Seale, *Seize the Time* (New York: Random House, 1970), 66–69.

Growing tensions and the attitudes of ghetto residents reinforced Martin Luther King's concerns about his ability to maintain the civil rights movement's commitment to nonviolence as he organized in the North. The intransigence of Chicago's Mayor Richard Daley, the hostility between ghetto blacks and the police, and the enormity of the problems poor African Americans faced in the cities were all portents of future trouble. As he had done in Los Angeles after the Watts riots, King took time in Chicago to listen to the ghetto's young people, to discuss their views, and to talk to them about nonviolence. King had talked through the night with gang leaders in the living room of his Chicago apartment and understood that there was a wide gulf between their perceptions of racism and their future prospects and the perspectives of most white Americans. He believed that growing unrest in the North required a more militant nonviolent strategy. Attempting to formulate a plan that would appeal to his new constituency without alienating former supporters and more moderate civil rights leaders, amid speculation that his waning popularity signaled the end of his influence in the movement, King took on economic issues directly and decided to wage a Poor People's Campaign.[37]

SCLC had already identified problems associated with poverty—poor housing, inferior education, and unemployment—as the appropriate targets for their northern campaign. They began to organize a march on Washington, D.C., for April 1968 that would focus attention on the economic issues. King called racism America's sickness and preached his jeremiad:

> There is confusion in the land. Now this is why we've made a decision to come to the seat of government . . . and will seek to say to the nation that if you don't straighten up, and that if you do not begin to use your vast resources of wealth to lift God's children from the dungeons of despair and poverty, then you are writing your own obituary.[38]

President Lyndon Johnson took the plans for a poor people's march as a personal affront, evidence of a singular lack of appreciation for his efforts to address the needs of the poor.

Years before, in the early summer of 1964, Johnson had laid out his plans for wiping out poverty and improving the quality of life for all Americans in a second New Deal, called his "Great Society," to be administered by the federal government. He was convinced that his remarkable presidential victory that year had provided a popular mandate to move ahead with his vision of a general war on poverty, and he wanted to get his social programs through Congress while the glow of victory remained. During the congressional sessions of 1965–1966, Johnson guided into law a dazzling array of legislation, aiding education, supporting public health care with the Medicare program, subsidizing rents, aiding cities and urban transport systems, training people for jobs, regulating environmental and job safety, protecting the consumer, supporting mental health, and more. He used the civil rights theme in a speech before Congress in which he urged the passage of the Voting Rights Act. There was much work to be done to ensure the rights of individual Americans, to abolish poverty, and to overcome racial prejudice, Johnson said. But he assured the nation that the federal government was concerned about the people, and he echoed the famous civil rights anthem, declaring, "We shall overcome."[39]

African Americans had welcomed Johnson's expressions of concern. In 1966 one-third of black families—three times the proportion of whites—survived on less than three thousand dollars a year, and the black unemployment rate was over 7 percent, more than twice the white rate. In his stunning autobiography, *Manchild in the Promised Land,* published that year, Claude Brown provided the nation with a stark picture of growing up in poverty-stricken, drug-infested Harlem.[40] By every measure, including literacy, educational level, housing quality, hunger, and health, African Americans fared much worse than white Americans.[41] Segregationists attributed these differences to black inferiority, but most social scientists found the explanation in U.S. racial history. In 1965 Assistant Secretary of Labor Daniel Patrick Moynihan had published his analysis of what he considered the general pathology of black urban life, concluding that "at the heart of the deterioration of the fabric of Negro society [was] the deterioration of the Negro family." He asserted that slavery had destroyed the black family and robbed black men of their authority over the household. As evidence of the disastrous effects of this history, he offered the high rates of broken marriages, higher rates of female-headed families among African Americans, higher rates of illegitimate births, and "a startling increase in welfare dependency."[42]

Liberal social scientists, including Moynihan, recognized that African Americans had lacked the opportunities historically offered to white Americans, and assumed that generations of deprivation had had adverse effects on the development of black culture. Working for the Johnson administration, they devised Great Society programs to replace this supposed "culture of poverty" with middle-class values that would allow African Americans to take advantage of enhanced opportunities, build strong families, dedicate themselves to education, find employment, and be faithful workers. In this way, they believed, the cycle of poverty and welfare dependency would be broken, and what they saw as the pathology of the ghetto would be eradicated. Most African Americans, and more radical social scientists, had a different analysis of the problem, however. As they saw it, job discrimination, not a failure to learn the value of work, led to the higher rate of black unemployment. Families were more precarious because the lowest-paying jobs created tensions born of economic insecurity and forced both parents to work. Higher rates of crime and poverty, they believed, were consequences of the long history of discrimination and political and economic powerlessness in neighborhoods policed by hostile authorities. When some Great Society programs, such as the Community Action Program (CAP), enabled black communities to challenge the power of the authorities, city and state politicians strenuously objected and pressured the federal government to cut back the programs. Many of Johnson's War on Poverty, or Great Society, programs enabled African Americans to make progress, improving education, job training, and employment opportunities for some people in the black community, but clashes with urban authorities also exacerbated both growing black anger and the white backlash to programs designed for black advancement.[43]

During the summer and fall of 1966, racial violence erupted in forty-three cities. In Omaha, Chicago, San Francisco, and smaller cities in Michigan and Illinois, the National Guard was called out to stop race riots.[44] In a Chicago demonstration for open housing, Martin Luther King was among those stoned by angry white counterdemonstrators. King also faced criticism for his increasingly vocal opposition to Americans' growing role in the war in Vietnam. As early as the spring of 1965, he had been publicly critical of the Johnson administration's incremental escalation of troop commitments and massive bombing raids in Vietnam. In a speech at Howard University in Washington, D.C., early in March, King had spoken in favor of a negotiated settlement of the conflict. When he had appeared on the CBS television program *Face the Nation* in August with the same proposal, he had incurred the wrath of President Johnson, who brooked no dissent from his policy. That same month the board of SCLC had made it clear that they opposed the involvement of the organization in international affairs, particularly protests against the war. The board insisted that King's antiwar statements and actions expressed his individual conscience rather than the position of his organization.[45]

As moderate civil rights leaders counseled single-minded concentration on the national civil rights agenda, with some advising strategic support of Lyndon Johnson's policies, SNCC, the Black Panthers, and the mostly white college-campus-based Students for a Democratic Society (SDS), on the other hand, developed a political analysis linking the national and international issues of peace and racial justice. For these groups an anticolonial stance joined the struggles for liberation in many African countries, the war in Vietnam, and the condition of African Americans in urban ghettos. Young radicals' loyalties to people struggling against colonial oppression often pitted them against the policies of the American government.

Militant New York congressman Adam Clayton Powell, Jr., with members
of the Black Panther Party and the press after a meeting of the House Labor
and Education Committee seeking to curtail his powers as committee
chairman in 1966. Powell was expelled from the House in 1967,
but he won a special election and regained his seat a year later.
Photographs and Prints Division, Library of Congress, Washington, D.C.

There were also personal ties among members of these groups. Some leaders of SDS had been active in the civil rights activities in the South, including SNCC's voter registration drives. Tom Hayden, the drafter of the Port Huron
Statement, SDS's founding document, had established a field office in Atlanta
in the early 1960s and was arrested for his participation in a freedom ride in
1961. Members of SDS and the Panthers had worked in urban community organizations associated with Johnson's War on Poverty. Members of SDS, SNCC,
CORE, and other organizations had been arrested together for demonstrating against South African apartheid in front of the offices of the Chase Manhattan Bank in New York City in March 1965. That year, there were three major
demonstrations in Washington against the war, and late in the year, SNCC
leader Robert Moses went to teach in a remote village in the new African nation
of Tanzania.

At great cost to his own reputation, risking diminished contributions to
SCLC and criticized by white allies and some black leaders, Martin Luther King
preached antiwar sermons and spoke out against the war throughout 1967
and early 1968. As the historian James Cone characterized King's state of mind

during this period: "He was gripped by the suffering of the Vietnamese, espe-cially the children; he was angered that Americans would deprive their own poor to pay for an unjust war; and he was saddened that his antiwar position alienated many of his allies, black and white, in the freedom movement."[46]

The escalation of violence during the summer of 1967 reinforced King's sense of the urgency of his nonviolent message. More extensive rioting, including major riots in Newark, New Jersey, and Detroit, Michigan, in July, seemed to many observers to signal a black rebellion. According to a Senate committee, eleven people had been killed in twenty-one riots in 1966, but in 1967, eighty-three people were killed in seventy-five major riots.[47] Stud-ies of the riots' causes blamed American racism for the inferiority of housing and education for many blacks and their high rates of unemployment. As in many earlier riots, in 1967 the most common precipitating factor was a clash between residents and the white police, who were frequently perceived as an occupying military force. The National Advisory Commission on Civil Disorders, headed by Illinois governor Otto Kerner, issued a report at the end of February 1968 predicting that if no change in policy occurred, the United States would become "two societies, one black, one white—separate and unequal." The commission feared that this would eventually result in "the destruction of basic democratic values."[48] Commissioners linked poverty and racial discrimination; Martin Luther King included the Vietnam War: "A nation that spends $500,000 to kill one enemy soldier in Vietnam and only $50 to get one of its own citizens out of poverty is a nation that will be destroyed by its own moral contradictions," he declared.[49]

Since the early 1960s Martin Luther King and his organization had been the targets of intense scrutiny and attack by the federal government, a cam-paign headed by J. Edgar Hoover, the director of the Federal Bureau of Inves-tigation. Hoover had joined the bureau after World War I and early in his career worked in a counterintelligence operation that had targeted Marcus Garvey and A. Philip Randolph. He was a rabid anti-Communist who continually searched for subversive elements in leftist organizations, among which he counted associations dedicated to the achievement of racial justice. Under Hoover's directorship the FBI was especially alert to signs of the possible emergence of a black leader who could unite African Americans to attack the racial and economic status quo. As such, Malcolm X and Martin Luther King were among those who received attention. The FBI kept King under contin-ual surveillance and used particularly underhanded methods in attempts to discredit his moral leadership, including offering recorded material from the surveillance to the media, giving it to President Johnson, and mailing audio tapes to Mrs. King. In 1956 Hoover established an aggressive program called COINTELPRO, using extensive systems of informants and activities designed to promote conflict and disrupt leftist organizations, particularly the American Communist Party. In 1967 he officially extended COINTELPRO to "expose, disrupt, misdirect, discredit, or otherwise neutralize the activities of black nationalist, hate-type organizations and groupings, their leadership, spokesmen, membership and supporters."[50] The targets of this expanded COINTELPRO included the Nation of Islam, the Black Panthers, and SCLC and Martin Luther King. Hoover's conviction that King was dangerous to the nation's stability seemed confirmed when King linked the issues of race, class, and opposition to the war. King's statement to his staff in 1967 undoubtedly fueled Hoover's worst fears. King announced a change in aims and tactics from the earlier reform movement:

> The black revolution is much more than a struggle for the rights of Negroes. It is forcing America to face all its interrelated flaws— racism, poverty, militarism, and materialism. It is exposing evils that are rooted deeply in the whole structure of our society. It reveals systemic rather than superficial flaws and suggests that radical reconstruction of society itself is the real issue to be faced.[51]

Although King had added his concerns about poverty and war to his civil rights agenda, others moved from civil rights to other social concerns. Many whites withdrew their financial support from southern civil rights campaigns in response to the rise in black militancy and calls for black power and separate black action. The *New York Times* reported a decline in contributions to traditional southern civil rights projects in favor of antipoverty work and antiwar efforts.[52] Some traditional groups became more racially exclusive as they became more politically radical. In 1967 CORE redrafted its constitution and removed the word "multiracial" from the section on membership. Members of one the most radical new groups, the Revolutionary Action Movement (RAM), a Marxist-Leninist group formed in 1964, talked of black nationalism and guerrilla warfare.[53] The FBI placed RAM, SNCC, SCLC, and CORE in the same category, as if they were all equally dangerous, but there were great differences between them. In the summer of 1967, sixteen members of RAM were arrested for plotting to kill Roy Wilkins, Whitney Young, and other moderate civil rights leaders. It is questionable whether this plot ever existed—the FBI later admitted that RAM leaders were arrested frequently, and on "every possible charge"—but the hostility between members of different groups made the existence of such a scheme somewhat plausible.[54]

In many ways the split between black activists was generational and paralleled the divide apparent in the society as a whole. The oppositional youth culture embraced black liberation at home and abroad, the peace movement against the war in Vietnam, a generalized freedom from middle-class American mores, and a communal ethic. For some members of this generation, the counterculture became more a matter of style than politics, but all were drawn together by the music of black America. Even as the sentiment for black separatism in political organizing grew, young people of both races were joined in the common culture that made superstars of such Motown artists as Stevie Wonder, Marvin Gaye, Diana Ross and the Supremes, the Jackson Five, Martha Reeves and the Vandellas, and the Temptations. Jimi Hendrix, a young black guitar player from Seattle, Washington, seemed to exemplify the countercultural style. Hendrix had played with such rock and roll greats as Little Richard, Ike and Tina Turner, and the Isley Brothers. When he returned from England with his own band in 1968, his dress, Afro hairstyle, musical approach, and experimentation with drugs had great appeal for rebellious young people. Hendrix became a revolutionary musical icon.[55]

The interracial counterculture was centered on college campuses, and colleges and universities themselves often became the targets of radical demands. Black students were particularly interested in bringing the study of African American history and culture to the curriculum. At Yale University students formed a Black Student Alliance in November 1967. The following spring, they held a conference on Black Studies and brought together educators from across the nation to discuss the establishment of black studies programs.[56] Black students also demanded that more black students be enrolled and that black faculty be hired. Students sometimes pressed their demands with sit-ins, taking over buildings, and generally disrupting campus life. In the spring of 1968, for example, Tufts University outside Boston bowed to student demands and provided admissions programs and financial aid to encourage applications from black students. Student action produced similar results at Trinity University in Connecticut, Radcliffe College in Boston, Mount Holyoke College in western Massachusetts, Brown University in Providence, Rhode Island, and elsewhere in the Northeast. The following fall many Midwestern schools took action in response to student protests. At Kent State University in Ohio, black students joined with white students from SDS to protest, and black students and white students at Washington University in St. Louis took over a campus building to call attention to racism at their school. Protests on the West Coast led to the establishment of several black studies programs at colleges and universities, including the University of California at Berkeley and San Francisco State College. In many colleges radical white students and black students stood together to make common demands for a broader curriculum and a more diverse student body and faculty. To satisfy student protests, some universities added a course or two in Afro-American studies, but radical students continued to demand more fundamental changes in the presentation and analysis of American history and culture.[57]

The Jackson 5, one of Motown Records' most popular singing groups of the 1970s. Later they changed their name to The Jacksons. Clockwise from the top left: Jackie, Tito, Marlon, Michael, and Randy Jackson, 1977.

By 1968 Martin Luther King was also seeking more fundamental changes. He was focusing much of his attention on class issues and working for political power and racial and economic justice. He was dogged by threats and dispirited by outbreaks of violence. In March he went to Memphis, Tennessee, to support striking city garbage collectors and led a march to dramatize the workers' demands. Despite his efforts to keep the march nonviolent, marchers clashed with police, about 150 buildings were set ablaze, one person was killed, at least fifty were injured, and three hundred were arrested. Finally four thousand National Guardsmen were called in to calm the city. King returned to Memphis on April 3 to continue the struggle with another march, and rallied his followers with an emotional sermon. "I've been to the mountaintop," he told the crowd, and "I've seen the promised land." Then he added, "I may not get there with you. But I want you to know tonight, that we, as a people will get to the promised land." Concluding his message, he reassured his listeners, "And so I'm happy tonight. I'm not worried about anything. I'm not fearing any man." The following evening, on April 4, while he stood on the balcony of the Lorraine Motel, where he regularly stayed, Martin Luther King, Jr., was shot and killed by a sniper.[58]

Word of King's assassination triggered a hopeless rage in American cities. Between April 4 and April 11, ghetto residents burned and looted and confronted police in more than 125 cities. Forty-one blacks and five whites were killed, more than 3,500 people were injured, and $45 million worth of property was destroyed. The largest riots were in Chicago, Baltimore, Pittsburgh, and Washington, D.C., where entire sections of the cities burned. Chicago's mayor Richard Daley ordered his police to shoot to kill if necessary to restore order. There were other riots later that spring and summer, and it seemed that nonviolent protest had died with Martin Luther King.[59]

Although President Johnson was more and more preoccupied with the quagmire of violence that the war in Vietnam had become, he maintained his opposition to racial discrimination. In 1967 he had named Thurgood Marshall to the Supreme Court, the first African American to hold that position. Johnson declared April 6, 1968, a national day of mourning for Martin Luther King, and on April 11 he signed the Civil Rights Act of 1968 into law, outlawing discrimination in the sale or rental of housing. The law was an ambiguous memorial to King. It made it a crime to interfere with civil rights workers, but it also outlawed crossing state lines to incite a riot, an accusation often leveled at civil right workers.[60] Early that summer Ralph Abernathy, King's close friend and loyal lieutenant, led about three thousand people in the Poor People's March on Washington that King had planned before his death. The marchers set up tents on the Mall and called their encampment Resurrection City. Fifty thousand people participated in Solidarity Day there on June 19 in support of the protest, but the police closed and demolished Resurrection City before the end of the month.

Even the most optimistic activists were disheartened by King's death and by the continually escalating war in Vietnam. African Americans were about 10 percent of the American military in Vietnam, as they were of the total population, but they were 20 percent of the combat troops in the field and more than 14 percent of those killed in action.[61] In 1968 Robert Kennedy ran for the Democratic presidential nomination and carried King's message forward. The younger brother of the assassinated president, and thus personally touched by America's violence, he warned a group in Cleveland that "violence breeds violence" and declared that only a "cleansing of our whole society can remove this sickness from our soul." He urged a black crowd in Indianapolis to "say a prayer for our country and for our people." He had supported the civil rights movement in its early days, and many blacks supported his candidacy. "Kennedy is on our side," they believed. "We know it. He doesn't have to say a word."[62] Robert Kennedy spoke for poor children, calling them victims of the violence of the nation's institutions, and encouraged poor people of all races to unite in common cause. John Lewis of SNCC and Charles Evers, the late Medgar Evers's brother, took up Kennedy's banner, as did Latino labor activist Cesar Chavez. Kennedy had been slow to declare his candidacy, and in the process had alienated the primarily white leadership of the antiwar movement, who had given up hope he would champion their cause and had turned instead to the intellectual Eugene McCarthy. By the time they reached the end of the primary campaigns in California, Kennedy's activist spirit and passionate commitment to humanitarian values had spoken to the hopes of disheartened people and had won him increasing support. Then, in Los Angeles in June, immediately after winning the close California primary, Robert Kennedy was assassinated. Martin Luther King had feared that the failure of nonviolence would mean a right-wing victory, repression, and a loss of democracy. The violent deaths of these two champions of the poor and oppressed within a few months threw the Left into despair. Pitched battles occurred between the Chicago police and demonstrators outside the Democratic National Convention that summer, and many progressives' fears of a conspiracy against dissidents, blacks, and the poor were fueled by crippling factional conflict within the Left, presidential candidate George Wallace's strong showing outside the South, and the election of Richard Nixon to the presidency that fall.[63]

Periodic rioting continued; police exchanged gunfire with snipers in Chicago; arrested five hundred to end disturbances in Hartford, Connecticut; and battled rioters in Springfield, Massachusetts; Jacksonville, Florida; and Cairo, Illinois. The National Guard was called into Baton Rouge, Louisiana, and Fort Lauderdale, Florida. In the spring of 1969 police and National Guardsmen fired on black student demonstrators at the predominantly black North Carolina A&T College, killing one of the students. Police in Oakland, California, engaged in a shoot-out with the Black Panthers, killing seventeen-year-old Bobby Hutton as he emerged, hands raised, from a building set afire by the police. Panther and author Eldridge Cleaver had stripped naked to show that he was not armed, but he was also shot. In Chicago police and FBI agents invaded an apartment and killed Black Panther leader Fred Hampton as he slept. They shot Mark Clark through the heart; he was pronounced dead on arrival at the hospital.[64] A subsequent federal grand jury left no doubt that the FBI and local law enforcement were waging a war on the Panthers, symbol of the terrifying possibilities of black revenge. At Cornell University black students were harassed by white students who called them names, made obscene telephone calls, threw rocks through their windows, and burned a cross in front of a dormitory housing a number of black female students. Several armed black male students provided protection for the women, and black students occupied the student union building to protest the unwillingness of the school administration to act against racism at the university. The black students armed themselves when they received word that a white fraternity had organized a one-hundred-member armed force to remove them. This discouraged the attack, encouraged the university to bargain, and ended the standoff. When the protesters emerged from the occupied building, the pictures of armed black students transmitted by the television cameras shocked the nation. The pictures seemed to confirm white fears that a racial revolution was close at hand. Black patience was at an end, and angry voices demanded "Freedom now!"[65]

Chapter 14

1971   Congressional Black Caucus created

Jesse Jackson organizes People United to Save Humanity

United States bombs Cambodia; Vietnam War spreads to Laos and Cambodia

1972   Congresswoman Shirley Chisholm is first black woman to run for president

Angela Davis acquitted of murder and conspiracy charges

1973   Vietnam peace accord signed; African Americans had been disproportionately represented among volunteers and draftees

Marian Wright Edelman organizes Children's Defense Fund

1974   House Judiciary Committee recommends three articles of impeachment in Watergate scandal; President Nixon resigns; President Gerald Ford grants Nixon a preemptive pardon; President Ford offers limited amnesty to draft dodgers and deserters

1975   North Vietnamese Communists take over South Vietnam

1976   Representative Andrew Young becomes U.S. ambassador to the United Nations

1977   The televised version of Alex Haley's *Roots* reaches more than 130 million viewers

Public Works Employment Act reserves 10 percent of federal public works projects for minority-owned businesses

1978   Sociologist William Julius Wilson publishes *The Declining Significance of Race,* arguing for the growing importance of economics in determining opportunities for black Americans

1979   Ku Klux Klan kills five people at an anti-Klan rally in Greensboro, North Carolina

1980   California governor Ronald Reagan elected president

Black Entertainment Television founded by Robert L. Johnson

1981   More than 300,000 people from labor and civil rights organizations join Solidarity Day demonstration protesting Reagan administration policies

1983   Martin Luther King, Jr.'s birthday becomes federal holiday

Alice Walker wins Pulitzer Prize for *The Color Purple*

Vanessa Williams is first black woman crowned Miss America; resigns in July 1984 after nude photographs taken before the contest are published in national magazine; succeeded by first runner-up, Suzette Charles, another black woman

Harold Washington elected Mayor of Chicago

1987   Toni Morrison wins Pulitzer Prize for *Beloved*

1988   Jesse Jackson wins presidential primaries in five states

1989   Gen. Colin Powell named chair of the U.S. Joint Chiefs of Staff

Ronald H. Brown heads Democratic National Committee

David Dinkins elected mayor of New York City

Douglas Wilder elected governor of Virginia; the first African American elected governor of any state

Conservatism and Race in Multicultural America

*B*y the end of the 1960s the American polity was fractured, and any semblance of a civil society seemed to be disintegrating. Most of the leaders of the nonviolent movement were dead or dispirited. White radical antiwar factions used the rhetoric of revolution, black militants threatened revolution, and urban violence seemed to confirm the prospect. In 1970 the fears of many blacks about abuses of police power were corroborated when UCLA philosophy instructor Angela Davis was arrested in connection with a courtroom shoot-out. Angela Yvonne Davis was born into the black middle class of the urban South in 1944. Her parents, both active in the NAACP, were schoolteachers in Birmingham, Alabama, until her father became the proprietor of a gas station, a better-paying job than teaching. Davis was a very bright child; she learned to read, write, and do basic arithmetic before she entered school. She did very well in school, was active in civil rights activities early in life, and earned a scholarship to a private high school in New York City from the American Friends Service Committee when she was fifteen. The school was a haven for leftist teachers who had been blacklisted from New York's public schools. Davis found their political ideas compatible with her own beliefs, and she joined a Marxist-Leninist group in high school.[1]

She attended Brandeis University near Boston, spending her junior year in 1963 at the Sorbonne in Paris. That year international issues, national politics, and personal experience converged for Davis. She discussed world affairs with students from Algeria who were active in the fight against French colonialism. She also learned that four young girls she knew in Birmingham had been murdered by a Ku Klux Klan bombing, killed while they attended Sunday school at the Sixteenth Street Baptist Church. Davis continued her education at Brandeis, where she took courses from the philosopher Herbert Marcuse, a member of a group of prominent scholars from Frankfurt's Institute of Social Research who had fled Hitler's Germany. Marcuse's strongly moral Marxist stance greatly influenced Davis. She graduated from Brandeis in 1965 and studied two additional years at the Goethe University in Frankfurt, Germany. She then returned to the United States to continue her studies with Marcuse, who had moved to the University of California at San Diego.[2]

Davis entered the volatile world of black activism in southern California in 1967. She joined the SNCC chapter in Los Angeles and the local chapter of the Communist Party. She found the sexism of the men in SNCC difficult to tolerate. Finally she resigned when some SNCC members complained about her Communist affiliation, although she maintained close ties with a few of the group's radicals. A few years later Davis was hired to teach philosophy at UCLA. The job did not last long, however; under pressure from California governor Ronald Reagan, UCLA fired her because of her Communist ties. Her dismissal and her affiliation with the Black Panther Party attracted the attention of the press and made her a national figure in the late 1960s.[3]

The Panthers were popular among young men, but it is difficult to estimate their membership. They were reluctant to reveal precise numbers, though at one rally in North Richmond, California, Newton claimed that the party took in more than three hundred applications. Boys too young to carry guns legally were enrolled in the Junior Panthers and attended classes in black history. By the early 1970s Panther members had been arrested and tried on charges ranging from conspiracy to commit murder to bombing police stations and assaulting the police. Angela Davis became an advocate for prisoners, arguing that many blacks were being held for political reasons. She befriended George Jackson, an inmate at California's Soledad Prison, who had already served ten years of an indeterminate sentence for a seventy-dollar robbery. While in jail, Jackson was alleged to have killed a prison guard. She encouraged Jackson to publish *Soledad Brother,* a series of philosophical and autobiographical reflections on the lives of black prison inmates and the pervasive racism in the American prison system.[4] African Americans were one-half of the prison population in America in 1970; Jackson's book attracted national attention and became the principal document in the emerging prisoners' rights movement.

Just two months before George Jackson's book was published in 1970, his younger brother, Jonathan, invaded a trial at a San Rafael, California, county courthouse. In the ensuing shoot-out, Jackson, a judge, and two defendants were killed. When authorities learned that the weapons Jackson used were registered in Angela Davis's name, they issued a warrant for her arrest. Fearing the police, Davis went underground and for two months was on the FBI's Ten Most Wanted list. Finally she was captured and jailed for sixteen months before coming to trial. After deliberating for thirteen hours, an all-white jury acquitted her of the charges of murder, kidnapping, and conspiracy, but the fact that she could be arrested and held for so long on extremely weak evidence was sobering. James Baldwin wrote her an open letter expressing the dread that many blacks felt: "If they come for you in the morning, they will be coming for us that night."[5]

One year later, in August 1971, George Jackson was killed by prison guards. He was shot in the back during an alleged escape attempt, but most of the country's black prison inmates believed he had been murdered for his political activism. It was unlikely, some pointed out, that he would attempt to escape just two days before he was to receive a new trial. Inmate anger over Jackson's death gave rise to hundreds of prison protests all over the country. In the largest, most violent protest in 1971, inmates seized control of Attica Prison in upstate New York, taking thirty-nine hostages. They demanded reforms in prison living conditions, the recruitment of African American and Latino guards, and the payment of the state's minimum wage for prison labor. State authorities negotiated with the inmates for five days before 211 state troopers and police stormed the prison. More than four hundred shots were fired. Ten hostages and twenty-nine inmates were killed. Later investigation showed that all those killed had been shot, but no guns were found in the inmates' possession.[6]

The Black Panthers saw themselves as the servants and protectors of the community. But the media gave little attention to their free breakfast programs for hungry children, legal aid to the poor, or their pressuring city officials to serve the black community fairly. Few outside the black communities saw more than the confrontational style that made the Panthers targets of the FBI, which considered them dangerous lawbreakers who should be arrested, disbanded, or destroyed. The press and some government agencies encouraged wildly exaggerated fears of a radical conspiracy, but a U.S. House Internal Security Committee study concluded that though the Panthers posed a threat to the authority of the police, they were not capable of violently overthrowing the government. Panthers were convinced that many of the FBI informants who had infiltrated their organization were agents who provoked violence to discredit the party. Revelations in 1975 of the FBI'S COINTELPRO campaigns against black leaders and organizations lent credence to their charges.[7]

The aggressive stance of black power that threatened authorities was especially appealing to young black men because it expressed a type of manhood they had traditionally been denied. Through slavery and segregation, black people had been expected to suppress their anger, to hide their offense at public indignities, and to submit to white authority. In the South even by the late 1960s, racial etiquette dictated that African Americans avert their eyes, since making direct eye contact with whites was considered aggressive. Even militant nonviolence appeared to some young African Americans raised in the North to continue the passivity that seemed an admission of inferiority.

The impression made by the style and image of the Black Panthers was vividly described by best-selling author Eldridge Cleaver in his insightful and startling book of autobiographical essays, *Soul on Ice*. Cleaver, a small-time drug dealer who had become a Black Muslim in prison, was introduced to the Black Panther Party in 1967. When the Panthers entered the room, "I spun round in my seat and saw the most beautiful sight I had ever seen," he recalled, "four black men wearing black berets, powder blue shirts, black leather jackets, black trousers, shiny black shoes—and each with a gun!" It was a transforming moment for Cleaver. "Where was my mind at?" he asked rhetorically. "Blown." Panthers Bobby Seale and Huey Newton had come to provide security for Betty Shabazz, Malcolm X's widow. Moments after he met them, Cleaver saw Newton face down a policeman angered by the Panthers' swagger. Newton challenged the officer to draw his gun, the policeman retreated, and Newton turned his back and walked away. The astounded Cleaver became the Panthers' minister of information in charge of press relations. Many young black men in northern cities reacted as Cleaver had in the late 1960s, shocked but filled with pride to see black men stand against the police.[8]

The self-assertion and militancy that attracted young black men often left black women in the difficult position of having to confirm black manhood by assuming the role of supportive women. Although "they were allowed to wear pants and expected to pick up the gun," one female member recalled, they were often treated like children, expected to give "doe-eyed looks to our leaders . . . while the Brotha was doing his thing, or had moved on to bigger and better things." Panther communications secretary Kathleen Cleaver, married to Eldridge, found she never received the credit for her work that the men received for theirs. "It seemed that it had something to do with the egos of the men involved," she mused. Although the Panthers declared their commitment to "absolute equality between male and female," and Bobby Seale and Huey Newton were conscious of the need to rid the organization of male chauvinism, even they were often paternalistic toward female members.[9]

The attitudes of Black Panthers toward women were far from unique. The roles of black women in SNCC, SCLC, and other civil rights organizations were generally limited by the sexism of male colleagues. Angela Davis denounced the chauvinism of black men in these groups who used the stereotypes about emasculating black women as a weapon against women in the movement, "whenever we women were involved in something important."[10] Nor was this phenomenon limited to black groups. White women in civil rights and anti-war groups met similar obstacles, but the history of African Americans gave it a unique and complex dimension. During the generations of slavery, gender roles for slaves were determined primarily by the demands of the labor system rather than social conventions, and women and men were both required to do heavy labor with little accommodation for differences between the sexes. Since slaves were under the nearly complete authority of the slave master, black men were not accorded the customary familial authority of men in a patriarchal society. Thus slavery, and to some extent the system of seg-regation that followed it, was perceived as an attack on black manhood. Limited opportunities for jobs and education for black men in contemporary society continued the attack. An important imperative for women in black society from the time of slavery to the present has been accepting the respon-sibility for overcoming the consequences of that history and supporting black men in their efforts to achieve an independent and powerful manhood. During the centuries of struggle for freedom and justice, the complexities of gender roles complicated the relationships between black men and women and even the operation of civil rights organizations.[11]

A tentative black feminism emerged in the late 1960s, partly as a result of black women's experiences in civil rights and black power organizations. Pauli Murray, a black lawyer, civil rights worker, and poet, was one of the founders of the predominantly white National Organization for Women and described the new organization as a civil rights organization for women. For most black women, however, racial oppression seemed more immediate and debilitating than gender discrimination. Their loyalty to racial progress made it difficult for them to identify with the early feminist movement. Initially white feminists were generally middle class, and many black women saw their analysis of women's problems as anti-male. In the early 1970s middle-class professional women formed the National Black Feminist Organization and Black Women Organized for Action, but they attracted few members. A decade later, black feminist Michele Wallace observed, "there is still no Black women's movement, and it appears there won't be for some time to come."[12]

In the 1980s black feminism found its expression in highly acclaimed literary works. Alice Walker won the 1983 Pulitzer Prize for her novel *The Color Purple,* made into a popular and controversial movie a few years later. Walker's book portrayed the life of Celie, a woman who was sexually and emotionally abused her entire life by black men, from her stepfather to the emotion-ally detached husband she called "Mister." On black radio talk shows, tele-vision interview shows, and in newspapers and magazines, black men reacted vehemently to what many perceived as the negative portrayal of black men, or "male bashing."[13] For a time controversy raged over whether or not black female writers were receiving more favorable attention than their work war-ranted. Some theorized that the white literary power structure might be ignoring the work of black male writers, finding the women's work somehow less threatening. Perhaps, they conjectured, attacks on black men reinforced racial stereotypes. Controversy heightened when black writer Toni Morrison's novel *Beloved* won the Pulitzer Prize and was nominated for both the National Book Award and the National Book Critics Circle Award in 1987. In much of their writing, black women seemed willing to say in public what had been traditionally reserved for private conversation—that black men generally shared American male chauvinism and were unwilling to treat black women as equals despite their history of equally sharing the burdens of race. Bell Hooks echoed the admonition by the nineteenth-century abolitionist and women's rights activist Sojourner Truth when she warned, in 1981, that "there can be no freedom for black men as long as they advocate subjection of women."[14]

As national organizations came under increased governmental assault during the 1970s, local groups led the civil rights campaign, devising strategies to attack de facto segregation and customary racial discrimination. To integrate public schools in residentially segregated cities and towns outside the South, some concluded that busing children to schools in other neighborhoods could be an interim solution. Few parents relished sending their children out of their communities to school, but white resistance to residential integration and the difficulty of finding affordable housing for blacks in predominantly white neighborhoods seemed to make it necessary. The differences in facilities between most white schools and predominantly black schools was obvious even to the casual observer. "When we would go to white schools," wrote one black Bostonian, "we'd see these lovely classrooms, with a small number of children in each class. The teachers were permanent. We'd see wonderful materials." This contrasted sharply with the underfunded, understaffed, underequipped schools serving African American students. In 1971 the Supreme Court confirmed the constitutionality of busing to integrate schools, and state and local courts ordered many cities to devise and implement busing plans. When Boston's school committee refused to design such a plan, U.S. District Court Judge W. Arthur Garrity, Jr., ordered students to be bused from predominantly black Roxbury schools to those in Irish-American South Boston. Longtime Boston residents knew this plan would be difficult to enforce and feared for the safety of black children. "As a child I had encountered the wrath of people in South Boston," recalled Ruth Batson, a veteran of the movement for equal education in the city. "They made it clear that they didn't like black people."[15]

South Boston fought the court order. Louise Day Hicks, a member of Boston's city council, and her antibusing group called Restore Our Alienated Rights (ROAR), held rallies protesting the plan. When Senator Edward Kennedy, the pride of Boston's Irish community, attempted to calm the crowd, he was shouted down. It was extremely popular to oppose busing in Boston during the 1970s. Councilwoman Hicks became a formidable political force in the city. Urban working-class schools close to black neighborhoods were more likely than middle-class suburban schools to be affected by these plans, and the reaction of white ethnic working-class communities was sometimes extreme. In Pontiac, Michigan; Denver, Colorado; Lamar, South Carolina, and other white communities, as in South Boston, voters elected local representatives who opposed busing, and opposing "busing" became a code for opposing racial integration and black rights in general. The underlying racial intolerance that dated from at least the mid–nineteenth century in Boston burst into plain view as local whites attacked school buses and harassed black children. Many liberal Bostonians were shocked to see the Ku Klux Klan march through the streets of their city.[16]

In the early 1970s George Wallace's political appeals to racial antagonisms drew great support from northern working-class voters, building on his successes in the Democratic presidential primaries in 1968. In that year he had shocked most political observers by winning 40 percent of the vote in the liberal state of Wisconsin and making an impressive showing in several other northern states, thereby expanding his traditional southern base. Recognizing the political advantage of capitalizing on the backlash to black advances, President Nixon and his combative vice president, Spiro Agnew, also encouraged antibusing campaigns. While Agnew railed against demands for racial justice, Nixon weakened civil rights activities in the Justice Department and the Health, Education, and Welfare Department; cut programs; and vetoed bills to aid the poor. As part of his strategy to appeal to Wallace supporters, he nominated judges to the Supreme Court who were opposed to busing, and at least one, G. Harrold Carswell, who was an admitted white supremacist. White backlash to civil rights gains was further fueled by an economic downturn in the 1970s that caused massive industrial layoffs and by a dramatic rise in inflation that further strained working-class budgets. The contracting economy once more pitted black workers against white workers as black demands seemed to threaten the economic security of the white working class.[17]

Most African Americans had already considered the Nixon White House to be among the most powerful opponents of civil rights. In the spring of 1970 the chair of the NAACP board of directors denounced the administration as "anti-Negro," saying it encouraged right-wing extremists. Yet blacks were acquiring political power. In 1970 there were twelve African Americans in Congress, Edward W. Brooke was a U.S. senator from Massachusetts, and blacks were the mayors of the major American cities of Gary, Indiana; Cleveland, Ohio; Newark, New Jersey; and Washington, D.C. That year the African Americans in Congress came together to form the Congressional Black Caucus (CBC) to help set a national agenda for black progress and to counter attacks from the Republican administration. When Nixon delivered his annual State of the Union Address in January 1971, members of the caucus refused to attend, protesting the president's refusal to meet with them to discuss pressing racial issues. The next year eight thousand African Americans gathered in Gary, Indiana, for the first National Black Political Convention and agreed to form a permanent organization to set a national political and social agenda for African Americans. Two controversial resolutions passed at the convention contributed to the organization's failure. One called for black control of black schools and opposed busing as a remedy for segregation in public education. The other called for self-determination for all people of color, and many liberal civil rights supporters saw this as a condemnation of Israel and an endorsement of the Palestine Liberation Organization (PLO). The Congressional Black Caucus did not want to alienate longtime Jewish supporters and immediately issued a statement making their position clear. "We vigorously oppose the efforts of any group that would seek to weaken or undermine Israel's right to exist," they declared. Many black nationalists rejected the CBC's statement, reasserted their support for the PLO, and denounced Israel's military and economic ties with the apartheid government of South Africa. As the presidential campaign of 1972 approached, the CBC continued to distance itself from the resolutions of the Gary convention.[18]

Race, sometimes code-worded "law and order," "the Silent Majority," or "busing," and the war in Vietnam were the central issues of the presidential election of 1972. The strong right-wing challenge to Nixon's reelection ended when a would-be assassin's bullet crippled Governor George Wallace for life. A series of campaign blunders and Republican sabotage destroyed Maine's Senator Edmund Muskie's chances for the Democratic nomination. New York Democratic representative Shirley Chisholm, elected in 1969 as the first African American woman ever to sit in Congress, mounted a challenge from the political left, but the party all but ignored her spirited campaign. Finally the liberal antiwar arm of the party secured the Democratic nomination for Senator George McGovern of South Dakota. Nixon won by one of the largest margins in American history, despite suspicions of his connection to campaign abuses and a burglary at the Democratic National Committee headquarters. He carried forty-nine of the fifty states, more than 60 percent of the popular vote; and blacks were the only traditionally Democratic group that voted for McGovern. The massive black vote did help secure the election of sixteen African Americans to Congress, including Andrew Young of Georgia, Barbara Jordan of Texas, and Yvonne Brathwaite Burke of California, and returned liberal Republican Edward W. Brooke of Massachusetts to the Senate.[19]

The Republicans had retained the White House, but Nixon faced crises both at home and abroad. Just weeks before the U.S. presidential election, Nixon had stepped up the bombing of North Vietnam and mined its major harbors in order to counter an earlier North Vietnamese offensive that had brought them to within thirty miles of the South Vietnamese capital of Saigon. He continued to escalate the bombing, which reached a historic high that Christmas.

Shirley Chisholm, elected to Congress in 1969, the first African American woman to hold national legislative office.

Photographs and Prints Division, Library of Congress, Washington, D.C.

The destruction of civilian targets at Christmastime was so massive that some U.S. pilots and ground crews refused to fly or support the missions. Each escalation of the war brought intensified opposition, particularly on college campuses at home and even within the military. Contentious antiwar demonstrations, growing black militancy, and the repressive government reaction to them created bitter and increasingly violent fragmentation among the American people.

The earliest opposition to the war among black groups had come mainly from young people, with the traditional civil rights organizations generally supporting America's foreign policy. Martin Luther King's outspoken opposition in the early 1960s, though partly based on his unswerving commitment to nonviolence, had alienated him from many in his own organization. As early as 1965 young blacks in the Mississippi Freedom Democratic Party urged African Americans to resist the draft on the grounds that "no Mississippi Negroes should be fighting in Viet Nam for the White man's freedom, until all the Negro People are free in Mississippi."[20] In 1967 Muhammad Ali (formerly Cassius Marcellus Clay), then a member of the Black Muslims, refused to be drafted on religious grounds. He was convicted of violating the Selective Service Act, sentenced to five years in prison, and stripped of his heavyweight championship title. Although the U.S. Supreme Court overturned his conviction in 1970, he did not regain his title until 1974. As opposition to the war grew, black antiwar activists identified with the anticolonialist struggles of the Vietnamese people, objected to the war's draining of resources from antidiscrimination and antipoverty efforts at home, and expressed their resentment of the widespread discrimination African Americans faced in the military.

Although Muhammad Ali came to symbolize the stand against the war, few African American men followed his example. Facing unemployment and limited opportunities at home, they were as likely as whites to enlist in the armed forces and were twice as likely to reenlist. The greater likelihood of African Americans to be in combat positions in the military resulted in approximately twice as many black casualties as might have been expected from their numbers in the armed services. More and more black leaders, especially the most militant young leaders, pointed to the obvious contradiction— black men were giving their lives to kill brown men in the name of a country where white men discriminated against people of color. Racial tensions spawned racial confrontations on military bases, and as early as 1968, commanders in Vietnam reported that racial disturbances were becoming "a serious and explosive problem." Given the high proportion of southern-born whites in the military, assertions of black rights were almost certain to result in racial confrontations as more militant young black men entered the service. Disputes occurred on military bases in the United States and abroad; in 1972 forty-six sailors were injured in a clash aboard the aircraft carrier *Kitty Hawk*. Despite such racial confrontations, however, Vietnam-era veterans often formed lasting bonds that transcended race.[21]

When the United States finally withdrew its troops from Vietnam in 1973, there were no victory parades for returning war heroes. Disillusioned soldiers, often cynical about the government and apprehensive about their future, came home to a country in turmoil where racial strife remained a central issue. African Americans returning to civilian life faced an unemployment rate almost twice that of whites. They were more likely to be the victims of crime, more likely to fall prey to drug addiction, more likely to live in inadequate housing, and less likely to cope successfully with the transition to civilian life.

As American involvement in the war wound down, the Nixon administration's illegal campaign activities, including the Watergate burglary, began to come to light. By the summer of 1973, televised Senate hearings and subpoenaed tapes of White House conversations began to illuminate the break-ins, bribery, and illegal use of government agencies that the administration had engaged in to counter its political enemies and opponents of the war. In July 1974, with the extent of Nixon's participation in such activities clear, the House Judiciary Committee conducted a formal debate on articles of impeachment, and on August 8 Richard Nixon resigned. Nixon's prosecution was fore-

Barbara Charline Jordan, congresswoman from Texas, elected in 1972,
was a member of the House Judiciary Committee that investigated the
Watergate scandal. Selected as *Time* magazine's Woman of the Year in 1976,
she electrified the country with her powerful keynote address at the
Democratic National Convention.

Photographs and Prints Division, Schomburg Center for Research in Black Culture,
The New York Public Library, Astor, Lenox, and Tilden Foundations.

stalled by former Vice President Gerald Ford, then president, who granted
Nixon a pardon for any wrongdoing of which he might be accused.[22]

Barbara Jordan, U.S. representative from Texas, was an outspoken member of the House Judiciary Committee, and in that position she gained
national attention for her eloquence in expressing her belief in the Constitution and support for the articles of impeachment. Jordan became the first
black woman to deliver the keynote address before the Democratic National
Convention during the presidential campaign of 1976. That convention
nominated Jimmy Carter, the former governor of Georgia, as Democratic candidate for the presidency to oppose the Republican incumbent Gerald Ford.
Carter attempted not to identify himself too closely with African American
support. He had been lukewarm toward local black leaders during the primary
elections and refused to attend conferences sponsored by the Black Caucus
and other major black organizations during the presidential campaign. Still,
blacks overwhelmingly supported him. Carter won the election with 55 percent of the popular vote and swept the South, winning every southern state
except Virginia. Black voters made the difference especially in the South, where

the Republican strategy designed in the Nixon administration delivered the majority of the southern white votes to Ford. For blacks, well aware of Republican appeals to southern whites, there seemed little choice. More than 90 percent of African American voters backed Carter, and black spokespersons gained greater access to the White House. Carter appointed a significant number of blacks to important positions in his administration. He named corporate lawyer Patricia Harris secretary of housing and urban development; minister and aide to Martin Luther King, Andrew Young, ambassador to the United Nations; Judge Wade McCree solicitor general; John Reinhardt to head the International Communications Agency; and a host of other blacks to posts in the executive branch. African Americans served in ambassadorial positions representing the United States in Europe, Africa, and the Caribbean.[23]

Yet, many African Americans saw these appointments as more symbolic than substantive, as Carter seemed more concerned with fighting inflation than with providing relief for the poor. Shortly after he took office Carter declared a moratorium on new social welfare, educational, and health care programs. Taking a page from the Republican policy book, he increased military spending and championed corporate-sponsored wage and benefit limitations and price guidelines. He also cut federal benefits to economically hard-pressed cities. Meanwhile the poor, suffering the effects of inflation, saw cuts in the social programs that had reduced the black poverty rate from 55 percent in 1959 to 31 percent by 1973. By late 1977 even many of Carter's middle-class black supporters felt betrayed by his economic policies, which neglected the poor.[24]

Economic discontent and racial tensions provided a fertile field for the continued growth of radical conservatism. National membership in the Ku Klux Klan nearly tripled between 1971 and 1980, and there was an upsurge in Klan violence throughout the South as the Klan firebombed black churches, schools, and residences. In November 1979 television videotape captured the murder of five demonstrators in Greensboro, North Carolina, by seventy-five Klansmen and neo-Nazis. Though the evidence seemed clear, an all-white jury acquitted the six who were accused of the killings. In the 1980 election a Klan leader won the Democratic Party primary for a congressional seat in Southern California.[25]

The conservative reaction to civil rights gains that began in the 1960s and accelerated under Nixon culminated in the election of Ronald Reagan as president in 1980. This triumph of the right wing encouraged blatant racism and prompted more racial violence than had occurred in twenty years. Under Reagan's policies the economic difference between the very rich and the very poor continued to grow, and those in the middle lost ground. *Washington Post* columnist William Raspberry declared, "Everything you thought you knew about the economic gap between black and white Americans is worse than you thought." While conservatives complained about blacks' unfair advantage and the "reverse racism" supposedly associated with affirmative-action programs, by 1985 college attendance for blacks, especially black males, was declining, while it continued to increase for whites.[26] Conservatives attacked affirmative action while they cut the combined effective tax rate for the top fifth of the population by more than 3 percent and increased the rate for those at the bottom by more than 2 percent in five years. White workers facing economic uncertainty believed that for every black person who moved forward, a white person lost ground. While complaining that welfare programs were too expensive, Reagan pushed federal spending on Cold War weaponry to almost $3 trillion. He tripled the national debt, bringing it to an all-time high during his presidency.[27]

Civil rights veteran Jesse Jackson ran for the Democratic presidential nomination in 1984 and again in 1988, on a platform opposing Reagan's economic and social conservatism. Surprisingly Jackson drew significant support even among working-class whites, but Americans retained the Republicans, first returning Reagan and then electing his vice-president, George Bush, to the White House. Reagan appointed hundreds of conservative judges to federal courts from which they could invalidate programs for racial progress. With appointments by Nixon and Reagan, the Supreme Court gradually became more conservative. In 1977 Allan Bakke, a white student denied admission to medical school at the University of California at Davis, had challenged the university's affirmative-action plan. By a single vote the Supreme Court agreed that Bakke had been discriminated against, and while it did not strike down all affirmative-action plans, it did make their implementation more difficult. In other cases in 1979 and 1980, the Court seemed to approve affirmative action as a means to equal opportunity, but by the time Reagan had appointed four judges and George Bush had appointed two, the shift to the right brought the Supreme Court firmly under conservative control.[28]

Uneven political and economic progress during the 1960s and 1970s had profoundly affected the structure of black society. Observing the changes in conditions for African Americans over the previous generation, William Julius Wilson, a black sociologist at the University of Chicago, theorized that class had become a more important factor in determining status and quality of life than race for blacks in America. In his book *The Declining Significance of Race,* Wilson noted the growth of a successful black middle class and contended that the nation was developing a permanent black underclass located primarily in the inner cities.[29] The hallmark of this underclass was a high rate of unemployment for black men and a high proportion of black households headed by single women. By 1978 40 percent of black families were headed by single women, and these family heads were generally poorly edu-cated, unskilled, low paid, or unemployed. Two-parent black families, on the other hand, were likely to have two wage earners, making a middle-class lifestyle more possible for their families. The proportion of African Americans in the middle class had increased from less than 28 percent in 1970 to more than 38 percent in 1980.[30]

The breakdown in legalized segregation made it easier for African Ameri-cans to live where they could afford to buy or rent. Although the Supreme Court had declared in 1948 that restrictive covenants (clauses in deeds that forbid selling the property to blacks or Jews) were unconstitutional, discrimination had continued. Open-housing provisions and other antidiscrimination poli-cies enacted during the 1960s and 1970s finally encouraged some change in customary segregation, and new middle class suburbs proved easiest to inte-grate. Gradually many African Americans settled in these middle-class sub-urbs, where there were better houses, better schools, and lower crime rates. The withdrawal of many middle-class blacks from the city left behind more concentrated poverty and its attendant problems, and a more isolated black lower class. The poorer inner-city population had less political power—power necessary to encourage authorities to address such growing urban prob-lems as deteriorating schools and rising crime in the face of the cutbacks in the war on poverty during the mid-1970s and the conservative 1980s. Iron-ically, many declining cities had elected black mayors. Beginning in 1967 with Carl Stokes in Cleveland, Ohio, and Richard Hatcher in Gary, Indiana, African Americans served as mayors of 135 cities by 1975. By Ronald Reagan's second term, one-third of all African Americans and two-thirds of the chil-dren living in households headed by single black women still lived in poverty, but the general perception in white America was that discrimina-tion had been overcome, and the growing black middle class was proof of the nation's success.[31]

The black middle class had made great economic progress. The incomes of college-educated and professional blacks steadily advanced, and in 1977, for example, the unemployment rate for black professional and technical work-ers was roughly one-third the unemployment rate for black workers gener-ally.[32] Though African Americans in the middle class were far more secure, when they left the ghetto, they didn't escape racism. For the black lawyer, doc-tor, or college professor, racism was generally more inconvenient and uncom-fortable than life threatening, and often more subtle than confrontational, but it was maddening and frustrating nonetheless. A Georgetown University law professor with a Ph.D. from the University of Michigan and a law degree from Harvard, who had graduated in the top 10 percent of her class, remem-bered that as a teaching fellow she was confronted by a white student who

Harold Washington

In 1983 Harold Washington built a progressive interracial coalition and became Chicago's first black mayor. Richard J. Daley had been mayor from 1955 until his death in 1976, controlling the longest-lasting political machine in the country. Washington's coalition decentralized ward politics, and the more open politics enabled Jane Byrne to be elected Chicago's first woman mayor in 1979.

Harold Washington was born on Chicago's predominantly black South Side. He served in the army during World War II, returned home, attended Roosevelt University, and earned a law degree from Northwestern University. Washington became active in Democratic state politics and served fifteen years in the Illinois House and Senate, often dissenting from the party establishment. In 1969 he helped organize a black caucus in the Illinois legislature and championed the causes of the poor, the elderly, and other minorities. Elected to the U.S. Congress, Washington was drafted to run for mayor of Chicago during his first term. He won a plurality of the vote in the 1983 Democratic mayoral primary, outdistancing the white candidates, including incumbent Byrne. In the general election state and city Democratic leaders refused to help elect a black mayor and supported the Republican candidate, but Washington's coalition of blacks, Latinos, and liberal whites swept him into office with 51.5 percent of the vote.

During his first term Washington faced a hostile city council led by members of his own party. A federal court ruling increased Washington's power base by redrawing racially discriminatory district lines, his performance in office won over some white voters, and he was reelected in 1987. Washington's administration instituted campaign finance reform, provided women and minorities with greater opportunities for city contracts, brought greater diversity to city employment, established greater equality in service delivery to poor neighborhoods, and appointed the first black police chief. At the start of his second term, on November 25, 1987, Washington suffered a massive heart attack and died before the day was over. The interracial coalition he had established disintegrated, and many feared that Chicago would return to less inclusive "politics as usual." Two years later Richard M. Daley, son of Richard J. Daley, became mayor of Chicago; he was reelected in 1991 and 1995.

Harold Washington, the first African American to hold the office of mayor of Chicago. Chicago Public Library.

asked her, "What gives you the right to teach this class?" Black scholars were assumed to be able to teach African American subjects, but regardless of their training, whites often doubted their abilities on other topics. The every-day pressures faced by middle-class blacks did not compare to those that confronted the inner-city poor, but "the pressure of being a black person under the microscope" generated anger, resentment, and debilitating stress.[33]

Some advances since the early civil rights movement provided opportunities for talented African Americans and gave the black middle class higher visibility. *Beulah, Amos 'n' Andy,* and other early television shows that featured working-class characters gave way to programs with more glamorous black roles. Bill Cosby won an Emmy Award in 1966 for his role in *I Spy,* a dramatic adventure series. Diahann Carroll brought *Julia,* a single mother with an adorable young son and a professional nursing career, to television in 1968. A year later Cosby was back, this time starring as a high school athletic coach in *The Bill Cosby Show.* Singer Della Reese briefly hosted her own show in 1969, and a host of black performers, including Flip Wilson and Redd Foxx, became television favorites in the 1970s. Alex Haley's 1976 best-selling family biography, *Roots,* attracted an audience of 130 million when it became a television miniseries the next year and was the most watched program in history. During the 1980s, surveys showed that blacks watched more television programs than whites, and networks hired more and more black actors.[34] In 1984 NBC premiered *The Cosby Show,* this time starring Bill Cosby as a black doctor married to a black lawyer living with their children in an upper-middle-class neighborhood. Though most Americans loved this show, many African Americans wondered about the impact of this highly unusual black family on white viewers' perceptions of black progress. Might the "Cosby family" become an argument for the belief that racism was no longer an impediment to black success?[35]

In other areas of popular culture, many African Americans were superstars. Black athletes dominated professional baseball, football, and basketball. Their dominance of basketball was so complete that some officials worried that white fans would not continue to follow the sport, and considered devising special programs to increase the number of white basketball players in the NBA. African Americans continued to define American popular music, as such stars as Quincy Jones, Tina Turner, Aretha Franklin, Whitney Houston, and Michael Jackson became international celebrities. In 1985 Michael Jackson's record album "Thriller" sold forty million copies, making it the best-selling record of all time, and the following year Jackson won an unprecedented eight Grammy awards.[36]

African Americans have always been important contributors to American popular culture, and they generally played visible roles in the world of entertainment. Though black people were active in shaping other aspects of the culture and were significant actors in major events, their roles have been less visible. The civil rights movement successfully attacked legal impediments to racial equality by striking down segregationist laws, but the racist assumptions underlying the inequalities remained, and those assumptions hid black achievement from view. The scholarship that followed the 1960s took on the task of examining those assumptions, and of discovering the lives, thoughts, and actions of Americans who had been excluded from the historical narrative. By its very nature this endeavor created a public role for academic history. This role of the public intellectual in African American studies was institutionalized in such organizations as the Social Policy Institute in Washington, D.C., and the W.E.B. Du Bois Center at Harvard University. Activist scholars in such institutions continued the work begun by earlier intellectuals such as Frederick Douglass, Du Bois, Pauli Murray, Zora Neale Hurston, James Baldwin, and Thurgood Marshall. The continuing study of the history and culture of African Americans led scholars to examine issues that ranged from joblessness in urban ghettos to conflicts over human rights in emerging African nations. Since such studies confronted comfortable assumptions about American society and created a different, less familiar history of the nation and its place in the world, they created a great deal of controversy and drew scholars into a contentious public arena. As it called the United States to recognize its diversity, African American history became a powerful weapon in the intensifying struggle for racial justice.

1990   Nelson Mandela, leader of the African National Congress in South Africa, freed after twenty-seven years in prison

1991   Clarence Thomas appointed to the Supreme Court after contentious Senate hearings

1992   Arkansas governor William J. Clinton elected president

      Carol Moseley Braun becomes first African American woman U.S. senator

1993   President Clinton appoints five African Americans, Michael Espy, Ronald Brown, Hazel O'Leary, and Jesse Brown, to his cabinet, and Joycelyn Elders as surgeon general

      South Africa adopts interim constitution ending apartheid

1994   Nelson Mandela elected president of South Africa

      Byron De La Beckwith convicted of Medgar Evers's murder in Mississippi more than thirty years before

1995   O. J. Simpson trial and acquittal for the murder of his wife and her friend becomes international media event

      Hundreds of thousands of black men participate in "Million-Man March" in Washington, D.C., to demonstrate commitment to families and communities

      U.S. troops join peacekeeping force in Bosnia

      Bomb destroys federal building in Oklahoma City, killing 168 people

      Truth Commission under Bishop Desmond Tutu begins to document human rights violations under apartheid in South Africa

1996   Rash of black church burnings in South prompts federal investigation

      President Clinton reelected

1997   FBI and Birmingham, Alabama, police reopen investigation of 1963 church bombing that killed four girls to consider evidence that Klansmen in addition to one convicted were involved

      Hundreds of thousands attend "Million-Women March" in Philadelphia, expressing the personal and collective concerns of black women

      White House names Presidential Advisory Board on Racial and Ethnic Relations; historian John Hope Franklin appointed chair.

1998   House Judiciary Committee holds televised impeachment hearing; House votes to impeach President Clinton for perjury and obstruction of justice in connection with his grand jury testimony regarding an intimate relationship with a White House intern

1999   Senate holds five-week-long impeachment trial of president; fails to reach two-thirds vote necessary for conviction

2000   NAACP mounts major boycott to pressure South Carolina to remove the Confederate flag from the dome of the state capitol

Race-ing to the Millennium

$\mathcal{P}$resident Ronald Reagan's much-touted "morning in America" was instead a dark time for most African Americans. This former actor presented a credulous nation with the Hollywood version of its story. He managed to assuage uneasiness about cutting benefits to the poor while redistributing resources to the affluent and greatly increasing the budget deficit and national debt. By the end of his second term, Reagan was a figure of nearly mythic proportions. In 1981 he had survived an assassin's bullet, and a year later, he reinforced his image as an unyielding free-market warrior by standing up to, and breaking, the striking air traffic controllers' union. Charging his Democratic predecessor with pessimism, he had reiterated again and again his belief that progress was unlimited in the United States for anyone with initiative and ambition.

The Reagan administration weakened the federal enforcement of civil rights laws, opposed strengthened voting rights for blacks, encouraged local opposition to busing for school integration, and attempted to eliminate the Legal Services Corporation, which provided legal aid to the poor. The Reagan Justice Department attacked the constitutionality of such affirmative-action agreements as those that had increased the number of blacks in the fire and police departments of Detroit, Boston, and New Orleans by filing suit against them in federal court. In the fall of 1983, Reagan fired three members of the federal Civil Rights Commission who opposed his efforts to reverse the advances made by 1960s civil rights laws. Drawing on the image of a fictional "welfare queen" who drove a "welfare Cadillac" and supposedly lived off the generosity of the U.S. social insurance system, Reagan cut social services to the poor. The Aid to Families with Dependent Children (AFDC) program was cut by more than 17 percent, food stamps by more than 14 percent, and community development grants by more than 37 percent; and the training and public employment program called CETA was eliminated. Reagan's tax cuts and business incentives raised the average household income of the top 1 percent of Americans by 75 percent, compared to a 7 percent rise for the 90 percent at the bottom and middle of the society. The percentage of African Americans in poverty rose from more than 30 percent in 1977 to more than 50 percent by 1993, returning to the levels of the 1950s.[1]

The distance between a small group of affluent blacks and the masses of black lower classes, begun during the 1970s, continued to grow during the 1980s. Many middle-class African Americans depended on the federal government for their employment, and the protection of federal civil service laws made them relatively secure. Their progress widened the income gap within black society, as the average yearly income of the top 5 percent of black Americans reached more than $93,000 by 1985, while the bottom 20 percent earned only about $5,000.[2] The vast majority of African Americans agreed with black journalist Carl Rowan when he wrote that Reagan's "administration encourages, subsidizes, and defends racism" and is "brutally hostile to the non-white people of America."[3] African Americans at all income levels steadfastly opposed Reagan's assault on social services and were angered by his use of oblique racial references for political advantage. They were particularly outraged at Reagan's cynical use of race as he showcased a small, but highly visible group of black conservatives who loyally supported his tactics. In 1983, in a move that horrified civil rights advocates, Reagan appointed black conservative Clarence M. Pendleton, Jr., a vigorous opponent of affirmative-action programs, to chair the National Civil Rights Commission. To head the Equal Employment Opportunity Commission, Reagan appointed Clarence Thomas, a black attorney who claimed to be "unalterably opposed to programs that force[d] or even cajole[d] people to hire a certain percentage of minorities."[4]

By the 1980s conservatism had become more sophisticated and better organized. Right-wing scholars such as economists George Gilder and Jude Waninski attacked what they considered the excesses of liberalism and provided the intellectual rationale for Reagan's economic policies. Republicans even enlisted the support of a few outspoken conservative African Americans, who shielded the Reagan administration from charges of racism as it pursued policies detrimental to general black progress. Economist Thomas Sowell of the Hoover Institute at Stanford University; former followers of Martin Luther King, Ralph Abernathy, and Hosea Williams; and former black power advocate Nathan Wright were among the small group of nationally prominent blacks to support the Republican agenda. Such black conservative academics as Shelby Steele and Glenn Loury chastised blacks for failing to take full advantage of opportunities open to them and preached that individual effort could overcome the problems of black Americans without government aid. One irony of the black conservatives' rejection of the value of government social programs was that middle-class educated blacks like themselves were the prime beneficiaries of these programs.[5]

By the mid-1980s changing policies were reflected in public opinion. In 1986 polls showed that 81 percent of white Americans opposed racial preferences in hiring and promotion as a way of redressing historic racial job discrimination, but almost 60 percent of blacks favored them. Two-thirds of whites opposed reserving places for blacks in colleges where they had been traditionally excluded, but almost three-quarters of African Americans supported such measures. Most alarming, from the standpoint of many black Americans, was the growing number of whites who argued that blacks had an unfair advantage in hiring, education, and government assistance, and charged that progressive policies had created a "reverse racism" that discriminated against whites. The Democratic presidential primaries of 1988 demonstrated both racial progress and the growing split between blacks and whites in America. Jesse Jackson, a powerful orator and popular black leader who had stood with Martin Luther King, Jr., in the civil rights campaign, made a strong showing in his second run for the presidency. Jackson won the presidential primary election in seven states and garnered nearly 25 percent of the primary vote (compared to his Democratic rival, Michael Dukakis, who won 43 percent). Jackson's vote also illustrated blacks' and whites' differing opinions. He received 92 percent of black votes but only 17 percent of white votes.[6]

During the Reagan years, rhetoric and changes in federal policies encouraged racial resentment, and when Reagan's vice president, George Bush, ran for president in 1988, his campaign played on racial fear and animosity. While Bush insisted that the country should "leave the tired baggage of bigotry behind," and said of himself, "There's not a racist bone in my body," his campaign relied heavily on stereotypes of black immorality and crime. Bush used the image of Willie Horton, a black man sentenced to life in prison in Massachusetts, to attack his Democratic opponent, Massachusetts governor Michael Dukakis. Under the state's prison furlough program, Horton had been granted a weekend pass, had escaped to Maryland, and had terrorized a white couple, beating the man and raping the woman repeatedly. The Bush campaign used this tragedy as a weapon against the Democratic candidate, labeling him a "liberal theorist" who cared more about the rights of criminals than about the safety of American families. One Republican-sponsored article appeared in the popular magazine *Reader's Digest* under the title "Getting Away with Murder" and warned that Dukakis would let criminals out of prison to commit more crimes. A flood of attacks branded Dukakis "soft on crime" and Willie Horton's dark menacing face was ubiquitous in campaign ads. Voters were told, "You, your children, your parents, and your friends can have the opportunity to receive a visit from someone like Willie Horton if Mike Dukakis becomes President."[7]

As Richard Nixon had used the call for "law and order" as a code phrase for race and the problems associated in the public mind with black people in the 1970s, the Bush campaign used crime and the name Willie Horton as codewords for race. Bush charged Dukakis with being soft on crime, and Horton came to symbolize the evidence. The message was conveyed by implication that only Republicans could save white America from that threat. The oblique racism that had become acceptable to many white Americans during the Reagan presidency became undeniably obvious in the late 1980s, despite Bush's disclaimers. Southern demagogues had used race to unite their white supporters for most of the twentieth century; Reagan's allusions to "welfare queens" had garnered support for cuts in social welfare; and Bush also found race a useful political tool. The Willie Horton campaign strategy was effective, front-runner Dukakis lost ground dramatically, and George Bush was elected to the presidency in 1988.

Since 90 percent of black voters had cast their ballots for Dukakis, George Bush had little political reason to focus on issues of importance to African Americans. He named two African Americans to important cabinet posts, Gen. Colin Powell as chairman of the Joint Chiefs of Staff and Louis Sullivan as the secretary of health and human services. These were popular appointments, but his veto of such measures as the Civil Rights Act of 1990, a bill to make voter registration easier, and an extension of unemployment benefits led to doubts that African Americans or the poor could expect much aid from the Bush administration. Nor could they expect support from the increasingly conservative federal courts filled with Republican appointments. Early in 1990 President Bush ignited a storm of controversy by nominating the black conservative head of the Equal Employment Opportunity Commission, Clarence Thomas, to replace longtime black civil rights advocate Thurgood Marshall on the Supreme Court. Thomas's nomination split African American organizations and leaders, who were torn between pride at maintaining a black presence on the court and fears about his conservatism and the consequences for beleaguered civil rights legislation. Serious questions about Thomas's qualifications and competence were obscured during the Senate hearings by the controversy over accusations by African American law professor Anita Hill that Thomas had sexually harassed her during the years she had worked for him at the Department of Education and EEOC. The nationally televised questioning and testimony by Hill and Thomas focused the debate on the seemingly conflicting issues of women's rights and black rights and drew the nation into the question of Hill's believability. Some black women joined the attacks on Hill, seeing her accusations against a prominent black man as disloyalty to the race. The case spawned an intense debate within the black community with conflicting views on Hill's responsibility to women and her right to publicly criticize Thomas. After contentious discussions the Senate confirmed Clarence Thomas's appointment to the Supreme Court.[8]

George Bush presided over a period of extended recession, a costly federal bailout of savings and loan associations, increasing trade deficits, industrial

The African American Civil War Memorial in Washington, D.C.
Courtesy of Frank Smith.

plant closings, business failures, and an ineffectual "war on drugs" with its associated crime affecting the central cities. The gap between the rich and poor continued to widen, and the black urban poor were particularly hard hit. In January 1991 the nation became involved in an extended war against Iraq, fighting for oil, as Bush confirmed. Although African Americans were just over 13 percent of the population, they were 25 percent of the troops who fought in the war in the Middle East. Support for the war was divided along racial lines. An ABC News/*Washington Post* poll taken in early 1991 revealed that 84 percent of whites but only 48 percent of blacks backed America's pursuit of the war.[9]

According to historians John Hope Franklin and Alfred A. Moss, Jr., the "frustration and rage" of urban blacks in the face of a multiplicity of economic and social problems found cultural expression in the new musical forms of rap and hip-hop. In April 1992 a more threatening expression of black alien-ation was broadcast to American homes when riots erupted in Los Angeles in response to the acquittal of four white policemen who had been videotaped beating a black man named Rodney King after apprehending him in a high-speed car chase. Tensions were heightened by the fact that there were no blacks on the jury in the policemen's lengthy trial. The four days of rioting that erupted in response to this verdict resulted in thirty-eight deaths, four thou-sand arrests, 3,700 burned-out buildings, damage estimated at five hundred million dollars, and a great deal of conflict between racial and ethnic groups in the multiethnic city. The renewed importance of the issues of race and poverty was apparent that spring as President Bush and presidential candi-date Bill Clinton visited Los Angeles in the aftermath of the riots.[10]

By 1992 the United States had experienced twelve consecutive years of conservative Republican presidencies. For most black Americans these had been difficult times of rising poverty and crime rates and shrinking social ser-vices, increasing health needs and decreasing health services, and a widen-ing gap between the financial assets of black households and white households. Under these circumstances the rhetoric of William Jefferson Clinton, the Demo-cratic candidate for the presidency that year, had great appeal. Clinton called for greater economic equity, sustainable job growth, and a social service sys-tem that would benefit middle- and lower-income Americans. He spoke to African Americans, face to face, in their churches and community organiza-tions, with sincerity and conviction, restoring the hope that had been miss-ing for more than a decade. He promised a diverse presidential cabinet that would represent Americans of all races and include many women. Clinton won the presidency with only 43 percent of the popular vote, but blacks voted for him in overwhelming numbers, with 82 percent casting Democratic bal-lots.[11] The victory celebration during the inauguration week in January 1993 promised a new era. That week President-elect Bill Clinton and his wife, Hillary, and Vice President–elect Al Gore and his wife, Tipper, sang "We Are the World" with their multiracial, multicultural supporters, and during the inauguration ceremony, black poet Maya Angelou told the excited multitude:

Lift up your eyes upon
This day breaking before you.
Give birth again
To the dream.[12]

The new president's cabinet met his supporters' expectations. Clinton appointed Latino Henry Cisneros as secretary of housing and urban development, African Americans Ronald Brown as secretary of commerce, Mike Espy as secretary of agriculture, Hazel O'Leary as secretary of energy, Jesse Brown as secretary of veterans affairs, Joycelyn Elders as surgeon general, and a host of other blacks to high-ranking positions in his administration. However, African American reaction to the first Clinton administration was mixed. Clinton was outspoken and supportive of liberal positions on social issues, but his positions on economic issues did not depart dramatically from those of his Republican predecessor. Clinton focused on the need for more police to fight urban crime, promoted programs for bettering community relations with police, and spoke about getting tough with criminals. Yet this focus seemed to ignore the connection between poverty and crime. In 1995 black unemployment remained twice the level of whites'.[13] Though African Americans were likely to be the victims of crime, without programs to expand economic opportunities, the Clinton crime initiative seemed to reinforce conservative assumptions that African Americans were more likely to be criminals. Clinton's political strategy, however, did refocus assumptions about crime by discussing the issue in meetings with members of the black community.

During the Reagan/Bush years, many whites had grown increasingly impatient with arguments that stressed the continuing significance of racism in American life. A growing number of whites believed that blacks received unfair advantages and preferential treatment. One poll showed that two-thirds of white Americans believed that most poor blacks were responsible for their own condition. More Americans reported living in integrated neighborhoods than a generation earlier, but stereotypical beliefs persisted about blacks being prone to crime, lacking in ambition, and not as smart as whites. Such attitudes were reinforced by a popular book entitled *The Bell Curve,* published by Richard Herrnstein and Charles Murray in 1994, which claimed to have found important connections between race and intelligence. This controversial study suggested that African Americans were genetically limited and best suited for society's lower-level jobs. Providing an apparently scientific rationale, this study gave conservative policy makers an argument for opposing affirmative-action programs that sought to remedy discrimination in employment or promotions without seeming to be prejudiced. Perhaps, they could argue, African Americans lacked the ability for more demanding positions.

By the mid-1990s political conservatives led by such Republican spokesmen as former presidential candidate Patrick Buchanan had joined such conservative religious leaders as Ralph Reed and his political Christian Coalition to attack affirmative-action programs in colleges and universities, in businesses, and in governmental employment. They believed the role of colleges and universities to be particularly dangerous. One outcome of the modern civil rights movement was exemplified by student demands for the establishment of African American Studies programs and resulted in an effort to rediscover the African American role in the creation of American history and culture. Developments in African American history since the 1970s had led scholars to rethink the central themes of the nation's development, recognizing the centrality of race, ethnicity, class, and eventually gender in shaping the way Americans see themselves and their society. Many of these scholars were inspired by the social activism of the 1960s and 1970s to pursue scholarship that contributed directly to progress in human rights. As their work challenged traditional historical interpretations, it came under attack from political conservatives unwilling to consider any but celebratory European-dominated conceptions of the American past. In the process the debates over historical authority, the legitimacy of historical sources, and revisions of the historical canon became central to the public discussion of such policy issues as affirmative action in education and employment, curriculum revision, social assistance and welfare, and the role of government in a democratic capitalist society.

A vast array of studies by a generation of scholars examined the institution of slavery and its economic, social, and political impact on America; the influence of Africa and African cultures on the United States and western culture; and the importance of the black family, community, and cooperative institutions in the survival and progress of black America. Scholars studied interethnic and interracial relationships in the conflicts and accommodations of a multicultural society and noted the significance of race for understanding the development of western civilization, illuminating the social psychology of black and white Americans, and creating the nation's identity. Conservative critics claimed that these efforts to tell the story of a more racially inclusive American history were dangerous and would eventually lead to the destruction of American civilization. During his 1992 run for the Republican presidential nomination, Buchanan had charged that there was under way a struggle for "the soul of America . . . a cultural war, as critical to the kind of nation we will one day be as was the Cold War itself."[14]

There were also disputes over the interpretation of history and culture within black society. Louis Farrakhan had established a new branch of the Nation of Islam as an offshoot of the Black Muslims in 1978 and become the major voice of black nationalism during the 1980s. Born Louis Eugene Walcott in 1933 in the Bronx, New York, to a mother who had emigrated from the West Indies, he had worked in New York and Boston as a musician, singing and playing the violin and the piano. Modeling himself on Malcolm X, Farrakhan spoke out against racism and urged black pride and autonomy. His anti-Semitic statements, however, created conflicts between him, the NAACP, and other traditional civil rights organizations, as well as antagonism between the Nation of Islam and the American Jewish community. Relations between blacks and Jews were further strained in 1991 by the publication of *The Secret Relationship between Blacks and Jews*, a book published by the Nation of Islam charging that Jews had financed and dominated the slave trade, a charge echoed later that year by Leonard Jeffries, then the head of the Black Studies Department at the City College of New York.[15] Tensions between blacks and Jews also underlay race riots in the Crown Heights section of Brooklyn in 1991 in which blacks and Hasidic Jews were pitted against one another. Black and Jewish civil rights leaders became concerned about a potentially permanent rift between these traditional allies. Around the country they attempted to reestablish more amicable relations by organizing informal groups to discuss conflicts arising from Farrakhan's remarks but also covering long-standing tensions associated with such issues as black nationalist support for Palestine, Jesse Jackson's ill-conceived anti-Semitic remarks during his presidential campaign, lingering antagonisms from conflicts over Jewish ownership of stores in black ghettos, and Jewish opposition to affirmative action.

In the fall of 1995 reactions to the verdict in the murder trial of former football star O. J. Simpson brought blacks' and whites' conflicting perceptions of America's racial situation into stark relief. When Simpson was acquitted of brutally murdering his wife, Nicole, and her friend Ronald Goldman, television networks carried pictures of gatherings of elated African Americans and interviews with disbelieving whites. Discussions ensued about the historical treatment of black men by the police and the courts. Disagreements over the justice of the Simpson verdict were heated. In the middle of the controversy, African Americans answered Louis Farrakhan's call for a million black men to march on Washington to demonstrate solidarity, strength, and support for black family and community. The success of this Million-Man March, as it was called, demonstrated that many of the broad concerns articulated by Farrakhan—ranging from disappointment that the civil rights movement

A poster from the Million-Man March
in Washington, D.C., October 16, 1995.
Gelman Library Photographic Collection, George Washington University.

had not brought true equality to fears that many of the gains of the 1970s
were being reversed and that economic conditions were worsening for lower-
class blacks—resonated with African American society.

In 1997 President Clinton encouraged debate on racial issues and called
for Americans to hold conversations on race as one way to encourage a dia-
logue across the color line. To lead his commission on race in the United States,
Clinton appointed Professor John Hope Franklin, one of America's most
accomplished and respected scholars and the best-known African American
historian in the country. Commission members had difficulty agreeing on how
to define the nation's racial problem. Some, including Chairman Franklin,
argued that the position of African Americans and the relative positions of
blacks and whites was of fundamental importance in American history and
culture. The troubled history of the difference between blacks and whites
defined the issues on which the adaptations of all other groups depended. Thus,
they argued, black-white issues constituted the commission's primary man-

John Hope Franklin

Born in the all-black town of Rentiesville, Oklahoma, John Hope Franklin is the son of Buck Colbert Franklin, a lawyer, and Mollie Parker Franklin, an elementary schoolteacher. He was deeply influenced by his father's practice of law and accompanied him to court on many occasions. On one occasion young John Hope stood watching as his father presented a motion to the court. Those in the courtroom were amused at the sight of the bright young boy so obviously engrossed in the proceedings. When the judge addressed the six-year-old, asking about his future plans, John Hope replied, "I intend to be the first Negro president of the United States when I grow up." The judge laughed heartily, and even Buck Franklin was startled at his son's answer. Here was a person of great determination who would make his mark on the nation.

In 1921 Buck Franklin left the family temporarily in Rentiesville to set up a law office in Tulsa. There he witnessed a race riot during which whites destroyed the buildings in the city's black community, including his new law office. These and many other experiences during the Jim Crow era in segregated Oklahoma helped shape John Hope Franklin's commitment to civil rights and human equality. He went on to earn a B.A. at Fisk University in 1935 and a Ph.D. in history at Harvard University in 1941. His long and distinguished career combines scholarship and social activism, beginning with his undergraduate years at Fisk, when he carried a protest against lynching all the way to the White House. During the 1940s and 1950s he was an expert witness on segregation in higher education for the NAACP. He also served on

John Hope Franklin autographing one of his books at the Schomburg Center for Research in Black Culture in New York City. Photographs and Prints Division, Schomburg Center for Research in Black Culture, The New York Public Library, Astor, Lenox, and Tilden Foundations.

(continued)

(continued)

the NAACP research team for the case that ultimately produced the 1954 landmark Supreme Court *Brown* v. *Board of Education* decision, which declared segregation in public education unconstitutional.

John Hope Franklin's scholarship spans more than a half century. Perhaps his greatest contribution has been the scholarly rigor with which his books on southern history and African American history have set the issue of race within the mainstream of American history. Franklin's academic career has been extraordinary, and in addition to mentoring and inspiring a generation of prominent and promising historians, he has led the faculties of such respected institutions as Howard University, Brooklyn College, and the University of Chicago, and served as president of most of the major professional historical associations. He has been the subject of a major television film, has been awarded more than seventy honorary degrees by colleges and universities around the nation, and is the James B. Duke Professor of History Emeritus at Duke University. When President Bill Clinton sought a respected scholar and a great moral presence to head his Advisory Committee on Race, he selected John Hope Franklin for that difficult task.

date. Others believed that race had become such a complex issue that the problems of other racial and ethnic groups, such as Asians and Hispanics, were not necessarily subsumed under the issues of black and white. They argued for a much broader consideration that encompassed many ethnicities. The commission held hearings throughout the country, and the president himself took part in public conversations on race, but ultimately the topic proved difficult to focus and left the public with a sense that little had been accomplished.

In the academic world, however, the study and discussion of race flourished during the 1990s. As early as 1911 anthropologist Franz Boas had challenged the idea that race was based on systematic biological differences. By the end of the twentieth century most scholars agreed that race is not a biological phenomenon but is socially constructed. Historians have noted that racial designations changed over time to fit social needs and reflected political and economic power. They illustrated the mutability and constructed nature of race by showing that during the era of Jim Crow segregation, state laws created different definitions of race. In the early twentieth century Texas, Tennessee, and Alabama declared that a person with any African ancestry at all was a Negro, whereas in Virginia or Kentucky those with less than one-sixteenth African ancestry were defined as white, and in Florida any person with less than one-eighth African ancestry was considered white. Thus a person might have legally changed races by moving to a different state. Mississippi prohibited the marriage of a white person and a black person, but permitted marriage between a white person and a person with less than one-eighth African ancestry.[16] During the 1920s Virginia drew racial distinctions between whites and American Indians but ruled that white persons could retain their racial standing if their American Indian heritage was traceable to Pocahontas. This was done mainly for the benefit of those affluent and politically powerful white families who believed they gained status by tracing their roots to the famous seventeenth-century Indian "princess."

Clearly race was a matter of law and convenience, not biology, and a series of publications under the new category of "whiteness studies" during the mid-1990s demonstrated the artificiality of the racial categories created by the powerful for their own benefit. Such works as *The Wages of Whiteness* and *Toward the Abolition of Whiteness,* by David Roediger; *How the Irish Became White,* by Noel Ignatiev; and *Race Traitor,* by Ignatiev and John Garvey; challenged the conventions of race, called for racial tolerance and equality, and noted the unfair privileges associated with a white identity. In *The Possessive Investment in Whiteness* George Lipsitz calculated the economic value of whiteness and found that discriminatory governmental policies in the allocation of home loans helped create the significant gap in wealth between the races still visible in the late 1990s. Great appreciation in property values over three decades allowed white parents to pass substantial wealth to children maturing in the 1980s and 1990s. Denied the same opportunities to purchase homes in the 1950s and 1960s, most African American parents thus had far less wealth to pass along to their offspring. Therefore, even though wage gaps narrowed slightly between blacks and whites, and the household income of two-parent black middle-class families approached that of white middle-class families, African Americans possessed less wealth than whites at comparable income levels.[17]

At the beginning of the twenty-first century, Americans still wrestle with the dilemma of race. W.E.B. Du Bois's prediction that the central problem of the twentieth century would be the color line proved remarkably accurate. However, the meaning and the consequences of race have changed. Race no longer defines the line between freedom and slavery. It is no longer a legal divide that defines place and opportunity in American society. African Americans exercise considerably more political power than at any time in history. Although perceptions differ about the remaining need for redressing past disabilities, it is more difficult for politicians to create policies and laws without considering the African American presence.

Within the middle class at least, the United States is a more integrated society. The influence of black culture is apparent in literature, film, music, and television programming. Few Americans are aware of the extent to which Africans helped shape the very foundations of American culture, but most are aware of the importance of black styles and traditions in the modern United States. Changes in media coverage, the integration of programming, and the higher visibility of black participation in mainstream sports, entertainment, and political life created awareness of the United States as a multiracial society. Greater integration and acceptance for the black middle class, however, has accentuated the gap between it and the poor and reinforced negative stereotypes of the black urban lower class. The popularity of public policies that blame the supposed characteristics and values of the poor for their own problems have focused attention particularly on lower-class African Americans and allowed politicians to play on fears about black crime. Despite the progress of the black middle class, race is still closely linked to economic, educational, political, and social standing.

In the poorest segments of today's African American community, it is difficult to focus on the progress made in the last few generations. There the unemployment rate is two, three, or more times higher than in the society at large. In poor urban areas people's vulnerability to crime and drug addiction is debilitating. Young people, in particular, have few attractive choices. What New York congressman Major Owens observed in 1989 remains true today, many young, black, unemployed males "have a choice between zero and the drug trade."[18] The appearance of crack cocaine in the inner city during the early 1980s exacerbated an already critical situation. Extremely addictive and relatively inexpensive, crack was widely available from the mid-1980s. As a result of the growing drug addiction and increasing sales in inner-city black neighborhoods, the arrest and incarceration rate of young black men increased dramatically. Racial disparities also increased as new laws punished crack users and dealers particularly severely. They are more likely to be sent to jail and to receive longer sentences, for example, than cocaine users, who are more likely to be middle class and white. African Americans' general suspicions about the police and the legal system, born of negative experiences over a long history, have led some to see the availability of crack in the inner city as a systematic plot against black communities. A survey taken in 1990 revealed that an astounding 67 percent of college-educated African Americans believed in, or at least would not dismiss the possibility of, such a plot.[19] Such beliefs may perhaps be understandable, since the police have been more intent on controlling than protecting black people for most of the nation's history. Media accounts of violence and crime in poor black communities that generally portray blacks as the perpetrators rather than the victims of crime do little to counteract poor blacks' sense of injustice. A 1993 study of Chicago's predominantly black South Side found that most people worried about their community becoming more dangerous. As one respondent put it, "More people are dying and being killed" as a result of rising crime in the neighborhood. Yet even today, a call for law and order conjures up images of black lawlessness and dangers in the minds of the majority of white middle-class people. Ironically white middle-class residences are far less vulnerable to crime than are those in the inner city.[20] Most hopeful is the growing use of community policing projects to "take back the night," projects in which hundreds of neighbors parole their communities, forming partnerships with the police to discourage crime. Boston, parts of New York City, and other cities showed encouraging progress, and by the end of the 1990s, the overall rate of violent crime declined. A historical view of crime in America gives a better understanding of both the long-standing black vulnerability to white fears and the dangers criminals have posed to residents of poor black communities.

The best historical scholarship of the past generation has rediscovered the history and culture of black America. Under the influence of the civil rights movement of the 1950s and 1960s, scholars redoubled their efforts to research and write about the common people in history. This new social history led to a renaissance in African American history, as well as in labor history, women's history, and ethnic histories. The portrait these histories have painted is of an America that was a multiracial society from the first European settlement. They have demonstrated that the millions of Africans who were forced to migrate to the New World not only contributed a large part of the labor on which the country's wealth was built, they also helped shape its very culture as they brought their skills, languages, music, art, religions, values, and philosophies. Part of African Americans' contribution to the United States came from their dreams while an enslaved people. From the very beginning of their enslavement, Africans struggled to be free. They engaged in fierce rebellions, they sabotaged the work process, they ran away, and they used slave owners' own religious and philosophical principles to argue for their freedom. When emancipation, both immediate and gradual, came to northern states in the aftermath of the Revolutionary War, freed blacks organized to protest southern slavery and to work for full citizenship for all African Americans. Black Americans fought in every American war and each time were asked to prove themselves and their commitment to the country. Each time they fought overseas, they returned to face racial inequality at home. From the earliest days of the Republic, African Americans spoke as the conscience of a nation that preached human freedom and equality. With their long tradition of protest and commitment to the struggle for freedom, contemporary black leaders and organizations continue to call on the United States to live up to its principles.

Throughout American history, new immigrant populations have entered a racial reality that slavery and segregation first created in black and white.

In earlier times ethnic immigrants fitted into this bipolar system, but today integration, black political power, and greater global awareness have created a much more complex world of color. Changes in the immigration laws in the mid-1960s opened the United States to non-Europeans as never before in the twentieth century. Although more than 60 percent of the nation's foreign-born residents are white, 20 percent are Asians and Pacific Islanders. More than 7 percent of the newcomers are black. Latinos, who may be of any race, account for more than 45 percent of foreign immigrants. At the beginning of the twentieth century 85 percent of the nation's immigrants came from Europe. Today Mexico accounts for the largest number of immigrants. Clearly Americans are changing, and although the nation has always had a multiracial and multicultural population, by the beginning of the twenty-first century it had become increasingly difficult to pretend otherwise.[21]

In the early decades of the new millennium, nonwhite Americans, including Hispanics, will constitute the majority of the population. This reality may demand a rethinking of traditional political and social alliances. It may even provide the opportunity for a reconsideration of the definition of race. The future challenges for black America are to seek new opportunities for political action by joining with people of other colors, including progressive whites and people of all ethnicities; to bridge the chasm of class within black society; and to continue the struggle along the hard road to freedom, justice, and equality.

Notes

Introduction

1. William L. Andrews, *To Tell a Free Story: The First Century of Afro-American Autobiography, 1760–1865* (Urbana: University of Illinois Press, 1986).
2. R.J.M. Blackett, *Beating against the Barriers: Biographical Essays in Nineteenth-Century Afro-American History* (Baton Rouge: Louisiana State University Press, 1986); James Oliver Horton and Lois E. Horton, *Black Bostonians: Family Life and Community Struggle in the Antebellum North,* rev. ed. (New York: Holmes and Meier Publishers Inc., 1999).
3. John Hope Franklin, *George Washington Williams: A Biography* (Chicago: University of Chicago Press, 1985).
4. Northwestern University awarded a Ph.D. to Rufus Clement in 1930; Benjamin Quarles received his doctorate from the University of Wisconsin in 1940; and John Hope Franklin received a Ph.D. from Harvard University in 1941.

Chapter 1 ▪ *Africa and the Atlantic Slave Trade*

1. Olaudah Equiano, *The Interesting Narrative of the Life of Olaudah Equiano, or Gustavus Vassa, the African* (1789), reprinted in *Great Slave Narratives,* edited by Arna Bontemps (Boston: Beacon Press, 1969), 7. Recently discovered documents have led scholars to question whether Equiano's description of Africa was based on personal experience or oral history. See Vincent Carratta, "Olaudah Equiano or Gustavas Vasa? New Light on an Eighteenth-Century Question of Identity," *Slavery and Abolition* 20:3 (1999), 96–105.
2. Philip Curtin, Steven Feierman, Leonard Thompson, and Jan Vansina, *African History,* 9th ed. (New York: Longmans, 1991); A. J. Arkell, *A History of Sudan from the Earliest Times to 1821* (University of London Athlone Press, 1961).
3. Basil Davidson, *The Search for Africa: History, Culture, Politics* (New York: Random House, 1994), 73; Colin A. Palmer, *Passageways: An Interpretive History of Black America, 1619–1863,* vol. 1 (Fort Worth, Tex.: Harcourt Brace College Publishers, 1998), 5.
4. Quoted from Philip S. Foner, *History of Black Americans,* vol. 1 (Westport, Conn.: Greenwood Press, 1975), 40–41. See also Jean Rouch, *Les Songhay* (Paris: Presses Universitaires de France, 1954), and R. E. Bradbury, *The Benin Kingdom and the Edo-speaking Peoples of Southwestern Nigeria* (London: International African Institute, 1957).
5. John Hope Franklin and Alfred P. Moss, Jr., *From Slavery to Freedom: A History of Negro Americans,* 6th ed. (New York: Knopf, 1988).
6. Foner, *History of Black Americans,* vol. 1, 43–47.
7. David Brion Davis, *The Problem of Slavery in Western Culture* (Ithaca, N.Y.: Cornell University Press, 1966), 52; Ronald Sanders, *Lost Tribes and Promised Lands: The Origins of American Racism* (New York: Harper Perennial, 1992); Curtin et al., *African History,* 183–189.

8. Philip D. Curtin, "Migration in the Tropical World," *Immigration Reconsidered,* edited by Virginia Yans-McLaughlin (New York: Oxford University Press, 1990), 21–36.

9. Slaves in Africa retained an acknowledged humanness, for slavery was a condition of their lives and a status of the society into which they had fallen. Slavery was not, as it would later become in the United States, a racially defined, permanent state connoting a supposed genetic inferiority.

10. Equiano in Bontemps, *Great Slave Narratives,* 11.

11. Donald R. Wright, *African Americans in the Colonial Era: From African Origins through the American Revolution* (Arlington Heights, Ill.: Harlan Davidson, Inc., 1990). Dahomey was most transformed by its access to firearms and became committed to the slave trade as the principle foundation of its national economy by the early sixteenth century. The Dutch established trade in Allada, the major trading state in the region, before the end of the century. See I. A. Akinjogbin, *Dahomey and Its Neighbors, 1708–1818* (Cambridge, England: Cambridge University Press, 1967).

12. Colin Palmer, "African Slave Trade: The Cruelest Commerce," *National Geographic* 182:3 (September 1992), 67–68.

13. Akinjogbin, *Dahomey.*

14. Sanders, *Lost Tribes,* 17.

15. Davis, *The Problem of Slavery,* 53.

16. Winthrop D. Jordan, *White over Black: American Attitudes Towards the Negro, 1550–1812* (Chapel Hill, N.C.: University of North Carolina Press, 1968), 7.

17. Equiano in Bontemps, *Great Slave Narratives,* 28–29.

18. Ibid., 30.

19. Jay Coughtry, *The Notorious Triangle: Rhode Island and the African Slave Trade, 1700–1807* (Philadelphia: Temple University Press, 1981).

20. Alexander Falconbridge, *An Account of the Slave Trade on the Coast of Africa* (London, 1788), 16–22.

21. William Loren Katz, *Eyewitness: The Negro in American History* (Belmont, Calif.: Fearon Pitman Publishers, Inc., 1974), 6.

22. "Samuel Waldo to Captain Samuel Rhodes, 1734," in *Documents Illustrative of the History of the Slave Trade in America,* vol. 3, edited by Elizabeth Donnan (Washington, D.C.: Carnegie Institution of Washington, 1932), 45.

23. Vincent Harding, *There Is a River: The Black Struggle for Freedom in America* (New York: Harcourt Brace Jovanovich, Publishers, 1981), 12–13.

24. Ivan van Sertima, *They Came before Columbus* (New York: Random House, 1976).

25. William D. Piersen, *From Africa to America: African American History from the Colonial Era to the Early Republic, 1526–1790* (New York: Twayne Publishers, 1996), 37–44.

26. Germany later broadened its participation in the slave trade but never became a dominant player, in large part because it did not develop substantial American holdings.

27. Wright, *African Americans in the Colonial Era,* 40.

28. Darold Wax, "Preferences for Slaves in Colonial America," *Journal of Negro History* 58:4 (1973), 375–376.

29. Curtin, Feierman, Thompson, and Vansina, *African History,* 219–221.

Chapter 2 ▪ **The Evolution of Slavery in British North America**

1. Winthrop D. Jordan, *White over Black: American Attitudes toward the Negro, 1550–1812* (New York: W. W. Norton, 1977), 75, 79.

2. Jordan, *White over Black,* 75.

3. Jordan, *White over Black,* 81.

4. David Brion Davis, *The Problem of Slavery in Western Culture* (Ithaca, N.Y.: Cornell University Press, 1966), 102.

5. Paul C. Palmer, "Servants into Slaves: The Evolution of the Legal Status of the Negro Laborer in Colonial Virginia," *South Atlantic Quarterly* 65 (Summer 1966).

6. *Pennsylvania Gazette,* October 8, 1747; *Journal and Baltimore Advisor,* October 10, 1779.

7. Carl N. Degler, "Slavery and the Genesis of Race Prejudice," *Comparative Studies in Society and History* 2 (1959), 61.

8. Edward Pearson, "From Stono to Vesey: Slavery, Resistance, and Ideology in South Carolina, 1739–1822" (Ph.D. dissertation, University of Wisconsin, 1991). Pearson provides an account of the establishment of slavery in South Carolina and the transition from timber producing and herding to rice cultivation. He offers a fascinating argument on the impact of this transition on the gender conventions of African slaves. Donald R. Wright, *African Americans in the Colonial Era: From African Origins through the American Revolution* (Arlington Heights, Ill.: Harlan Davidson, Inc., 1990), 67; Ira Berlin, *Many Thousands Gone: The First Two Centuries of Slavery in North America* (Cambridge, Mass.: Harvard University Press, 1998), 149, 370. Slaveholders believed that Africans were immune to malaria. This was not true, but many Africans did display a resistance to the disease that was greater than that of Europeans.

9. Philip D. Morgan, *Slave Counterpoint: Black Culture in the Eighteenth-Century Chesapeake & Lowcountry* (Chapel Hill: University of North Carolina Press, 1998), 394, 264–265.

10. William Loren Katz, *Eyewitness: The Negro in American History* (Belmont, Calif.: Fearon Pitman Publishers, Inc., 1974), 22.

11. Darold Wax, "Georgia and the Negro before the American Revolution," *Georgia Historical Quarterly* 51 (March 1967), 63–75.

12. Berlin, *Many Thousands Gone,* 369–370.

13. William D. Piersen, *From Africa to America: African American History from the Colonial Era to the Early Republic, 1526–1790* (New York: Twayne Publishers, 1996), 57–65; Philip S. Foner, *History of Black Americans,* vol. 1 (Westport, Conn.: Greenwood Press, 1975), 228; Clement Alexander Price, *Freedom Not Far Distant: A Documentary History of Afro-Americans in New Jersey* (Newark: New Jersey Historical Society, 1980), 35. Population numbers are estimates, since there was no official Pennsylvania census during the colonial period.

14. Gary Nash, *Forging Freedom: The Formation of Philadelphia's Black Community, 1720–1840* (Cambridge, Mass.: Harvard University Press, 1988); Israel Acrelius, *A History of New Sweden; or, The Settlements on the Delaware* (Philadelphia: Historical Society of Pennsylvania, 1874); Katz, *Eyewitness,* 23.

15. Jean R. Soderlund, *Quakers and Slavery: A Divided Spirit* (Princeton, N.J.: Princeton University Press, 1985), 15–16.

16. New York and New Jersey blacks frequently spoke both English and Dutch because the area was controlled by the Netherlands until the 1660s. *Pennsylvania Gazette,* September 24, 1741; June 6, 1746; July 31, 1740; July 4, 1745; September 20, 1764; *New York Gazette,* July 31, 1766.

17. A. Leon Higginbotham, Jr., *In the Matter of Color: Race and the American Legal Process: The Colonial Period* (New York: Oxford University Press, 1978); Joyce D. Goodfriend, *Before the Melting Pot: Society and Culture in Colonial New York City, 1664–1730* (Princeton, N.J.: Princeton University Press, 1992), 111–132. See also Shane White, *Somewhat More Independent: The End of Slavery in New York City, 1770–1810* (Athens: University of Georgia Press, 1991), and Edgar J. McManus, *Black Bondage in the North* (Syracuse, N.Y.: Syracuse University Press, 1973), 57–58.

18. Ira Berlin, "Time, Space, and the Evolution of Afro-American Society," *American Historical Review* 85 (February 1980), 44–78; McManus, *Black Bondage,* 84.

19. McManus, *Black Bondage,* 208–211; White, *Somewhat More Independent,* 3.

20. James Oliver Horton and Lois E. Horton, *In Hope of Liberty: Culture, Community, and Protest among Northern Free Blacks* (New York: Oxford University Press, 1977), 10, 37.

21. Jane G. Austin, *Dr. LeBaron and His Daughters* (Cambridge, Mass.: Riverside Press / Boston: Houghton, Mifflin & Co., 1892), 55.

22. Austin, *Dr. LeBaron,* 91.

23. Arthur Zilversmit, *The First Emancipation: The Abolition of Slavery in the North* (Chicago: University of Chicago Press, 1967), 33; James A. Henretta, "Economic Development and Social Structure in Colonial Boston," *William and Mary Quarterly* 22 (1965), 75–92; Lorenzo J. Greene, *The Negro in Colonial New England 1620–1766* (1942; reprint, N.Y.: Atheneum Press, 1968), 84.

24. Greene, *The Negro in Colonial New England;* Piersen, *Black Yankee;* Nash, *The Urban Crucible.* See also Robert C. Twombly and Robert M. Moore, "Black Puritan: The Negro in Seventeenth Century Massachusetts," *William and Mary Quarterly,* 3rd series, 24 (April 1967), 224–242.

25. Higginbotham, *In The Matter of Color,* 203.

26. The Stono Rebellion is described in chapter 3.

27. Peter Wood, *Black Majority: Negroes in Colonial South Carolina from 1670 through the Stono Rebellion* (New York: W. W. Norton, 1974), 152.

28. Free blacks were taxed more heavily than whites and had to pay a poll tax from age twelve. Whites did not have to pay the poll tax until age sixteen. After 1760 blacks were required to possess fifty acres of land in order to be eligible to vote. There is reason to believe that some free blacks in South Carolina voted. See Higginbotham, *In the Matter of Color,* 204.

29. See examples of conspiratorial free blacks in Robert Olwell, "Becoming Free: Manumission and the Genesis of a Free Black Community in South Carolina, 1740–90," in Jane Landers, ed., *Against the Odds: Free Blacks in the Slave Societies of the Americas* (Portland, Ore.: Frank Cass, 1996), 1–19.

30. *New England Weekly Journal,* May 1, 1732.

31. Katz, *Eyewitness,* 24.

32. Winthrop Jordan, *White over Black,* 139; Greene, *The Negro in Colonial New England;* Debra L. Newman, "Black Women in the Era of the American Revolution in Pennsylvania," *Journal of Negro History* 61:3 (July 1976), 276–289.

33. Horton and Horton, *In Hope of Liberty,* 30–54; Katz, Eyewitness, 27.

34. Horton and Horton, *In Hope of Liberty,* 39.

35. Jack D. Forbes, *Black Africans and Native Americans: Color, Race, Cast in the Evolution of Red-Black Peoples* (New York: Basil Blackwell, 1988).

36. Lamont D. Thomas, *Rise to Be a People: A Biography of Paul Cuffe* (Urbana: University of Illinois Press, 1986).

37. Horton and Horton, *In Hope of Liberty.*

38. Alice Morse Earle, *Colonial Days in Old New York* (1896; reprint, New York: Empire Book Company, 1926), 196–200. See also White, *Somewhat More Independent;* and Sterling Stuckey, *Slave Culture: Nationalist Theory and the Foundations of Black America* (New York: Oxford University Press, 1987).

39. Albert J. Raboteau, *Slave Religion: The "Invisible Institution" in the Antebellum South* (New York: Oxford University Press, 1978), 15; Berlin, *Many Thousands Gone.*

40. Samuel E. Morrison, "A Poem on Election Day in Massachusetts about 1760," *Proceedings of the Colonial Society of Massachusetts* 18 (February 1915), 54–61.

41. Eileen Southern, ed., *Readings in Black American Music* (New York: W. W. Norton, 1971), 41.
42. Wood, *Black Majority.*
43. Reports by eighteenth-century European doctors traveling in West Africa and anthropological studies in the twentieth century confirm that inoculation was an ancient practice in West Africa. For an important recent argument on the impact of African medicine on American medicine see William D. Piersen, *Black Legacy: American's Hidden Heritage* (Amherst: University of Massachusetts Press, 1993), 101–102.
44. Ibid.

Chapter 3 ▪ *Slavery and Freedom in the Age of Revolution*

1. Robert Olwell, *Masters, Slaves and Subjects: The Culture of Power in the South Carolina Low Country, 1740–1790* (Ithaca, N.Y.: Cornell University Press, 1998), 22–23.
2. These Africans are generally referred to as Angolans, but John Thornton provides a convincing argument that they were most likely to have been from the Kingdom of Kongo in modern Angola. See John K. Thornton, "African Dimensions of the Stono Rebellion," *American Historical Review* 96:4 (October 1991), 1101–1114.
3. Jane G. Landers, "Acquisition and Loss on a Spanish Frontier: The Free Black Homesteaders of Florida, 1784–1821," in Jane G. Landers, ed., *Against the Odds: Free Blacks in the Slave Societies of the Americas* (Portland, Ore.: Frank Cass, 1996), 85–101.
4. Olwell, *Masters, Slaves and Subjects,* 22.
5. Thornton, "African Dimensions of the Stono Rebellions," 1111.
6. Olwell, *Masters, Slaves and Subjects,* 24.
7. Ibid., 26–29.
8. Ira Berlin, *Many Thousands Gone: The First Two Centuries of Slavery in North America* (Cambridge, Mass.: Harvard University Press, 1998), 171–173.
9. Ibid.; James Oliver Horton and Lois E. Horton, *In Hope of Liberty: Culture Community, and Protest among Northern Free Blacks, 1700–1860* (New York: Oxford University Press, 1997), 42–43.
10. Alan Gallay, "Planters and Slaves in the Great Awakening," in *Masters and Slaves in the House of the Lord: Race and Religion in the American South, 1740–1870,* edited by John B. Boles (Lexington: University Press of Kentucky, 1988), 19–36; Nathan O. Hatch, *The Democratization of American Christianity* (New Haven, Conn.: Yale University Press, 1989).
11. Leonard W. Labaree, "The Conservative Attitude toward the Great Awakening," *William and Mary Quarterly* 1 (1944), 339, 336.
12. *New York Weekly Journal,* August 9, 1742.
13. Daniel Horsemanden, *The New York Conspiracy,* edited by Thomas J. Davis (Boston: Beacon Press, 1971); Thomas J. Davis, *A Rumor of Revolt: The Great Negro Plot in Colonial New York* (New York: Free Press, 1985).
14. Davis, *A Rumor of Revolt.*
15. Gary Nash, "Up from the Bottom in Franklin's Philadelphia," *Past and Present* 77 (1977), 57–83; Eric Foner, *Tom Paine and Revolutionary America* (New York: Oxford University Press, 1976), 48.
16. For a description of the process of the concentration of colonial wealth and political power see James A. Henretta, *The Evolution of American Society, 1700–1815: An Interdisciplinary Analysis* (Lexington, Mass.: D. C. Heath, 1973). Gary Nash has analyzed the tax records for Boston, New York, and Philadelphia from the late seventeenth to the late eighteenth century and found that

in all three cities the rich increased their share of the community's wealth. See Nash, *The Urban Crucible*.

17. Josiah Quincy, Jr., *Reports of Cases Argued and Adjudged in the Superior Court of Judicature of the Province of Massachusetts Bay, between 1761 and 1772*, edited by Samuel M. Quincy (Boston: Little Brown, 1865), 237–238; Nash, *Urban Crucible*, 8.

18. Benjamin Colman to Mr. Samuel Holden, Boston, May 8, 1737, "Colman Papers," unpublished papers, vol. 2, Massachusetts Historical Society.

19. Jesse Lemisch, "Jack Tar in the Streets: Merchant Seamen in the Politics of Revolutionary America," *William and Mary Quarterly* 25 (1968), 371–407; Howard Zinn, *A People's History of the United States* (New York: Harper & Row, 1980), 51; Nash, *Urban Crucible*, 221–223.

20. Roi Ottley and William J. Weatherby, eds., *The Negro in New York: An Informal Social History, 1626–1940* (New York: New York Public Library, 1967), 36–37.

21. William C. Nell, "Crispus Attucks Once a Slave in Massachusetts," *Liberator*, August 5, 1859, 124. See the *Boston Gazette and Weekly Journal*, October 2, November 13, and November 20, 1750, for the runaway ad for Attucks.

22. Ibid.

23. John Adams, quoted in Howard Zinn, *A People's History of the United States* (New York: Harper & Row, 1980), 67. See *Boston Gazette*, March 12, 1770, for an eyewitness account of this event.

24. Benjamin Thatcher, *Traits of the Tea Party, Being a Memoir of George R. T. Hewes* (New York, 1835), 103–104. See also William Cooper Nell, *The Colored Patriots of the American Revolution* (Boston: Robert F. Wallcut, 1855; reprint, Salem, N.H.: Ayer Company, 1986).

25. One of those initially wounded died later. Thatcher, *Traits of the Tea Party*, 123–124.

26. John Adams's diary, July 1773, in Sidney Kaplan, *The Black Presence in the Era of the American Revolution, 1770–1800* (Washington, D.C.: Smithsonian Institution Press, 1973), 9. The original diary is housed at the Massachusetts Historical Society, Boston, Massachusetts.

27. Jack P. Greene, ed., *The Reinterpretation of the American Revolution* (New York: Harper & Row, 1968), 169. There is evidence that Revolutionary leaders such as Samuel Adams tended to disqualify African Americans from consideration as persons deserving freedom from British rule, conveniently separating the actual slavery of blacks from the metaphorical slavery of white colonists. See Patricia Bradley, *Slavery, Propaganda, and the American Revolution* (Jackson: University of Mississippi Press, 1998).

28. Sidney Kaplan, *The Black Presence in the Era of the American Revolution, 1770–1800* (Greenwich, Conn.: New York Graphic Society, 1973), 11–13.

29. James Otis, *The Rights of the British Colonies Asserted and Proved* (Boston: Edes and Gill, 1764), 37; Abigail Adams to John Adams, September 22, 1774, in Lyman H. Butterfield, ed., *Adams Family Correspondence* (Cambridge, Mass.: Harvard University Press, 1963), vol. 1, 162, 12–14.

30. The Boston Tea Party in 1773 was part of the protest over England's tax on tea. Revolutionaries dressed as American Indians boarded a vessel in the port and dumped the ship's cargo of tea overboard. Philip S. Foner, *History of Black Americans: From Africa to the Emergence of the Cotton Kingdom*, vol. 1 (Westport, Conn.: Greenwood Press, 1975), 307.

31. Benjamin Quarles, *The Negro in the American Revolution* (Chapel Hill: University of North Carolina Press, 1961).

32. Zinn, *A People's History of the United States*, 81.

33. *Pennsylvania Gazette,* June 12, 1780; Clement Alexander Price, *Freedom Not Far Distant: A Documentary History of Afro-Americans in New Jersey* (Newark, N.J.: Historical Society, 1980), 68; for information about the banditti, see Rachel N. Klein, *Unification of a Slave State: The Rise of the Planter Class in the South Carolina Backcountry, 1760–1808* (Chapel Hill: University of North Carolina Press, 1990), 95–99.

34. Paul Finkelman, *Slavery in the Courtroom: An Annotated Bibliography of American Cases* (Washington, D.C.: Library of Congress, 1985); Foner, *History of Black Americans,* vol. 1, 296–297; Bradley, *Slavery, Propaganda,* 66–80.

35. Wilson, *The Loyal Blacks,* 21; Franklin and Moss, *From Slavery to Freedom,* 70.

36. Quotes in Foner, *History of Black Americans,* vol. 1, 316. Benjamin Quarles suggested that Washington was also moved by black requests to be included in the American forces, and although this undoubtedly did play a role in his decision, we agree with Philip Foner that military considerations were mainly responsible for the change in policy. See Benjamin Quarles, *The Negro in the American Revolution,* and Foner, *History of Black Americans.*

37. Revolutionary War Pension Records, Prince Hazeltine, Records of the Veteran's Administration, Record Group #15, National Archives and Record Service, Washington, D.C.

38. Quarles, *The Negro in the American Revolution,* ix; Sylvia R. Frey, *Water from the Rock: Black Resistance in a Revolutionary Age* (Princeton, N.J.: Princeton University Press, 1991), 121–122.

39. "The Negro in the Military Service of the United States: A Compilation of Official Records, State Papers, Historical Records, Etc.," National Archives, Washington, D.C.: 206–214, 220, cited in Foner, *History of Black Americans,* vol. 1, 333.

40. British slaveholders in the West Indies or those in North America who remained loyal to the Crown expressed similar fears about Lord Dunmore's arming slaves to fight for the British Empire. Many believed that before the war was over British troops would have to be used to defend against the armed rebellion of their slave allies. See "The Negro in the Military Service of the United States: A Compilation of Official Records, State Papers, Historical Records, Etc.," National Archives, Washington, D.C.

41. Revolutionary War Pension Records, Cato Cuff, Samuel Coombs, Prince Whipple, Oliver Cromwell, and Prince Bent.

42. Wilson, *Loyal Blacks;* Robin W. Winks, *The Blacks in Canada: A History* (Montreal: McGill–Queen's University Press, 1997).

43. Quarles, *The Negro in the American Revolution,* 172; Wilson, *Loyal Blacks,* 42; Ottley and Weatherby, *The Negro in New York,* 40.

44. Wilson, *Loyal Blacks,* 70–77, 135–153.

45. John H. Watson, "In Re Vermont Constitution of 1777 . . . ," *Proceedings of the Vermont Historical Society, 1919–1920,* cited in Foner, *History of Black Americans,* vol. 1, 347.

46. Foner, *History of Black Americans,* vol. 1, 347. In 1857 free blacks were also declared to be full citizens of the state of New Hampshire. For a similar petition from Connecticut, see Herbert Aptheker, ed., *A Documentary History of the Negro People in the United States* (New York: New Citadel Press, 1951), 10–12.

47. Zilversmit, *The First Emancipation;* Horton and Horton, *In Hope of Liberty,* 80.

48. Ira Berlin, *Slaves without Masters: The Free Negro in the Antebellum South* (New York: Pantheon Books, 1974); *Negro Population in the United States, 1790–1915* (New York: Arno Press, 1968).

49. Paul Finkelman, *An Imperfect Union* (Chapel Hill: University of North Carolina Press, 1981), 80.

50. "Removal to the South, 1818," quoted in Price, *Freedom Not Far Distant,* 85–86.
51. For quotes see Jacqueline Bernard, *Journey toward Freedom: The Story of Sojourner Truth* (New York: Feminist Press at the City University of New York, 1990), 71. Also see Bert James Loewenberg and Ruth Bogin, eds., *Black Women in Nineteenth-Century American Life* (University Park: Pennsylvania State University Press, 1976), 234–242; Harriet Beecher Stowe, "Sojourner Truth, The Libyan Sibyl," *Atlantic Monthly* (April 1863), 473–481.
52. Revolutionary War Pension Records, Cato Howe; James Deetz, *In Small Things Forgotten: The Archeology of Early American Life* (Garden City, N.Y.: Anchor Doubleday, 1977), 138–161.

Chapter 4 ■ **The Early Republic and the Rise of the Cotton Kingdom**

1. James Oliver Horton and Lois E. Horton, *In Hope of Liberty: Culture, Community and Protest Among Northern Free Blacks, 1700–1860* (New York: Oxford University Press, 1997), 69–70; Gary Nash, *Forging Freedom: The Formation of Philadelphia's Black Community, 1720–1840* (Cambridge, Mass.: Harvard University Press, 1988), 52.
2. Gary B. Nash, *Race and Revolution* (Madison, Wis.: Madison House, 1990), 6.
3. Ibid.; David P. Szatmary, *Shays' Rebellion: The Making of an Agrarian Insurrection* (Amherst: University of Massachusetts Press, 1980); Horton and Horton, *In Hope of Liberty,* 177. The African Americans' petition for funds to transport them to Africa was unsuccessful. In 1787 Shays's followers won control of the Massachusetts legislature and later secured a pardon for their leader.
4. Thomas Jefferson attempted to include the southwestern territories as part of the area in which slavery was outlawed, but his recommendation failed to be adopted by Congress by a single vote. Apparently the New Jersey representative who would have voted for its inclusion missed the vote because of illness. Had slavery been prohibited from taking root in the Southwest as well as the Northwest, the course of American history during the nineteenth century and beyond might well have been considerably different. See Staughton Lynd, *Class, Conflict and Slavery, and the United States Constitution* (Indianapolis, Ind.: Bobbs-Merrill, 1967); Emma Lou Thornbrough, *The Negro in Indiana: A Study of a Minority* (Indianapolis, Ind.: Bobbs-Merrill, 1957); and Paul Finkelman, "Slavery and the Northwest Ordinance: A Study in Ambiguity," *Journal of the Early Republic* 6 (Winter 1986), 343–370.
5. Leon Litwack, *North of Slavery: The Negro in the Free States, 1790–1860* (Chicago: University of Chicago Press, 1961), 72. Indiana's black population increased from less than three hundred in 1800 to fourteen hundred by 1820, to more than eleven thousand by 1850. Ohio's blacks, numbering less than four hundred in 1800, stood above twenty-five thousand by mid–nineteenth century. *Negro Population in the United States, 1790–1915* (Washington, D.C.: Government Printing Office, 1918; reprint, New York: Arno Press, 1968), 45.
6. James Walvin, *An African's Life: The Life and Times of Olaudah Equiano, 1745–1797* (New York: Cassell, 1998).
7. Equiano's narrative style influenced the nineteenth-century antislavery autobiographies of former slaves such as Frederick Douglass. See the introduction by Henry Louis Gates, Jr., to *The Classic Slave Narratives* (New York: Penguin Books, 1987), xiii.
8. C.L.R. James, *The Black Jacobins* (1938; reprint, New York: Vintage Books, 1963); Donald R. Hickey, "American's Response to the Slave Revolt in Haiti, 1791–1806," *Journal of the Early Republic* 2 (Winter 1982), 361–379.
9. Gary B. Nash and Jean R. Soderlund, *Freedom by Degrees: Emancipation in Pennsylvania and Its Aftermath* (New York: Oxford University Press, 1991).

Philadelphia was the seat of the national government from 1790 to 1800, when Washington became the capital.

10. Paul A. Gilje, *The Road to Mobocracy* (Chapel Hill: University of North Carolina Press, 1987), 149.

11. Douglas R. Egerton, "Gabriel's Conspiracy and the Election of 1800," *Journal of Southern History* 56 (May 1990), 191–214. See also Douglas R. Egerton, *Gabriel's Rebellion: The Virginia Slave Conspiracies of 1800 and 1802* (Chapel Hill: University of North Carolina Press, 1993). Egerton speculates that Gabriel favored the Republicans in any struggle with the Federalists, failing to appreciate that the Republican commitment to freedom and liberty did not apply to blacks. This interpretation is intriguing in light of the fact that in Philadelphia, New York, and even in the Upper South, Federalists were those who founded the antislavery societies of the late eighteenth century. If Gabriel was aware of the international tensions between the United States and France, it seems likely that he would have also been aware of the antislavery leanings of many Federalists in Philadelphia and Virginia. See also Gerald W. Mullin, *Flight and Rebellion: Slave Resistance in Eighteenth-Century Virginia* (New York: Oxford University Press, 1972), and Stuckey, *Slave Culture.*

12. Donald R. Wright, *African Americans in the Early Republic, 1789–1831* (Arlington Heights, Ill.: Harlan Davidson, 1993); Edward W. Phifer, "Slavery in Microcosm: Burke County, North Carolina," in Allan Weinstein and Frank Otto Gatell, eds., *American Negro Slavery: A Modern Reader* (New York: Oxford University Press, 1968), 74–97.

13. Richard B. Morris and Jeffrey B. Morris, eds., *Encyclopedia of American History* (New York: Harper & Row, 1976), 757, 759; Douglas C. North, *The Economic Growth of the United States, 1790–1860* (New York: W. W. Norton, 1966), 128.

14. North, *The Economic Growth of the United States*, 75–76.

15. Ann Patton Malone, *Sweet Chariot: Slave Family and Household Structure in Nineteenth-Century Louisiana* (Chapel Hill: University of North Carolina Press, 1992), 52; Charles Duncan Rice, *The Rise and Fall of Black Slavery* (New York: Harper & Row, 1975), 286–287.

16. Gavin Wright, *The Political Economy of the Cotton South: Households, Markets and Wealth in the Nineteenth Century* (New York: W. W. Norton, 1978).

17. Lewis Clarke, *Narrative of the Sufferings of Lewis Clarke, during a Captivity of More than Twenty-Five Years among the Algerines of Kentucky* (Boston: D. H. Eli, 1845), 121; James Williams, *Narrative of James Williams, An American Slave, Who Was for Several Years a Driver on a Cotton Plantation in Alabama* (New York: American Anti-Slavery Society, 1838), 32; Benjamin Drew, ed., *A North-Side View of Slavery: The Refugee, or the Narratives of Fugitive Slaves in Canada Related by Themselves* (Boston: John P. Jewett, 1856; reprint, New York: Negro Universities Press, 1968), 178; Israel Campbell, *Bond and Free; or, Yearnings for Freedom, from My Green Briar House; Being the Story of My Life in Bondage and My Life in Freedom* (Philadelphia, 1861), 18.

18. Michael Tadman, *Speculators and Slaves: Masters, Traders, and Slaves in the Old South* (Madison, Wis.: University of Wisconsin, 1989), 21–46; Malone, *Sweet Chariot*, 15, 193.

19. Gary B. Nash, "Forging Freedom: The Emancipation Experience in the Northern Seaport Cities, 1775–1820," in Ira Berlin and Ronald Hoffman, eds., *Slavery and Freedom in the Age of the American Revolution* (Charlottesville: United States Capitol Historical Society/University Press of Virginia, 1983), 3–48; quote, 7; Leonard P. Curry, *The Free Black in Urban America 1800–1850* (Chicago: University of Chicago Press, 1981), 244–248. In addition to these free blacks,

Philadelphia still had about fifty slaves and New York City nearly three thousand slaves in 1800.

20. Thomas, *Rise to Be a People: A Biography of Paul Cuffe* (Urbana: University of Illinois Press, 1986).

21. James B. Browning, "The Beginnings of Insurance Enterprise among Negroes," *Journal of Negro History* 22:4 (October 1937), 417–432; Robert L. Harris, Jr., "Early Black Benevolent Societies, 1780–1830," *Massachusetts Review* 20:3 (Autumn 1979), 603–625.

22. Harris, "Early Black Benevolent Societies, 1780–1830," 603–625; Browning, "The Beginnings of Insurance Enterprise among Negroes," 417–432; "Colored Population of Philadelphia," *National Enquirer and Constitutional Advocate of Universal Liberty* 1:7 (October 22, 1836), 27.

23. Horton and Horton, *Black Bostonians* (New York: Holmes & Meier, 1999), 41–55; see also C. Eric Lincoln and Lawrence H. Mamiya, *The Black Church in the African American Experience* (Durham, N.C.: Duke University Press, 1990); Edward Smith, *Climbing Jacob's Ladder: The Rise of Black Churches in Eastern American Cities, 1740–1877* (Washington, D.C.: Smithsonian Institution Press, 1988).

24. Charles V. Hamilton, *The Black Preacher in America* (New York: William Morrow, 1972); David E. Swift, *Black Prophets of Justice: Activist Clergy before the Civil War* (Baton Rouge: Louisiana State University Press, 1989).

25. Ira Berlin, *Slaves without Masters: The Free Negro in the Antebellum South* (New York: Pantheon, 1974), 284–315.

26. Ibid. Berlin argues that the role of free blacks differed from one region of the South to another and over time. Also see Horton and Horton, *In Hope of Liberty,* for important distinctions between the role of free blacks, especially mulattoes, in the North and in the South.

27. Thomas, *Rise to Be a People.*

28. Foner, *History of Black Americans,* vol. 1, 485.

29. *New York Evening Post,* August 20, 1814, quoted in Shane White, *Somewhat More Independent* (Athens: University of Georgia Press, 1991), 150.

30. Quoted in Foner, *History of Black Americans,* vol. 1, 486.

31. Ibid., 487.

32. William Cooper Nell, *Colored Patriots of the American Revolution* (Boston: Robert F. Wallcut, 1855; reprint, New York: Arno Press, 1968), 190–191. Sailors were commonly called tars.

33. W. Jeffrey Bolster, *Black Jacks: African American Seamen in the Age of Sail* (Cambridge, Mass.: Harvard University Press, 1997), 127.

34. Donald E. Everett, "Emigrés and Militiamen: Free Persons of Color in New Orleans, 1803–1815," *Journal of Negro History* 38:4 (October 1953), 377–402.

35. James Roberts, *The Narrative of James Roberts: Soldier in the Revolutionary War and at the Battle of New Orleans* (Chicago, 1858), 32.

36. Arnett G. Lindsay, "Diplomatic Relations between the United States and Great Britain Bearing on the Return of Negro Slaves, 1783–1828," *Journal of Negro History* 5 (October 1920), 391–419.

37. William S. McFeely, *Frederick Douglass* (New York: W. W. Norton, 1991), 318.

Chapter 5 ■ **Slavery and the Slave Community**

1. Peter Kolchin, *American Slavery, 1619–1877* (New York: Hill & Wang, 1993), 242.

2. Solomon Northup, *Twelve Years a Slave* (Auburn, N.Y.: Derby and Miller, 1853; reprint, edited by Sue Eakin and Joseph Logsdon, Baton Rouge, La.: Louisiana State University Press, 1968).

3. Walter M. Brasch, *Black English and the Mass Media* (Amherst: University of Massachusetts Press, 1981), 26–31; Charles Joyner, *Down by the Riverside: A South Carolina Slave Community* (Urbana: University of Illinois Press, 1984).

4. Austin Steward, *Twenty-Two Years a Slave and Forty Years a Freeman* (Rochester, N.Y.: W. Alling, 1857), 33–38. For a description of retribution taken against Virginia slaves after the Nat Turner rebellion see Jacobs, *Incidents in the Life of a Slave Girl.*

5. William F. Cheek, *Black Resistance before the Civil War* (Beverly Hills, Calif.: Glencoe Press, 1970), 99.

6. Norrece T. Jones, Jr., *Born a Child of God Yet a Slave: Mechanisms of Control and Strategies of Resistance in Antebellum South Carolina* (Hanover, N.H.: University Press of New England, 1990).

7. Benjamin Drew, ed., *North-Side View of Slavery, the Refugee; or, The Narrative of Fugitive Slaves in Canada. Related by Themselves* (Boston: John P. Jewett, 1856), 223.

8. Bernard E. Powers, *Black Charlestonians: A Social History, 1822–1885* (Fayetteville: University of Arkansas Press, 1994), 31–33.

9. Eric Foner, ed., *Nat Turner* (Englewood Cliffs, N.J.: Prentice-Hall, 1971); Ira Berlin, *Slaves without Masters: The Free Negro in the Antebellum South* (New York: Pantheon Books, 1974), 188–189, 195; Henry Irving Tragle, *The Southampton Slave Rebellion of 1831: A Compilation of Source Material* (Amherst: University of Massachusetts Press, 1971).

10. John Hope Franklin, *The Militant South, 1800–1860* (Cambridge, Mass.: Harvard University Press, 1956); Sterling Stuckey, *Slave Culture: Nationalist Theory and the Foundation of Black America* (New York: Oxford University Press, 1987); Eugene D. Genovese, *Roll, Jordan, Roll: The World the Slaves Made* (New York: Pantheon Books, 1974).

11. Bertram Wyatt-Brown, *Southern Honor: Ethics and Behavior in the Old South* (New York: Oxford University Press, 1982). Wyatt-Brown describes the violence in Southern society but attributes it to cultural factors imported from ancient Ireland. Although he may well be correct, slavery almost certainly necessitated its regular practice and helped to create the atmosphere in which this violence took on a racial dimension.

12. Ibid., 88, 366. Wyatt-Brown has interesting information comparing northern and southern crime rates generally and concludes that northern society's lower crime rate reflected its less violent culture. One might ask if the early abolition of slavery in the North, an institution that was never as widespread or as significant there as in the South, was not a major factor in this cultural difference.

13. Northup, *Twelve Years a Slave.*

14. Ibid., 61–69.

15. Ibid., 122–144.

16. Quoted in James Oliver Horton and Lois E. Horton, "Black Theology and Historical Necessity," in Miles L. Bradbury and James B. Gilbert, eds., *Transforming Faith: The Sacred and Secular in Modern America* (Westport, Conn.: Greenwood Press, 1989), 25–37; quote, 28.

17. Melville J. Herskovits, *Dahomey* (New York: Augustin, 1938); Robert Farris Thompson, *The Four Movements of the Sun* (Washington, D.C.: National Gallery of Art, 1981). For an important interpretation of the ring shout and its significance as a link between West African culture and that of African America see Stuckey, *Slave Culture.*

18. James Lindsay Smith, *Autobiography of James Lindsay Smith* (Norwich, Conn: Press of the Bulletin Co., 1881), 27.

19. Francis Fedric, *Slave Life in Virginia and Kentucky* (London: Wertheim, MacIntosh, and Hunt, 1863), 5.
20. Charles Joyner, *Down by the River Side: A South Carolina Slave Community* (Urbana: University of Illinois Press, 1984), 232.
21. Quoted in Horton and Horton, "Black Theology and Historical Necessity," 29.
22. Northup, *Twelve Years a Slave,* 172.
23. Ann Patton Malone, *Sweet Chariot: Slave Family and Household Structure in Nineteenth-Century Louisiana* (Chapel Hill: University of North Carolina Press, 1992), 16–17. See also Herbert Gutman, *The Black Family in Slavery and Freedom* (New York: Pantheon Press, 1976), and Leslie Howard Owens, *This Species of Property: Slave Life and Culture in the Old South* (New York: Oxford University Press, 1976).
24. Owens, *This Species of Property,* 198.
25. Brenda Stevenson, "A Heroine's Heroine: Slave Women Choose," paper presented at the Intercollegiate Department of Black Studies' Conference, Claremont Colleges, Claremont, California, January 1994.
26. Gutman, *Black Family in Slavery and Freedom,* 191. Elizabeth's father and mother belonged to different masters, and before her father was moved to the West he was able to visit only twice a year.
27. Frederick Douglass, *My Bondage and My Freedom,* edited and with an introduction by William L. Andrews (Urbana: University of Illinois Press, 1987), 27–32.
28. James W. C. Pennington, *The Fugitive Blacksmith,* in Arna Bontemps, ed., *Great Slave Narratives* (Boston: Beacon Press, 1969), 193–267; quote, 207.
29. Harriet A. Jacobs, *Incidents in the Life of a Slave Girl, Written by Herself,* edited by Jean Fagan Yellin (Cambridge, Mass.: Harvard University Press, 1987), 77.
30. Northup, *Twelve Years a Slave,* 151–152.
31. Ibid., 116, 123–125.
32. Ibid.
33. Frederick Law Olmsted, *The Slave States: Before the Civil War* (1856; reprint, revised and enlarged, New York: Capricorn Books, 1959), 203.
34. Northup, *Twelve Years a Slave,* 125.
35. Joyner, *Down by the River Side,* 23–24, 42. See also John Michael Vlach, *The Afro-American Tradition in Decorative Arts* (Athens: University of Georgia Press, 1990).
36. John Brown, *Slave Life in Georgia: A Narrative of the Life, Suffering, and Escape of John Brown, A Fugitive Now in England* (London: W. M. Watts, 1855), 186–187.
37. Joyner, *Down by the River Side,* 43–45. Joyner gives a detailed description of the task system and its advantages to the slaves over the gang system used in cotton cultivation.
38. Charles Joyner, "The World of the Plantation," in Edward D. C. Campbell, Jr., with Kim S. Rice, eds., *Before Freedom Came* (Charlottesville and Richmond: University Press of Virginia and The Museum of the Confederacy, 1991), 51–99; quote, 82.
39. Olmsted, *The Slave States,* 115.
40. Lawrence W. Levine, *Black Culture and Black Consciousness: Afro-American Folk Thought from Slavery to Freedom* (New York: Oxford University Press, 1977), 5–19; see also Miles Mark Fisher, *Negro Slave Songs in the United States* (1953; reprint, New York: Carol Publishing Group, 1990).
41. Northup, *Twelve Years a Slave,* 135–136.
42. Henry Clay Bruce, *The New Man: Twenty-nine Years a Slave, Twenty-nine Years a Free Man: Recollections of H. C. Bruce* (York, Pa.: P. Anstadt and Sons, 1895).
43. Booker Taliaferro Washington, *Up from Slavery: An Autobiography* (1900; reprint, New York: Dell, 1965), 26.

44. James Oliver Horton, *Free People of Color: Inside the African American Community* (Washington, D.C.: Smithsonian Institution Press, 1993), 66.
45. James Oliver Horton, "Links to Bondage," ibid., 53–74.

Chapter 6 ▪ *Free People of Color and the Fight against Slavery*

1. Just before the Civil War, the South Carolina legislature considered a provision that would have deprived all free blacks in the state of their freedom. See James Roark and Michael Johnson, *Black Masters: A Free Family of Color in the Old South* (New York: W. W. Norton, 1984).
2. Gary B. Nash, "Forging Freedom: The Emancipation Experience in the Northern Seaport Cities, 1775–1820," in *Slavery and Freedom in the Age of the American Revolution,* Ira Berlin and Ronald Hoffman, eds. (Charlottesville: University Press of Virginia, for the United States Capitol Historical Society, 1983), 3–48; quote, 32–33.
3. David Walker, *David Walker's Appeal to the Coloured Citizens of the World* (1829), introduction by Sean Wilentz (New York: Hill & Wang, 1995), 21.
4. *Freedom's Journal,* March 16, 1827.
5. Walker, *David Walker's Appeal.*
6. Peter P. Hinks, *To Awaken My Afflicted Brethren: David Walker and the Problem of Antebellum Slave Resistance* (University Park: Pennsylvania State University Press, 1997).
7. Henry Mayer, *All on Fire: William Lloyd Garrison and the Abolition of Slavery* (New York: St. Martin's Press, 1998), 101; *Liberator,* January 1, 1831.
8. James O. Horton and Lois Horton, *In Hope of Liberty: Culture, Community, and Protest among Northern Free Blacks* (New York: Oxford University Press, 1997), 213, chap. 9, n. 1.
9. James Oliver Horton and Lois E. Horton, *Black Bostonians: Family Life and Community Struggle in the Antebellum North* (New York: Holmes & Meier Publishers, 1999).
10. Donald M. Jacobs, "David Walker: Boston Race Leader, 1825–1830," *Essex Institute Historical Collection* 107 (January 1971), 94–107.
11. Philip S. Foner, *History of Black Americans,* vol. 2 (Westport, Conn.: Greenwood Press, 1983), 399, 401.
12. Horton and Horton, *In Hope of Liberty,* 244–245.
13. Ibid., 102–103.
14. Ibid.
15. Howard Holman Bell, ed., *Minutes of the Proceedings of the National Negro Conventions 1830–1864* (New York: Arno Press / New York Times, 1969). For an account of the Cincinnati race riot see Richard Wade, *The Urban Frontier: The Rise of Western Cities, 1790–1830* (Cambridge, Mass.: Harvard University Press, 1959), 222–229.
16. Horton and Horton, *In Hope of Liberty,* 193–196.
17. Ibid., 262.
18. C. Peter Ripley, Roy E. Finkenbine, Michael F. Hembree, and Donald Yacovone, eds., *The Black Abolitionist Papers: Canada, 1830–1865,* vol. 2 (Chapel Hill: University of North Carolina Press, 1991), 109–112.
19. Dorothy Sterling, *Speak Out in Thunder Tones: Letters and Other Writings by Black Northerners, 1787–1865* (New York: Da Capo Press, 1998); James Stewart, *William Lloyd Garrison and the Challenge of Emancipation* (Arlington Heights, Ill.: H. Davison Press, 1992).
20. Former slave and renowned abolitionist speaker Frederick Douglass promoted the manual-labor-school idea for blacks both at conventions and in his newspapers during this later period. See Horton and Horton, *Black Bostonians,* 84.

21. Carlton Mabee, *Black Education in New York State* (Syracuse, N.Y.: Syracuse University Press, 1979), 108–166; C. Peter Ripley, Roy E. Finkenbine, Michael F. Hembree, and Donald Yacovone, eds., *The Black Abolitionist Papers,* vol. 3 (Chapel Hill: University of North Carolina Press, 1991), 337 n.; Nat Brandt, *The Town That Started the Civil War* (Syracuse, N.Y.: Syracuse University Press, 1990), 38.
22. "Report of the Condition of the People of Color in the State of Ohio" (April 1835), reprinted in Aptheker, *Documentary History,* 157–158; Horton and Horton, *Black Bostonians,* 33.
23. Horton, *Free People of Color,* 49–50.
24. Christine Stansell, *City of Women* (New York: Alfred A. Knopf, 1982), 63–73; Barbara Meil Hobson, *Uneasy Virtue* (New York: Basic Books, 1987), 51–54.
25. *Colored American,* March 15, 1838.
26. Stewart, *Garrison,* 82.
27. Ripley, Finkenbine, Hembree, and Yacovone, eds., *The Black Abolitionist Papers,* vol. 3, 482.
28. Horton and Horton, *In Hope of Liberty,* 243.
29. Frederick Douglass, *Narrative of the Life of Frederick Douglass,* edited by David W. Blight (New York: Bedford Books, 1993).
30. William McFeely, *Frederick Douglass* (New York: W. W. Norton, 1991).
31. Ibid., 82–92; see also Blight, *Narrative of the Life of Frederick Douglass.*
32. John G. Whittier, *Narrative of James Williams an American Slave* (New York: Isaac Knapp, 1838), 97–99.
33. Ibid.
34. Dorothy B. Parker, "David B. Ruggles, An Apostle for Human Freedom," *Journal of Negro History* (January 1943), 23–50.
35. Ripley, Finkenbine, Hembree, and Yacovone, *The Black Abolitionist Papers,* vol. 4, 184–185 n.
36. J. C. Furnas, *Goodbye to Uncle Tom* (New York: William Sloane Associates, 1956), 214.
37. Horton and Horton, *Black Bostonians.*
38. Sarah H. Bradford, *Scenes in the Life of Harriet Tubman* (Auburn, N.Y., 1869).
39. "James G. Birney to Lewis Tappan, February 27, 1837," in Dwight L. Dumond, ed., *Letters of James Gillespie Birney* (1938; Gloucester, Mass.: Peter Smith, 1966), vol. 2, 379; Levi Coffin, *Reminiscences of Levi Coffin* (Cincinnati: Western Tract Society, 1876), 106. Coffin was speaking specifically of Newport, Indiana, but it was also more generally true.
40. Calvin Fairbank, *How the Way Was Prepared* (1890; reprint, New York: Negro University Press, 1969), 46–93.
41. Jonathan Walker, *Trial and Imprisonment of Jonathan Walker* (1845; reprint, Gainesville: University Presses of Florida, 1974); John W. Blassingame, *The Frederick Douglass Papers, 1841–1846* (New Haven, Conn.: Yale University Press, 1979), vol. 1, 226.
42. William Jeffrey Bolster, *Black Jacks: African American Seamen in the Age of Sail* (Cambridge, Mass.: Harvard University Press, 1997); *Richmond Enquirer,* November 15, 1850.
43. Horton, *Free People of Color,* 68–71.
44. "Original Records of the Union Baptist Church, Cincinnati, Ohio, 1834," Cincinnati Historical Society.
45. Brandt, *The Town That Started the Civil War,* 212.
46. *Colored American,* December 9, 1837.
47. *Colored American,* September 9, 1837.
48. "Minutes of the National Convention of Colored Citizens, Held in Buffalo, 1843," in Howard Holman Bell, ed., *Minutes of the Proceedings of the National*

Negro Conventions, 1830–1864 (New York: Arno Press and *New York Times,* 1969), 7.

49. Henry Highland Garnet, *Walker's Appeal, with a Brief Sketch of His Life, and Also Garnet's Address to the Slaves of the United States of America* (New York: J. H. Tobitt, 1848), 90–96.

50. "Minutes of the National Convention . . . ," 23.

51. *Colored American,* April 18, 1840.

52. *Colored American,* August 29, 1840.

53. "The Poor Man's Party" broadside dated October 17, 1846, Peterboro, N.Y., Cornell University Archives, Ithaca, N.Y.

54. In October 1845 blacks from western New York State held a meeting in Geneva, New York, to protest racial restrictions on voting. They alerted the state's blacks to be ready to act if a convention was called to amend the state constitution. Among those attending were William Wells Brown and Samuel Ringold Ward. See *Ithaca Chronicle,* October 1, 1845.

55. "Gift of Land and Money to Negroes" (undated list of names) and "To Gerrit Smith Grantees" (broadside dated October 4, 1854), box 145, Gerrit Smith Papers, George Arents Research Library, Syracuse University, Syracuse, NY.

56. Ripley, Finkenbine, Hembree, and Yacovone, *The Black Abolitionist Papers,* vol. 3, 409.

57. Foner, *History of Black Americans,* vol. 2, 543.

58. *National Anti-Slavery Standard,* October 15, 1846, 77.

Chapter 7 ▪ **From Militancy to Civil War**

1. Quoted in James Oliver Horton and Lois E. Horton, *Black Bostonians: Family Life and Community Struggle in the Antebellum North,* rev. ed. (New York: Holmes and Meier, 1999), 102.

2. "State Convention of Colored Citizens of Ohio, Columbus," in Philip S. Foner and George W. Walker, eds., *Proceedings of the Black State Conventions, 1840–1865* (Westport, Conn.: Greenwood Press, 1979), 229.

3. *North Star,* February 9, 1849, quoted in Robert C. Dick, *Black Protest: Issues and Tactics* (Westport, Conn.: Greenwood Press, 1974), 138.

4. Fillmore is not known for antislavery sentiments, but his past indicated that he had some sympathy for the fugitives. When Fillmore was a lawyer in Buffalo during the 1830s, according to William Wells Brown, he served without charge as defense counsel for a fugitive slave. William E. Farrison, "William Wells Brown in Buffalo," *Journal of Negro History* 39:4 (October 1954), 298–314.

5. William Loren Katz, *Eyewitness: The Negro in American History,* 3rd ed. (Belmont, Calif.: Fearon Pitman Publishers, 1974), 189; James Oliver Horton and Lois E. Horton, "A Federal Assault: African Americans and the Impact of the Fugitive Slave Law of 1850," *Chicago-Kent Law Review* 68:3 (Fall 1993), 1179–1197; Carol Wilson, *Freedom at Risk: The Kidnapping of Free Blacks in America, 1780–1865* (Lexington: University Press of Kentucky, 1994).

6. Olivia Mahoney, "Black Abolitionist," *Chicago History* 20:1–2 (1991), 22–37.

7. *Liberator,* October 18, 1850.

8. *Liberator,* October 25, 1850.

9. Foner and Walker, *Proceedings,* 318; Horton and Horton, *Black Bostonians,* 130–131.

10. Fred Landon, "The Negro Migration to Canada after the Passing of the Fugitive Slave Act," *Journal of Negro History* 5:1 (January 1920), 22–36.

11. *Liberator,* October 4, 1850.

12. *Pennsylvania Telegraph,* October 2, 1850.

13. Horton and Horton, *Black Bostonians,* 112. See also Mechal Sobel, *Trabelin' On: The Slave Journey to an Afro-Baptist Faith* (Princeton, N.J.: Princeton University Press, 1988), 216; *Liberator,* April 25, 1851; James K. Lewis, "Religious Nature of the Early Negro Migration to Canada and the Amherstburg Baptist Association," *Ontario History* 58 (1966), 117–132.

14. *Liberator,* December 13, 1850; Michael F. Hembree, "The Question of 'Begging': Fugitive Slave Relief in Canada, 1830–1865," *Civil War History* 37:4 (December 1991), 314–327; quote, 315.

15. "Slave-Hunters in Boston," *Liberator,* November 1, 1850.

16. For a more complete account of the Crafts in Boston see Horton and Horton, *Black Bostonians,* 112–113.

17. Gary Collison, *Shadrach Minkins: From Fugitive Slave to Citizen* (Cambridge, Mass.: Harvard University Press, 1997); Foner, *History of Black Americans,* vol. 3, 35–36.

18. Foner, *History of Black Americans,* vol. 3, 35–36; Thomas P. Slaughter, *Bloody Dawn: The Christiana Riot and Racial Violence in the Antebellum North* (New York: Oxford University Press, 1991).

19. Horton and Horton, *Black Bostonians,* 120–123; Albert J. Von Frank, *The Trials of Anthony Burns: Freedom and Slavery in Emerson's Boston* (Cambridge, Mass.: Harvard University Press, 1998).

20. Foner, *History of Black Americans,* vol. 3, 87–91; Julius Yanuck, "The Garner Fugitive Slave Case," *Mississippi Valley Historical Review* 40 (June 1953), 47–66; Steven Weisenburger, *Modern Medea: A Family Story of Slavery and Child-Murder from the Old South* (New York: Hill & Wang, 1998).

21. Yanuck, "The Garner Fugitive Slave Case"; Weisenburger, *Modern Medea.*

22. Philip S. Foner, ed., *The Life and Writings of Frederick Douglass,* vol. 4 (New York: International Publishers, 1950), 227.

23. Donald E. Liedel, "The Antislavery Publishing Revolution in the 1850s," *Library Journal* 2 (1972), 67–80.

24. Ripley, Finkenbine, Hembree, and Yacovone, *The Black Abolitionist Papers,* vol. 4, 144; James M. McPherson, *Battle Cry of Freedom: The Civil War Era* (New York: Oxford University Press, 1988), 90.

25. Eugene D. Genovese, *The Slaveholders' Dilemma* (Columbia: University of South Carolina Press, 1992).

26. Merton L. Dillon, *The Abolitionists: The Growth of a Dissenting Minority* (DeKalb: Northern Illinois University Press, 1974), 86.

27. *Frederick Douglass' Paper,* May 26, 1854.

28. Benjamin Quarles, *Allies for Freedom: Blacks and John Brown* (New York: Oxford University Press, 1974), 32–36.

29. Eric Foner, *Free Labor, Free Soil, Free Men* (New York: Oxford University Press, 1970); Frederick Douglass, "The Unholy Alliance of Negro Hate and Antislavery," *Frederick Douglass' Paper,* April 5, 1856.

30. David R. Roediger, *The Wages of Whiteness: Race and the Making of the American Working Class* (New York: Verso, 1991); Eric Lott, *Love and Theft: Blackface Minstrelsy and the American Working Class* (New York: Oxford University Press, 1993).

31. Benjamin Quarles, *Black Abolitionists* (New York: Oxford University Press, 1969), 189.

32. *Liberator,* September 5, 1856.

33. *Liberator,* October 1, 1858.

34. Millard Fillmore, former president, ran on the nativist American Party (Know-Nothing) ticket and got just under nine hundred thousand votes.

35. Quoted in Foner, *History of Black Americans,* vol. 3, 213.

36. Foner, *Life and Writings of Frederick Douglass,* vol. 2, 406.
37. *Dred Scott* v. *Sanford* (1857), 19 Howard, 393.
38. Leon F. Litwack, *North of Slavery: The Negro in the Free States, 1790–1860* (Chicago: University of Chicago Press, 1961), 57.
39. Wilson Jeremiah Moses, *The Golden Age of Black Nationalism, 1850–1925* (New York: Oxford University Press, 1978).
40. *Frederick Douglass' Paper,* September 7, 1855; *Liberator,* November 27, 1857.
41. *Liberator,* August 13, 1858.
42. "Proceedings of the State Convention of Colored Men of the State of Ohio, Held in the City of Columbus, January 21st, 22d & 23d, 1857," in Foner and Walker, *Proceedings,* vol. 1, 320.
43. Ripley, Finkenbine, Hembree, and Yacovone, *The Black Abolitionist Papers,* vol. 4, 319.
44. *Liberator,* November 11, 1959.
45. Benjamin Quarles, *Allies for Freedom: Blacks and John Brown* (New York: Oxford University Press, 1974), 86–87.
46. McFeely, *Frederick Douglass,* 198–203; Quarles, *Allies for Freedom.*
47. *Weekly Anglo-African,* December 1859.
48. *Liberator,* December 9, 1859.
49. Benjamin Quarles, ed., *Blacks on John Brown* (Urbana: University of Illinois Press, 1972), 20–21.
50. *Liberator,* March 12, 1858.
51. Broadside signed by Harvey C. Jackson, Simcoe, Canada West, December, 7, 1859, in Boyd B. Stutler Collection of the John Brown Papers, Mss. 42, Roll 5, Ohio Historical Society; *Weekly Anglo-African,* December 31, 1859.
52. Quoted in Foner, *History of Black Americans,* vol. 3, 270–271.
53. *Liberator,* January 27, 1860, quoted in James M. McPherson, *The Negro's Civil War: How American Negroes Felt and Acted during the War for the Union* (New York: Vintage Books, 1965), 5.
54. *Anglo-African,* February 4, 1860; *Liberator,* October 19, 1860. See also McPherson, *The Negro's Civil War,* 10.
55. Hondon B. Hargrove, *Black Union Soldiers in the Civil War* (Jefferson, N.C.: McFarland & Co., 1988).
56. Quoted in McPherson, *Negro's Civil War,* 163.
57. *New York Tribune,* February 12, 1862; *Douglass' Monthly,* September 1861.
58. Quoted in McPherson, *Negro's Civil War,* 11. See also James O. Horton, "'Making Free': African Americans and the Civil War," in Frances H. Kennedy, ed., *The Civil War Battlefield Guide* (Boston: Houghton Mifflin Co., 1990), 261–263.
59. McPherson, *Negro's Civil War,* 17–18.
60. *Pine and Palm,* May 25, 1861, also quoted in McPherson, *Negro's Civil War,* 29.
61. Quoted in McPherson, *Negro's Civil War,* 166–167.
62. R.J.M. Blackett, ed., *Thomas Morris Chester: Black Civil War Correspondent* (Baton Rouge: Louisiana State University Press, 1989).
63. Quoted in McPherson, *Negro's Civil War,* 168.
64. *New York Tribune,* March 28, 1863.
65. James M. McPherson, *What They Fought For, 1861–1865* (Baton Rouge: Louisiana State University Press, 1994), 66–67.
66. Blackett, *Thomas Morris Chester,* 33.
67. Ibid., 34–38. Only when Harrisburg, Pennsylvania, faced Confederate invasion were black defenders considered. They were quickly rejected after the threat receded.
68. McPherson, *Negro's Civil War,* 178–179.

69. Although in 1864 Congress authorized equal pay for blacks who had been free before the war, until March 1865 it did not include those who had been slaves at the time of enlistment. At that time equal pay was made retroactive to their date of enlistment. Ira Berlin, Joseph P. Reidy, and Leslie S. Rowland, *Freedom: A Documentary History of Emancipation, 1861–1867* (Cambridge, England: Cambridge University Press, 1982), series 2, 363, 367–368.

70. Virginia M. Adams, ed., *On the Altar of Freedom: A Black Soldier's Civil War Letters from the Front* (Amherst: University of Massachusetts Press, 1991), 83.

71. McPherson, *Negro's Civil War*, 199.

72. Berlin, Reidy, and Rowland, *Freedom*, 365–366.

73. Susie King Taylor, *Reminiscences of My Life in Camp with the 33d United States Colored Troops Late First S.C. Volunteers* (Boston, 1902).

74. Joseph T. Glatthaar, *Forged in Battle: The Civil War Alliance of Black Soldiers and White Officers* (New York: Free Press, 1990), 91.

75. Foner, *History of Black Americans,* vol. 3, 374.

76. Ibid., 375.

77. Ibid., 376.

Chapter 8 ■ **From Reconstruction to Jim Crow**

1. R.J.M. Blackett, ed., *Thomas Morris Chester: Black Civil War Correspondent* (Baton Rouge: Louisiana State University Press, 1989), 5, 10–12.

2. Ibid., 41.

3. Jack Hurst, *Nathan Bedford Forrest: A Biography* (New York: Alfred A. Knopf, 1993), 172–178, 186; Blackett, *Thomas Morris Chester,* 125.

4. James M. McPherson, *What They Fought For, 1861–1865* (Baton Rouge: Louisiana State University Press, 1994), 67.

5. James M. McPherson, *For Cause and Comrades: Why Men Fought in the Civil War* (New York: Oxford University Press, 1997), 138. Some wives of U.S. troops also sent letters asking their men to return home.

6. McPherson, *For Cause and Comrades,* 172; Ira Berlin, Joseph P. Reidy, and Leslie S. Rowland, eds., *Freedom: A Documentary History of Emancipation, 1861–1867* (New York: Cambridge University Press, 1982), 295; see also Joseph T. Wilson, *The Black Phalanx: African American Soldiers in the War of Independence, the War of 1812 and the Civil War* (1890; reprint, New York: Da Capo Press, 1994).

7. *Liberator,* April 7, 1865.

8. Benjamin Quarles, *The Negro in the Civil War* (Boston: Little, Brown, 1969), 331.

9. Leon Litwack, *Been in the Storm So Long: The Aftermath of Slavery* (New York: Alfred A Knopf, 1979), 167–168.

10. Litwack, *Been in the Storm So Long,* 168; Virginia M. Adams, ed., *On the Altar of Freedom: A Black Soldier's Civil War Letters from the Front* (Amherst: University of Massachusetts Press, 1991), 18–19.

11. Litwack, *Been in the Storm So Long,* 168–169; see also Mark E. Neely, Jr., *The Last Best Hope on Earth: Abraham Lincoln and the Promise of America* (Springfield: Illinois State Historical Library, 1993).

12. James M. McPherson, *Battle Cry of Freedom: The Civil War Era* (New York: Oxford University Press, 1988), 852.

13. *Rochester Democrat,* April 17, 1865; Noah Andre Trudeau, *Like Men of War: Black Troops in the Civil War, 1862–1865* (Boston: Little, Brown, 1998), 434.

14. Eric Foner, *Reconstruction: America's Unfinished Revolution, 1863–1877* (New York: Harper & Row, 1989), 49.

15. Willie Lee Rose, *Rehearsal for Reconstruction* (New York: Random House, 1964).

16. Litwack, *Been in the Storm So Long,* 485.

17. Foner, *Reconstruction,* 152.

18. Litwack, *Been in the Storm So Long,* 401.

19. Foner, *Reconstruction,* 104; Litwack, *Been in the Storm So Long,* 402.

20. Foner, *Reconstruction.*

21. Whitelaw Reid, *After the War: A Tour of the Southern States, 1865–66* (1866; reprint, New York: Harper & Row, 1965), 564–565, quoted in William H. Harris, *The Harder We Run* (New York: Oxford University Press, 1982), 9.

22. Litwack, *Been in the Storm So Long,* 402; Foner, *Reconstruction.*

23. The oldest black college in the United States was founded in the North in 1854. Ashmun Institute, begun by Presbyterians, was renamed Lincoln University after the Civil War.

24. W.E.B. Du Bois, *Black Reconstruction in America, 1860–1880* (New York: Atheneum, 1973), 389–399.

25. Ibid., 399.

26. Thomas Holt, *Black over White: Negro Political Leadership in South Carolina during Reconstruction* (Urbana: University of Illinois Press, 1977), 34–35.

27. *Loyal Georgian,* July 6, 1867, cited in Litwack, *Been in the Storm So Long,* 547.

28. Noralee Frankel, *Freedom's Women: African American Women and Family in Civil War Era Mississippi* (Bloomington: Indiana University Press, 1999).

29. Holt, *Black over White,* 35.

30. Litwack, *Been in the Storm So Long,* 252.

31. Ibid., 448.

32. Steven Mintz, ed., *African American Voices: The Life Cycle of Slavery* (St. James, N.Y.: Brandywine Books, 1993), 170.

33. Ibid., 166.

34. Ibid.

35. Ira Berlin, ed., *Freedom: A Documentary History of Emancipation, 1861–1867* (Cambridge: Cambridge University Press, 1982), 754–755.

36. Litwack, *Been in the Storm So Long,* 486.

37. Mintz, *African American Voices,* 169.

38. Du Bois, *Black Reconstruction,* 686.

39. Ibid., 687.

40. Hurst, *Nathan Bedford Forrest,* 305; Foner, *Reconstruction.*

41. Litwack, *Been in the Storm So Long,* 269; George C. Wright, *Racial Violence in Kentucky, 1865–1940* (Baton Rouge: Louisiana State University Press, 1990), 58–60.

42. See, for example, David M. Chalmers, *Hooded Americanism: The History of the Ku Klux Klan* (New York: New Viewpoints, 1981), 13–21.

43. Howard Zinn, *A People's History of the United States,* rev. ed. (New York: Harper Perennial, 1995), 199.

44. Wright, *Racial Violence in Kentucky,* 162.

45. Foner, *Reconstruction,* 532. For the Supreme Court cases from the *Slaughter House Cases* in 1873 to the *Civil Rights Cases* in 1883, see A. Leon Higginbotham, Jr., *Shades of Freedom: Racial Politics and Presumptions of the American Legal Process* (New York: Oxford University Press, 1996).

46. Foner, *Reconstruction,* 599.

47. Edwin S. Radkey, *Black Exodus: Black Nationalist and Back-to-Africa Movements, 1890–1910* (New Haven, Conn.: Yale University Press, 1969), 22.

48. Franklin, *From Slavery to Freedom,* 278.

49. Henry King, "A Year of the Exodus in Kansas," *Scribner's Monthly* 8 (June 1880), 211–215; William Loren Katz, *The Black West: A Documentary and Pictorial*

History of the African American Role in the Westward Expansion of the United States (New York: Simon & Schuster, 1996), 167–198; Nell Irvin Painter, *Exodusters: Black Migration to Kansas after Reconstruction* (New York: W. W. Norton, 1976).

50. Ibid.
51. Philip Durham and Everett L. Jones, *The Negro Cowboys* (Lincoln: University of Nebraska Press, 1965), 173–174.
52. Leslie H. Fishel and Benjamin Quarles, eds., *The Black American: A Documentary History* (Glenview, Ill.: Scott, Foresman, 1970), 339. See the *Slaughter House Cases* (1873) and *United States* v. *Cruikshank* (1876). In 1883 the Supreme Court struck down the Civil Rights Act of 1875.

Chapter 9 ▪ **Populism, Industrial Unions, and the Politics of Race**

1. "Constitution and Address to the Nation of the Afro-American National League," New York, January, 25, 1890, in Leslie H. Fishel, Jr., and Benjamin Quarles, eds., *The Black American: A Documentary History* (Glenview, Ill.: Scott, Foresman, 1970), 325–327.
2. William Loren Katz, *Eyewitness: The Negro in American History*, 3rd ed. (Belmont, Calif.: Fearon Pitman Publishers, 1974), 302.
3. *Proceedings of the Colored National Labor Convention Held in Washington* (Washington, D.C., 1870), in Katz, *Eyewitness*, 303–304.
4. John Hope Franklin and Alfred A. Moss, Jr., *From Slavery to Freedom*, 7th ed. (New York: McGraw-Hill, 1994), 257; Howard Zinn, *A People's History of the United States*, rev. ed. (New York: Harper Perennial, 1995), 280.
5. Ibid., 280.
6. Edward L. Ayers, *The Promise of the New South: Life after Reconstruction* (New York: Oxford University Press, 1992), 272.
7. Ibid., 272–273.
8. David M. Oshinsky, *"Worse Than Slavery": Parchman Farm and the Ordeal of Jim Crow Justice* (New York: Free Press, 1996), 46.
9. Charles M. Christian, *Black Saga: The African American Experience: A Chronology* (Washington, D.C.: Civitas, 1995), 262, 275, 277; Leon Litwack, *Trouble in Mind: Black Southerners in the Age of Jim Crow* (New York: Alfred A. Knopf, 1998), 156; Alfreda M. Duster, ed., *The Autobiography of Ida B. Wells* (Chicago: University of Chicago Press, 1970), 62–63.
10. John Bodnar, Roger Simon, and Michael P. Weber, *Lives of Their Own: Blacks, Italians, and Poles in Pittsburgh, 1900–1960* (Urbana: University of Illinois Press, 1982), 18.
11. William H. Harris, *The Harder We Run: Black Workers since the Civil War* (New York: Oxford University Press, 1982), 46–48.
12. There was no truly effective AFL–affiliated African American union until Asa Philip Randolph established the Brotherhood of Sleeping Car Porters in 1925. Harris, *The Harder We Run*, 44.
13. Katz, *Eyewitness*, 371.
14. Lerone Bennett, Jr., *Before the Mayflower: A History of Black America*, 6th edition (New York: Penguin Books, 1993), 511.
15. Katz, *Eyewitness*, 373.
16. Booker T. Washington, *Up from Slavery* (1901; reprint, New York: Dell, 1965), 156–158.
17. C. Vann Woodward, *The Strange Career of Jim Crow* (New York: Oxford University Press, 1966), 65.
18. Quoted in Bennett, *Before the Mayflower*, 265.
19. Theodore Roosevelt to General Curtis Guild, Jr., Washington, D.C., October 28, 1901 (at the Gilder Lehrman Collection of American History, Pierpont Mor-

gan Library, New York); Joel Williamson, *The Crucible of Rage: Black–White Relations in the American South since Emancipation* (New York: Oxford University Press, 1984), 351.

20. W.E.B. Du Bois, *The Philadelphia Negro: A Social Study* (1899; reprint, New York: Schocken Books, 1967).

21. Harvey Wish, ed., *The Negro since Emancipation* (Englewood Cliffs, N.J.: Prentice-Hall, 1964), 49.

22. "Address before Brooklyn Institute of Science," February 2, 1903, *Booker T. Washington Papers*, 7, 88–89, quoted in David Blight, *Race and Reunion* (Cambridge, Mass.: Harvard University Press, in press).

23. Walter White, *A Man Called White* (New York: Viking Press, 1948), 9–12.

24. Williamson, *The Crucible of Rage*, 354–355; Katz, *Eyewitness*, 375.

25. Rayford W. Logan, *The Betrayal of the Negro* (New York: Collier Books, 1965); Katz, *Eyewitness*, 375.

26. Edward A. Berlin, *King of Ragtime: Scott Joplin and His Era* (New York: Oxford University Press, 1994).

27. Ibid.

28. Blacks were never more than 9 percent of the total population in any northern city during this period. Jacqueline Jones, *Labor of Love, Labor of Sorrow: Black Women, Work, and Family from Slavery to the Present* (New York: Basic Books, 1985), 156; Leonard Dinnerstein, Roger L. Nichols, and David M. Reimers, *Natives and Strangers: A Multicultural History of Americans* (New York: Oxford University Press, 1996), 140. See also Neil Fligstein, *Going North: Migration of Black and Whites from the South, 1900–1950* (New York: Academic Press, 1981).

29. Jones, *Labor of Love, Labor of Sorrow*, 157.

30. Ibid., 164.

31. Ibid., 166–167.

32. Howard H. Long, "The Negro Soldier in the Army of the United States," *Journal of Negro Education* 12 (Summer 1943), 311–312.

33. Bennett, *Before the Mayflower*, 349.

34. Fishel and Quarles, *The Black American*, 411–412.

35. Wilhelmina Guess Howell, "Eyewitness to Grief: The Death of My Uncle in the Tulsa Race Riot of 1921" (n.d.) in the Papers of the Tulsa Oral History Project, Oklahoma Historical Society, Oklahoma City.

36. Claude McKay, "If We Must Die," in James A. Emanuel and Theodore L. Gross, eds., *Dark Symphony: Negro Literature in America* (New York: Free Press, 1968), 94.

Chapter 10 ▪ **The Harlem Renaissance between the Wars**

1. Addison Gayle, *Richard Wright: Ordeal of a Native Son* (Garden City, N.Y.: Anchor Press/Doubleday, 1980).

2. James R. Grossman, *Land of Hope: Chicago, Black Southerners, and the Great Migration* (Chicago: University of Chicago Press, 1989), 39, 41–47.

3. Ibid., 57, 59.

4. Edmund David Cronon, *Black Moses: The Story of Marcus Garvey and the Universal Negro Improvement Association* (Madison: University of Wisconsin Press, 1969), 64–65, 70.

5. Mildred I. Thompson, *Ida B. Wells-Barnett: An Exploratory Study of an American Black Woman, 1893–1930* (Brooklyn, N.Y.: Carlson Publishing, 1990).

6. Gayle, *Richard Wright*, 57.

7. Wilson Jeremiah Moses, *The Golden Age of Black Nationalism, 1850–1925* (New York: Oxford University Press, 1978); Eric J. Sundquist, *The Oxford W.E.B. Du Bois Reader* (New York: Oxford University Press, 1996), 265.

8. Sundquist, *The Oxford W.E.B. Du Bois Reader,* 274.

9. Cronon, *Black Moses,* 18.

10. Ibid., 41.

11. Ibid., 131.

12. Sundquist, *The Oxford W.E.B. Du Bois Reader,* 265, 267, 268.

13. Jules Tygiel, *Baseball's Great Experiment: Jackie Robinson and His Legacy* (New York: Oxford University Press, 1983), 17, 16.

14. Eileen Southern, *The Music of Black America: A History,* 2nd ed. (New York: W. W. Norton, 1983), 362.

15. Burton W. Peretti, *The Creation of Jazz: Music, Race and Culture in Urban America* (Urbana: University of Illinois Press, 1994), 39.

16. David Levering Lewis, *When Harlem Was in Vogue* (New York: Oxford University Press, 1989), 209.

17. Lois E. Horton, "The Harlem Renaissance," in James Oliver Horton and Lois E. Horton, eds., *A History of the African American People* (New York: Smithmark Publishers, 1995), 126–127.

18. African Americans became popular performers of many kinds of music. Operatic singer Roland Hayes, originally from Georgia, thrilled audiences in New York, Boston, Philadelphia, and in the capitals of Europe. He sang for King George V in 1920 and toured Russia before the decade was over. Southern, *The Music of Black America,* 400–402.

19. Angela Y. Davis, *Blues Legacies and Black Feminism* (New York: Vintage Books, 1998).

20. Peretti, *The Creation of Jazz,* 62–63.

21. Davis, *Blues Legacies and Black Feminism,* 154, 151.

22. Peretti, *The Creation of Jazz,* 64.

23. Davis, *Blues Legacies and Black Feminism,* 154, 151; Daphne Duval Harrison, *Black Pearls: Black Queens of the 1920s* (New Brunswick, N.J.: Rutgers University Press, 1988).

24. Lil Armstrong, "Lil Armstrong Reminisces," *Down Beat* (June 1, 1951), 12, cited in David N. Bagaus, "Lillian Hardin: My Heart" (unpublished paper, St. Petersburg, Fla., 1995); Peretti, *The Creation of Jazz,* 69.

25. Horton, *Free People of Color;* Joel Williamson, *New People: Miscegenation and Mulattoes in the United States* (New York: Free Press, 1980).

26. Peretti, *The Creation of Jazz,* 59.

27. Ibid., 60.

28. Langston Hughes, *The Big Sea: An Autobiography* (New York: Hill & Wang, 1963), 227.

29. Katz, *Eyewitness,* 401–402; Lewis, *When Harlem Was in Vogue.*

30. *New York Times,* October 27, 1921.

31. Harvard Sitkoff, *A New Deal for Blacks: The Emergence of Civil Rights as a National Issue, The Depression Decade* (New York: Oxford University Press, 1981).

32. There is disagreement over the exact number of Klanspeople who marched. The *Washington Evening Star* reported the number at fifty thousand. See *Washington Evening Star,* August 19, 1925; *Baltimore Afro-American,* August 15, 1925; Katz, *Eyewitness,* 398.

33. Sitkoff, *A New Deal for Blacks,* 28.

34. Ibid., 85; Allen B. Ballard, *One More Day's Journey: The Story of a Family and a People* (New York: McGraw-Hill, 1984).

35. Michael Rogin, *Blackface, White Noise: Jewish Immigrants in the Hollywood Melting Pot* (Berkeley: University of California Press, 1996).

36. James Weldon Johnson, *Along This Way: The Autobiography of James Weldon Johnson* (New York: Viking Press, 1933), 380.

Chapter 11 ▪ **Depression and War**

1. Louis Banks, in Studs Terkel, *Hard Times* (New York: Avon Books, 1970), 57.
2. David Levering Lewis, *When Harlem Was in Vogue* (New York: Oxford University Press, 1989), 240.
3. Phyllis Palmer, *Domesticity and Dirt: Housewives and Domestic Servants in the United States, 1920–1945* (Philadelphia: Temple University Press, 1989), 74.
4. Allen B. Ballard, *One More Day's Journey* (New York: McGraw-Hill, 1984), 232. A domestic might work as many as six days each week for a total wage of $7.50.
5. Jacqueline Jones, *Labor of Love, Labor of Sorrow: Black Women and the Family from Slavery to the Present* (New York: Basic Books, 1985), 230.
6. "Colored Women as Industrial Workers in Philadelphia," Philip S. Foner and Ronald L. Lewis, eds., *The Black Worker: A Documentary History from Colonial Times to Present,* vol. 4 (Philadelphia: Temple University Press, 1981), 139–159.
7. Lewis, *When Harlem Was in Vogue,* 241.
8. Terkel, *Hard Times,* 57.
9. Jones, *Labor of Love, Labor of Sorrow,* 230.
10. Claude McKay, "'There Goes God!' The Story of Father Divine and His Angels," in Herbert Aptheker, ed., *A Documentary History of the Negro People in the United States, 1933–1945* (Secaucus, N.J.: Citadel Press, 1974), 156–163; William Loren Katz, *Eyewitness: The Negro in American History,* 3rd ed. (Belmont, Calif.: Fearon Pitman Publishers, 1974), 433.
11. Marilyn Halter, *Between Race and Ethnicity: Cape Verdean American Immigrants, 1860–1965* (Urbana: University of Illinois Press, 1993).
12. This movement had particular appeal to former Garveyites. Malcolm X, formerly Malcolm Little, was its chief and most influential spokesman during the 1960s. Albert J. Raboteau, *A Fire in the Bones: Reflections on African American Religious History* (Boston: Beacon Press, 1995), 110; C. Eric Lincoln, *The Black Muslims in America* (Boston: Beacon Press, 1961).
13. Lerone Bennett, Jr., *Before the Mayflower: A History of Black America,* 6th ed. (New York: Penguin Books, 1993), 359; John Hope Franklin and Alfred A. Moss, Jr., *From Slavery to Freedom,* 7th ed. (New York: McGraw-Hill, 1994), 384.
14. Roy Wilkins, "The Bonuseers Ban Jim Crow," *Crisis* 39 (October 1932), 316–317.
15. Howard Zinn, *A People's History of the United States,* rev. ed. (New York: Harper Perennial, 1995), 382.
16. Katz, *Eyewitness,* 425; Mark Naison, *Communists in Harlem during the Depression* (Urbana: University of Illinois Press, 1981); Dan Carter, *Scottsboro: A Tragedy of the American South* (Baton Rouge: Louisiana State University Press, 1969).
17. Theodore Rosengarten, *All God's Dangers: The Life of Nate Shaw* (New York: Alfred A. Knopf, 1975), 296, 312, 446–447.
18. Angelo Herndon, "You Cannot Kill the Working Class," in Joanne Grant, ed., *Black Protest: History, Documents, and Analyses* (Greenwich, Conn.: Fawcett Publications, 1968), 231.
19. Aptheker, *A Documentary History of the Negro People,* 1–2; Nell Irvin Painter, *The Narrative of Hosea Hudson: His Life as a Negro Communist in the South* (Cambridge, Mass.: Harvard University Press, 1979); Robin D. G. Kelley, *Hammer and Hoe: Alabama Communists during the Great Depression* (Chapel Hill: University of North Carolina Press, 1990), 85.
20. Kelley, *Hammer and Hoe,* 25.
21. The Communist Party made a bid for African American votes by running James W. Ford, a black man, for vice president in 1932, 1936, and 1940, but few blacks voted Communist.

22. "Mary Fitzbutler Waring to Mr. Franklin D. Roosevelt," May 11, 1933, in Aptheker, *A Documentary History of the Negro People,* 22–23.

23. *Crisis,* November 1934, reprinted in Aptheker, *A Documentary History of the Negro People,* 57–58.

24. Luther C. Wandall, "A Negro in the CCC," *Crisis* 42 (August 1935): 244–254.

25. Franklin and Moss, *From Slavery to Freedom,* 382.

26. Joe William Trotter, "From Hard Times to Hope," in James Oliver Horton and Lois E. Horton, *A History of the African American People* (New York: Smithmark Publishers, 1995), 119–151.

27. Adam Clayton Powell, Jr., "The Fight for Jobs," *Amsterdam News,* May 7, 1938, reprinted in Aptheker, *A Documentary History of the Negro People,* 317; Trotter, "From Hard Times to Hope," 136–142.

28. Katz, *Eyewitness,* 431.

29. Franklin and Moss, *From Slavery to Freedom,* 400.

30. Michael H. Kater, *Different Drummers: Jazz in the Culture of Nazi Germany* (New York: Oxford University Press, 1992), 19; Katz, *Eyewitness,* 433.

31. McKay, "'There Goes God!'" 159; W.E.B. Du Bois, "Segregation in the North," *Crisis* 41 (April 1934): 115–116, reprinted in Aptheker, *A Documentary History of the Negro People,* 77–82.

32. Richard Wright, "Joe Louis Uncovers Dynamite," *New Masses* 17 (October 8, 1935), 18–19, reprinted in Aptheker, *A Documentary History of the Negro People,* 194–197; Naison, *Communists in Harlem during the Depression,* 174.

33. Naison, *Communists in Harlem during the Depression,* 139.

34. Kennell Jackson, *America Is Me* (New York: HarperCollins, 1996), 277; Trotter, "From Hard Times to Hope," 142.

35. Naison, *Communists in Harlem During the Depression,* 96.

36. Ibid., 287–288.

37. Max Yergan, "Democracy and the Negro People Today," in Aptheker, *Documentary History of the Negro People,* 386–396; quotes, 392 and 393.

38. Jones, *Labor of Love, Labor of Sorrow,* 237; Paula Giddings, *When and Where I Enter: The Impact of Black Women on Race and Sex in America* (New York: William Morrow, 1984).

39. Jones, *Labor of Love, Labor of Sorrow,* 240.

40. Trotter, "From Hard Times to Hope," 146; Terkel, *Hard Times,* 60.

41. Peter M. Bergman and Mort N. Bergman, eds., *The Chronological History of the Negro in America* (New York: New American Library, 1969), 501.

42. Grant Reynolds, "What the Negro Soldier Thinks about This War," in Aptheker, *A Documentary History of the Negro People,* 487–507; quote, 488.

43. Rosalyn Baxandall and Linda Gordon, *America's Working Women: A Documentary History, 1600 to the Present,* rev. ed. (New York: W. W. Norton, 1995), 254–255.

44. Jules Tygiel, *Baseball's Great Experiment: Jackie Robinson and His Legacy* (New York: Oxford University Press, 1983), 59.

45. Bergman, *The Chronological History,* 494; Leslie H. Fishel, Jr., "The Negro in the New Deal Era," in Eric Foner, ed., *Americans' Black Past: A Reader in Afro-American History* (New York: Harper & Row, 1970), 388–413.

46. Katz, *Eyewitness,* 452.

Chapter 12 ▪ *The Postwar Civil Rights Movement*

1. William Loren Katz, *Eyewitness: The Negro in American History,* 3rd ed. (Belmont, Calif.: Fearon Pitman Publishers, Inc., 1974), 454.

2. Ronald Takaki, *A Different Mirror: A History of Multicultural America* (Boston: Little, Brown, 1993), 376.

3. Takaki, *A Different Mirror,* 396.
4. *Chicago Defender,* April 21, 1945.
5. John Hope Franklin and Alfred A. Moss, Jr., *From Slavery to Freedom: A History of African Americans,* 7th ed. (New York: McGraw-Hill, 1994), 458.
6. Howard Zinn, *A People's History of the United States,* rev. ed. (New York: Harper Perennial, 1995), 413.
7. Donald G. Nieman, *Promises to Keep: African Americans and the Constitutional Order, 1776 to the Present* (New York: Oxford University Press, 1991), 143–144.
8. Takaki, *A Different Mirror,* 400.
9. Katz, *Eyewitness,* 461.
10. James Baldwin, *Notes of a Native Son* (Boston: Beacon Press, 1955), 99.
11. Ibid., 100.
12. Slow to implement the president's order, the military finally integrated during the Korean War in the 1950s.
13. William H. Chafe, *The Unfinished Journey: America since World War II* (New York: Oxford University Press, 1986).
14. Robert L. Harris, Jr., "Ralph Bunche," in Eric Foner and John A. Garraty, eds., *The Reader's Companion to American History* (New York: Houghton Mifflin, 1991), 136; Brian Urquhart, *Ralph Bunche: An American Life* (New York: W. W. Norton, 1993), 109; Dean Acheson, *Present at the Creation: My Years in the State Department* (New York: W. W. Norton, 1969), 259.
15. Moses Fleetwood Walker played for the Toledo team in the American Association, an early major league association, in 1884, but no African Americans played in the majors during the modern era until Robinson.
16. Jules Tygiel, *Baseball's Great Experiment: Jackie Robinson and His Legacy* (New York: Oxford University Press, 1983).
17. Eileen Southern, *The Music of Black Americans: A History* (New York: W. W. Norton, 1971), 487.
18. Ibid., 488.
19. Ibid., 423.
20. Peter M. Bergman and Mort N. Bergman, *The Chronological History of the Negro in America* (New York: New American Library, 1969), 542–543.
21. Henry Hampton and Steve Fayer, *Voices of Freedom: An Oral History of the Civil Rights Movement from the 1950s through the 1980s* (New York: Bantam Books, 1990), 6–8.
22. Ibid., 6.
23. Stephen J. Whitfield, *A Death in the Delta: The Story of Emmett Till* (New York: Free Press, 1988), 72.
24. Hampton and Fayer, *Voices of Freedom,* 19.
25. John M. Glen, *Highlander: No Ordinary School, 1932–1962* (Lexington: University of Kentucky Press, 1988); Howell Raines, *My Soul Is Rested: The Story of the Civil Rights Movement in the Deep South* (New York: Penguin Books, 1983), 43.
26. Clayborne Carson, "A Season of Struggle," in James Oliver Horton and Lois E. Horton, eds., *A History of the African American People* (New York: Smithmark Publishers, 1995), 153–177; Hampton and Fayer, *Voices of Freedom,* 21.
27. James Cone, *Martin & Malcolm & America: A Dream or a Nightmare* (Maryknoll, N.Y.: Orbis Books, 1991).
28. Raymond Arsenault, "Bayard Rustin and the Miracle in Montgomery," in James Oliver Horton and Lois E. Horton, eds., *A History of the African American People* (New York: Smithmark Publishers, 1995), 156–157.
29. Carson, "A Season of Struggle."
30. Hampton and Fayer, *Voices of Freedom,* 42.

31. Roy Wilkins with Tom Mathews, *Standing Fast: The Autobiography of Roy Wilkins* (New York: Penguin Books, 1984), 248–252.
32. Hampton and Fayer, *Voices of Freedom,* 49.
33. Ibid., 51.
34. Chafe, *The Unfinished Journey,* 159–161.
35. Robert Sherrill, *Gothic Politics in the Deep South* (New York: Ballantine Books, 1969), 314.
36. Hampton and Fayer, *Voices of Freedom,* 56.
37. Mary King, *Freedom Song: A Personal Story of the 1960s Civil Rights Movement* (New York: William Morrow, 1987), 44.
38. Hampton and Fayer, *Voices of Freedom,* 62.
39. Clayborne Carson, *In Struggle: SNCC and the Black Awakening of the 1960s* (Cambridge, Mass.: Harvard University Press, 1982).
40. Hampton and Fayer, *Voices of Freedom,* 69.
41. Ibid., 74.
42. Hampton and Fayer, *Voices of Freedom,* 78; Juan Williams, *Eyes on the Prize: America's Civil Rights Years, 1954–1965* (New York: Penguin Books, 1987).
43. Hampton and Fayer, *Voices of Freedom,* 80; Williams, *Eyes on the Prize,* 149.
44. Williams, *Eyes on the Prize,* 151.
45. Ibid., 153.
46. Ibid., 158.
47. David L. Lewis, *King: A Biography,* 2nd ed. (Urbana: University of Illinois Press, 1978).
48. Wilkins with Mathews, *Standing Fast,* 281.
49. Tom Cowan and Jack Maguire, *Timelines of African American History* (New York: Berkeley Publishing Group, 1994), 244.
50. Taylor Branch, *Parting the Waters: America in the King Years, 1954–63* (New York: Simon & Schuster, 1988), 756–802.
51. Ibid.

Chapter 13 ▪ **From Civil Rights to Black Power**

1. William H. Chafe, *The Unfinished Journey: America since World War II* (New York: Oxford University Press, 1986), 312; LeRoi Jones, *Blues People* (New York: William Morrow, 1963); John Hope Franklin, *The Emancipation Proclamation* (Garden City, N.Y.: Doubleday, 1963).
2. Peter M. Bergman and Mort N. Bergman, *The Chronological History of the Negro in America* (New York: New American Library, 1969), 581.
3. Chafe, *Unfinished Journey,* 312–320.
4. Malcolm X with Alex Haley, *The Autobiography of Malcolm X* (New York: Ballantine Books, 1984).
5. James H. Cone, *Martin & Malcolm & America: A Dream or a Nightmare* (Maryknoll, N.Y.: Orbis Books, 1991), 113.
6. Malcolm X, *The Autobiography of Malcolm X,* 301; King, quoted in Clayborne Carson, "A Season of Struggle," in James Oliver Horton and Lois E. Horton, eds., *A History of the African American People* (New York: Smithmark Publishers, 1995), 152–177; quote, 165.
7. Harvard Sitkoff, *The Struggle for Black Equality, 1954–1980* (New York: Hill & Wang), 1981.
8. Doug McAdam, *Freedom Summer* (New York: Oxford University Press, 1988), 108.
9. Clayborne Carson, *In Struggle: SNCC and the Black Awakening of the 1960s* (Cambridge, Mass.: Harvard University Press, 1981), 96–97.
10. Ibid.; Sitkoff, *The Struggle for Black Equality,* 172–173.

11. Bergman and Bergman, *Chronological History of the Negro,* 587. McAdam records four murders during this period. See his *Freedom Summer,* 96.

12. Carson, *In Struggle,* 164–165.

13. Ibid., 117.

14. Mary King, *Freedom Song: A Personal Story of the 1960s Civil Rights Movement* (New York: William Morrow, 1987), 347.

15. Sitkoff, *The Struggle for Black Equality,* 184.

16. King, *Freedom Song,* 351; Sitkoff, *The Struggle for Black Equality,* 185. Malcolm X's reference is to the Mau Mau uprising in Kenya in the 1950s.

17. Bergman and Bergman, *Chronological History of the Negro,* 585.

18. Ibid., 586. George Wallace received one-third of the vote in Wisconsin, 30 percent in Indiana, and 43 percent in Maryland.

19. Robert Fogelson, *Violence as Protest: A Study of Riots and Ghettos* (Garden City, N.Y: Doubleday, 1971), 3, 27.

20. Cone, *Martin & Malcolm;* David J. Garrow, *Bearing the Cross: Martin Luther King, Jr. and the Southern Christian Leadership Conference* (New York: William Morrow, 1986), 440.

21. Cone, *Martin & Malcolm,* 193, 195, 204.

22. Malcolm X, *The Autobiography of Malcolm X,* 340.

23. Peter Goldman, *The Death and Life of Malcolm X,* 2nd ed. (Urbana: University of Illinois Press, 1979), 168.

24. Cone, *Martin & Malcolm,* 207.

25. Malcolm X, *The Autobiography of Malcolm X,* 427–436.

26. Garrow, *Bearing the Cross;* Roger Wilkins, *A Man's Life: An Autobiography* (New York: Simon & Schuster, 1982), 208.

27. Henry Hampton and Steve Fayer with Sarah Flynn, *Voices of Freedom: An Oral History of the Civil Rights Movement from the 1950s through the 1980s* (New York: Bantam Books, 1990).

28. Hampton and Fayer, *Voices of Freedom,* 289–291; Clayborne Carson, et al., eds., *A Reader and Guide: Eyes on the Prize: America's Civil Rights Years* (New York: Penguin Books, 1987), 194.

29. Cone, *Martin & Malcolm,* 116.

30. Ibid., 261–262.

31. Hampton and Fayer, *Voices of Freedom,* 294.

32. Ibid., 294; Wilkins, *A Man's Life,* 185, 184.

33. Garrow, *Bearing the Cross.*

34. *Playboy* (January 1965), 73.

35. Carson, "A Season of Struggle"; Bobby Seale, *Seize the Time: The Story of the Black Panther Party and Huey P. Newton* (New York: Vintage Books, 1970), 59–60.

36. Seale, *Seize the Time,* 68.

37. Garrow, *Bearing the Cross;* Wilkins, *A Man's Life;* Carson, "A Season of Struggle."

38. Cone, *Martin & Malcolm,* 234.

39. Chafe, *The Unfinished Journey,* 235.

40. Bergman and Bergman, *Chronological History of the Negro,* 595; Claude Brown, *Manchild in the Promised Land* (New York: Macmillan, 1965).

41. Bergman and Bergman, *Chronological History of the Negro,* 595.

42. Lee Rainwater and William L. Yancey, *The Moynihan Report and the Politics of Controversy* (Cambridge, Mass.: M.I.T. Press, 1967), 5. At that time the rates of female-headed households and illegitimate births in black society were about 25 percent each.

43. Chafe, *The Unfinished Journey,* 236–243.

44. Lerone Bennett, Jr., *Before the Mayflower: A History of Black America,* 5th rev. ed. (New York: Penguin Books, 1982), 576–577.

45. Garrow, *Bearing the Cross,* 394, 437–439; Cone, *Martin & Malcolm.*
46. Cone, *Martin & Malcolm,* 235.
47. Bennett, *Before the Mayflower,* 580.
48. Ibid., 425.
49. Cone, *Martin & Malcolm,* 240.
50. FBI directive quoted in Clayborne Carson, *Malcolm X: The FBI File,* edited by David Gallen (New York: Carroll & Graf Publishers, 1991), 30.
51. Chafe, *The Unfinished Journey,* 365.
52. Bergman and Bergman, *Chronological History of the Negro,* 602.
53. Max Stanford, the leader of this group, had grown up in Harlem and was a long-time friend of Stokely Carmichael.
54. Bergman and Bergman, *Chronological History of the Negro,* 602; Carson, *In Struggle,* 261–263.
55. Pat Romero, *In Black America, 1968: The Year of Awakening* (Washington, D.C.: United Publishing Corp., 1969), 296.
56. Armstead L. Robinson, Craig C. Foster, and Donald H. Ogilvie, eds., *Black Studies in the University* (New York: Bantam Books, 1969).
57. Romero, *In Black America,* 125–131; William Loren Katz, *Eyewitness: The Negro in American History* (Belmont, Calif.: Fearon Pitman Publishers, 1974).
58. Garrow, *Bearing the Cross,* 621.
59. Bergman and Bergman, *Chronological History of the Negro,* 609–610.
60. Richard Bardolph, ed., *The Civil Rights Record: Black Americans and the Law, 1849–1970* (New York: Thomas Y. Crowell Company, 1970), 425–426.
61. Bergman and Bergman, *Chronological History of the Negro,* 613. Yet African Americans reenlisted at a rate three times the white reenlistment rate.
62. Chafe, *Unfinished Journey,* 368–369.
63. Ibid.
64. Hampton and Fayer, *Voices of Freedom,* 533–538.
65. "Dr. Gloria I. Joseph to William Loren Katz," August 8, 1969, in Katz, *Eyewitness,* 551–552.

Chapter 14 ▪ *Conservatism and Race in Multicultural America*

1. Kathleen Thompson, "Angela Davis," in Darlene Clark Hine, ed., *Black Women in America: An Historical Encyclopedia,* vol. 1 (Brooklyn, N.Y.: Carlson Publishing, 1993), 304–306.
2. Angela Davis, *Angela Davis: An Autobiography* (New York: Random House, 1974).
3. Davis, *Angela Davis.*
4. George Jackson, *Soledad Brother: The Prison Letters of George Jackson* (New York: Bantam Books, 1970).
5. Henry Hampton and Steve Fayer, *Voices of Freedom: An Oral History of the Civil Rights Movement from the 1950s through the 1980s* (New York: Bantam Books, 1990), 540–542; William Loren Katz, *Eyewitness: The Negro in American History* (Belmont, Calif.: Fearon Pitman Publishers, Inc., 1974), 521.
6. Hampton and Fayer, *Voices of Freedom,* 539–563; Ward Churchill and Jim Vander Wall, *The Cointelpro Papers: Documents from the FBI's Secret Wars Against Dissent in the United States* (Boston: South End Press, 1990).
7. Clayborne Carson, *Malcolm X: The FBI File,* edited by David Gallen (New York: Carroll and Graf Publishers, 1991), 45–46; Richard Gid Powers, *Secrecy and Power: The Life of J. Edgar Hoover* (New York: Free Press, 1987), 338–345.
8. Gene Marne, *The Black Panthers* (New York: New American Library, 1969), 51–52, 55; Katz, *Eyewitness,* 519–520.

9. Jacqueline Jones, *Labor of Love, Labor of Sorrow: Black Women, Work, and the Family from Slavery to the Present* (New York: Basic Books, 1985), 314; see, for example, Bobby Seale, *Seize the Time* (New York: Vintage Books, 1970), 393–403.

10. Jones, *Labor of Love, Labor of Sorrow*, 314.

11. James Oliver Horton, *Free People of Color: Inside the African American Community* (Washington, D.C.: Smithsonian Press, 1993), 94–95; Lois E. Horton, "Ambiguous Roles: The Racial Factor in American Womanhood," in *The Invention of Identity and the Practice of Intolerance: Nationalism, Racism, and Xenophobia in Germany and the United States,* Dietmar Schirmer and Norbert Finzsch, eds. (Washington, D.C.: German Historical Institute and Cambridge University Press, 1998), 295–311.

12. Jones, *Labor of Love, Labor of Sorrow*, 319.

13. Patricia Hill Collins, *Black Feminist Thought: Knowledge, Consciousness, and the Politics of Empowerment* (New York: Routledge, Chapman & Hall, 1991), 185–188.

14. Bell Hooks, *Ain't I a Woman: Black Women and Feminism* (Boston: South End Press, 1981), 117.

15. Hampton and Steve Fayer, *Voices of Freedom*, 596.

16. J. Anthony Lukas, *Common Ground: A Turbulent Decade in the Lives of Three American Families* (New York: Vintage Books, 1986).

17. Joel Williamson, *The Crucible of Race: Black-White Relations in the American South since Emancipation* (New York: Oxford University Press, 1984), 508; William H. Chafe, *The Unfinished Journey: American since World War II* (New York: Oxford University Press, 1986), 386. Carswell's nomination was rejected by the U.S. Senate.

18. Manning Marable, *Race, Reform, and Rebellion: The Second Reconstruction in Black America, 1945–1982* (Jackson: University Press of Mississippi, 1984), 149–150.

19. Howard Zinn, *A People's History of the United States*, rev. ed. (New York: Harper Perennial, 1995), 532; Charles M. Christian, *Black Saga: The African American Experience, A Chronology* (Washington, D.C.: Civitas, 1995), 460–462.

20. Zinn, *A People's History*, rev. ed., 475.

21. Tom Wells, *The War Within: America's Battle over Vietnam* (Berkeley: University of California Press, 1994), 282.

22. Ibid.

23. Marable, *Race, Reform, and Rebellion*, 166, 182–184.

24. Roger Wilkins, "Race, Culture, and Conservatism," in James Oliver Horton and Lois E. Horton, eds., *A History of the African American People* (New York: Smithmark Publishers, 1996), 179–199; Marable, *Race, Reform, and Rebellion*, 184.

25. Marable, *Race, Reform, and Rebellion*, 188.

26. Ibid., 202–204; William Raspberry, "The Black-White Gap," *Washington Post*, December 4, 1989.

27. Thomas Byrne Edsall and Mary D. Edsall, *Chain Reaction: The Impact of Race, Rights, and Taxes on American Politics* (New York: W. W. Norton, 1991), 159; Ronald V. Dellums, "Our Congressional Black Caucus Budget," *Washington Post*, April 26, 1990.

28. Donald G. Nieman, *Promises to Keep: African Americans and the Constitutional Order, 1776 to the Present* (New York: Oxford University Press, 1991); Manning Marable, *The Crisis of Color and Democracy* (Monroe, Me.: Common Courage Press, 1992), 215; Edsall and Edsall, *Chain Reaction*, 126–127.

29. William Julius Wilson, *The Declining Significance of Race: Blacks and Changing American Institutions* (Chicago: University of Chicago Press, 1978), 129.

30. U.S. Bureau of the Census, *Census of Population and Housing* (Washington, D.C.: U.S. Government Printing Office, 1970, 1980).

31. Lerone Bennett, Jr., *Before the Mayflower: A History of Black America,* 6th rev. ed. (New York: Penguin Books, 1988), 437; Michael B. Katz, *The Undeserving Poor: From the War on Poverty to the War on Welfare* (New York: Pantheon Books, 1989), 241–242.

32. Marable, *Race, Reform, and Rebellion,* 170–171.

33. Ellis Cose, *The Rage of a Privileged Class* (New York: HarperCollins, 1993), 21.

34. Tom Cowan and Jack Maguire, *Timeline of African American History* (New York: Perigee Books, 1994), 308.

35. Phillip Brian Harper, "Around 1969: Televisual Representation and the Complication of the Black Subject," in Werner Sollors and Maria Diedrich, eds., *The Black Columbiad: Defining Moments in African Amrican Literature and Culture* (Cambridge, Mass.: Harvard University Press, 1994), 265–274.

36. Cowan and Maguire, *Timeline of African American History.*

Chapter 15 ▪ **Race-ing to the Millennium**

1. Thomas Byrne Edsall and Mary D. Edsall, *Chain Reaction: The Impact of Race, Rights and Taxes on American Politics* (New York: W. W. Norton, 1991), 192–193; William Julius Wilson, *When Work Disappears: The World of the New Urban Poor* (New York: Vintage Books, 1996), 194.

2. Wilson, *When Work Disappears,* 195.

3. Ronnie Dugger, *On Reagan: The Man and His Presidency* (New York: McGraw-Hill, 1983), 218.

4. Edsall and Edsall, *Chain Reaction,* 191.

5. George Gilder, *Wealth and Poverty* (New York, Basic Books, 1981), and Jude Wanniski, *The Way the World Works* (New York: Simon & Schuster, 1978); Manning Marable, *The Crisis of Color and Democracy* (Monroe, Me.: Common Courage Press, 1992), 212–221.

6. John Hope Franklin and Alfred A. Moss, Jr., *From Slavery to Freedom,* 7th ed. (New York: McGraw-Hill, 1994), 545.

7. Donald R. Kinder and Lynn M. Sanders, *Divided by Color: Racial Politics and Democratic Ideals* (Chicago: University of Chicago Press, 1996), 238, 235.

8. Toni Morrison, ed., *Race-ing Justice, En-gendering Power: Essays on Anita Hill, Clarence Thomas, and the Construction of Social Reality* (New York: Pantheon Books, 1992).

9. Franklin and Moss, *From Slavery to Freedom,* 567; Howard Zinn, *A People's History of the United States,* rev. ed. (New York: Harper Perennial, 1995), 610.

10. Franklin and Moss, *From Slavery to Freedom,* 552–553. Two of the four white policemen were convicted of violating Rodney King's civil rights (a federal charge) in 1993.

11. Clinton also drew a large percentage of Jewish voters (78 percent) and Latino voters (62 percent). Manning Marable, *Beyond Black and White: Transforming African American Politics* (New York: Verso, 1995), 64.

12. Quoted in Martin Carnoy, *Faded Dreams: The Politics and Economics of Race in America* (New York: Cambridge University Press, 1994), 222.

13. *Washington Post,* July 20, 1995.

14. Quoted in Lawrence W. Levine, *The Opening of the American Mind: Canons, Culture, and History* (Boston: Beacon Press, 1996), 4.

15. Eli Faber, *Jews, Slaves and the Slave Trade: Setting the Record Straight* (New York: New York University Press, 1998), 6–7.

16. John Hope Franklin, ed., *The Negro in 20th Century America* (New York: Vintage Books, 1967), 4–7.

17. David Roediger, *The Wages of Whiteness: Race and the Making of the American Working Class* (New York: Verso, 1991), and *Towards the Abolition of Whiteness: Essays on Race, Politics, and Working Class History* (New York: Verso, 1994); Noel Ignatiev, *How the Irish Became White* (New York: Routledge, 1995); Noel Ignatiev and John Garvey, eds., *Race Traitor* (New York: Routledge, 1996); George Lipsitz, *The Possessive Investment in Whiteness: How White People Profit from Identity Politics* (Philadelphia: Temple University Press, 1998); Melvin L. Oliver, *Black Wealth/White Wealth* (New York: Routledge, 1995).

18. Robert P. Hey, "Minorities: Congress Studies Aid to Black Males," *Christian Science Monitor,* August 1, 1989, 7.

19. Twenty-nine percent of college-educated blacks believed that such a plot did exist, and 38 percent believed that it might exist. Stephan Thernstrom and Abigail Thernstrom, *America in Black and White: Race in Modern America* (New York: Simon & Schuster, 1997), 515.

20. William Julius Wilson, *When Work Disappears: The World of the New Urban Poor* (New York: Alfred A. Knopf, 1997), 59–60.

21. Spencer Rich, "U.S. Immigrant Population at Postwar High," *Washington Post,* August 29, 1995, A1.

Index

Note: Page numbers in italics indicate illustrations.

About the Authors

James Oliver Horton, the Benjamin Banneker Professor of American Studies and History at George Washington University, directs the African American Communities Project at the Smithsonian Institution. He is a regular panelist on The History Channel's *The History Center.* **Lois E. Horton** is a professor of sociology and American studies at George Mason University. They are coauthors of several books, including *In Hope of Liberty: Free Black Culture and Community and Protest among Northern Free Blacks, 1700–1860* and *Black Bostonians: Family Life and Community Struggle in the Antebellum North.*